Baking Memories

Delicious ways to share the holidays

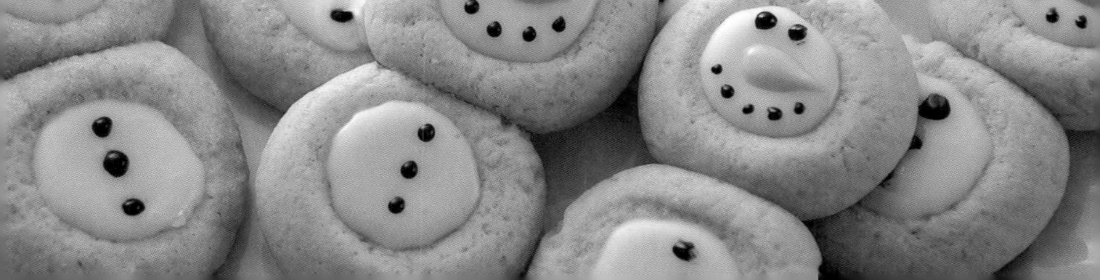

Holiday Treasures

Whether it's a snack mix, candy, bread, or cookies, a food gift – big or small – is a great way to spread some joy this holiday season.

ISBN-13: 978-1-56383-504-9
Item #7138

Printed in the USA
by G&R Publishing Co.

Distributed By:

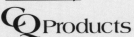

CQ Products

507 Industrial Street
Waverly, IA 50677

www.cqbookstore.com

gifts@cqbookstore.com

CQ Products

CQ Products

@cqproducts

@cqproducts

It truly is... the Most Wonderful Time of the Year

Enjoy your traditions and consider making some new ones. Set aside time to hang out with your favorite people. Bake together. Eat together. Sip some eggnog. Laugh.

This book will become a holiday favorite, with enough recipes to load your dessert table with delicious sweets and treats for the entire family.

And if it's gift-giving you enjoy, these recipes are guaranteed to put a smile on the faces of those lucky recipients. Keep the packaging simple so you can delight in the pure joys of the season.

As you work your way through these pages, let the recipes conjure up memories of the past, or try something completely new. Either way, it's going to be a delicious holiday!

Cranberry Burst Mini Loaves

- 4 C. flour
- 1¾ C. sugar
- 1 tsp. baking soda
- 1 T. baking powder
- 1 tsp. salt
- 2 eggs
- 2 T. orange zest
- 1½ C. orange juice
- 1 T. vanilla
- 1 tsp. orange flavoring
- ½ C. melted butter, cooled slightly
- 2 C. whole fresh or frozen & thawed cranberries
- 1½ C. mini semi-sweet chocolate chips

Preheat your oven to 350° and grease eight 3 x 5½" mini loaf pans; set aside.

In a big bowl, sift together the flour, sugar, baking soda, baking powder, and salt.

In a separate bowl, whisk together the eggs, orange zest, orange juice, vanilla, orange flavoring, and butter. Add to the flour mixture, stirring until just blended *(don't over-mix)*. Gently fold in the cranberries and chocolate chips and divide among the prepped loaf pans. Bake 30 to 35 minutes, until done.

Cool on a wire rack before removing the loaves from the pans.

As a perfect little gift for a teacher, slip one of these mini loaves into a cellophane bag and tie with a pretty ribbon. Very festive!

makes
8 mini loaves

makes about
3 dozen

Peanut Butter-Chocolate Wishes

- ½ C. butter, softened
- ½ C. creamy peanut butter
- 1 C. powdered sugar
- ¾ C. brown sugar
- 1 egg
- 1 tsp. vanilla
- 1 C. flour
- ½ C. unsweetened cocoa powder, plus more for sprinkling
- ¼ tsp. salt
- Your favorite decorator frosting
- Powdered sugar, optional

In a big bowl, beat butter, peanut butter, powdered sugar, and brown sugar until fluffy. Add egg and vanilla and beat until smooth.

In a separate bowl, mix flour, ½ cup cocoa powder, and salt; add to butter mixture a little at a time, stirring until a soft dough forms. Cover and chill several hours or overnight.

Preheat your oven to 375° and line cookie sheets with parchment paper.

Put chilled dough on a work surface lightly coated with cocoa powder; sprinkle dough lightly with more cocoa. Roll out dough to ¼" thickness and use alphabet cookie cutters *(ours were about 2" tall)* to cut dough into letters to spell out words. Reroll scraps and cut more cookies, chilling dough again as needed. Bake on prepped cookie sheets 7 to 9 minutes or until edges are firm. Transfer to a rack to cool.

Pipe on frosting and sprinkle with powdered sugar as desired.

Gift Idea

Give a wish spelled out in cookies by lining a gift box with scrapbook paper, creating several dividers. Stack cookie letters on a nest of tissue paper in each section.

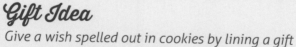

makes about
13 cups

Honey-Nut Caramel Corn

- 12 C. popped popcorn
- 1 C. almonds *(we used salted caramel and toasted coconut flavors)*
- ¾ C. creamy almond butter
- 1½ T. coconut oil
- ½ C. honey
- ¾ C. brown sugar
- ½ tsp. cinnamon
- ½ tsp. coarse salt, plus more for sprinkling
- ½ tsp. baking soda
- 2 tsp. vanilla

Preheat your oven to 325°. Line two rimmed baking sheets with parchment paper and put the popcorn in a big bowl. Coarsely crush the almonds if you'd like. Set all aside.

In a medium saucepan over medium heat, whisk together the almond butter, oil, honey, brown sugar, cinnamon, and ½ teaspoon salt. Bring the mixture to a full boil, whisking occasionally, then add the baking soda, whisking until it foams up and turns a lighter opaque color. Remove from the heat and stir in the vanilla.

Pour the caramel over the popcorn and toss on the chopped almonds. Toss with a rubber spatula until everything is coated, then spread the mixture out on the prepped baking sheets. Bake on the middle rack of the oven for 6 minutes. Stir and bake 6 minutes more. Slide the parchment paper and popcorn onto a rack to cool.

Give a bag of this special caramel corn to all of your co-workers. They'll love you for it.

serves 8

Everyone's Favorite Pumpkin Pie

For the crust

1¾ C. flour, plus more for rolling

2 tsp. sugar, plus more for sprinkling

¾ tsp. salt

6 T. cold unsalted butter, cubed

¼ C. shortening

7 to 8 T. ice water

1 egg yolk

Milk

For the filling

1 (15 oz.) can pumpkin purée

1 (14 oz.) can sweetened condensed milk

2 eggs

1 tsp. cinnamon

½ tsp. each ground ginger and nutmeg

½ tsp. salt

Pinch of black pepper

For the crust, in a big bowl, stir together 1¾ cups flour, 2 teaspoons sugar, and salt. Add the butter and rub between your fingers until the ingredients hold together; add the shortening and mix until pea-sized pieces form. Drizzle in half the water; mix until just moistened. Stir in the remaining water a little at a time *(don't over-mix)*. Flatten, wrap in plastic, and chill 30 minutes.

Preheat your oven to 425°. Roll the chilled dough on a lightly floured surface to a 10" circle; press into a 9" pie plate, flute, trim, and set aside. Cut small shapes from dough scraps. Whisk the egg yolk with a little milk; brush lightly over cut-outs. Sprinkle with sugar and bake for 10 minutes, until golden; set aside.

For the filling, whisk together the pumpkin, sweetened condensed milk, eggs, cinnamon, ginger, nutmeg, salt, and black pepper. Pour into the crust and bake for 15 minutes. Reduce oven temperature to 350°; bake an additional 35 minutes, until a knife inserted 1" from the edge comes out clean. Cool before cutting. Garnish with cut-outs.

You can skip the cut-out step and just bake crust scraps with cinnamon-sugar like Grandma did. Kids love 'em!

Pie Crust Spirals

Make the crust as directed at left; roll out to 8 x 12". Sprinkle generously with cinnamon-sugar. Starting at a short end, roll crust into a tight log. Cut into 1" slices, place cut side down on a baking sheet, and bake at 350° for 15 to 18 minutes, until just done. Move to a rack to cool. When cool, drizzle with powdered sugar icing.

Chocolate-Almond Toffee

Toast 1¼ C. coarsely chopped almonds; set aside ¼ C. and put the remainder in a single layer in a 9 x 13" pan lined with parchment paper. In a saucepan over medium heat, heat 1 C. unsalted butter *(cubed)*, 1 C. sugar, ½ tsp. vanilla, and ¼ tsp. salt 10 to 15 minutes, until caramel-colored, whisking constantly; drizzle evenly over the almonds in the pan and sprinkle with 1½ C. mini semi-sweet chocolate chips. When the chips have softened, spread evenly and sprinkle with the set-aside almonds. When cool, break into pieces.

Red Hot Divinity

In the bowl of a stand mixer, beat 2 egg whites until foamy; add ¼ tsp. cream of tartar and beat until stiff peaks form. Butter a 5 x 9" loaf pan; set aside. In a heavy saucepan over medium heat, mix 2½ C. sugar, ½ C. light corn syrup, ½ C. hot water, ¼ tsp. salt, and ½ C. Red Hots candies until boiling, stirring constantly; cover and boil 3 minutes undisturbed. Uncover, attach a candy thermometer, and heat to 260°, without stirring; pour into the egg whites in a slow, steady stream, beating constantly. Add 1 tsp. vanilla and beat until stiff peaks form. Immediately spread into prepped pan. Cool, then cut into squares.

A new twist to an old favorite.

serves 10

Gingerbread Cake Roll

For the cake

3 eggs
½ C. sugar
¼ C. sugar-free applesauce
½ C. molasses
1 C. flour
1 tsp. baking powder
2 tsp. cinnamon
½ tsp. ground allspice
1 tsp. ground ginger
½ tsp. salt
Powdered sugar

For the filling

1 C. heavy cream
2 T. powdered sugar
½ tsp. clear vanilla
5 T. purchased eggnog
(or see recipe, pg. 19)

Preheat your oven to 350°. Spritz a 10 x 15" rimmed baking sheet with cooking spray, line with parchment paper, and spritz the paper. Set aside.

For the cake, in a big mixing bowl, beat the eggs on high speed for 5 minutes. Gradually beat in the sugar, applesauce, and molasses. In a separate bowl, mix the flour, baking powder, cinnamon, allspice, ginger, and salt and add to the egg mixture. Beat until blended and spread evenly into the prepped pan. Bake 15 to 18 minutes, until done. Immediately turn the cake out onto a kitchen towel sprinkled liberally with sifted powdered sugar; remove paper. Starting at a narrow end, roll up the towel and cake together. Let stand a couple hours, until cool.

For the filling, beat the cream, powdered sugar, and vanilla until soft peaks form. Add eggnog a little at a time, beating until stiff peaks form. Carefully unroll the cooled cake and spread about half the whipped cream over the top; reroll the cake without the towel. Chill up to 24 hours before slicing. Serve with the remaining whipped cream.

makes about
2 dozen

Stained Glass Cut-Outs

1 C. unsalted butter, softened

¾ C. sugar

1 egg

1 tsp. vanilla

¼ tsp. salt

2½ C. flour, plus more for rolling

Small hard candies, crushed *(we used red and green Life Savers and blue candy canes)*

Cookie cutters in two sizes *(ours were 4" and 2")*

Cream the butter in a mixing bowl on medium speed and gradually beat in the sugar. Beat in the egg, vanilla, and salt until well mixed. Stir in the flour, ⅓ at a time, until incorporated. Divide the dough in half, flatten, wrap in plastic, and chill overnight.

Once the dough is chilled, preheat your oven to 375°. Line cookie sheets with parchment paper and coat with cooking spray; set aside.

Remove one chilled dough portion from the fridge and place on a lightly floured surface; let stand 10 minutes to soften slightly. Lightly flour the dough, cover with a sheet of waxed paper, and roll to ¼" thickness. Remove the paper and use the larger cookie cutter to cut shapes from the dough; transfer to the prepped cookie sheets. Remove the centers of the cookies with the smaller cookie cutter. Reroll scraps and repeat. Fill the cut-out part of each cookie with some crushed candy *(make sure to get all those nooks and crannies, too)* and bake for 10 minutes, until the edges start to brown and the candy is melted. Cool at least 10 minutes, then transfer to cooling racks covered with waxed paper. Repeat with the remaining chilled dough.

Store cookies on waxed paper to prevent the candy from sticking.

Fun Idea

Poke a small hole in the top of cookies before baking. When cool, attach ribbon and use as a decoration.

Eggnog Biscotti

For the biscotti

½ C. butter, softened

1 C. sugar

2 eggs

½ C. purchased eggnog *(or see recipe, pg. 19)*

1 tsp. rum flavoring

3¼ C. flour

2 tsp. baking powder

2 tsp. ground nutmeg

½ tsp. salt

For the glaze

1 C. powdered sugar

½ tsp. rum flavoring

2 to 3 T. eggnog

Preheat your oven to 350° and line a big baking sheet with parchment paper; set aside.

For the biscotti, in a big mixing bowl, beat butter, sugar, and eggs until well blended. Mix in eggnog and rum flavoring just until blended.

In a separate bowl, stir together flour, baking powder, nutmeg, and salt. Stir the flour mixture into the butter mixture a little at a time until well blended.

Divide the dough in half. On a floured surface, shape each half into a 14"-long roll and set on the prepped baking sheet, 3" apart; flatten slightly. Bake for 25 minutes, until golden brown. Move from the pan to a cooling rack.

When cool enough to handle, carefully cut rolls crosswise into ½"-thick slices. Place slices cut side down on the baking sheet and bake for 10 minutes. Flip slices over and bake 10 minutes longer, until firm and lightly browned. Transfer to racks set over waxed paper to cool completely.

For the glaze, mix the powdered sugar, rum flavoring, and enough eggnog to make a drizzling consistency. Drizzle over the biscotti.

Homemade Eggnog

In a saucepan, whisk together 8 egg yolks, ⅓ C. sugar, and ½ tsp. salt until light in color. Stir in 4 C. whole milk, 2 C. heavy cream, 2 tsp. ground nutmeg, 2 tsp. vanilla, 2 tsp. almond extract, and 1 tsp. rum flavoring. In a bowl, beat 8 egg whites until soft peaks barely form; fold into the milk mixture. Heat gradually to 140°, then cook for 3 minutes, stirring often; chill. Whisk before serving.
Serves 16

Pecan Snowballs

- 2 C. flour
- ¾ tsp. salt
- 2 C. chopped pecans, divided
- 1 C. unsalted butter, softened
- ⅓ C. sugar
- 1½ tsp. vanilla
- Powdered sugar

Preheat your oven to 325° and line cookie sheets with parchment paper; set aside.

Mix the flour, salt, and 1 cup pecans. Pulse the remaining 1 cup pecans in a food processor until finely ground, then stir them into the flour mixture.

In a separate bowl, cream together the butter and sugar. Beat in the vanilla and the flour mixture until incorporated, scraping down the bowl as needed. Roll the dough into scant tablespoon-sized balls, arrange on prepped cookie sheets, and bake for 18 minutes or until the bottoms are golden brown. Cool 2 minutes, then move to racks to cool.

Roll the cooled cookies in powdered sugar. Let stand 1 hour, then roll in powdered sugar again.

makes about
4 dozen

Chocolate-Dipped Cherry Meringues

- 4 egg whites
- ½ tsp. cream of tartar
- ½ tsp. salt
- 1⅓ C. sugar
- 1½ tsp. cherry flavoring
- Pink paste food coloring
- ½ C. semi-sweet chocolate chips
- 6 oz. chocolate almond bark
- Piping bag and large star tip

Put the egg whites in a big mixing bowl and let stand at room temperature for 30 minutes. Preheat your oven to 225° and line cookie sheets with parchment paper; set aside.

Add cream of tartar and salt to the egg whites and beat on high speed until soft peaks form. Gradually add sugar, 1 tablespoon at a time, beating well after each addition. Continue to beat on high speed until egg whites are glossy and stiff, 5 to 8 minutes. Beat in cherry flavoring and food coloring.

Transfer the mixture to the piping bag fitted with the star tip. Pipe 2" swirls about 1" apart on the prepped cookie sheets. Bake for 1 hour, until dry, firm to the touch, and lightly browned on the bottom.

Turn the oven off, keeping the meringues in the oven with the door closed for 1 hour or until cool.

In a small microwavable bowl, melt the chocolate chips and almond bark together, stirring until smooth. Carefully dip the bottoms of the cooled meringues into the melted chocolate, allowing the excess to drip off. Set on clean parchment paper until the chocolate is set. Store in an airtight container.

Sugarplums

Toast 2 C. almonds and dump into a food processor; pulse until finely chopped. Add ¼ C. honey, 1½ tsp. cinnamon, ½ tsp. ground nutmeg, ¼ tsp. ground cloves, 1½ C. whole dried apricots, ½ C. dried plums (prunes), ½ C. pitted dates, the zest of an orange, and a pinch of salt. Pulse until well chopped and beginning to hold together. Roll into balls using a rounded tablespoonful for each. Dust with powdered sugar. ***Makes 2½ dozen***

Thumbprint Snow People

For the cookies

½ C. butter, softened

¼ C. sugar, plus more for rolling

¼ C. brown sugar

1 tsp. baking powder

½ tsp. salt

1 egg

1 T. milk

1 tsp. vanilla

2 C. flour

For the icing

1¼ C. powdered sugar, sifted

2 T. milk

½ tsp. almond extract

Orange and black paste food coloring

Preheat your oven to 375° and line cookie sheets with parchment paper; set aside.

For the cookies, in a big bowl, beat butter on medium speed about 30 seconds. Beat in ¼ cup sugar, brown sugar, baking powder, and salt, scraping bowl occasionally. Mix in egg, milk, and vanilla, then beat in the flour until well mixed. For each cookie, shape dough into two ¾" balls and place beside each other on the prepped cookie sheets, sides touching. Press a thumb or the back of a small round measuring spoon into each ball to form an indentation. Repeat with remaining dough. *(Or make face-only cookies by using one dough ball.)* Bake 7 to 9 minutes, until the edges are light brown. Press indentation again. Transfer cookies to a rack to cool.

For the icing, stir together the powdered sugar, milk, and almond extract until smooth; fill the cooled cookie indentations with icing and let set several hours to dry. Tint half the remaining icing orange; tint the other half black. When the white icing is dry, decorate the cookies with the colored icing.

Sure to become a highly anticipated treat.

makes about
28 cookies

makes about 4½ dozen

Chocolate-Covered Cherries

On paper towels, drain 2 (10 oz.) jars maraschino cherries *(with stems)*. Mix 3½ C. powdered sugar, ½ C. softened butter, 1 T. milk, and 2 tsp. vanilla and use about 1 teaspoonful to cover each cherry; roll between your palms to make smooth balls. Chill overnight on waxed paper.

Melt 12 oz. chocolate almond bark with 1 C. dark chocolate chips; dip covered cherries to coat, letting excess drip off before setting on waxed paper to harden. Drizzle with more chocolate or dip halfway into melted white almond bark if you'd like.

serves 6

Pecan Cinnamon Roll Bake

Preheat your oven to 375° and coat a 9 x 9" deep baking dish with cooking spray. Pour 2 T. melted butter into the dish. Separate 2 (12.4 oz.) cans refrigerated cinnamon rolls *(the kind with icing included)*, cut each roll into six pieces, and place over the butter. In a bowl, whisk together 4 eggs, ½ C. heavy cream, 2 tsp. vanilla, and 2 tsp. cinnamon and pour evenly over the rolls. Sprinkle on 1 C. chopped pecans and drizzle with ¼ C. pure maple syrup. Bake for 45 minutes, until golden brown, covering with foil toward the end to prevent over-browning. Cool 10 minutes. Mix the icing with 1 tsp. maple syrup and drizzle over the warm rolls.

Serves 20

Fudgy Mint Brownies

For the brownies

1 (18.3 oz.) pkg. fudge brownie mix

Water, oil, and eggs as directed on brownie mix

For the filling

4 C. powdered sugar

3 oz. cream cheese, softened

¼ C. butter, softened

1 tsp. vanilla

¼ to ½ tsp. mint extract

Green food coloring

¼ to ⅓ C. milk

For the frosting

1 C. semi-sweet chocolate chips

¼ C. butter

¼ C. heavy cream

Preheat your oven to 350° and spray the bottom only of a 7 x 11" baking pan with cooking spray. For the brownies, stir together the brownie mix, water, oil, and eggs as directed on package, and bake about 40 minutes or until done. Cool completely.

For the filling, in a big mixing bowl, beat the powdered sugar, cream cheese, butter, vanilla, mint extract, food coloring, and enough of the milk to make a spreading consistency. Spread evenly over the cooled brownies. Refrigerate about 1 hour.

For the frosting, in a small saucepan, melt the chocolate chips with the butter and cream over low heat until smooth, stirring constantly. Remove from the heat and cool 10 minutes, then pour over the chilled brownies, spreading evenly. Refrigerate about 1 hour, until the chocolate is set. Cut into bars and store any leftovers in the fridge.

A brownie mix makes these convenient; the homemade filling and frosting makes them memorable!

makes about
2 dozen

Orange-Fennel Roundabouts

For the cookies

1 C. unsalted butter, softened

¾ C. sugar

1 tsp. salt

2½ C. flour, plus more for rolling

1 T. fennel seed, crushed to nearly a powder

1½ T. orange zest

1 egg at room temperature

1 tsp. vanilla

1 tsp. orange flavoring

For the frosting

2 C. powdered sugar, sifted

½ tsp. orange zest, plus more for sprinkling

Orange juice

For the cookies, in a mixing bowl, beat the butter, sugar, and salt on high speed for 5 minutes, until fluffy, scraping the bowl often.

In a separate bowl, 2½ cups flour, fennel seed, and orange zest. Add the egg, vanilla, and orange flavoring, stirring until combined; add to the butter mixture and beat on low speed until just combined. Form the dough into two disks, wrap in plastic, and chill at least an hour.

Preheat your oven to 350° and line cookie sheets with parchment paper; spritz the paper with cooking spray. Set aside.

Let one dough disk stand at room temperature a few minutes to soften. On a lightly floured surface, roll out the dough about ¼" thick and cut out 3" rounds; set on prepped cookie sheets, 1" apart. Bake 13 to 15 minutes or until just golden around the edges. Transfer to a cooling rack set over waxed paper. Repeat with remaining dough.

For the frosting, whisk together the powdered sugar, ½ teaspoon orange zest, and enough orange juice to make spreading consistency; frost the cooled cookies. Sprinkle with more zest if you'd like.

Hot Cocoa Gifts

Use a funnel to pour one serving of your favorite hot cocoa mix into a clear food-safe plastic ball ornament (ours was 3¼"). Ramp up the flavor with your favorite add-ins like white, mint, or chocolate chips, Red Hots candies, and/or mini marshmallows. Tie on a bow for gift-giving.

Lacy Ginger-Almond Snaps

For the snaps

Butter for coating pans, plus ½ C. for snaps

½ C. sugar

⅓ C. dark corn syrup

¾ C. flour

½ tsp. ground ginger

1 T. half & half

For the filling

2 C. heavy cream

⅓ C. powdered sugar

2½ tsp. almond extract

Sliced almonds

Maraschino cherries, drained

Preheat your oven to 350° and line cookie sheets with foil, making sure foil is smooth and flat. Lightly butter the foil and the underside of several mini muffin cups.

For the snaps, in a medium saucepan, combine sugar, syrup, and the ½ cup butter. Cook over low heat until butter melts; remove from heat. In a bowl, stir together the flour and ginger and stir into the butter mixture. Add the half & half and stir to combine.

Drop batter by rounded teaspoonful a few inches apart on prepped cookie sheets, making only three or four at a time *(they will increase in size)*. Bake 9 to 10 minutes, until bubbly and golden brown. Let cool 1 to 2 minutes, until set but still pliable; promptly remove with a spatula and drape over the prepped muffin cups, pressing to form a basket shape. Let cool a few minutes, then remove from cups to cool completely. Repeat with remaining batter.

For the filling, beat cream and powdered sugar in a chilled bowl with chilled beaters until it will hold its shape. Stir in almond extract. Pipe filling into each basket and sprinkle with almonds; top with a cherry.

makes about
3 dozen

makes about 3 dozen

Peppermint Dips

1 C. flour

½ C. unsweetened cocoa powder, plus more for rolling

½ tsp. baking soda

½ tsp. baking powder

½ tsp. salt

5 T. unsalted butter, softened

¾ C. sugar

1 egg plus 1 egg yolk

¾ tsp. peppermint extract

1¼ lbs. white or chocolate almond bark, coarsely chopped

15 round peppermint candies, crushed

Sift the flour, ½ cup cocoa powder, baking soda, baking powder, and salt into a bowl. In a mixing bowl, beat butter and sugar on medium-high speed for 1 minute; reduce speed to medium-low and add egg, then egg yolk, beating well after each addition. Beat in peppermint extract. Slowly beat in the flour mixture until just incorporated. Shape into two flat disks, wrap in plastic, and refrigerate at least 1 hour.

Working with one portion at a time, lightly coat both sides of dough with cocoa powder and roll between two pieces of parchment paper to ⅛" thickness; chill for 15 minutes.

Preheat your oven to 325°. Cut 2" circles from dough and arrange on parchment paper-lined baking sheets. Roll and cut scraps once. Freeze cookies 15 minutes.

Bake for 12 minutes or until cookies are dry to the touch. Transfer to racks to cool. Let the baking sheets cool and line with clean parchment paper.

Melt the almond bark in a double boiler over low heat. Using a fork, dip each cookie into the melted bark to coat, letting excess drip off; gently scrape the bottom against the edge of the pan. Set on prepped baking sheets and sprinkle with candy. Repeat with the remaining cookies. Let dry.

Package Idea

Cut pretty paper to fit inside a cellophane bag and tuck in some cookies. Add a paper topper and a ribbon for a gift that's sure to please.

makes 1½ dozen

Super Soft Butter Rolls

- ¾ C. milk
- ¼ C. butter
- 1 tsp. salt
- ¼ C. plus 1 tsp. sugar, divided
- 2 (.25 oz.) pkgs. active dry yeast
- ½ C. warm water *(110°)*
- 1 egg, lightly beaten
- 3½ C. bread flour, plus more for kneading
- Butter for brushing, softened

Pour milk into a glass 2-cup measuring cup and microwave until it boils. Add the butter, salt, and ¼ cup sugar; set aside until the temperature drops below 110°.

In a big bowl, dissolve the yeast and the remaining 1 teaspoon sugar in the warm water; let stand until it foams, about 10 minutes.

Pour the milk mixture into the yeast mixture; add the egg and 2 cups of the bread flour. Stir until smooth. Stir in the remaining flour, ½ cup at a time, until the dough is smooth and a little tacky. Knead lightly on a floured surface to pull dough together. Shape into a ball and place in a big oiled bowl; turn to coat the dough. Cover with a towel and let rise in a warm place for 30 minutes.

Preheat your oven to 350° and line two 8 x 8" baking pans with parchment paper. Divide dough into 18 even pieces, forming smooth balls with floured fingers; arrange half in each pan. Bake 20 to 25 minutes, until golden brown. Remove from the oven and immediately butter the tops.

Bake in disposable pans and give to a neighbor. Add a jar of flavored butter, too.

Flavored Butters

Cran-Orange Butter

Whisk together ½ C. very soft butter, 3 T. chopped cranberries, 2 T. honey, and orange zest to taste.

Cinna-Honey Butter

Whisk together ½ C. very soft butter, 2 T. sifted powdered sugar, 2½ T. honey, 1 tsp. vanilla, and 1 tsp. cinnamon.

These make great gifts! Just pack into small jars and attach a spoon.

Candy Cane Cookies

½ C. shortening
½ C. butter, softened
1 C. powdered sugar
1 egg
1½ tsp. peppermint extract
1 tsp. vanilla
2½ C. flour, plus more for rolling
¾ tsp. salt
Red food coloring
Powdered sugar

Preheat your oven to 375° and line cookie sheets with parchment paper.

Beat together the shortening, butter, and powdered sugar just until well combined. Add the egg, peppermint extract, and vanilla and mix well. Stir in 2½ cups flour and salt.

Transfer half the dough to another bowl and stir in food coloring until well blended. Chill both bowls for 15 minutes. On a lightly floured surface, roll about ½ tablespoon red dough into a 1" ball and then roll it into a rope about 5" long; do the same with the plain dough. Lay the ropes side by side and twist together. Set on prepped cookie sheets and curve the top to look like a candy cane. Repeat with the remaining dough. Bake for 6 to 9 minutes, until cookies are set and are just barely turning golden brown underneath.

Let cookies cool on the pan for a minute or two before removing to a rack to cool completely. Sprinkle with a little powdered sugar.

Flavored with peppermint, these old-time cookies will bring smiles to young and old alike.

makes about
2½ dozen

Microwave Caramels

Grease a 12 x 17" rimmed baking sheet with butter. In a big glass bowl, melt 1 C. butter in the microwave. Stir in 1 C. brown sugar, 1 C. sugar, and 1 C. light corn syrup. Add 1 (14 oz.) can sweetened condensed milk and stir to combine. Microwave on high for 12 minutes, whisking well halfway through cooking time. Stir in 1 tsp. vanilla. Pour hot caramel mixture into the prepped pan and spread evenly. Let cool completely. Cut into pieces and wrap in waxed paper *(we cut ours about ½" x 3")*. Can be stored in the refrigerator.

Ginger-Spice Nuts

Preheat your oven to 350°. In a medium bowl, mix ¾ tsp. cinnamon, ¾ tsp. ground ginger, ¼ tsp. ground allspice, ¼ tsp. ground nutmeg, ⅛ tsp. ground cloves, 3 T. brown sugar, a pinch of coarse salt, and 2 T. coconut oil. Stir in 1½ C. each walnut and pecan halves. Dump everything in a single layer on a parchment paper-lined rimmed baking sheet. Bake 10 to 12 minutes, until fragrant. Remove from the oven and stir until most of the spices cling to the nuts.

Cinnamon Wreath Bread

For the rolls

2 (.25 oz.) pkgs. active dry yeast

A pinch plus ½ C. sugar

¼ C. warm water *(110°)*

1 C. whole milk

½ C. butter, softened

1 egg

½ tsp. salt

1 tsp. ground cardamom

4 C. flour, plus more for kneading

For the filling

2 T. butter, melted

¼ C. plus 2 T. brown sugar

1½ T. sugar

1 T. cinnamon

1 C. golden raisins

¾ C. chopped almonds

¼ C. plus 2 T. almond paste, chopped into small pieces

For the rolls, dissolve the yeast and a pinch of sugar in the warm water and set aside. Warm the milk in a small saucepan over medium heat until steaming *(but not boiling)*. Remove from the heat and stir in the butter and ½ cup sugar until dissolved. Pour into a big mixing bowl and beat in the yeast mixture and egg. Mix in the salt and cardamom and slowly add 2 cups of the flour. Gradually add the remaining 2 cups flour until a soft dough forms and pulls away from the sides of the bowl.

Knead the dough on a floured surface 7 to 10 minutes *(or use a dough hook in a stand mixer)*, adding a little more flour as needed to keep the dough from being too sticky. Transfer dough to an oiled bowl, turn to coat, and cover bowl with plastic wrap. Let rise for an hour or until doubled in size. Punch down dough and divide in half. On a lightly floured surface, roll half the dough to an 8 x 16" rectangle.

For the filling, brush dough with half the melted butter to about ½" from the edges. Mix the brown sugar, sugar, and cinnamon and sprinkle half of it over the butter. Add half the raisins, half the almonds, and half the almond paste. Starting with one long side, roll up; pinch ends. Transfer to a greased baking sheet seam side down and form the dough into a circle, pinching ends together. With scissors, cut from outside edge about ⅔ of the way through the dough at 1" intervals; separate slices slightly and twist, filling side up. Repeat with the remaining dough. Cover and let rise until nearly doubled, about an hour.

Preheat your oven to 350° and bake 20 to 30 minutes, until golden brown, covering with foil toward the end of baking if the top is getting too dark. Cool completely.

To decorate, dust with powdered sugar and garnish with extra almonds, cranberries, star anise, and cinnamon sticks, or frost if desired.

makes about 2 dozen

Sugar Cookie Swirls

- ⅔ C. shortening
- ⅔ C. butter
- 1½ C. sugar
- 2 eggs, lightly beaten
- 3½ C. flour
- 1 tsp. salt
- 2 tsp. baking powder
- 2 tsp. vanilla
- Red and green paste food coloring
- Decorating sprinkles

In a mixing bowl, beat shortening, butter, sugar, and eggs. Beat in the flour, salt, baking powder, and vanilla on low speed until incorporated. Increase speed to medium and beat until well blended.

Divide the dough into three separate bowls. Mix red food coloring into one bowl – you'll need quite a bit to get a deep, rich color. Do the same to another bowl using green. Keep the third bowl plain. Roll out each color on separate pieces of waxed paper to about ⅛" thickness, making them all about the same size. Carefully flip one on top of the other, lining up edges of dough as much as possible and removing the waxed paper after flipping. Once stacked, use a pizza cutter to trim edges straight.

Starting at one long side, roll the layers tightly together, lifting up the waxed paper underneath to help roll. Wrap the waxed paper around the roll and chill overnight.

Preheat your oven to 375°. Use a sharp knife to cut dough into ⅝"-thick slices. Roll the edges in decorating sprinkles and set on a parchment paper-lined cookie sheet. Bake about 10 minutes, until just barely done.

Cupcake Toppers

Melt green candy melts; pour into a zippered plastic bag, zip shut, and cut off a tiny corner. Lay pretzel sticks several inches apart on waxed paper. Starting about ½" above each pretzel, pipe green tree shapes, continuing over all but the bottom 1" of the pretzel; while still wet, toss on decorating sprinkles. When dry, peel trees off the paper and poke uncoated end into frosted cupcakes.

makes 1 loaf

Iced Fruit Bread

For the bread

½ C. butter, softened

1 C. sugar

2 eggs

2 C. flour

1 tsp. baking soda

¾ to 1 C. mashed ripe banana

⅓ C. chopped maraschino cherries

⅓ C. toasted chopped walnuts or pecans

For the icing

¾ C. sifted powdered sugar

1 tsp. cherry flavoring

Milk

Preheat your oven to 350° and generously grease a 5 x 9" loaf pan; set aside.

For the bread, in a mixing bowl, cream the butter and sugar together until light and fluffy. Add the eggs one at a time, beating well after each.

In a separate bowl, sift together the flour and baking soda. Add to the butter mixture alternately with the banana, beating until just incorporated. Stir in the cherries and nuts and pour into the prepped loaf pan. Bake 55 to 60 minutes or until done. Set the pan on a cooling rack for 10 minutes, then remove the bread from the pan.

For the icing, mix the powdered sugar, cherry flavoring, and enough milk to make a drizzling consistency. Drizzle over warm or cool bread; cool before slicing.

For gift-giving, don't ice. Just wrap in a pretty dish towel and tie a ribbon around the whole thing.

serves 16

Peppermint Bark Cheesecake

For the crust

20 Oreos, finely crushed

3 T. unsalted butter, melted

For the filling

6 oz. white baking chocolate, chopped

½ C. heavy cream

3½ (8 oz.) pkgs. cream cheese, softened

1 C. sugar

4 eggs

1 tsp. peppermint extract

1½ tsp. vanilla

½ C. sour cream

5 oz. semi-sweet baking chocolate, chopped

⅓ C. peppermint bits or crushed peppermint candies

For the topping

2 oz. white baking chocolate, chopped

1 C. heavy cream

2 T. sugar

½ (8 oz.) pkg. cream cheese, softened

¼ tsp. peppermint extract

Preheat your oven to 350°. Cover the outside and underside of a 9" springform pan with heavy-duty foil; spritz the inside of the pan with cooking spray and set aside.

For the crust, stir together the Oreos and butter until moistened; press firmly into the bottom of the prepped pan. Bake 10 minutes, then set on a cooling rack. Reduce oven temperature to 325°.

For the filling, melt the white chocolate and cream together in the microwave at 50% power, stirring every 20 seconds; whisk until smooth and set aside. In a mixing bowl, beat together the cream cheese and sugar until smooth. Beat in eggs one at a time; stir in peppermint extract, vanilla, and sour cream. Stir in the melted white chocolate. Tap the bowl on the counter several times to eliminate air pockets. Fold in the semi-sweet chocolate and peppermint bits and spread over the crust. Set in a big roasting pan on the center rack of the oven. Pour enough boiling water into the roasting pan to cover half the springform pan. Bake 1½ hours or until the edges of the cheesecake are beginning to set, but the center jiggles slightly.

Carefully remove the pan from the water and set on a cooling rack for 45 minutes. Cover with plastic wrap leaving a small opening for heat to escape, then chill overnight.

For the topping, melt the white chocolate in the microwave at 50% power; set aside. In a mixing bowl, beat the cream until soft peaks form; add sugar and beat until very stiff peaks form. In a separate mixing bowl, beat cream cheese until smooth; stir in the peppermint extract and melted white chocolate. Fold in the whipped cream and spread evenly over the chilled cheesecake; chill 1½ hours longer. Run a knife around the edge of the pan to loosen; remove the sides of the pan, slice the cheesecake, and garnish any way you'd like.

makes about
3 dozen

Salted Caramel Pretzel Bites

For the cookies

1 C. flour

⅓ C. unsweetened cocoa powder

¼ tsp. salt

½ C. unsalted butter, softened

⅓ C. sugar

⅓ C. light brown sugar

1 egg yolk

1½ tsp. vanilla

2 T. buttermilk

1 C. finely chopped pretzels

For the filling

15 caramels, unwrapped

2½ T. heavy cream

Coarse sea salt

½ C. milk chocolate chips

1 tsp. vegetable oil

For the cookies, in a bowl, mix flour, cocoa powder, and salt. In a big mixing bowl, beat butter, sugar, and brown sugar until pale and fluffy. Mix in egg yolk and vanilla. Blend in the buttermilk. Slowly add the flour mixture, beating on low speed until just incorporated. Cover dough and chill at least an hour.

Preheat your oven to 350° and line cookie sheets with parchment paper. Shape the chilled dough into 1" balls and roll in the pretzels to coat. Arrange on prepped baking sheets and use your thumb to make a deep indentation in the center of each. Bake 10 to 12 minutes.

Remove the cookies from the oven and use a rounded measuring spoon to press down on the existing indentation. Cool several minutes before moving to a rack to cool.

For the filling, combine caramels and cream in a glass bowl and microwave until melted and smooth, stirring every 30 seconds. Spoon caramel into the cookies' indentation; sprinkle with sea salt.

Melt chocolate chips with oil in the microwave at 50% power. Transfer to a small zippered plastic bag; zip shut, cut off a tiny corner, and drizzle chocolate over cookies. Let stand until cool.

Starlight Ornaments

Preheat your oven to 350° and line a baking pan with parchment paper. Spray metal cookie cutters with cooking spray; arrange in pan. Fill cutters with a single layer of peppermint candies. Bake 5 minutes or until candies have melted together. While hot, use a toothpick coated with cooking spray to poke a hole in the top of each. Let harden, remove from the cutters, and attach ribbon.

makes about
6 dozen

Dressed-Up Peanut Blossoms

For the cookies

1 C. shortening

1 C. creamy peanut butter

1 C. brown sugar

1 C. sugar, plus more for rolling

2 eggs

¼ C. milk

2 tsp. vanilla

3½ C. flour

2 tsp. baking soda

1 tsp. salt

For the frosting

½ C. butter, softened

½ tsp. vanilla

2½ C. powdered sugar

½ C. unsweetened cocoa powder, sifted

2 T. milk

2 T. light corn syrup

Piping bag and large star tip

Preheat your oven to 375° and grease cookie sheets; set aside. For the cookies, cream together the shortening, peanut butter, brown sugar, and 1 cup sugar until smooth. Beat in the eggs one at a time; stir in the milk and vanilla. In a separate bowl, mix the flour, baking soda, and salt; stir into the peanut butter mixture until well blended. Shape tablespoonfuls of dough into balls and roll in more sugar. Arrange 2" apart on prepped cookie sheets. Bake 12 to 14 minutes, until golden brown and cracked.

Remove from the oven and immediately use a rounded measuring spoon to gently press an indentation into the center of the cookies. Transfer to a rack to cool.

For the frosting, mix the butter and vanilla. Slowly beat in the powdered sugar and cocoa powder; stir in the milk and syrup. Beat on high speed to desired consistency and transfer the mixture to the piping bag fitted with the star tip; pipe into the center of the cooled cookies.

Neapolitan Fudge

Melt 3 C. semi-sweet chocolate chips with 1 (14 oz.) can sweetened condensed milk and 2 T. butter. Stir in 1 tsp. vanilla and 1 C. chopped walnuts. Spread evenly into a 9 x 9" foil-lined and greased pan. Boil together ¾ C. unsalted butter, 2 C. sugar, ¾ C. heavy cream, and a pinch of salt for 5 minutes, stirring constantly; remove from heat. Use a hand mixer to beat in 2 C. white baking chips and 1 (7 oz.) jar marshmallow crème until smooth; pour half over the chocolate layer. To the remainder, beat in 2 T. dry strawberry gelatin; drop by spoonfuls into pan and swirl gently with a knife. Chill before cutting.

Reindeer Bark

Line a jellyroll pan with parchment paper. Remove ¼ C. of chips from a 12 oz. bag of dark chocolate chips and set aside; toss the remainder into a double boiler with 1 C. butterscotch chips and melt over medium heat, stirring constantly. When smooth, remove from the heat and stir in the set-aside chips and 1 T. shortening until melted. Spread evenly in prepped pan. Make reindeer faces on the soft mixture using candy eyes, red M&M noses, and small pretzel twists for antlers *(cut pretzels with a sharp knife for best results)*. Toss on some decorating sprinkles for good measure; chill. When cool, but not completely set, cut into pieces around the faces; when set, break on the cut lines. Keep chilled.

serves 16

Pumpkin-Spice & Maple Poke Cake

For the cake

1 (15.25 oz.) pkg. spice cake mix

3 (3.4 oz.) pkgs. instant pumpkin spice pudding, divided

1 tsp. cinnamon

½ tsp. pumpkin pie spice

3 eggs

½ C. vegetable oil

4¾ C. milk, divided

½ C. sour cream

For the topping

2 C. heavy cream

2 tsp. cinnamon

3 T. pure maple syrup

¾ C. Heath milk chocolate toffee bits

Preheat your oven to 350° and grease a 9 x 13" baking pan.

For the cake, in a mixing bowl, stir together the cake mix, 1 package pudding mix, cinnamon, and pie spice. Beat in eggs, oil, ¾ cup milk, and sour cream until well combined. Pour into the prepped baking pan and bake 18 to 22 minutes, until done. Set the pan on a cooling rack for 15 minutes.

After 15 minutes, in a bowl, whisk together the remaining 2 packages pudding mix and the remaining 4 cups milk until smooth. Poke holes in the warm cake using the handle of a wooden spoon and pour the pudding mixture slowly over the cake, filling the holes. Refrigerate at least 1 hour.

For the topping, in a chilled bowl, beat together the cream and cinnamon until soft peaks form. Slowly add syrup, one tablespoon at a time, making sure the syrup is incorporated before adding more. Beat until stiff peaks form. Spread the whipped cream over the cooled cake and sprinkle with toffee bits.

Holly Jolly Crunch

In a big bowl, mix 7 C. Rice or Corn Chex cereal, 1 C. dried cranberries, 2 C. pretzels, 2 C. mini marshmallows, and 2 C. nuts (any of your favorites). Melt 1 (20 oz.) pkg. white almond bark according to package directions and stir into cereal; mix until coated. Add 1½ C. M&Ms and stir again. Spread on waxed paper to cool. ***Makes about 15 cups***

makes about
8 dozen

Cream Cheese Spritz

- 2 C. butter, softened
- 1 (8 oz.) pkg. cream cheese, softened
- 1 C. plus 3 T. sugar
- 2 tsp. vanilla
- 4½ C. sifted flour
- Paste food coloring, optional
- Colored sugars and/or decorating sprinkles, optional
- Almond bark or candy melts, any color, optional
- Cookie press

Whether you color them, dip them, or eat 'em straight-up plain, these cookies practically scream nostalgia!

Preheat your oven to 375° and chill your cookie sheets.

In a mixing bowl, cream together the butter and cream cheese until smooth. Add sugar and beat until well combined. Beat in vanilla and slowly add the flour, beating until well mixed. Stir in the food coloring if you're using it.

Transfer the dough to a cookie press fitted with the desired decorating plate. Form cookies on an ungreased chilled cookie sheet by setting the end of the cookie press against the cookie sheet and pressing out the shapes you want. Decorate cookies with colored sugars or decorating sprinkles now if you're not going to coat them in almond bark later.* Bake 8 to 10 minutes, until lightly browned underneath. Move to a rack to cool. For coated cookies, after baking, melt almond bark or candy melts in a small bowl in the microwave at 50% power, stirring until smooth. Set a cooled cookie on a fork above the bowl while drizzling the bark over the top and sides of the cookie; tap the fork against bowl to remove excess and set on a rack over waxed paper. Decorate with sugars or sprinkles. Repeat with remaining cookies. Let stand until the coating is dry.

** Some decorating sprinkles hold up to oven heat better than others – test on one cookie before decorating them all.*

Cookie Plate

Using enamel acrylic paint (for glass and ceramics), paint a design on a white ceramic plate; set on a baking sheet and place in a cold oven. Set oven temperature to 300° and heat the plate for 30 minutes, then set aside to cool. Now just pile on the cookies!

Gingerbread Village Centerpiece

½ C. plus 1 T. butter
½ C. brown sugar
½ C. light corn syrup
2 tsp. ground ginger
½ tsp. cinnamon
1 tsp. ground nutmeg
½ tsp. ground cloves
2½ C. flour, sifted
1 tsp. baking soda
Powdered sugar
Frosting and decorating sprinkles, optional
Tall bowl
Sugar

In a mixing bowl, cream together the butter and brown sugar until fluffy. Add the syrup, ginger, cinnamon, nutmeg, and cloves. In a separate bowl, mix the flour and baking soda and add it to the butter mixture, beating until well blended. Divide dough in half, flatten into disks, and wrap in plastic; chill until firm.

Let one disk soften slightly, then roll out 3⁄16" thick between sheets of parchment paper. Cut house and tree shapes using cookie cutters *(ours were about 4" to 7" tall)* or cut out free-hand. Press details like shingles and doors into the dough using a knife or toothpick. Slide parchment and cookies onto a tray and chill 15 to 20 minutes.

Preheat your oven to 375°. Transfer parchment and cookies to cookie sheets. Bake 8 to 10 minutes, until done. Transfer to racks to cool. Roll, cut, and bake remaining chilled dough.

Sprinkle powdered sugar liberally over cooled cookies and gently rub in. Cover with waxed paper and let stand 30 minutes. Decorate with frosting and sprinkles if you'd like. Fill the bowl with a few inches of sugar and arrange the cookies in the sugar.

makes about 12 cookies

makes about
1½ dozen

Lemon Tartlets

For the shells

½ C. butter, softened
½ C. sugar
1 egg
¾ tsp. lemon flavoring
¼ tsp. vanilla
2 tsp. lemon zest
1½ C. flour
⅛ tsp. salt

For the filling

½ C. heavy cream
3 T. powdered sugar
1 (10 oz.) jar lemon curd
½ C. sour cream
½ tsp. vanilla
1 lemon
Sugar
Spray whipped cream
Fresh berries
2½" tart tins *(or lined standard muffin cups)*

Preheat your oven to 375°.

For the shells, cream the butter, then beat in sugar until well blended. Mix in the egg, lemon flavoring, vanilla, and lemon zest. Add the flour and salt, mixing to make a stiff dough; chill at least 2 hours. Roll dough into 1¼" balls and press one into a thin even layer over the bottom and up the side of the tart tins. Bake about 10 minutes, until edges start to brown. Set tins upside down and when cool enough to handle, pinch edges slightly to remove the shells; cool completely.

For the filling, beat the cream with powdered sugar until stiff peaks form. In a separate bowl, whisk together lemon curd, sour cream, and vanilla; fold in the prepped whipped cream. Spoon into cool shells and freeze at least 4 hours.

Just before serving, peel thin strips of rind from the lemon and toss with sugar. Remove tartlets from freezer and top with whipped cream, berries, and lemon strips.

Index

POCKET GUIDE TO

Health Assessment

POCKET GUIDE TO

Health Assessment

Patricia A. Potter, RN, MSN

Doctoral Student
Saint Louis University School of Nursing
St. Louis, Missouri

Fourth Edition

*with **169** illustrations*

Mosby

St. Louis Baltimore Boston Carlsbad
Chicago Minneapolis New York Philadelphia Portland
London Milan Sydney Tokyo Toronto

Mosby
Dedicated to Publishing Excellence

A Times Mirror Company

Publisher: Nancy L. Coon
Senior Editor: Susan R. Epstein
Associate Developmental Editor: Jerry Schwartz
Project Manager: John Rogers
Senior Production Editor: Lavon Wirch Peters
Designer: Yael Kats
Manufacturing Manager: Linda Ierardi

Fourth Edition

Printed in the United States of America
Composition by Clarinda Company
Printing/binding by R.R. Donnelley & Sons Company

Mosby, Inc.
11830 Westline Industrial Drive
St. Louis, Missouri 63146

International Standard Book Number 0-8151-8396-8

98 99 00 01 02 / 9 8 7 6 5 4 3 2 1

Reviewers

Sue A. Beeson, MSN, PhD
Assistant Professor of Nursing
The University of North Carolina at Greensboro
Greensboro, North Carolina

Margie E. Brown, RNC, BSN, MS, ANP
Professor of Nursing, School of Health/Science
Long Beach City College
Long Beach, California

Lisa Kless-Kern, BSN, MSN
Professor
Community College of Southern Nevada
Las Vegas, Nevada

Cathleen Opperman, RN, MS, CPN
Nurse Educator
Pickerington, Ohio

Preface

Health assessment is the process of gathering, verifying, analyzing, and communicating data about a client. The purpose of the initial assessment is to establish a database about the client's level of wellness, health practices, past illnesses and related experiences, and health care goals. This database is derived from a health history, physical examination, and the results of laboratory and diagnostic test results. The information contained in the database is the basis for an individualized plan of care.

The *Pocket Guide to Health Assessment,* fourth edition, is a useful guide for performing physical examinations and health assessments in any type of clinical setting. The organization of the guide provides a quick reference when assessment focuses on a specific body system or when conducting a complete physical examination.

Features of the guide include the following:

- Summary of client and equipment preparation
- Step-by-step approach to body system assessment
- Review of normal and abnormal findings of the adult
- Listing of potential nursing diagnoses
- Special gerontologic and pediatric factors
- Teaching considerations
- Nurse alerts incorporated throughout caution about techniques to avoid or symptoms to be alert for
- Standard precautions alerts advise when to use protective garments

Several new features have been added in response to user requests and to address changes in health care. These include the following:

- Broadside 3-column format that lists the area assessed, normal findings, and variations
- A critical thinking model describes the application of critical thinking to health assessment
- Cultural variations alert the nurse to individual clients' preferences and pertinent assessment findings

- Delegation considerations address the appropriate role of unlicensed assistive personnel in health assessment
- Spiral binding that lays flat for easy reference

With the addition of these features, this trusted resource is made even more practical and more user-friendly.

Patricia A. Potter

Contents

I

PRELIMINARY SKILLS

1 Critical Thinking and Nursing Judgment

Nursing, as defined in the American Nurses Association (ANA) social policy statement, is "the diagnosis and treatment of human responses to actual or potential health problems" (ANA, 1980). To assist a person in maintaining, regaining, or improving health, a nurse must be able to make appropriate clinical judgments. Clinical decision making is central to nursing practice. Clinical decision making requires a nurse to think critically by analyzing and applying knowledge, reflecting on experience, exercising appropriate professional standards, solving problems, and making decisions. Health assessment is a key component of clinical decision making. Expertise in clinical decision making contributes to the advancement of nursing practice.

Consider a situation in which a nurse meets a female client who is visiting the local health clinic with a complaint of recent weight loss, fatigue, and recurrent headaches. The nurse observes the client initially, noting a poor postural stance, slow but purposeful body movements, and a grimaced facial expression suggesting "discomfort." Making the observation that the client has "discomfort" may result from the nurse's experience with other clients or from having seen the same client 6 months earlier and knowing that a change has occurred.

The nurse assesses the client further. As the client begins to describe her symptoms more specifically, the nurse begins to consider the client's reason for seeking health care, asks her occupation, observes for subtle signs in body position, and begins to ask focused questions. The questions may be direct, such as "Tell me how you are feeling" or "Where are the headaches located?" Measurement of the client's weight, assessment of vital signs, and a focused review of the head and neck area may provide additional information about the client's status. How the nurse uses the information to reason, make inferences, and form a mental picture of what is happening to this client is called *critical thinking*. Over time the nurse learns to almost simultaneously review, interpret, analyze, and evaluate information about clients. The nurse considers a client's situation without jumping to a single solution but rather by focusing on deciding what to believe and do (Kataoka-Yahiro and Saylor, 1994).

Facione and Facione (1996) define critical thinking as purposeful self-regulatory judgment that is centrally evident in expert clinical judgment. Whenever a nurse directs thinking toward understanding and finding solutions to a client's health problems, the process becomes purposeful and goal directed. It becomes a conscious habit.

The American Philosophical Association (APA) has developed a consensus description of critical thinking skills (Box 1-1). An awareness of these skills can help the nurse clinician appreciate the detail and attention necessary to be a successful critical thinker.

Model for Critical Thinking

Critical thinking is a complex cognitive process. Understanding the elements of critical thinking can make a nurse a better practitioner. This text is designed to provide a comprehensive approach for health assessment that adopts a critical thinking model.

Kataoka-Yahiro and Saylor (1994) have adapted a model of critical thinking for nursing judgment (Fig. 1-1). The model graphically displays the many dimensions and components of critical thinking (Box 1-2). The model also defines the outcome of critical thinking as the clinical judgment of nurses relevant to nursing problems in a variety of settings. The five components of critical thinking in the model include the following:

- *Specific knowledge base*—A specific knowledge base in nursing,

BOX 1-1 Critical Thinking Skills Proposed by the 1990 APA Consensus Definition: Critical Thinking Cognitive Skills and Subskills

Interpretation

- Categorization
- Decoding sentences
- Clarifying meaning

Analysis

- Examining ideas
- Identifying arguments
- Analyzing arguments

Evaluation

- Assessing claims
- Assessing arguments

Inference

- Querying evidence
- Conjecturing alternatives
- Drawing conclusions

Explanation

- Stating results
- Justifying procedures
- Presenting arguments

Self-Regulation

- Self-examination
- Self-correction

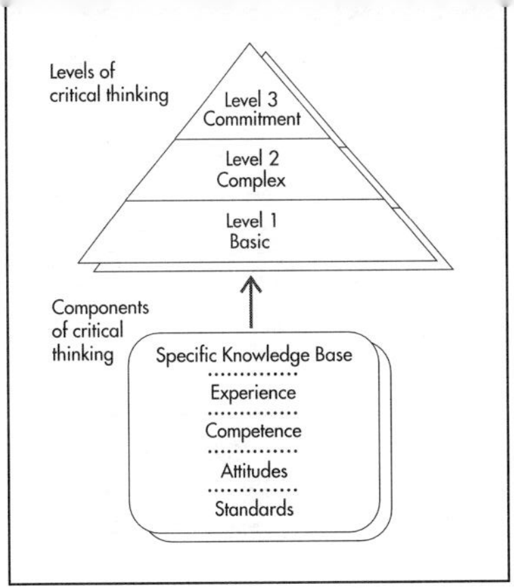

Fig. 1-1
Critical thinking model.
(Redrawn from Kataoka-Yahiro M, Saylor C: A critical thinking model for nursing judgment, *J Nurs Educ* 33(8):351, 1994. Modified from Glaser, 1941; Miller and Malcolm, 1990; Paul, 1993; and Perry, 1970.)

BOX 1-2 Components of Critical Thinking in Nursing

Specific Knowledge Base in Nursing
Experience in Nursing
Critical Thinking Competencies

- General competencies
- Specific competencies in clinical situations
- Specific competency in nursing

Attitudes for Critical Thinking

- Confidence
- Independence
- Fairness
- Accountability
- Risk taking
- Discipline
- Perseverance
- Creativity
- Curiosity
- Integrity
- Humility

Standards for Critical Thinking

Intellectual standards

- Clear
- Precise
- Specific
- Accurate
- Relevant
- Plausible
- Consistent
- Logical
- Deep
- Broad
- Complete
- Significant
- Adequate
- Fair

Professional standards

- Ethical criteria for nursing judgment
- Criteria for evaluation
- Professional responsibility

Modified from Kataoka-Yahiro M, Saylor C: A critical thinking model for nursing judgment, *J Nurs Educ* 33(8):351, 1994.

the sciences, and humanities is necessary to think about nursing problems. For example, a nurse caring for a client who has low back pain will draw on knowledge from pain physiology, pathophysiology of muscular skeletal injuries, nursing concepts in nonpharmacologic pain relief, cultural concepts, and principles of psychology to accurately interpret the significance pain has for the client and to determine the measures that will likely bring relief.

- *Experience*—Unless a nurse has the opportunity to practice in a clinical setting and make decisions about client care, critical thinking will not develop. The nurse learns from each client. When a nurse encounters a client, a wealth of information can be learned from observing, sensing, talking with the client, and then reflecting actively on the experience. Experience helps the expert nurse understand the context of a clinical situation, recognize cues, and interpret them as relevant or irrelevant.
- *Competence*—There are three cognitive competencies that the Kataoka-Yahiro and Saylor model (1994) address: general critical thinking competencies (hypothesis formation, problem solving, and decision making); specific critical thinking competencies in clinical situations (diagnostic reasoning, clinical inferences, and clinical decision making); and a specific critical thinking competency in nursing (the nursing process). The nursing process gives a nurse a systematic way of thinking through client problems.
- *Attitudes*—These are central values of a critical thinker (Paul, 1993). The model includes the values of confidence, independence, fairness, responsibility, risk taking, discipline, perseverance, creativity, curiosity, integrity, and humility. A nurse cannot achieve the best results with a client without being fair in weighing the views of other practitioners, taking risks to generate new solutions to chronic problems, or demonstrating humility when his or her knowledge about a problem is limited.
- *Standards*—Intellectual and professional standards (see Box 1-2) are essential for critical thinking to lead to the right decisions. For

example, when assessing a client's pain, the nurse seeks clear information from the client and clarifies any confusing statements. Any measurements, such as the degree of range of motion, are precisely made. As the examination proceeds the nurse asks additional questions to be sure information is in-depth and complete. Professional standards such as ethical criteria or clinical practice standards provide an additional frame of reference for critical thinking.

A critical thinking model shows the complexity of the cognitive processes used in making clinical decisions. Although Kataoka-Yahiro and Saylor's model requires more testing, it is an exciting approach to show the relationship of critical thinking and clinical judgment.

Applying Critical Thinking to Health Assessment

Health assessment and physical examination are two domains of practice that a nurse will use in a variety of clinical situations (Box 1-3). The successful use of the knowledge and skills employed in assessment and examination requires critical thinking (Table 1-1).

A nurse assesses a client by drawing on a scientific knowledge base to anticipate possible findings. For example, assessing the client with low back pain will require the nurse to refer to knowledge about potential pathophysiologic causes of low back pain. This knowledge will alert the nurse to assess not only the character of the pain but also potential musculoskeletal and neurologic changes. The nurse's experience will be needed to help recognize physical findings and

BOX 1-3 Using a Health History and Physical Examination in Practice

- To conduct a complete history and examination for any health risks or preexisting health problems
- To conduct a focused assessment when clients exhibit specific signs and symptoms
- To perform ongoing assessments of clients' health status to identify problems early
- To evaluate clients' responses to medical and nursing therapies and clients' overall clinical progress; physical assessment findings reveal if a client's status is changing

Table 1-1 Application of the critical thinking model to health assessment and physical examination

Components of Critical Thinking	Health Assessment and Physical Examination Skills
Specific knowledge base	Understanding normal findings for each body system
	Understanding normal anatomy and physiology
	Recognition of variations in findings resulting from aging
	Knowledge of select pathologies and their related symptomatology
Experience	Familiarity with skills of physical examination (inspection, palpation, percussion, and auscultation)
	Recognition of client symptoms seen previously
	Ability to organize examination over time
Competencies	Collecting thorough nursing history
	Using general and appropriately focused examination techniques
	Forming accurate nursing diagnoses
	Evaluation of nursing care through reassessment of findings
Attitudes	Validating findings with another nurse when uncertain
	Using discipline in being sure examination is systematic and thorough
Standards:	
Intellectual	Applying criteria for symptom analysis
Professional	Knowing “classic” signs and symptoms of abnormalities
	Identifying all characteristics of a symptom
	Telling the client results of the examination

interpret their normalcy. Clients with low back pain will likely have some common patterns of symptomatology, yet the nurse will also recognize that each client is unique. It is important for the nurse to apply critical thinking attitudes (e.g., curiosity and perseverance) when a client's clinical signs are subtle. The nurse must be responsible for conducting a detailed, well-focused exam. Similarly, the nurse will apply both intellectual and professional standards when examining clients. All physical measurements should be specific and precise. In the example of ruling out the potential source of a client's pain, the nurse will apply knowledge from anatomy and physiology and make assessments specific to the client's complaint (e.g., measurement of range of motion of the lower back and assessment of sensation in the extremities). As for professional standards, the nurse learns that to gain a comprehensive pain assessment, a standard of care will include assessment of the client's functional abilities. The nurse will integrate critical thinking competencies from a clinical perspective, as well as from the nursing process approach. As a critical thinker, the nurse will use diagnostic reasoning in making any ongoing assessments on the basis of a client's medical problem. The client's low back pain, if related to a herniated disk, will result in clinical signs for which the nurse must be alert. In applying the nursing process, the nurse considers how the client's response to pain affects lifestyle, occupation, and daily living activities.

A nurse will become more adept at health assessment and physical examination by recognizing how the use of both requires a systematic and rigorous application of critical thinking. A thorough health assessment and physical examination will allow the nurse to identify client problems appropriately and to select those nursing therapies designed to meet desired outcomes.

Critical Judgment in Nursing

From a thorough health assessment and physical examination a nurse gathers objective and subjective data from which recognizable patterns are formed. Data are reviewed and analyzed from the client's physical, developmental, intellectual, emotional, social, cultural, and spiritual dimensions. Accurate clinical judgment requires a complete and thorough assessment, accurate diagnosis identification (nursing and collaborative), and selection of therapies that are appropriate for the diagnoses identified and their related cues.

The subtle and overt signs and symptoms gained from a health history and physical examination provide cues or defining characteristics that lead to formulation of nursing diagnoses. Nursing diagnoses provide a language that enables all nurses to understand the client's health care alterations. A nursing diagnosis is a clinical judgment about individual, family, or community responses to actual and potential health problems and life processes (NANDA, 1997). A nursing diagnosis gives clear direction for a nurse to select with the client the outcomes and associated therapies for which the nurse is accountable and licensed and competent to implement. A nursing diagnosis has three essential components, known by the acronym PES: problem, etiology, and symptomatology (defining characteristics) (Gordon, 1976).

P—Health problems or status of an individual, family, or community. Problems such as pain, body image disturbance, or anxiety are short, clear, precise statements. Actual problems or problems for which the client may be at risk may be diagnosed.

E—Related or etiologic factors contribute to the existence or maintenance of a client's health problems. For example, pain may be related to reluctance to take pain medications or failure to follow activity restriction. Related factors may be either external or internal to the client. Identification of a related factor helps nurses focus on the right interventions for eventual elimination or management of the client's response to health problems. This is very important. The diagnosis of pain suggests a variety of therapies. However, if a therapy is not selected on the basis of a client's diagnostic related factor, it is less likely the client will gain pain relief.

S—The final component in the definition of a nursing diagnosis is the defining characteristics or objective and subjective findings that indicate the presence of a nursing diagnosis. It is a combination of signs and symptoms that reveal a client's health problems (Table 1-2).

The nurse uses clinical reasoning to cluster the PES data and to form the most appropriate nursing diagnoses.

Table 1-2 Sample nursing diagnosis statements

P Problem	E Etiologic Factors	S Symptomatology (Defining Characteristics)
Impaired skin integrity	Shearing force from positioning and immobilization	Disruption of skin surface Erythema of surrounding skin
Ineffective breathing pattern	Reduced lung expansion from postoperative pain	Shortness of breath Splinting with reduced excursion Tachypnea
Anticipatory grieving	Perceived loss of spouse from terminal illness	Expression of denial Alterations in sleep Expression of sorrow Loss of appetite

Collaborative Problems

After a nurse completes an assessment of a client, it may be determined that other health care problems exist that are outside the nurse's independent scope of practice. Nursing therapies alone will not solve this type of problem. Carpenito (1995) describes this in her bifocal clinical practice model, which identifies two clinical situations in which nurses intervene—one as primary prescriber and the other in collaboration with other disciplines. In the latter case, the health problems that require collaborative care are certain physiologic complications that a nurse monitors to detect onset or changes in status and manages by implementing both physician-prescribed and nurse-prescribed interventions to minimize

Table 1-3 Collaborative problems and nursing diagnoses

Collaborative Problems	Nursing Diagnoses
Clinical scenario: A client is admitted through the emergency room with a diagnosis of closed head injury and cerebral contusion. At this time the client is unresponsive to verbal stimuli, the right pupil is dilated and slow to react to light, and the client withdraws the left side in response to pain. Glasgow coma scale is 10.	
Potential complication: increased intracranial pressure	Impaired physical mobility Tissue perfusion, altered cerebral Risk for impaired skin integrity
Clinical scenario: A client enters an acute care medical division with a medical diagnosis of acute lymphocytic leukemia. The client has a fever, pallor, fatigue, and anorexia with a recent 5-lb weight loss. Laboratory data reveal a reduced white blood cell count (neutropenia), reduced platelets (thrombocytopenia), and anemia.	
Potential complication: bleeding Potential complication: infection	Risk for infection Risk for activity intolerance Altered nutrition: less than body requirements Fatigue

Table 1-3 Collaborative problems and nursing diagnoses—cont'd

Collaborative Problems	Nursing Diagnoses
Clinical scenario: A client comes to a community clinic with a 10-year history of rheumatoid arthritis. In the past 12 months the client's condition has worsened, with symptoms of increasing fatigue, weight loss, and increased pain and stiffness of the hands. Joint range of motion of hands and fingers is making performance of activities of daily living more difficult. The client is placed on steroid therapy for 4 weeks, along with methotrexate.	
Potential complication: systemic inflammation Potential complication: joint deformity	Pain Impaired physical mobility Fatigue Altered nutrition: less than body requirements Self-care deficit

complications of the events (Carpenito, 1995). For example, a client with the medical diagnosis of coronary artery disease may have a collaborative problem such as "Potential complication: cardiac dysrhythmias." This diagnosis will require the nurse's ongoing monitoring, as well as actions to reduce any risk factors that might increase the incidence of the dysrhythmia. For example, the nurse will avoid exertional client care activities that might increase frequency of dysrhythmias. The same client might also have related nursing diagnoses such as "knowledge deficit regarding disease process related to newly diagnosed status" and "activity intolerance related to oxygen imbalance." For each nursing diagnosis the nurse is able to implement independent measures. Carpenito (1995) notes that not all physiologic complications are collaborative problems. If a nurse is able to prevent the onset of a complication, such as the development of a pressure ulcer, or provide primary treatment, such as exercises for an ineffective cough, then the diagnosis is a nursing diagnosis. It is also important to remember that a medical diagnosis is not a collaborative problem. Table 1-3 outlines collaborative problems in comparison with nursing diagnoses.

Nurses do not care for clients by themselves. A significant part of a nurse's practice is with other health care professionals (e.g., physicians, dietitians, social workers, physical therapists). Many times these professionals are comfortable with the nursing language and can collaborate on problems labeled as nursing diagnoses. Other times, professionals may wish to use language with which they are most familiar and to which the nurse can easily relate. For example, a problem familiar to the nurse as "activity intolerance" may be stated as "reduced cardiac reserve" by a physical therapist. With the nurse and thera pist collaborating, each can define the realm of practice for which he or she is responsible.

The nurse often serves as the leader of the health care team because of the independent nursing care that must be delivered and the nursing implications related to collaborative problems. Success in helping clients regain function or maintain existing functions is best ensured when critical thinking and clinical judgment go hand-in-hand.

Nursing Health History and Interview Process

2

From the moment a nurse first meets a client, the nurse learns to exhibit a sense of caring and respect that wins trust from the client. When successful, the relationship that eventually forms between nurse and client enables the nurse to discover information about the client's health status, collaborate with the client on a health care plan, and initiate therapies that maintain and/or improve the client's health.

Health History

In today's complex health care environment, nurses must be able to solve problems accurately, thoroughly, and quickly. This means that the nurse must be able to review a tremendous amount of information to critically think and make the correct judgments (Potter and Perry, 1997). The nurse's assessment includes collection of data from a primary source (the client) and secondary sources (family, friends) initially in the form of a nursing history. A physical examination of the client then follows. The nursing health history is a client's subjective account of current and past health status. Gathered during an interview with a client, the health history alerts the nurse to key areas the physical examination must later cover.

The nursing health history can take many forms. Health care settings will design forms so that nurses may collect histories quickly and easily. The forms usually are designed on the basis of a particular model or framework, which helps to conceptualize the health setting's standards for practice. A form that uses a nursing model helps to conceptualize the scope of nursing practice. Regardless of the model, the history form requires the nurse to collect information thought to be most important in assessing a client's needs. A nursing history form serves as a guideline only. It is the nurse who decides what and how much information needs to be collected about a client's status.

The nursing assessment must include data that either support existence of a problem or demonstrate absence of a problem. In other words, data must be relevant. A nurse therefore must know what to assess in terms of subjective and objective data. This does not mean that the nurse goes through the same series of routine questions for each and every client. Instead the nurse must have the ability to critically think and know what direction assessment must take on the basis of the client's presenting history, physical signs, and known physiologic or psychologic problems.

Clinical situations offer the nurse the opportunity to either conduct a quick overview of a client's condition or collect a comprehensive database about the client's health. When a nurse first meets a client, an overview includes a brief series of questions aimed toward the client or family member and the measurement of specific physical findings. This overview will usually be based on the nurse's specialty of practice or the treatment situation: an emergency room nurse uses the A-B-C (airway-breathing-circulation) approach; a psychiatric nurse may focus on the client's reality, anxiety level, and violence potential (Carnevali and Thomas, 1993). Of course, it is possible that important cues may be missed with such an intense focused assessment. However, the nurse interprets cues from the client to determine how in-depth an assessment should be.

A comprehensive database can provide a more complete view of a client's health status. Carnevali and Thomas (1993) suggest two ways to collect comprehensive data. One is a structured comprehensive database, and the other is a problem-oriented approach focusing on the client's current situation. The comprehensive approach moves from the general to the specific.

Data are collected for each client within a variety of established categories. A comprehensive assessment covers all potential health problem areas. As data begin to reveal a problem or strength in a particular area, the nurse can then choose to expand the assessment to analyze the client's situation correctly and thoroughly.

The problem approach to assessment begins with problematic areas, such as pain, and spreads out to relevant areas of the client's life. A comprehensive pain assessment will begin with a review of the nature of the pain itself and then broaden to categories such as the effect of pain on mobility, lifestyle, and family relationships. Once completed, the problem of pain will be thoroughly analyzed so that a comprehensive approach can be used to manage the client's pain.

Gordon's Functional Health Patterns

One model that is commonly used to guide nurses in data collection is Gordon's Functional Health Patterns (Gordon, 1987; 1991) (Box 2-1). Various health care organizations have used Gordon's model to develop their history forms. Professional staff use the 11 functional health patterns as their organizing framework and then develop a history tool with a series of questions that will best assess a client's status for each health pattern. The functional patterns focus on both physiologic and psychosocial, cultural, and environmental factors affecting clients' health. An actual history tool can organize the 11 categories in whatever way the practitioners of the organization prefer.

Nurses gather data in all 11 categories and then review and analyze the information to see if patterns of problems are revealed. For each of the 11 patterns the nurse assesses clients by organizing patterns of behavior and physiologic responses that pertain to a functional health category. The nurse then compares the client's baseline (e.g., usual blood pressure, weight, and nutritional intake); established norms based on age, gender, height, and weight; and cultural, social, or other norms and health care practices (Gordon, 1987). Description and evaluation of health patterns assist the nurse in identifying functional patterns (client strengths) and dysfunctional patterns (nursing diagnoses and collaborative problems) on which a plan of care is based. Gordon's tool is just one model that may be used to orga-

Text continued on p. 27

BOX 2-1 Health History Organized by Gordon's Functional Health Patterns

1. **Health-Perception–Health-Management Pattern** describes clients' perceived patterns of health and well-being and how their health is managed.

   Possible questions on a health history form:

   Perception of health problem

   How would you describe your own health?

   What is your understanding of your current health problem?

   What are your health goals?

   Tell me what you know about current and proposed treatments.

   Attitudes regarding health care providers

   Who is your principal health care provider?

   What is your opinion of the care you have received?

   When do you usually visit a health care provider (for both preventive and episodic care)? How often are checkups?

   Compliance with existing therapies

   What are the current therapies prescribed for your health problem?

   Are you following your medication schedule? (Have the client describe drugs, dosages, and times of administration.)

   Are you able to regularly purchase the medications/therapies you need?

   Do you have transportation to get to your doctor/pharmacy?

2. **Nutritional-Metabolic Pattern** describes consumption relative to metabolic need and nutrient supply, including pattern of food and fluid consumption; condition of skin, hair, nails, and mucous membranes; body temperature; height; and weight.

   Possible questions on a health history form:

   Intake pattern

   Describe for me what you usually eat during the day.

Continued

BOX 2-1 Health History Organized by Gordon's Functional Health Patterns—cont'd

How many meals do you eat a day, and when?
Are there certain food preferences that you have?
Estimate the amount of fluids you drink during a day.
What fluids or beverages do you prefer?

Weight gain/loss pattern

How many pounds have you gained/lost over the last month?
How long have you noticed a weight change?
Can you associate your weight loss with anything (e.g., change in activity, meals eaten, gastrointestinal intolerance)?
Describe for me any stresses in your life.

See Chapters 5, 7, 12, and 22 for additional questions.

3. **Elimination Pattern** describes patterns of excretory function (bowel, bladder, and skin); includes individual's daily pattern, changes or disturbances, and methods used to control excretion.

Possible questions on a health history form:

Daily urinary pattern

How many times do you usually void/urinate/pass urine each day?
Can you estimate for me how much you void each time?
Have you noticed any recent changes?
Describe what your urine looks like (color, clarity, presence of material in urine).

Daily bowel pattern

How often do you have a bowel movement?
What time of day?
Describe your intake of fruits, vegetables, and other bulk-forming foods.

Changes in function

Have you had any abdominal or anal pain?
Have you noticed any blood in your stool?
When was your last bowel movement? (If there is a change, ask client about possible cause.)

Have you noticed any urgency to void, dysuria, frequency, polyuria, dribbling, nocturia, or retention?

Have you experienced pain in the flank, groin, or low back?

See Chapters 15, 16, and 17 for additional questions.

4. **Activity-Exercise Pattern** describes pattern of exercise, activity, leisure, and recreation; includes activities of daily living, type and quality of exercise, and factors affecting activity pattern (e.g., neuromuscular, respiratory, circulatory).

Possible questions on a health history form:

Activity profile

Describe your usual daily activities.

What type of formal exercise do you participate in daily? Weekly?

How long do you exercise each time?

Describe how you respond to exercise.

Do you participate in any recreational sports? If so, how often?

Activities of daily living

Describe any difficulties you have with dressing, eating or preparing food, bathing and hygiene, or toileting. (This is a good question to use in gathering additional information from family members.)

Do you use any assistive devices or mobility aids?

Activity tolerance

NOTE: The nurse may refer to questions used in the review of systems regarding cardiac and pulmonary function.

Does the client experience symptoms of shortness of breath, dyspnea, dyspnea on exertion, cough, or chest pain?

How much activity produces shortness of breath or dyspnea?

Are symptoms relieved when exercise ceases?

5. **Sleep-Rest Pattern** describes pattern of sleep, rest, and relaxation and any aids to change those patterns.

Possible questions on a health history form:

Sleep pattern

What time do you usually go to sleep?

How quickly do you fall asleep?

How many hours do you sleep on average each night?

Continued

BOX 2-1 Health History Organized by Gordon's Functional Health Patterns—cont'd

How many times do you awaken at night?

When do you usually awaken in the morning? (Adapt to client's sleep cycle; some clients may sleep during the day.)

Describe your intake of coffee, tea, cola, chocolate, and other caffeinated beverages and foods.

Rest and relaxation

What do you do to relax?

Are you able to relax this way daily?

Aids to sleep

What do you do to help yourself fall asleep?

Are you currently taking any over-the-counter sleep medications?

Describe the conditions in your bedroom (noise, lighting, temperature).

6. **Cognitive-Perceptual Pattern** describes sensory-perceptual and cognitive patterns; includes adequacy of sensory modes (vision, hearing, touch, taste, and smell), reports of pain perception, and cognitive functional abilities.

Possible questions on a health history form:

Sensory-perceptual function

Assess the client's ability to see, hear, smell, taste, and feel (see Chapters 8, 9, 10, 11, and 19).

Does the client use any sensory aids (e.g., contact lenses, glasses, hearing aids)?

How does the client rate his or her own sensory loss (excellent, good, fair, poor, or bad) (Janken and Lewis-Cullinan, 1990)?

Assess any alternative communication methods the client may use as a result of a sensory loss.

Pain

Describe your pain for me: When did pain begin? How long has it lasted? Does it occur the same time each day? How often does it recur? Show me the location of your pain. Rate the severity of your pain on a scale of 0 to 10, with 0 as no pain and 10 as severe, unbearable pain. What worsens or relieves the pain? Do you have any other symptoms (e.g., nausea, dizziness) when the pain occurs?

How does pain affect your ability to perform daily activities?

Does the pain affect your ability to sleep?

Does the pain influence your ability to perform work activities?

Cognitive function

NOTE: This assessment may begin with a mini–mental examination (see Chapter 5).

Tell me what you know about your current health status.

Describe for me the schedule you follow for your medications and the amount you take of each.

Describe for me any treatments your health care provider has you perform at home.

Include in the assessment the client's ability to make decisions, perceive messages, and make judgments.

7. **Self-Perception–Self-Concept Pattern** describes how persons perceive themselves; includes their capabilities, body image, and feelings.

Possible questions on a health history form:

Education

What was the last grade in school that you completed?

What additional schooling/training have you had?

Financial status

Determine client's level of income and whether it is adequate to meet lifestyle and health care requirement demands.

Self-perception

Tell me how you feel about yourself and what you have accomplished in life so far.

Describe for me your strengths.

Have you experienced a recent loss (e.g., job change, divorce or separation, moving away from home, death of loved one)?

Body image

Has the client experienced an alteration or loss of a body part (e.g., amputation, mastectomy, colostomy)?

If there has been an alteration or loss, how does this affect the client's ability to work?

Continued

BOX 2-1 Health History Organized by Gordon's Functional Health Patterns—cont'd

Does the client have difficulty in performing activities of daily living? (See *Activity-Exercise Pattern.*)

8. **Role Relationship Pattern** describes pattern of role engagements and relationships; includes perception of major roles and responsibilities in current life situation.
   Possible questions on a health history form:
   Family
   Describe for me who is in your family.
   Do you live alone? If not, with whom do you live?
   What relationship does the client have with spouse, parents, siblings, and friends?
   How do you share tasks in your family?
   How long have you been married, widowed, or divorced?
   Has there been a recent loss within your family?
   Whom does the client seek out for support?
   How does the family normally cope in times of stress?
   Do family members respect each other's point of view?
   Occupation
   Tell me about your current occupation.
   How long have you worked with your current employer?
   How would you describe your current level of satisfaction with your job?
   Has illness threatened your ability to perform your job?
   Tell me about the type and amount of stress you experience at work.
   What do you do to relieve it? (See *Coping–Stress Tolerance Pattern.*)
9. **Sexuality-Reproductive Pattern** describes patterns of satisfaction or dissatisfaction with sexuality; includes female's reproductive state.
   Possible questions on a health history form:
   Sexual satisfaction
   How do you feel about the sexual part of your life?
   How has your illness, medication, or impending surgery affected your sex life?

It is not unusual for people with your condition to have some sexual problems. Has that been a concern for you?

Tell me more about those concerns: When did they begin, and have they changed? What do you see as the cause for the concerns? How would you like this concern resolved?

Domestic violence

NOTE: Should be asked when client is alone.

Are you in a relationship in which someone is hurting you?

Have you ever been forced to have sex when you did not want to?

10. **Coping–Stress Tolerance Pattern** describes general coping pattern and effectiveness of coping skills in stress tolerance.

Possible questions on a health history form:

Current coping status

Tell me about any current health problems that you have.

Do you feel you have been able to cope or deal with these problems as you would like to?

Has the client experienced a situational crisis or loss? (See *Self-Perception–Self-Concept Pattern.*)

Is there acceptance or denial of the situation?

Does the client ask questions or request information about problems?

During discussion, does the client have the ability to problem solve?

Behavioral changes

Does the client's affect or mood reveal anxiety (restlessness, insomnia, poor eye contact, trembling, facial tension) or depression (blunt affect, helplessness, guilt, poverty of speech, apathy, lowered self-esteem)?

Have you had any changes in eating habits, sleep, and activity?

Do you have difficulty concentrating on tasks, remaining productive, or attending to details?

Does the client have a tendency to exhibit unprovoked emotional outbursts?

Coping resources

Is the client able to ask for help?

Whom do you depend on during a crisis?

Continued

BOX 2-1 Health History Organized by Gordon's Functional Health Patterns—cont'd

Is that person available?
What coping method works best for you during stress?
How long does it take for the client to get over a crisis?

11. **Value-Belief Pattern** describes patterns of values, goals, or beliefs that guide lifestyle choices and decisions.

Cultural

What is the client's cultural heritage? (Where were you born? Where did you grow up? Are you and your parents from the same or different ethnoreligious backgrounds?)
Is the client able to communicate in English, or is a translator necessary?
What can you tell me about your specific health and illness beliefs?
Within your culture, are there certain rituals you follow when one becomes ill?
Are there certain remedies you take?

Spiritual

Tell me about your source of hope and strength.
How would you describe your own philosophy of life?
Is there something threatening your spirituality as a result of your illness?
Has illness affected your ability to express your spirituality?
Does the client have a fellowship with other persons (includes immediate family; close friends; associates at work, school, or church)?
What is the level of support received from this group?
Does the client follow a particular religion? If so, what is it?
Are there customary religious rituals the client practices (e.g., singing, use of a rosary, meditating, scripture reading, making offerings)?
Does the ritual offer support at a time of illness?

nize a comprehensive history. It is a nursing model, whereas other common models incorporate more of a medical orientation.

Medical Model for a Health History

Most medical models used in acquiring a health history contain six to seven categories. Although this model is referred to as a medical model, valuable data can be used by the nurse in client assessment. Many health care settings develop health history forms that are a combination of nursing and medical models.

Adult Health History

The following provides an example of a format that can be used for an adult client's health history. The rationale explains the importance information in each category plays in developing a clear picture of a client's health status. Historical information is to be collected directly from the client or a family member or significant other. In some cases a previous medical record can be used to complete data collection.

1. Biographic information:

   Client's name, age, and date of birth
   Sex, race, ethnic origin
   Marital status
   Address and phone number
   Working status and occupation
   Names and phone numbers of close family members or significant others (including person to contact in an emergency)
   Religious preferenceSource of health insurance; Medicare/Medicaid number, other insurance name and phone number

Rationale:

The biographic information provides a quick reference for information that allows a health care provider to identify the client and to make contact with the client and family members. Information regarding sex, race, and ethnicity will influence how the nurse interprets physical examination findings collected later.

Assessment tips:

What is your name?
When were you born?
Are you currently working? If so, tell me a little bit about what you do.
Do you have a religious preference?
Who is the person closest to you whom you would want to be kept informed about your illness/hospitalization?

2. Reason for seeking health care (client's chief complaint):

This should be revealed in the client's own words, describing the reason for the visit to a health care provider. This is also a good time to ask the client what expectations he or she might have of the visit.

Rationale:

The client's chief complaint often can be very useful in helping the nurse focus and direct the nursing history and physical examination. Caution must be used in case the client is a poor historian.

Assessment tips:

Tell me what brings you to the clinic today.

Describe for me the reason you came to see us.

What do you expect from the care you are to receive?

3. Present health history:

This is an overview of the reason the client is seeking health care. A chronologic summary of any symptoms and signs, beginning with the onset of the problem and ending with present day, gives a complete view of the client's principal complaint. Each symptom should be described in detail on the basis of the following characteristics: location, character or quality, severity, timing (onset, duration, frequency), setting or situation when the symptom occurs, aggravating or relieving factors, associated symptoms, and client's interpretation of what the symptoms mean.

Rationale:

The present health history provides an excellent starting point for the nurse to begin to organize mentally how the remainder of the history and examination will progress. Certain symptoms will likely represent potential problems in particular body systems or functional areas. For example, a client who complains of nausea and weight loss will require a focused review of gastrointestinal function, diet, and medication history. As a result, the nurse may not review all body systems as thoroughly, depending on whether findings reinforce the client's description.

Assessment tips:

Describe the symptoms you have had.

Show me exactly where you have felt your pain, discomfort, nausea, headache, or swelling.

What causes your symptom to worsen? Get better?

What do you do to relieve your symptoms at home?

When you feel your pain/nausea/swelling, are there any other symptoms you notice?

Tell me what you think is causing your symptoms.

4. Past health history:

This is an overview of any past illnesses (including childhood illnesses), hospitalizations, or surgeries that the client might have experienced. Included in the assessment is a review of the client's allergies, medications, immunizations, and most recent visits to health care providers. For females, the past health history includes an obstetric history.

Rationale:

Information from the past health history often can immediately explain the related cause for the client's symptoms. Throughout the history, the nurse puts together information, referring to past experiences and a knowledge base that helps to interpret data from the client. If the past health history fails to reveal a cause for the client's problem, the information will prove useful later as the nurse plans therapies that adapt to the client's strengths and weaknesses. In addition, information is useful in assessing the client's health promotion activities.

Assessment tips:

Can you recall for me what common childhood illnesses you have had (measles, mumps, rubella, chickenpox, whooping cough [pertussis], strep throat, rheumatic fever, scarlet fever, poliomyelitis)?

Have you had any previous illnesses (e.g., cancer, diabetes, heart disease, hypertension, thyroid problems, stroke, seizure disorder)?

Have you had any accidents or injuries?

Do you have a record of your childhood immunizations? Were they kept up to date?

When have you last had a flu shot, tetanus immunization, and tuberculosis skin test? (For health care workers, ask if they have had a hepatitis vaccine.)

Tell me when you last visited your physician, dentist, and optometrist.

Tell me what foods, medicines,

or environmental agents (e.g., pollen, dog hair, latex) you are allergic to. What happens when you have an allergic reaction?

List for me all of the medications you are currently taking, including prescribed and over-the-counter medications. (See Appendix A for guidelines for assessment of substance abuse.)

How do the medications make you feel?

Tell me about any surgeries you have had.

How many times have you been pregnant? How many deliveries occurred in which the fetus reached viability? Have you had any miscarriages or abortions?

5. Family history:

This portion of the health history includes the health status of the immediate family and living blood relations, as well as cause of death of blood relatives.

Rationale:

The family history can reveal risk factors for major illnesses such as alcoholism, arthritis, cancer, heart disease, diabetes mellitus, hypertension, sickle cell disease, and mental disorders. The client's presenting signs and symptoms could prove to be the first indication of a serious illness developing.

Assessment tips:

Have any of your family members had heart disease, cancer, stroke, high blood pressure, diabetes, sickle cell disease, kidney disease? If so, who?

Do any family members have illnesses similar to that of the client's illness?

Has any family member suffered from a mental illness?

What was the cause of death of your parents? How old were they at the time of their death?

If there is a hereditary disease, assess the history of grandparents, aunts, uncles, siblings, and cousins (assess both sides of the client's family for at least two generations).

A pedigree diagram or genogram is a useful way to record the occurrence of hereditary disease (Fig. 2-1).

6. Environmental history:

This portion of the history reviews the environmental setting in which the client lives and works. The nurse will review whether the client lives or works around pollutants or hazardous wastes and chemicals. Exposure

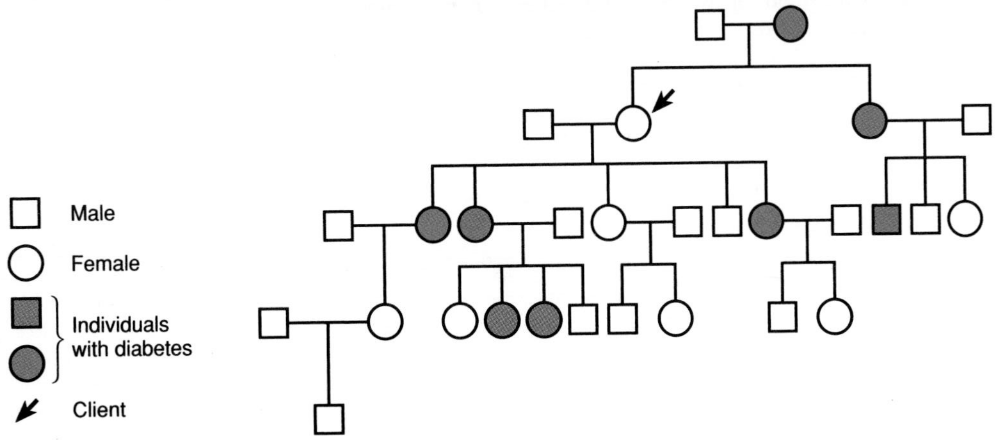

Fig. 2-1
Example of pedigree diagram for diabetes.

to noise and physical safety risks will also be assessed.

Rationale:

A client can be at risk for a variety of chronic diseases as a result of exposure to pollutants and hazardous materials. Chronic exposure to loud noise can cause hearing problems. The client's failure to use safety equipment during work and recreation will reveal additional risks.

Assessment tips:

Are you exposed to any sources of pollution or hazardous wastes where you live?

What hazards are you exposed to at your workplace?

When you participate in sports or hobbies, do you wear protective equipment (e.g., helmet, safety glasses)?

Are you exposed to extremely loud noise at work?

7. Review of systems:

The nurse will gather historical information before a head-to-toe examination of each of the major body systems. Some nurses may choose to integrate this portion of the history during the examination itself. NOTE: The review of systems can be found under the history section of each body system (see Chapters 6 to 19).

Rationale:

There are typical patterns of signs and symptoms and client behaviors that can be associated with alterations in particular body systems. When revealed, the nurse will thoroughly assess the system most likely to be affected. For example, if a nurse assesses that a client has been a smoker for 10 years; smokes three packs a day; and has a chronic, productive cough, the physical examination should include a thorough review of respiratory and cardiovascular function. Information from the review of systems helps the nurse to prioritize those portions of the examination that require more attention.

Interview

The collection of an appropriate and thorough health history requires the nurse to gather subjective information through an interview. The interview is a pattern of communication initiated for a specific purpose and focused on a specific content area. During a health history the nurse interviews a client to learn not only about the client's level of wellness but also about many issues that can often be of a sensitive nature. The nurse also helps clients to understand changes that are occurring or will occur in their pattern of living. Therapeutic communication skills are essential. The nurse must also convey the image of a professional in dress, grooming, and demeanor.

It is helpful to always remain focused on the subject at hand. Collecting a health history is a serious responsibility. All information shared by the client must be kept confidential. The choice of words the nurse uses is important to avoid confusion or misinterpretation on the part of the client. Always maintain good eye contact with the client. It is also important for the nurse to be able to show an understanding of the client's intellectual and emotional needs before the client is willing to discuss important issues about his or her health.

Phases of the Interview

Preparation

The nurse prepares by reviewing available information about the client in the medical record. At times this may be limited if the nurse is the first person to see the client. If the nurse is familiar with a client's situation, it may be helpful to review in advance information in the literature related to the client's health problem. The interview should take place in a comfortable, quiet setting when possible.

One additional step in preparation is knowing oneself (Seidel et al., 1995). The nurse should understand what he or she brings to an interaction. Does the nurse have any preexisting biases about the client? Is the nurse angry over reasons unrelated to the client but which are difficult to control? Is the nurse overzealous in wanting to be liked by the client? It is important for the nurse to understand himself or herself and to be aware of personal emotions and thoughts. Displacement of anger or nonverbal expressions of disapproval can destroy a client relationship.

Orientation

The interview begins with an introduction to the client. The nurse clearly states his or her name, the role he or she will play in the history and examination process, and the approximate length of time the interview and examination will last. It is also important to address the client properly. Ask whether the client prefers to be called by a first or last name. Orientation is a time to become acquainted with the client. Often it helps to be seated at an easy distance from the client. Both the nurse and client should be comfortable.

The client learns about the type of questions that will be asked. Clarification is given regarding confidentiality of information. The nurse's professional approach evokes the client's trust. This is particularly important if the nurse is to learn about a client's motivations, strengths, and resources. The nurse helps the client resolve any anxiety, feelings of helplessness, and concerns about the personal nature of information to be shared.

Working phase

The nurse focuses the interview on the client's health dimensions, using a model that forms a database for eventual nursing diagnosis identification. The nurse uses interviewing skills to clarify and validate information so that appropriate clinical problem solving takes place. Data collected are later confirmed by findings from the physical examination. The nurse and client work together to identify problems and select goals of care.

Termination

The nurse closes the interview by summarizing information collected. Problems or diagnoses and goals of care are validated with the client. The nurse explains how additional contact will be made with the client, including preparation for the physical assessment. It helps to give a client a clue as to when the interview will end; for example, "We will finish in about 5 minutes." Thus the client can maintain attention without wondering when the interview will end.

Interview Techniques

Problem seeking

The problem-seeking technique identifies the client's potential problems, and subsequent data collection then focuses on these problems. For example, the nurse may ask the client about changes in diet, appetite, or the onset of nausea and vomiting. If the client admits to similar symptoms, the nurse will use questions that focus on the specific changes to identify the problem.

Problem solving

The problem-solving technique focuses on gathering in-depth data on specific problems identified by the client or nurse (Ivey, 1988). For example, if the client reports pain, the nurse gathers information about the onset, character, duration, and precipitating factors.

Direct questions

Direct questions ask for specific information that often clarifies previous information or offers additional data. With this technique the questions do not encourage the client to volunteer more information than is specifically requested. Direct questions can be answered with short, one- or two-word answers or with a *Yes* or *No* response. The technique is useful in gathering biographic information or in dealing with a rambling historian.

Open-ended questions

Open-ended questions are aimed at obtaining a response of more than one or two words, leading to a discussion in which clients actively describe their health status. Examples of open-ended questions are: "Tell me about the pain you are having" and "Describe how you have been feeling."

Basic Communication Strategies

Silence—Communicates to the client that he or she has time to organize thoughts and present complete information without the nurse's interruption. During this time the nurse can observe any nonverbal behavior, physical deformities, or limitations.

Attentive listening—Shows the nurse's interest and concern and helps ensure that accurate data are collected. Notice client's posturing, body movement, and voice tone while listening to what is said.

Conveying acceptance—Communicates a willingness to listen nonjudgmentally. EXAMPLE: Sitting at eye level with the client, assuming a comfortable and open posture, and using good eye contact.

Related questions—Focuses the interview on particular health issues or body systems to prevent rambling. For example, the client might report, "I have had this pain in my stomach for so long, it just never seems to go away." A related question might be, "Tell me specifically what you were doing when the pain began."

Paraphrasing—The nurse restates what he or she has heard the client communicating. This validates in more specific terms what the client has said. It lets the client know how another person is understanding the message. For example, the client might say, "I guess this illness will be a problem for my family. I have been able to live by myself for a long time. I'm worried about what I will be able to do for myself. My daughter has talked about me moving to Arizona with her." The nurse may paraphrase, "Let me see if I understand. You are concerned as to how your illness will limit your ability to live alone. You feel your family may want you to live with them?"

Clarifying—Asking the client to restate information in more specific or different terms when the client's word choice is confusing. This helps the nurse understand the client's intended message better. Having the client give examples to clarify meaning is very helpful. For example, the client might report, "I seem to notice a twinge in my back whenever I try to sleep on my side or I notice it when I dress in the morning." The nurse's clarifying remark might be, "Now tell me what part of your back is affected. Are you saying your back hurts whenever you turn or rotate your body?"

Focusing—Helps eliminate vagueness in communication by asking follow-up questions, requesting the client to be more complete with data. The nurse may point to inconsistencies in statements. For example, the nurse might say, "Now you told me that you have difficulty sleeping at night. Let's be specific; are you having difficulty falling asleep, reawakening, or both?"

Stating observations—Allows client to get feedback and encourages the client to offer additional pertinent information. EXAMPLE: "You seem to be holding your right arm still when you move in that direction."

Confronting—A constructive approach informing a client what the nurse thinks or feels about a behavior, feeling, or statement that the client has communicated during the interaction. The nurse may describe the client's visible behavior, using responses aimed at understanding and using constructive feedback. This skill focuses on the nurse's perception of a client's overt or subtle behavior. For example, "You look nervous; would you like to talk about it?" or "You said your knee does not hurt, but when I palpated it you winced."

Giving feedback—Giving client information about what the nurse observes or deduces. Effective feedback:

Focuses on behavior rather than on the client.

Focuses on observations rather than inferences.

Focuses on description rather than judgment.

Focuses on exploration of alternatives rather than answers or solutions.

Focuses on its value to client rather than on catharsis it provides the nurse.

Focuses on what is said rather than why it is said.

Is limited to appropriate time and place (Kneisl and Wilson, 1984).

EXAMPLE: "As I watch you now, you are able to prepare the medication much more quickly in the syringe. Plus, you did not contaminate the needle."

Offering information—Statements that give information help the client by supplying additional data (Kneisl and Wilson, 1984). Information offered should not be mistaken for advice. Similarly, if a nurse shares personal information, the interaction may no longer be therapeutic.

EXAMPLE: "When you have a cataract, it is normal to have a reduction in depth perception. It can be difficult to make out the edges of stairs, for example."

Summarizing—Highlights the main ideas of any interview or discussion. This validates data from the client and signals the end of one part of the interview before continuing with the next part. EXAMPLE: "Let me quickly review what you have shared. You are wanting to start an exercise plan to help manage the stress you have been feeling at work and to help you control your weight better. You prefer swimming and walking. Your husband wants to exercise with you as well. Setting up a daily schedule would help you plan time for exercise."

Cultural Phenomena Influencing Health Assessment

A client's cultural heritage presents the need for a unique approach to health assessment and physical examination. Giger and Davidhizar (1995) provide an excellent model for assessing clients from multicultural backgrounds (see Appendix E). Their model includes six important variables to incorporate in any interaction with a client: communication, space, social organization, time, environmental control, and biologic variation. Each factor influences how a nurse approaches a physical examination. For example, nurses must understand the importance of nonverbal communication and use of silence in different cultures so as to not assume they are indicative of a physiologic or psychologic abnormality. Touch is an important skill to use during palpation and may not be well received by clients from a variety of cultures (Table 2-1). A client's comfort with the nurse will be influenced by the space he or she maintains with the client. If the nurse makes biased assumptions about a client's social organization and the type of familial support that should be present, the nursing history may be inaccurate. The client's orientation to time will be significant, especially if the nurse is attempting to assess the ability of the client to follow a treatment regimen. Environmental control becomes important in understanding a client's perception of his or her health problem and the value placed on health promotion. Finally, biologic variations must be considered when analyzing physical findings.

Special Considerations for Collecting a Nursing History

- Assessment data sources include the client, family or significant other, health team members, and the client's health record.
- Do not allow interruptions to occur during the interview.
- Data collected on the nursing history tool are subjective; the nurse does not challenge this information but explores it with the client to clarify any vagueness.
- When the client is critically ill, disoriented, confused, mentally handicapped, or very young, the family, significant others, or previously recorded health histories are necessary sources of information for the nursing history.
- Approaching sensitive issues (e.g., death, sex, drug or alcohol use, history of abuse) can be uncomfortable for both the client and nurse. Seidel et al. (1995) recommend the following tips: privacy is essential; do not waffle but be direct and firm; do not apologize for asking a question, because you are doing nothing wrong; do not pass judgment; be patient and give the client time to respond to your questions; do not push too hard—if the client is defensive, proceed slowly.
- Clients with physical or emotional handicaps require an assessment approach that adapts to their needs. The client must be involved even if mental or physical limitations prevent full discussion and participation. Family members and friends can be useful resources, but do not allow them to make decisions for the client when the client is capable of doing so independently. Often

Table 2-1 Cross-cultural variations in clients' response to touch

Nation of Origin	Space
Asian China Hawaii Philippines Korea Japan Southeast Asia	Noncontact people (however, Japanese require less personal space)
African West coast (as slaves) African countries West Indian Islands Dominican Republic Haiti Jamaica	Close personal space
European Germany England Italy Ireland Other European countries	Noncontact people: aloof; distant Southern countries: closer contact and touch
Native American 170 Native-American tribes Aleuts Eskimos	Space very important and has no boundaries
Hispanic countries Spain Cuba Mexico Central and South America	Tactile relationships: touch; handshakes; embracing Value physical presence
Arabic countries	Require less personal space; common to touch persons of same sex

Modified from Giger JN, Davidhizar RE: *Transcultural nursing: assessment and intervention,* ed 2, St Louis, 1995, Mosby. In Potter PA, Perry AG: *Fundamentals of nursing: concepts, process, and practice,* ed 4, St Louis, 1997, Mosby.

family members know tips on making the client comfortable or communicating more effectively with the client. Deaf clients often read, write, or read lips. Blind persons can usually hear; talking louder is unnecessary.

Pediatric Considerations

- Routine examinations of children have a focus on illness prevention, particularly for care of well children with competent parenting and no serious health problems (Wong, 1995). The focus is on growth and development, sensory screening, dental examination, and behavioral assessment.
- Children who are chronically ill, disabled, foster children, or foreign-born adopted may require additional examination visits.
- When obtaining histories for infants and children, gather all or part of the information from the parent or guardian. Institutions that provide health care services for children will have specially adapted assessment forms.
- Parents often think they are being tested by the interviewer. Offer support and do not pass judgment.
- Use first names with children and last names with parents (unless parents prefer otherwise).
- If a young child becomes restless or uncooperative, divide the assessment into two sessions. Use of a toy, as well as the presence of parents, may have a calming effect.
- Interviewing children in the presence of parents or guardians allows the nurse to observe parent-child interactions.
- Children are often unable to express their feelings and tend to act out their problems instead.
- Children who experience a traumatic event, such as loss of a parent, a pet, or close friend, may experience an acute episode of depression.
- Children with psychosocial problems may have difficulty at school.
- Adolescents tend to respond best when treated as adults and individuals. Ask adolescents how they prefer to be addressed (e.g., "Billy" or "Mr. Smith").
- Parents' reliability in providing a health history can vary. Concrete facts such as birth weight and birth date tend to be recalled most accurately; minor illnesses tend to be forgotten more easily than major ones; parents of several children tend to be less accurate in their recall of most items than are parents of single children; and

the parents' educational level is directly related to the accuracy of recall for some data, such as immunizations.

Gerontologic Considerations

- In addition to the basic components of a health history, assess the following categories with an older adult: functional, cognitive, affective, and social well-being (Lueckenotte, 1996).
- Older adults often have lengthy and complicated histories. It is important to stay focused and help the client share pertinent information.
- Do not stereotype aging clients. They are able to adapt to change and learn about their health.
- Sensory or physical limitations (especially hearing or visual impairments) can affect how quickly the nurse can interview and assess a client. Plan for more than one examination period.
- Clients may find that giving certain types of health information is stressful; they may not discuss change or problems confirming their fear of illness or old age.
- Data provided depend on what the older adult feels is important at the time.
- Touch is often well accepted by older adults (Burnside, 1988; Lueckenotte, 1996). Use touch with respect and sensitivity.
- Ask about the client's unfulfilled hopes or aspirations.

3 Physical Assessment Skills

The four basic skills used during a physical examination are inspection, palpation, percussion, and auscultation. The specific uses of these skills are outlined in the assessment sections for the different body systems. In addition, olfaction is an important skill the nurse uses throughout an examination, detecting and analyzing the nature and source of odors associated with bodily alterations. The following sections summarize general principles for the use of the basic physical assessment skills.

Inspection

Inspection is the process of observation. It is a visual examination of body parts to detect normal characteristics or significant physical signs.

Critical Thinking

- Learn to make several observations at once, while becoming perceptive of early warnings of abnormalities.
- Know normal physical characteristics of clients of all ages before trying to distinguish abnormal findings. Experience helps the nurse to recognize normal variations among clients.

- There are variations among clients, as well as ranges of normal in an individual. Experience is needed to distinguish abnormal findings.

Skill Techniques

- Be thorough and systematic in inspecting every body part. If hurried, an examiner may overlook significant findings or make incorrect conclusions about a client's condition.
- Good lighting and exposure of body parts are essential for careful inspection.
- Inspect each area for size, shape, color, symmetry, position, and the presence of any abnormalities.
- Compare each area with the same area on the opposite side of the body.
- Pay attention to detail.
- Inspection is a visual skill, but the examiner should also include olfaction. The sense of smell can sometimes detect abnormalities that may not be recognized by other means.
- Ask a colleague to confirm findings if you are unsure about an odor.
- Table 3-1 lists common characteristic odors and their potential causes.

Palpation

Palpation involves use of the sense of touch. Through palpation the hands can make delicate and sensitive measurements of specific physical signs, including resistance, resilience, roughness, texture, temperature, and mobility.

Critical Thinking

Use palpation with or after visual inspection. (The only exception to this is after inspection of the abdomen; see Chapter 15.) This allows the examiner to focus on any abnormalities noted during inspection. Know the normal location of body organs. Experience will improve your ability to detect subtle differences in qualities such as texture, temperature, and resistance.

Skill Techniques

- Use different parts of the hand to detect characteristics (e.g., texture, shape, temperature, perception of vibration, or movement and consistency) (Fig. 3-1).
- Be sure client is relaxed and positioned comfortably to avoid muscle tension that may distort palpation findings.
- Have the client take slow, deep breaths to enhance muscle relaxation.
- Palpate any suspected area of tenderness last.

Table 3-1 Assessment of characteristic odors

Odor	Site or Source	Potential Causes
Alcohol	Oral cavity	Ingestion of alcohol; diabetes
Ammonia	Urine	Urinary tract infection
Body odor	Skin, particularly in areas where body parts rub together (e.g., under arms, breasts)	Poor hygiene, excess perspiration (hyperhidrosis), foul-smelling perspiration (bromidrosis)
Feces	Wound site	Wound abscess
	Vomitus	Bowel obstruction
	Rectal area	Fecal incontinence
Foul-smelling stools in infant	Stool	Malabsorption syndrome
Halitosis	Oral cavity	Poor dental and oral hygiene, gum disease
Sweet, fruity ketones	Oral cavity	Diabetic acidosis
Stale urine	Skin	Uremic acidosis
Sweet, heavy, thick odor	Draining wound	*Pseudomonas* (bacterial) infection
Musty odor	Casted body part	Infection inside cast
Fetid, sweet odor	Tracheostomy or mucous secretions	Infection of bronchial tree (*Pseudomonas* bacteria)

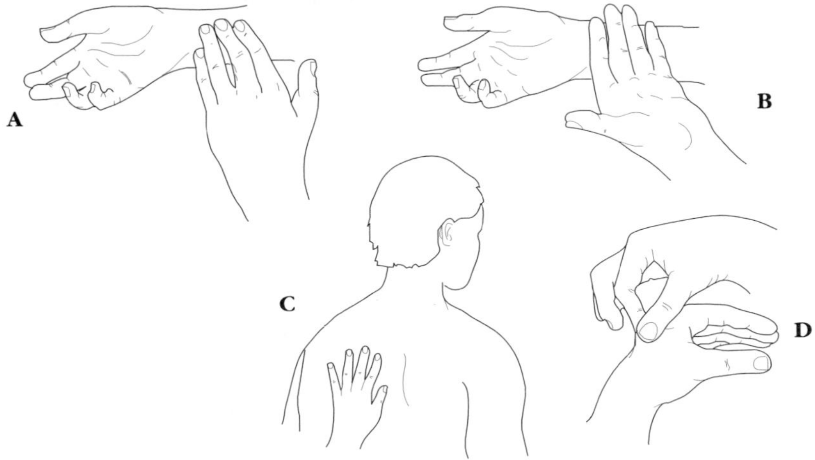

Fig. 3-1
A, Fingertips are most sensitive parts of the hand and are used to assess texture, shape, size, and consistency. **B,** Dorsum or back of hand assesses temperature. **C,** Palm of hand is sensitive to vibration. **D,** Nurse grasps the skin with fingertips to assess turgor.

- Have the client point out more sensitive areas and note any nonverbal signs of discomfort.
- Keep fingernails short, warm hands before touching client, and use a gentle approach.
- Always use light palpation before deep palpation.
- Apply tactile pressure in a slow, gentle, deliberate manner.
- The sensation of touch is best preserved with light, intermittent pressure.
- Any tender areas should be examined further, because tenderness may reveal a serious abnormality.
- The three methods of palpation include the following (Fig. 3-2):
  Light palpation—fingers are gently applied over the skin surface; skin is depressed about 1 cm (½ inch).
  Deep palpation—used to examine the condition of organs and

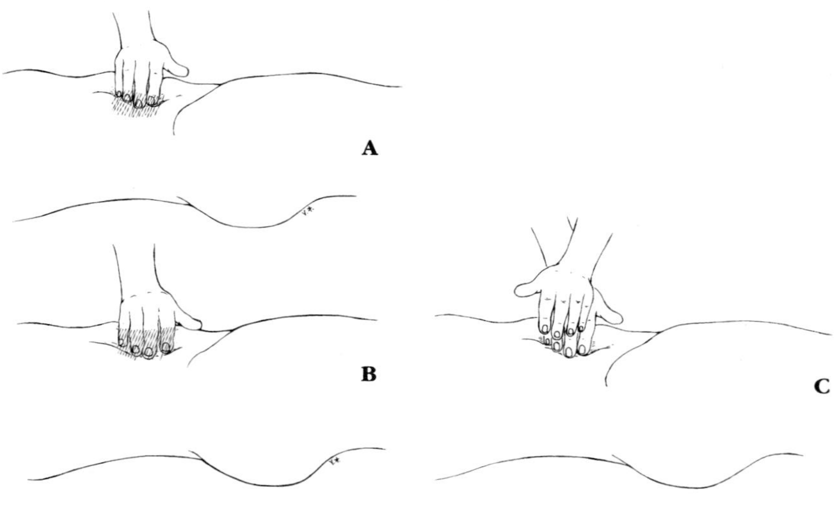

Fig. 3-2
Three techniques of palpation. **A,** Light palpation. **B,** Deep palpation. **C,** Bimanual palpation.

masses; skin is depressed 2.5 cm (1 inch). Caution is needed to prevent internal injury.

Bimanual palpation—both hands are used to palpate deeply; one hand (the sensing hand) is relaxed and placed lightly on the client's skin. The active hand applies pressure to the sensing hand. The lower sensing hand remains sensitive to detect organ characteristics.

- Palpation techniques depend on the body area being examined and the client's condition. For example, when there is risk of a fractured rib, palpate with extreme care; when palpating an artery, avoid applying pressure that may obstruct the blood flow.
- Characteristics measured by palpation in major body areas are listed on pp. 50-51.

Percussion

Percussion is tapping the body with the fingertips to evaluate the size, borders, and consistency of body organs and to discover fluid in body cavities. Percussion determines the location, size, and density of underlying structures to verify abnormalities assessed by palpation and auscultation.

Critical Thinking

Know the location of body organs in relation to typical anatomic landmarks such as the costal margin, umbilical area, and costovertebral angle. Much experience is needed to become competent at percussion.

Skill Techniques

- Table 3-2 describes the five basic percussion sounds, the sites at which they are normally heard, and the sound characteristics to assess.
- Direct method of percussion: The body surface is struck directly with one or two fingertips.
- Indirect method of percussion: The middle finger of the nondominant hand (pleximeter) is placed firmly against the body surface (Fig. 3-3). With palm and fingers staying off the skin, the tip of the middle finger of the dominant hand (plexor) strikes the base of the distal joint of the pleximeter. Use a quick, sharp stroke with the plexor finger, keeping the forearm stationary. Keep the wrist relaxed. Once the finger has struck, the wrist snaps back. A light, quick blow produces the clearest sounds.
- Apply the same force at each area of the body to make an accurate

Table 3-2 Sounds produced by percussion

Sound	Intensity	Pitch	Duration	Quality	Common Location
Tympany	Loud	High	Moderate	Drumlike	Enclosed, air-containing space; gastric air bubble, puffed-out cheek
Resonance	Moderate to loud	Low	Long	Hollow	Normal lung
Hyperresonance	Very loud	Very low	Longer than resonance	Booming	Emphysematous lung
Dullness	Soft to moderate	High	Moderate	Thudlike	Liver
Flatness	Soft	High	Short	Flat	Muscle

comparison of sounds produced by percussion.

- If the blow is not sharp, if the pleximeter hand is held loosely, or if the palm rests on the body surface, the sound is dampened or softened, preventing detection of underlying structures.

Auscultation

Auscultation is listening to sounds produced by the body. Some sounds can be heard with the unaided ear, although most sounds are heard only with a stethoscope.

Critical Thinking

Know normal sounds created by the body (e.g., passage of blood through an artery, bowel sounds, heart sounds). Also be aware of the location in which sounds can be most easily heard. Experience will help you learn what areas normally do not emit sounds.

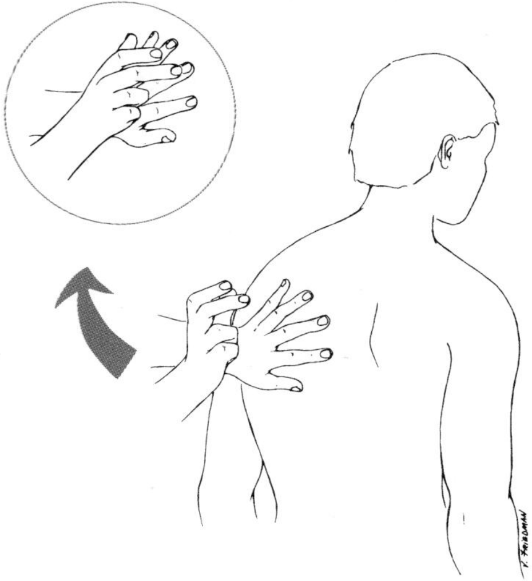

Fig. 3-3
Technique for performing indirect percussion.

Skill Techniques

- Listen in a quiet environment.
- Listen for the presence of sound, as well as its characteristics.
- Be sure earpieces of stethoscope fit snugly and comfortably, with binaurals angled and earpieces following the contour of the ear canal (most persons wear earpieces pointed toward the face).
- Rubber or plastic tubing of stethoscope should be flexible and 30 to 40 cm (12 to 18 inches) in length.
- Examiners with hearing disorders should use a stethoscope with greater amplification or ask colleagues to validate findings.
- Always place the stethoscope on naked skin, because clothing obscures sound.
- Use the stethoscope bell for low-

Area of Body Examined	Criteria Assessed by Palpation
Skin	Temperature Moisture Resistance Texture Turgor and elasticity Tenderness Thickness
Organs such as the liver, intestine, and lung	Size Shape Presence of tenderness Presence or absence of masses Vibration of voice sounds (lung)
Glands such as the thyroid and lymph	Swelling Symmetry Mobility Size Presence of tenderness
Blood vessels such as the carotid or femoral artery	Pulse amplitude Elasticity Pulse rate Pulse rhythm

pitched sounds such as abnormal heart and vascular sounds.

- Use the diaphragm for high-pitched sounds such as bowel, lung, and normal heart sounds.
- With auscultation at any site, the nurse should consider the origin and cause of the sound, the exact site at which it is heard best, and the expected normal qualities of the sound to assess deviations from normal.
- Through auscultation note four characteristics of sound (Table 3-3).
- Box 3-1 outlines exercises to improve familiarity with the stethoscope.

Muscles	Size; shape; tone Presence of tenderness Presence of spasm or rigidity
Bones	Symmetry; shape Presence of deformity Presence of tenderness

Table 3-3 Characteristics of sound

Characteristic	Description
Frequency	Number of sound wave cycles generated per second by a vibrating object. The higher the frequency, the higher the pitch of a sound and vice versa.
Loudness	Amplitude of a sound wave. Auscultated sounds are described as *loud* or *soft*.
Quality	Sounds of similar frequency and loudness from different sources. Terms such as *blowing* or *gurgling* describe quality of sound.
Duration	Length of time sound vibrations last. Duration of sound is *short, medium,* or *long*.

BOX 3-1 Exercises to Increase Familiarity With Stethoscope

1. Place earpieces in both ears with tips of earpieces turned toward the face. *Lightly* blow into the stethoscope's diaphragm. Again place earpieces in both ears, this time with ends turned toward the back of the head. *Lightly* blow into the stethoscope's diaphragm. The earpiece should follow the contour of the ear canal. After learning the right fit for the loudest sound, wear the stethoscope the same way each time.
2. Put the stethoscope on and *lightly blow* into the diaphragm. If sound is barely audible, *lightly* blow into the bell. Sound is carried through only one part of the chestpiece at a time. If sound is greatly amplified through the diaphragm, the diaphragm is in position for use. If sound is barely audible through the diaphragm, the bell is in position for use.
3. Listen while moving the diaphragm lightly over the hair on your arm. The bristling sound created by rubbing of hair against the diaphragm mimics a sound heard in the lungs. Also, always be sure to keep the diaphragm stationary and firm to reduce extraneous sounds.
4. Place the stethoscope on and gently tap tubing. The sound can distract from being able to hear sounds created by body organs. Always avoid stretching or moving the tubing; it should hang freely.

Preparation for the Examination

4

Proper preparation of the environment, equipment, and client ensures a smooth physical examination with few interruptions. A disorganized approach when preparing for a physical examination can cause errors and incomplete findings.

Preparation of Environment

- Ensure privacy for the client. Conduct the examination in a well-equipped room if possible. If you are examining the client in a semi-private hospital room, close the room curtains or dividers. In the home use the client's bedroom.
- Be sure lighting is adequate, without distortion from shadows.
- A sound-proofed room is ideal; minimize any outside noise.
- Do not allow interruptions from other health care workers during the examination.
- Have the client wear an examination gown when possible.
- Ensure client comfort by offering a small pillow.
- Raise the head of the table about 30 degrees when the client is supine.
- Have examination bed or table at examiner's waist level.
- Help the client move onto and off the table.
- Do not leave confused, combative,

or uncooperative clients unattended on the examining table.

- Make sure the room is sufficiently warm to maintain comfort.
- Provide adequate space for an examination, particularly for older adults who use mobility aids.

Preparation of Equipment

- Wash hands thoroughly before preparing equipment for the examination.
- Have all equipment readily available and arranged in order of use before the examination begins.
- Be sure any equipment that touches the client's skin is warm (e.g., run warm water over speculum blades; rub diaphragm of stethoscope briskly between the hands).
- Be sure all equipment is functioning properly. Have spare batteries and light bulbs available for the otoscope and ophthalmoscope.
- Box 4-1 lists the equipment and supplies typically needed by examiners for physical assessment. (Special equipment for special procedures is listed in later chapters.)

Physical Preparation of Client

- Ensure the client's physical comfort before starting the examination. Ask the client to empty bladder or bowel if needed, and collect urine and fecal specimens at this time.
- Be sure client is dressed and draped properly.
  - Provide privacy while the client changes into a gown and give the client time to undress, assisting if necessasry. If the examination is limited to certain body systems (e.g., head and neck), it may be unnecessary for the client to undress.
  - Hospitalized clients usually wear a simple gown.
  - Outpatients can change into a linen or disposable gown.
  - After gowning, provide a drape for over the lap or lower trunk.
- Eliminate drafts, control room temperature, and provide warm blankets.
- Periodically ask whether the client is comfortable.
  - Seriously ill or older clients are more likely to become chilled.
  - Offer a drink of water, tissue, or pillow to help the client relax.
- Help the client assume proper positions (Table 4-1) during the examination so that body parts are

BOX 4-1 Equipment and Supplies for Physical Examination

- Cotton applicators
- Cytobrush
- Disposable pad
- Drapes
- Eye chart (e.g., Snellen chart)
- Flashlight and spotlight
- Forms (e.g., physical, laboratory)
- Gloves (sterile or clean)
- Goniometer
- Gown for client
- Water-soluble lubricant
- Ophthalmoscope
- Otoscope
- Glass microscope slides and slip covers
- Paper towels
- Percussion hammer
- Ruler
- Safety pin
- Scale with height measurement rod
- Specimen containers and microscope slides
- Sphygmomanometer and cuff
- Stethoscope
- Swabs or sponge forceps
- Tape measure
- Thermometer
- Tissues
- Tongue depressor
- Tuning fork
- Vaginal speculum
- Wristwatch with second hand or digital display

accessible and the client stays comfortable.

Adjust draping during positioning to be sure the body part being examined is not unnecessarily exposed.

Some positions are uncomfortable and/or embarrassing; keep the client in a position no longer than is necessary.

When alternative positions can be used for a particular examination, choose the position best suited for weakened clients.

Position older adults to avoid having them look into the source of light, which can cause discomfort from the light's glare.

Some clients have limited strength; provide assistance in assuming desired positions.

For disabled clients, special body

Table 4-1 Positions for examination

Position	Areas Assessed	Rationale	Limitations
Sitting 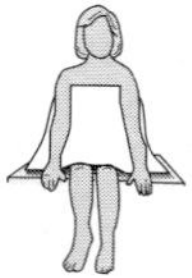	Head and neck, back, posterior thorax and lungs, anterior thorax and lungs, breasts, axillae, heart, vital signs, and upper extremities	Sitting upright provides full expansion of lungs and provides better visualization of symmetry of upper body parts.	Physically weakened client may be unable to sit. Examiner should use supine position with head of bed elevated instead.
Supine 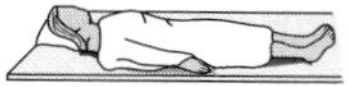	Head and neck, anterior thorax and lungs, breasts, axillae, heart, abdomen, extremities, pulses	This is most normally relaxed position. It provides easy access to pulse sites.	If client becomes short of breath easily, examiner may need to raise head of bed.
Dorsal recumbent 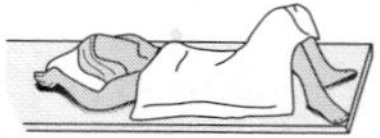	Head and neck, anterior thorax and lungs, breasts, axillae, heart, abdomen	Position is used for abdominal assessment because it promotes relaxation of abdominal muscles.	Clients with painful disorders are more comfortable with knees flexed.
Lithotomy* 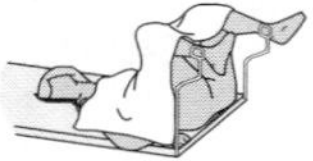	Female genitalia and genital tract	This position provides maximal exposure of genitalia and facilitates insertion of vaginal speculum.	Lithotomy position is embarrassing and uncomfortable, so examiner minimizes time that client spends in it. Client is kept well draped.

Sims' 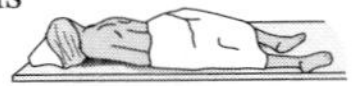	Rectum and vagina	Flexion of hip and knee improves exposure of rectal area.	Joint deformities may hinder client's ability to bend hip and knee.
Prone 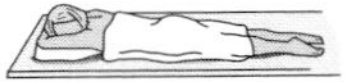	Musculoskeletal system	This position is used only to assess extension of hip joint.	This position is poorly tolerated in clients with respiratory difficulties.
Lateral recumbent 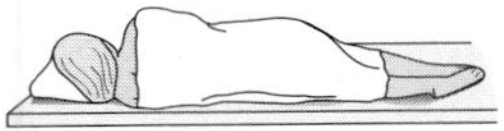	Heart	This position aids in detecting murmurs.	This position is poorly tolerated in clients with respiratory difficulties.
Knee-chest* 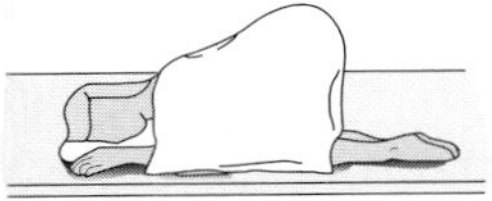	Rectum	This position provides maximal exposure of rectal area.	This position is embarrassing and uncomfortable.

*Clients with arthritis or other joint deformities may be unable to assume this position.

positions may be used (see Chapter 16).

- Sequence an examination to keep position changes to a minimum. Be efficient throughout the examination, to limit client movement.

Psychologic Preparation of Client

- Begin the assessment by explaining in general terms the purpose of the examination, how it will be performed, what the client should expect to feel, and how the client can cooperate.
  - Tell the client to feel free to ask any questions and to describe any discomfort felt during the examination. Provide an opportunity for those questions.

  EXAMPLE: Mrs. Smith, I am now going to perform a physical examination so I can have a good idea of whether you have any health problems. As we go along I will explain to you exactly what I will be doing. Please feel free to ask any questions. If you become uncomfortable, please tell me. We will start with an examination of the head and neck area.

- As you examine each body system, explain the procedure in greater detail.
  - Use simple terms when describing steps of the examination. If a client speaks a foreign language, determine if a family member or friend can interpret. Ask the client if the family member can be present during the examination.

  EXAMPLE: As I examine your breasts, I want you to relax lying down. First I will look at the color, size, and shape of your breasts. Then I'll gently use my hands to feel the breast tissue itself.

- Put the client at ease.
  - Convey an open, receptive, and professional approach.
  - Use a relaxed tone of voice and facial expression when making explanations.
  - Maintain good eye contact.
  - Perform each physical examination maneuver smoothly and confidently (take your time).
  - If a client seems highly anxious, back away and reexplain your intent. Then begin again.
- Have a third person (of the client's gender) in the examination room during the examination of the geni-

talia. Having a third person ensures that the examiner will behave ethically.

- Monitor the client's emotional responses throughout the examination. Observe fear or concern in facial expressions.
- Observe for body movements such as tensing when touched or clutching the drape around the body.
- If the client is overly afraid, anxious, or uncomfortable, postpone the examination until a time when relaxation and cooperation can lead to greater accuracy in the assessment.
- Never force a client to continue.
- Pace or time the examination process according to the client's physical and emotional tolerance. Older adults in particular take more time to assume necessary body positions.
- Respect the client's cultural differences. A client's health beliefs, use of alternative therapies, nutritional habits, relationships with family, and comfort with close physical contact during an examination must be considered.

5 General Survey and Vital Signs

Organization of the Examination

The nurse usually obtains a nursing history and general survey before the initial physical examination. Information from the history and survey provides a useful road map for the nurse to follow when making detailed physical measurements. Historical information, survey findings, and vital signs help to localize physical signs later during the examination. The client's health status, the health care setting, and the nurse's experience may require different approaches for organizing an examination. For example, a client in acute distress may require a focused physical examination before any historical information can be gathered. When a client is admitted to a hospital or is a first-time visitor to a clinic, a complete examination is usually performed. An experienced nurse often learns to incorporate history taking with an examination, especially if time with the client is limited. Again, critical thinking is important in deciding what information to gather from the client and how extensive an examination should be.

Once a complete examination is done, the nurse will perform ongoing assessments of a client's condition. The nature and extent of these focused examinations depend on the client's clinical status and needs. In hospital settings, nurses typically perform a portion of an examination at the beginning of each shift to gain a good sense of the client's status. This serves as a comparison with previous assessments, plus it gives the nurse a reference point from which to evaluate the client's progress during the remainder of the shift.

The physical examination follows certain priorities when a client is ill or has specific symptoms. Body systems most at risk for being abnormal should be examined first; noncritical parts of the examination can be deferred until the client can tolerate a more thorough examination. For example, a client who has shortness of breath usually first undergoes a complete thoracic (see Chapter 12) and cardiac (see Chapter 13) assessment. A more comprehensive examination can wait until the client's fatigue is relieved.

The following are general tips for organizing an examination:

- Follow a head-to-toe approach, using each of the four examination skills, to ensure that all body systems are reviewed.
- Always inspect, palpate, percuss, then auscultate *except during the abdominal examination*. Auscultate and percuss before palpating the abdomen, to avoid causing alterations in bowel sounds.
- Assess the structure and function of each body part and organ (e.g, the appearance of external eye structures, as well as visual function).
- Compare both sides of the body for symmetry. A degree of asymmetry is normal (e.g., the biceps muscle of the dominant arm may be more developed than the same muscle in the nondominant arm).
- Integrate client education throughout the examination. Demonstrations can often be given during an examination (e.g., breast self-examination).
- Perform painful assessment procedures near the end of the examination.
- If a client becomes fatigued, offer rest periods between assessments.
- Record quick notes during the examination to avoid keeping the client waiting.
- Complete all documentation after the examination. Use the institution's nursing history and physical examination form.

- Record findings in specific anatomic and scientific terms so that any professional can interpret the findings.
- Use common and accepted medical abbreviations to keep notes brief and concise.

Critical Thinking

Knowledge

Throughout the examination concentrate on one step at a time. Ask yourself the following questions: What are the skills appropriate for this part of an examination? What are my findings? What should the findings normally be? Is my technique causing the findings, or is there evidence of a true abnormality?

Experience

Use your experience. If you have ever cared for a client with similar abnormal findings, consider in what way the two clients are the same or different. This may help in determining the nature of any abnormalities. In addition, recall what approaches to examination were most effective with previous clients. For example, you may have learned that a certain positioning approach makes it easier for you to assess a client accurately.

Standards

Always apply appropriate standards for data gathering. For example, to assess any symptom, such as nausea or pain, always follow the standard of assessing location, onset, severity, frequency, aggravating and relieving factors, concomitant symptoms, and so on.

General Survey

The general survey begins a review of the client's primary health problems. It includes assessment of the client's mental status, general appearance and behavior, vital signs, and height and weight. The survey can effectively point out problems early. It provides information about characteristics of an illness, a client's hygiene and body image, emotional state, recent weight changes, and the client's developmental status. If abnormalities or signs of problems are found, the nurse directs attention to specific body systems later during the examination. The survey can also reveal important information about the client's behavior that can influence how the nurse communicates instructions to the client and conducts portions of the examination.

Delegation Considerations

The general survey requires problem solving and knowledge application unique to a professional nurse. An unlicensed assistive staff member may monitor assessment data (e.g., measure height and weight, take vital signs, record intake and output [I&O]) and report a client's subjective signs and symptoms. All monitoring data must be reported to the RN for assessment considerations. Delegation of this skill to unlicensed personnel for assessment is inappropriate.

Equipment

Electronic, disposable single-use, or mercury-in-glass thermometer
Soft tissue
Water-soluble lubricant for rectal temperature measurements
Disposable gloves
Standing platform scale or electronic scale with height measuring attachment
Stretcher scale (optional)
Table model or basket scale (optional)
Tape measure
Sphygmomanometer and cuff
Stethoscope
Watch with second hand or digital display

Client Preparation

- Conduct the general survey with the client sitting or standing. An experienced nurse can do this almost automatically before beginning the physical assessment.
- Before conducting the mental status examination, be sure the client is as fully awake as possible.
- Body temperature is usually measured orally, requiring the client to assume a comfortable sitting position. If a rectal temperature is to be measured, have the client lie in Sims' position with upper leg flexed; a child may lie prone. Temperatures measured via the axillary or tympanic membrane route require the client to sit comfortably.
- For pulse assessment, position the client supine with a forearm across the lower abdomen or chest or at the side of the body. If the client is seated, bend the elbow 90 degrees and support the lower arm on the chair or on your arm. Slightly extend the wrist with palm facing down.
- To assess respirations, have the client assume a comfortable position, sitting or lying with the head of the bed elevated 45 to 60 degrees.
- The client may sit or lie comfortably during blood pressure measurement.

- Ask the client to remove shoes and any heavy outer clothing before you measure height and weight.
- When weighing a hospitalized client, always weigh at the same time of day, with the same scale, and with the client wearing the same clothing.

History

- Data may be collected initially during the nursing history or as the nurse performs physical measurements.
- Note if client is in any acute distress (e.g., difficulty breathing, pain, anxiety). If present, defer general survey until later.
- Ask the client for current height and weight.
- Ask whether the client has had a recent change in weight, the amount, and period of time in which change occurred.
- Review client's past fluid I&O records (if available).
- Ask if client has recently been dieting or following an exercise program.
- Ask client what was eaten during the previous 24 hours.
- Determine type of client's diet.
- Before measuring body temperature ask if client is experiencing headaches, myalgia, chills, nausea, or weakness. Inspect condition of oral mucosa for coating, lesions, and decreased salivation.
- Ask if client has noticed recent change in pulse or heart rate.
- Identify the client's normal baseline heart rate.
- Consider any factors that might influence vital signs (Table 5-1).
- Does the client have a history of hypertension or hypotension?
- Ask the client's reason for seeking health care and expectations for this encounter.
- Review nursing history for the client's primary health problems.
- Review nursing history for medications client is currently taking.

Table 5-1 Factors that influence vital signs

Factor	Vital Sign	Effect
Exercise	Pulse	Short term—increases rate Long term—strengthens heart muscle, causing lower-than-normal rate at rest and quicker return to resting rate after exercise
	Respiration	Increases rate and depth
	Blood pressure	Increases cardiac output and mean arterial pressure
	Temperature	Strenuous exercise may raise temperature
Fever, heat	Pulse	Increases rate
	Respirations	Increases rate
Acute pain, anxiety	Pulse	Sympathetic stimulation—increases rate
	Respirations	Increases rate and depth; alters rhythm
	Blood pressure	Increases pressure
Unrelieved severe chronic pain	Pulse	Parasympathetic stimulation—slows rate
Medications		
Atropine	Pulse	Increases rate
Digitalis	Pulse	Slows rate

Modified from Hazinski MF: Children are different. In Hazinski MF, ed: *Nursing care of the critically ill child,* St Louis, 1984, Mosby; Kinney MR et al: *AACN's clinical reference for critical care nursing,* ed 3, St Louis, 1993, Mosby; and National High Blood Pressure Education Program; National Heart, Lung, and Blood Institute, National Institutes of Health: *The fifth report of the Joint National Committee on Detection, Evaluation, and Treatment of High Blood Pressure,* NIH Pub No 93-1088, Bethesda, Md, January 1993, NIH.

Continued

Table 5-1 Factors that influence vital signs—cont'd

Factor	Vital Sign	Effect
Medications—cont'd		
Beta blocker	Pulse	Slows rate
	Blood pressure	Lowers pressure
Antidysrhythmic	Pulse	Slows rate
Diuretics	Blood pressure	Lower pressure
Adrenergic inhibitors	Blood pressure	Lower pressure
Ace inhibitors	Blood pressure	Lower pressure
Narcotic analgesics	Respirations	Decrease rate and depth or affect rhythm
	Blood pressure	Lower pressure
General anesthetics	Respirations	Lower rate and depth
	Blood pressure	Lower pressure
Amphetamines and cocaine	Respirations	Increase rate and depth
Age	Respirations	From infancy to adulthood, lung vital capacity increases
		With old age, depth of respiration decreases
	Pulse	Infant 120 to 160 beats/min
		Toddler 90 to 140 beats/min
		Preschooler 80 to 110 beats/min
		School-age 75 to 100 beats/min
		Adolescent 60 to 90 beats/min
		Adult 60 to 100 beats/min

	Respirations	Newborn 35 to 40 breaths/min Infant 30 to 50 breaths/min Toddler 25 to 32 breaths/min Child 20 to 30 breaths/min Adolescent 16 to 19 breaths/min Adult 12 to 20 breaths/min
	Blood pressure	1 Month 85/54 1 Year 95/65 6 Years 105/65 10 to 13 Years 110/65 14 to 17 Years 120/75 Middle adult 120/80 Older adult 140/90
Body position	Pulse	Lying prone decreases rate Standing or sitting increases rate
	Respirations	Straight posture—full chest expansion Slumped posture—reduced rate and volume
	Blood pressure	Standing suddenly—may lower pressure

Modified from Hazinski MF: Children are different. In Hazinski MF, ed: *Nursing care of the critically ill child,* St Louis, 1984, Mosby; Kinney MR et al: *AACN's clinical reference for critical care nursing,* ed 3, St Louis, 1993, Mosby; and National High Blood Pressure Education Program; National Heart, Lung, and Blood Institute, National Institutes of Health: *The fifth report of the Joint National Committee on Detection, Evaluation, and Treatment of High Blood Pressure,* NIH Pub No 93-1088, Bethesda, Md, January 1993, NIH.

Assessment Techniques

Assessment	Normal Findings	Deviations From Normal
Mental Status		
For clients who are alert and responsive to conversation, conduct a mental status examination, using a mental status questionnaire such as the MSQ or Folstein's Mini–Mental State (MMS) (Box 5-1).	Test should only take 5 to 10 minutes to administer. Concentrating on cognitive function, the maximum score on the test is 30; average score is 27.	Scores below 20 may indicate dementia and delirium (see Chapter 19).
If client's alertness is questioned, assess client's level of consciousness (see Chapter 19 for neurologic examination).	Client is alert, oriented, and responds appropriately to all questions.	Client is confused, at times difficult to arouse by verbal stimulus. Client not consistently oriented to person, place, event, or time.
General Appearance		
Assess client's gender and race while observing client's physical features.	It will often be necessary to ask clients, "What is your race?"	

BOX 5-1 Folstein's Mini–Mental State

Maximum Score	Score	
Orientation		
5	( )	What is the (year) (season) (date) (day) (month)?
5	( )	Where are we (state) (county) (town) (hospital) (floor)?
Registration		
3	( )	Name 3 objects: 1 second to say each. Then ask the patient all 3 after you have said them. Give 1 point for each correct answer. Then repeat them until he learns all 3. Count trials and record.
Attention and calculation		
5	( )	Serial 7's. 1 point for each correct. Stop after 5 answers. Alternatively, spell "world" backwards.
Recall		
3	( )	Ask for the 3 objects repeated above. Give 1 point for each correct.
Language		
9	( )	Name a *pencil* and a *watch* (2 points) Repeat the following: "No ifs, ands, or buts" (1 point)

Modified from Folstein MF, Folstein S, McHugh PR: Mini–Mental State; a practical method for grading the cognitive state of patients for the clinician, *J Psychiatr Res* 12:189, 1975.

Continued

BOX 5-1 Folstein's Mini–Mental State—cont'd

Maximum Score	Score	
Language—cont'd		
		Follow a 3-stage command: "Take a paper in your right hand, fold it in half, and put it on the floor" (3 points)
		Read and obey the following: "Close your eyes" (1 point)
		Write a sentence (1 point)
		Copy design (1 point)
________		Total score

Assess level of consciousness along a continuum

Alert	Drowsy	Stupor	Coma

Instructions for Administration of Mini–Mental State Examination

Orientation

(1) Ask for the date. Then ask specifically for parts omitted (e.g., "Can you also tell me what season it is?"). One point for each correct.

(2) Ask in turn, "Can you tell me the name of this hospital?" (town, county, etc.). One point for each correct.

Registration

Ask the patient if you may test his memory. Then say the names of 3 unrelated objects, clearly and slowly, about 1 second for each. After you have said all 3, ask him to repeat them. This first repetition determines his score (0-3), but keep saying them until he can repeat all 3, up to 6 trials. If he does not eventually learn all 3, recall cannot be meaningfully tested.

Attention and calculation

Ask the patient to begin with 100 and count backwards by 7. Stop after 5 subtractions (93, 86, 79, 72, 65). Score the total number of correct answers.

If the patient cannot or will not perform this task, ask him to spell the word "world" backwards. The score is the number of letters in correct order (e.g., dlrow = 5, dlorw = 3).

Recall

Ask the patient if he can recall the 3 words you previously asked him to remember. Score 0-3.

Language

Naming: Show the patient a wristwatch and ask him what it is. Repeat for pencil. Score 0-2.

Repetition: Ask the patient to repeat the sentence after you. Allow only one trial. Score 0 or 1.

3-Stage command: Give the patient a piece of plain blank paper and repeat the command. Score 1 point for each part correctly executed.

Reading: On a blank piece of paper print the sentence "Close your eyes" in letters large enough for the patient to see clearly. Ask him to read it and do what it says. Score 1 point only if he actually closes his eyes.

Writing: Give the patient a blank piece of paper and ask him to write a sentence for you. Do not dictate a sentence; it is

Modified from Folstein MF, Folstein S, McHugh PR: Mini–Mental State; a practical method for grading the cognitive state of patients for the clinician, *J. Psychiatr Res* 12:189, 1975.

Continued

BOX 5-1 Folstein's Mini–Mental State—cont'd

to be written spontaneously. It must contain a subject and verb and be sensible. Correct grammar and punctuation are not necessary.

Copying: On a clean sheet of paper, draw intersecting pentagons, each side about 1 inch, and ask him to copy it exactly as it is. All 10 angles must be present and 2 must intersect to score 1 point. Tremor and rotation are ignored.

Estimate the patient's level of sensorium along a continuum, from alert on the left to coma on the right.

Modified from Folstein MF, Folstein S, McHugh PR: Mini–Mental State; a practical method for grading the cognitive state of patients for the clinician, *J. Psychiatr Res* 12:189, 1975.

Assessment	Normal Findings	Deviations From Normal
Note if client appears to be his or her stated age.	Normal physical characteristics vary according to age. A client's ability to participate in examination will also be affected.	
Observe client's dress. A person's culture, lifestyle, socioeconomic level, and personal preference affect the type of clothes that the person wears.	Type of clothing worn is appropriate for occasion, temperature, and weather conditions. Looks clean and fits the body. Older adults may wear extra clothing because of their sensitivity to cold.	Clothing is dirty or unkempt. Depressed or mentally ill persons may be unable to choose proper clothing.

Observe for signs of distress (e.g., shortness of breath, client's subjective complaint of chest pain or difficulty breathing). These signs help to establish priorities about what to examine first. For any acute sign or symptom, determine onset, duration, severity, predisposing and aggravating factors, and conditions that bring relief.		Defer the examination if the client's condition worsens, and attempt to relieve the distress.
Body Structure and Mobility		
Observe the following:		
Body type	Client appears fit, trim, and muscular. Body type reflects level of health, age, and lifestyle.	Client appears obese or extremely thin.
Posture	Normal standing posture is an upright comfortable stance with parallel alignment of hips and shoulders. Normal sitting involves some rounding of the shoulders.	Posture is slumped or bent. May reflect mood or presence of pain.

Assessment	Normal Findings	Deviations From Normal
Gait. Observe the client walk into the room or along the bedside (if ambulatory). Note whether movements are coordinated or uncoordinated.	Walks with the arms swinging freely at the sides and with the head and face leading the body.	Walks hesitantly or tends to list. May fall one way, backward, forward, consistent direction (see Chapter 19).
Body movements. Observe purposeful body movements (e.g., shaking of examiner's hand, grasping hold of an object).	Able to perform movement smoothly, without hesitation.	Tremors present, involving the extremities. Body part is limited in motion or immobile.
Behavior		
Facial expression. Note client's eye contact (be aware of cultural norms). Are expressions appropriate to the situation?	Maintains good eye contact during discussions. Smiles and shows thoughtful reflections to questions.	Facial expression does not match verbal message or other nonverbal signs. Makes no eye contact; motionless face, fixed stare. Hides mouth behind hand when speaking.
Hygiene and grooming. Note the client's level of cleanliness; observe the appearance of the hair, skin, and fingernails. A person's grooming may	Dressed for occasion. Hair is neatly groomed or brushed. Appears clean and groomed appropriately for age, culture, or socioeconomic group.	Appearance is unkempt and disheveled. Hair is not groomed. Fingernails and hands may appear soiled.

be affected by degree of illness, as well as the type of activities performed just before the examination. Also note the amount and type of cosmetics used.	Makeup is appropriate for age and culture.	
Note the presence of any body odor. An unpleasant body odor may simply be the result of physical exercise or may be caused by poor hygiene. Also look for any dressings, ostomy devices, or open wounds.	No body odor is noted.	Foul body odors; fetid breath, fruity odor. Note that the odor of alcohol does not always mean alcoholism. Foul odor can be localized to a draining wound or ostomy.
Mood and affect. Affect is a person's feelings as they appear to others. A person's mood or emotional state is expressed verbally and nonverbally. Observe whether the client's verbal expressions match nonverbal behavior and note whether the client's mood is appropriate for the situation.	Client is comfortable and cooperative with examiner; answers questions freely and appropriately.	Client appears unusually happy or withdrawn. Hesitates to answer questions; quick to anger.

Assessment	Normal Findings	Deviations From Normal
Speech. Note client's ability to articulate words and pace sentences. Does client speak in a normal tone of voice?	Follows simple instructions and answers questions. Normal speech is understandable, is moderately paced, and shows an association with the person's thoughts. Voice tone is moderate and changes appropriately with context of discussion.	Has difficulty responding to questions or instructions. Client talks rapidly or slowly. An abnormal pace may be caused by emotions or neurologic impairment. Speaks loudly or very softly.
Abuse		
The abuse of children, women, and older adults is a growing health problem. Assess for the following signs: Client has suffered obvious physical injury or neglect (e.g., evidence of malnutrition or presence of bruising on extremities or trunk). Client is fearful of spouse or partner, caregiver, parent, or adult child.	Client denies history or shows no physical sign of injury.	Presence of clinical indicators of abuse should be reported to a social service center.

Partner or caregiver has history of violence, alcoholism, or drug abuse.

Caregiver is unemployed, ill, or frustrated in caring for client.

! ***Nurse Alert*** *If abuse is suspected, interview further in private (Table 5-2).*

Vital Signs

Temperature Measurement

Wait 20 to 30 minutes after client ingests any hot or cold foods or liquids, after smoking, or after strenuous exercise.

Wash hands and apply disposable glove to dominant hand for measuring oral and rectal temperatures.

Table 5-2 Clinical indicators of abuse

Physical Findings	Behavioral Findings
Child Sexual Abuse	
Vaginal or penile discharge	Problem in sleeping or eating
Blood on underclothing	Fear of certain people or places
Pain or itching in genital area	Play activities recreate the abuse situation
Genital injuries	Regressed behavior
Difficulty sitting or walking	Sexual acting out
Pain while urinating	Knowledge of explicit sexual matters
Foreign bodies in rectum, urethra, or vagina	Preoccupation with other's or own genitals
Venereal disease	
Domestic Abuse	
Injuries and trauma are inconsistent with reported cause	Attempted suicide
Multiple injuries involving head, face, neck, breasts, abdomen, and genitalia (black eyes, orbital fractures, broken nose, fractured skull, lip lacerations, broken teeth, strangulation marks)	Eating or sleeping disorders
	Anxiety
	Panic attacks
	Pattern of substance abuse (follows physical abuse)

X-rays show old and new fractures in different stages of healing	Low self-esteem
Burns	Depression
Human bites	Sense of helplessness
	Guilt
	Increased forgetfulness

Older Adult Abuse

Injuries and trauma are inconsistent with reported cause (cigarette burn, scratch, bruise, or bite)	Dependent on caregiver
Hematomas	Physically and/or cognitively impaired
Bruises at various stages of resolution	Combative
Bruises, chafing, excoriation on wrist or legs (restraints)	Wandering
Burns	Verbally belligerent
Fractures inconsistent with cause described	Minimal social support
Dried blood	
Prolonged interval between injury and medical treatment	

Modified from Haviland S, O'Brien J: *Orthop Nurs* 8(4):11, 1989; Stanley SR: *Orthop Nurs* 8(1):33, 1989; and Moss VA, Taylor WK: *AORN J* 53(5):1158, 1991.

Assessment	Normal Findings	Deviations From Normal
Oral Temperature Place clean thermometer under client's tongue in sublingual pocket, lateral to center of lower jaw, for 3 minutes (mercury thermometer) (Holtzclaw, 1992); 60 seconds (disposable thermometer) (Erickson et al., 1996); or until audible signal occurs on electronic thermometer digital display.	Normal adult body temperature is 36° C (96.8° F) to 38° C (100.4° F). (For temperature conversions from Fahrenheit to centigrade see Appendix F.)	A single temperature reading does not indicate a fever. A persistent elevation above normal warrants therapy.
Rectal Temperature With client in Sims' position and upper leg flexed, separate buttocks and gently insert lubricated probe into anus in direction of umbilicus. Insert 1.2 cm (½ inch) for infant and 3.5 cm (1½ inches) for adult. *Do not force thermometer.* Hold in place for 3 minutes (mercury in glass) or until audible signal occurs on electronic digital display.	Rectal temperatures are usually 0.5° C (0.9° F) higher than oral temperatures (Pontious et al., 1994).	A persistent elevation above normal warrants therapy.

Axillary Temperature

Move clothing or gown from shoulder and arm. Insert thermometer into center of axilla, lower arm over thermometer, and place arm across client's chest. Leave in place 5 to 10 minutes (mercury in glass) or until audible signal occurs on electronic digital display.

Axillary temperatures are usually 0.5° C (0.9° F) lower than oral temperatures (Pontious et al., 1994).

A persistent elevation above normal warrants therapy.

Tympanic Membrane Temperature

Insert tympanic probe into ear canal, applying a gentle but firm pressure (Fig. 5-1). Initiate starter and leave in place until audible or visual signal indicates temperature reading is complete.

Accurate measure of core temperature.

Pulse Measurement

Wait 5 to 10 minutes before assessing pulse if client has been active or exercising.

Assessment	Normal Findings	Deviations From Normal

Radial Pulse

Place tips of first two fingers of hand over groove along radial or thumb side of client's inner wrist. Lightly compress against radius, obliterate pulse initially, and then relax pressure so that pulse becomes easily palpable. Count rate for 30 seconds if regular and multiply by 4. Count rate for 60 seconds if irregular. Assess the pulse for the following:

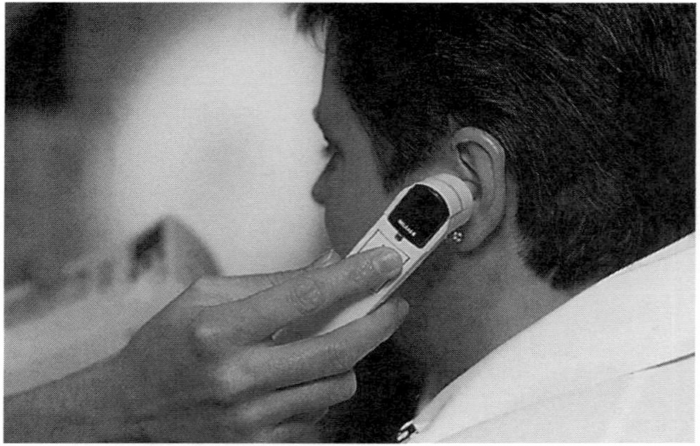

Fig. 5-1
Tympanic thermometer inserted into auditory canal.

Rate	See Table 5-1 for normal findings.	Rate > 100 beats/minute is tachycardia (abnormally elevated rate). Rate < 60 beats/minute is bradycardia (abnormally low rate; *exception is highly conditioned athletes*).
Rhythm	Normally a regular interval occurs between each pulse or heartbeat.	A dysrhythmia is indicated by an interval interrupted by an early or late beat or a missed beat.
Strength	Pulse strength or amplitude remains equally strong bilaterally.	Pulse strength may be graded: 0 Absent, not palpable 1+ Pulse diminished, barely palpable, easy to obliterate 2+ Easily palpable, normal 3+ Full, increased 4+ Strong, bounding, cannot be obliterated
Equality	Both radial pulses are symmetric.	One pulse is unequal in strength or absent.

Assessment	Normal Findings	Deviations From Normal

Apical Pulse

Expose client's sternum and left side of chest. Locate fifth intercostal space at left midclavicular line. Place diaphragm of stethoscope over apical impulse and auscultate until you hear normal S_1 and S_2 heart sounds (Fig. 5-2). Count rate for 1 full minute.

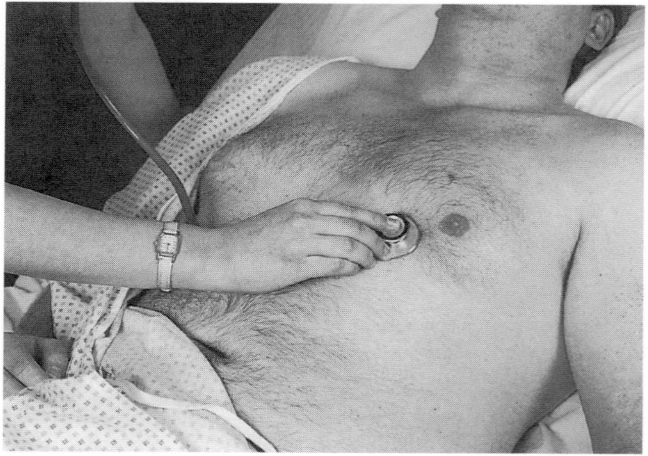

Fig. 5-2
Auscultation of apical pulse.

Rate	Normal rate is 60 to 100 beats/minute	Rate $>$ 100 beats/minute is tachycardia; rate $<$ 60 beats/minute is bradycardia.
Rhythm	Regular interval occurs between S_1 and S_2 and between S_2 and next S_1.	A dysrhythmia involves an interruption in successive heart sounds.
Respiration Assessment		
Wait 5 to 10 minutes if client has been active or exercising.		
Be sure client's chest is visible. Observe a complete respiratory cycle, then count rate for 30 seconds if regular and multiply by 2. If rhythm is irregular or rate is less than 12 or more than 20, count for 1 full minute.		
Assess the following:		
Rate	See Table 5-1 for normal findings.	Rate $<$ 12 breaths/minute is bradypnea; rate $>$ 20 breaths/minute is tachypnea.
Rhythm	A regular interval occurs after each respiratory cycle.	Intervals occur irregularly between respiratory cycles.

Assessment	Normal Findings	Deviations From Normal
Depth	Excursion or movement of chest wall is full and equal bilaterally.	Excursion is shallow or excessively deep. One side of chest may expand more than the other, indicating pain, positioning restriction, or possible pathology.
Blood Pressure		
Assess best site for obtaining blood pressure measurement. Avoid applying cuff to arm when intravenous catheter is in antecubital fossa and intravenous fluids are infusing, when client has arteriovenous shunt, when breast or axillary surgery has been performed on that side, when arm or hand has been traumatized or diseased, or when client has lower arm cast or bulky bandage.		

Try to have client avoid caffeine intake and smoking for 30 minutes before assessment (Joint National Committee on Detection, Evaluation, and Treatment of High Blood Pressure, 1993).

Table 5-3 outlines steps to avoid mistakes in measuring blood pressure.

Be sure restrictive clothing has been removed from client's arm. Palpate brachial artery and position cuff 2.5 cm (1 inch) above site of brachial pulsation. Center bladder of cuff above artery and wrap cuff evenly and snugly around upper arm. With manometer positioned vertically at eye level, palpate brachial or radial artery while inflating cuff rapidly to a pressure 30 mm Hg above point at which pulse disappears. Slowly deflate cuff. Point at which pulse reappears is approximate systolic pressure.

Table 5-3 Common mistakes in blood pressure measurement

Error	Effect
Bladder or cuff too wide	False low reading
Bladder or cuff too narrow	False high reading
Cuff wrapped too loosely	False high reading
Deflating cuff too slowly	False high diastolic reading
Deflating cuff too quickly	False low systolic and false high diastolic reading
Stethoscope that fits poorly or impairment of the examiner's hearing, causing sounds to be muffled	False low systolic and false high diastolic reading
Inaccurate inflation level	False low systolic reading
Multiple examiners using different Korotkoff sounds for diastolic readings	Inaccurate interpretation of systolic and diastolic readings

Assessment	Normal Findings	Deviations From Normal
Wait 30 seconds. Then place diaphragm of stethoscope over brachial artery. Inflate cuff to 30 mm Hg above palpated systolic pressure. Slowly release valve and allow mercury to fall at rate of 2 to 3 mm Hg per second. Note point on manometer when first	See Table 5-1 for normal blood pressure findings.	A high reading of 150/90 mm Hg warrants another checkup within 2 months (Table 5-4) for hypertension. The severity of hypertension is classified by stages (Table 5-5). Hypotension is present when the systolic blood pressure falls to 90 mm Hg or below.

clear sound is heard. Continue to deflate cuff, noting point when sound becomes muffled (diastolic pressure in child). Continue deflation, noting point when sound disappears (diastolic pressure in adult).

Height and Weight

Adult

Weigh clients capable of bearing weight on a standing scale. Use a stretcher scale for clients who are unable to bear weight.

Calibrate the scale by setting the weight at *zero;* note whether the balance beam registers in the middle of the mark. Scales with a digital display should read *zero* before use.

Table 5-4 Recommendations for follow-up based on initial set of blood pressure measurements for adults age 18 and older

Initial Screening Blood Pressure (mm Hg)*		
Systolic	Diastolic	Follow-Up Recommended†
<130	<85	Recheck in 2 years
130-139	85-89	Recheck in 1 year‡
140-159	90-99	Confirm within 2 months
160-179	100-109	Evaluate or refer to source of care within 1 month
180-209	110-119	Evaluate or refer to source of care within 1 week
≥210	≥120	Evaluate or refer to source of care immediately

From Joint National Committee on Detection, Evaluation, and Treatment of High Blood Pressure; National High Blood Pressure Education Program; National Heart, Lung and Blood Institute; National Institutes of Health: *Fifth report of the Joint National Committee on Detection, Evaluation, and Treatment of High Blood Pressure,* NIH Pub No 93-1088, Bethesda, Md, January 1993, NIH.

*If the systolic and diastolic categories are different, follow recommendations for the shorter time follow-up (e.g., 160/85 mm Hg should be evaluated or referred to source of care within 1 month).

†The scheduling of follow-up should be modified by reliable information about past blood pressure measurements, other cardiovascular risk factors, or target-organ disease.

‡Consider providing advice about lifestyle modifications.

Table 5-5 Classification of blood pressure for adults age 18 years and older*

Category	Systolic (mm Hg)	Diastolic (mm Hg)
Normal†	<130	<85
High normal	130-139	85-89
Hypertension‡		
Stage 1 (mild)	140-159	90-99
Stage 2 (moderate)	160-179	100-109
Stage 3 (severe)	180-209	110-119
Stage 4 (very severe)	≥210	≥120

Modified from Joint National Committee on Detection, Evaluation, and Treatment of High Blood Pressure; National High Blood Pressure Education Program; National Heart, Lung and Blood Institute; National Institutes of Health: *Fifth report of the Joint National Committee on Detection, Evaluation, and Treatment of High Blood Pressure,* NIH Pub No 93-1088, Bethesda, Md, January 1993, NIH.

*Not taking antihypertensive drugs and not acutely ill. When systolic and diastolic pressures fall into different categories, the higher category should be selected to classify the individual's blood pressure status. For instance, 160/92 mm Hg should be classified as Stage 2, and 180/120 mm Hg should be classified as Stage 4. Isolated systolic hypertension (ISH) is defined as SBP ≥ 140 mm Hg and DBP < 90 mm Hg and staged appropriately (e.g., 170/85 mm Hg is defined as Stage 2 ISH).

†Optimal blood pressure with respect to cardiovascular risk is SBP < 120 mm Hg and DBP < 80 mm Hg. However, unusually low readings should be evaluated for clinical significance.

‡Based on the average of two or more readings taken at each of two or more visits following an initial screening.

NOTE: In addition to classifying stages of hypertension based on average blood pressure levels, the clinician should specify presence or absence of target-organ disease and additional risk factors. For example, a patient with diabetes and a blood pressure of 142/94 mm Hg plus left ventricular hypertrophy should be classified as "Stage 1 hypertension with target-organ disease (left ventricular hypertrophy) and with another major risk factor (diabetes)." The specificity is important for risk classification and management.

Assessment	Normal Findings	Deviations From Normal
Be sure client is wearing light clothing and no shoes. Have client stand on scale platform and remain still. Adjust scale weight on the balance beam until the tip of the beam registers in the middle of the mark. Weight is measured in pounds or kilograms (2.2 lb = 1 kg). Digital scales display results in seconds.		A weight gain of up to 5 lb (2.3 kg) in a day may indicate a fluid retention problem.
With the client standing erect on a scale, raise the metal rod attached to the scale up and over the client's head. The rod should be placed level horizontally at a 90-degree angle to the measuring stick. Height is measured in inches or centimeters.	See Appendix B for standardized height and weight tables. The body mass index (BMI) is calculated by dividing the client's weight (in kg) by the height (in meters squared) (BMI = Wt [kg]/ht [m^2]). A BMI between 20 and 25 in men and 19 and 24 in women is expected.	A BMI above 27 corresponds with being at least 20% overweight. A BMI of 30 and above indicates obesity.

Assessment	Normal Findings	Deviations From Normal
Infants		
Using a table scale for infants, weigh the infant unclothed and protected from falling from the scale basket.	Healthy term newborns vary in weight between 2500 and 4000 g (5 lb 8 oz to 8 lb 13 oz). In general they double their birth weight by 4 to 5 months of age and triple their birth weight by 12 months of age (Seidel et al., 1995).	
Portable devices are available to measure infant length. Place the infant on the firm surface and have a parent or assistant hold the infant's head against the headboard. With the infant's legs straight at the knees, place the footboard against the bottom of the infant's feet. Record length in the nearest 0.5 cm or ⅕ inch.	See Appendix D for physical growth curves for children.	

Anthropometric Measures

Head Circumference

With the child supine, place the measuring tape snugly around the child's head at the occipital protuberance and supraorbital prominence (Fig. 5-3). Measure to the nearest 0.5 cm or ⅕ inch.

Head circumference for term newborns ranges from 12.5 to 14.8 inches (31.5 to 37 cm).

A head circumference increasing rapidly and rising above percentile curves suggests increased intracranial pressure. A head circumference growing slowly to fall off percentile curves suggests microcephaly.

Chest Circumference

Wrap the measuring tape around the infant's chest at the nipple line, firmly but not tight enough to cause an indentation of the skin. Take the measure midway between inspiration and expiration to the nearest 0.5 cm or ⅕ inch.

The newborn's head circumference may equal or exceed the chest circumference by 2 cm (⅘ inch) for the first 5 months of age (Seidel et al., 1995). Between 5 and 24 months of age the infant's chest circumference should closely approximate the head circumference. After 24 months the chest circumference exceeds the head circumference.

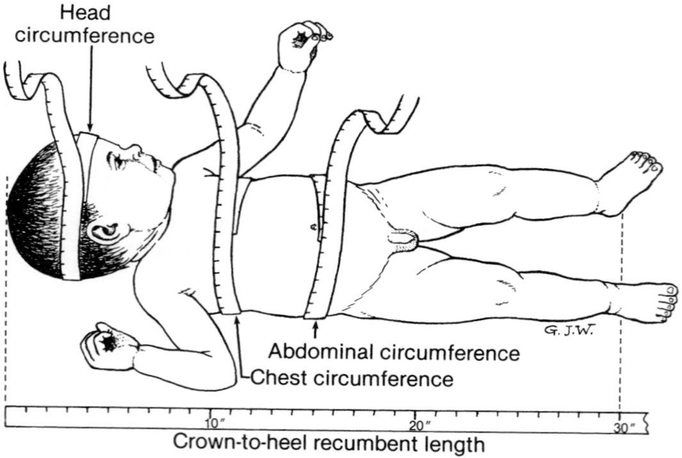

Fig. 5-3
Measuring infant's head, chest, and abdominal circumferences.

Nursing Diagnoses

Assessment data may reveal defining characteristics for the following nursing diagnoses:

- Nutrition, altered: less than body requirements, more than body requirements, or risk for more than body requirements
- Cardiac output, decreased
- Hyperthermia
- Hypothermia
- Altered peripheral tissue perfusion

Pediatric Considerations

- When weighing an infant in a basket scale, remove the infant's clothing and diaper. Be sure the room is warm. Place the infant in the basket and hold a hand lightly above to prevent an accidental fall.

- If a child is below minimum height on the standing scale, position the child against a wall, place a book on top of the child's head perpendicular to the wall, mark the wall at the point of contact, and measure the distance between the floor and the mark on the wall.
- Count respirations in infant or young child for a full minute. Infant respirations are primarily diaphragmatic and are thus observed by abdominal movement.
- Apnea monitors may be made available in the home for premature infants/newborns who are at risk for respiratory compromise or arrest.
- Wait at least 15 minutes after any activity or anxiety before measuring a child's blood pressure.

Gerontologic Considerations

- Many older adults assume a stooped, forward-bent posture, with hips and knees somewhat flexed and arms bent at the elbows, raising the level of the arms.
- Aging causes ossification of costal cartilage and downward slant of the ribs with an increase in the intercostal spaces, causing a more rigid rib cage and reduction in chest wall expansion.
- Older adults may have a decrease in height as a result of osteoporosis and kyphosis.
- Body weight changes because of a decline in lean body mass and a loss of body water. From age 25 to 75, the fat content of the body increases by 16% (Ebersole and Hess, 1994).
- Older adults have a diminished immune response to pyrogens, and therefore body temperature might not rise as high in the presence of a fever.

Cultural Considerations

- Italian, Jewish, African-American, and Spanish-speaking persons smile readily and use many facial expressions and gestures to communicate happiness, pain, or displeasure. Irish, English, and Northern European persons tend to have less facial expression (Giger and Davidhizar, 1995).
- Orientals and some Native Americans often find eye contact to be impolite and an invasion of privacy. Persons of certain Indian cultures avoid eye contact with persons of a higher or lower socioeconomic

status (Giger and Davidhizar, 1995). Vietnamese usually practice less eye contact as well (Rocereto, 1981).

- African-American infants generally weigh 181 to 240 g less than white infants at birth. Oriental, Filipino, Hawaiian, and Puerto Rican babies generally also weigh less than white infants (Crowell et al., 1992; Hulsey et al., 1991; Seidel et al., 1995; Yip et al., 1991).
- Mexican-American children tend to have greater weight-for-height values than the average white child (Seidel et al., 1995).
- African-Americans are less responsive to beta blockers for hypertension (McKenry and Salerno, 1995).

Client Teaching

- The general survey can be a time to instruct the client about the importance of regular health examinations.
- Encourage parents to keep postnatal care follow-up visits to assess child's ongoing growth pattern.
- All clients should know how to measure body temperature. It is particularly important to teach clients with febrile illnesses or conditions that increase the risk of infection. In addition to temperature measuring techniques, instruct on the evaluation parameters to report to the physician or to treat at home.
- Teach clients with preexisting respiratory disease preventive measures for avoiding respiratory infections, such as routinely having flu shots or pneumonia vaccines. Special breathing and coughing exercises may be necessary for clients with chronic lung disease.
- Educate clients about hypertension risk factors: family history, obesity ($>30\%$ overweight), cigarette smoking, excessive alcohol consumption, elevated blood cholesterol levels (total cholesterol ≥ 240 mg/dl or LDL cholesterol ≥ 160 mg/dl), and continued exposure to stress.
- Educate clients with hypertension about long-term follow-up care, medication schedules, and importance of a consistently followed treatment plan.

BODY SYSTEM ASSESSMENT

II

Integument

6

The integument, consisting of the skin, hair, and nails, provides external protection for the body, helps regulate body temperature, and is a sensory organ for pain, temperature, and touch. The nurse may initially inspect all integumentary structures or may conduct an assessment while other body systems are examined. The nurse will use the skills of inspection, palpation, and olfaction.

Anatomy and Physiology

The skin has three primary layers: epidermis, dermis, and subcutaneous tissue (Fig. 6-1). The epidermis, the outer layer, is composed of several thin layers undergoing different stages of maturation. It shields underlying tissue against water loss, mechanical injury, and chemical injury and prevents the entry of disease-producing microorganisms. The innermost layer of the epidermis generates new cells that migrate toward the skin's surface to replace dead cells that are continuously shed from the skin's outer surface. The innermost epidermis also resurfaces wounds and restores skin integrity. Special cells called *melanocytes* can be found in the epidermis. They produce melanin, the dark pigment of the skin. Darker-skinned clients have more active melanocytes.

The dermis is a thicker skin layer containing bundles of collagen and

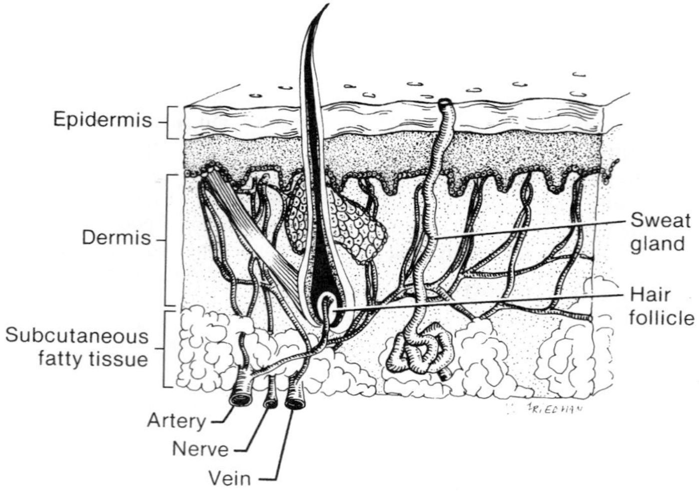

Fig. 6-1
A cross-section of the skin.

elastic fibers that support the epidermis. It is elastic and durable and contains a complex network of nerve endings, sweat glands, sebaceous glands, hair follicles, and blood vessels. The skin insulates the body against extremes of cold and facilitates heat loss. When the body's temperature rises, the skin acts as a radiator. It promotes the radiation of heat from the skin's surface by way of vasodilation and by providing a surface for the evaporation of sweat.

The third layer, subcutaneous tissue, contains blood vessels, nerves, lymph, and loose connective tissue filled with fat cells. The fatty tissue serves as a heat insulator and provides support for upper skin layers.

The skin exchanges oxygen, nutrients, and fluid with underlying blood vessels; synthesizes new cells; and eliminates dead, nonfunctioning cells.

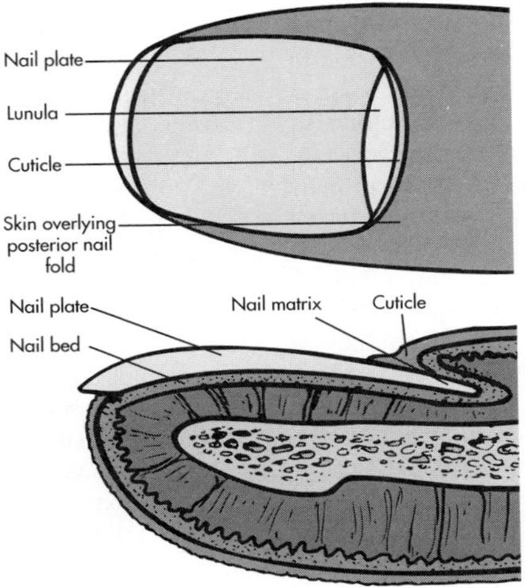

Fig. 6-2
Components of the nail unit.
(From Thompson SM et al: *Mosby's manual of clinical nursing,* ed 2, St Louis, 1989, Mosby.)

The cells require adequate nutrition and hydration to resist injury and disease. Adequate circulation is needed for cell life. The skin reflects changes in a person's physical condition by alterations in color, thickness, texture, turgor, temperature, and hydration.

The most visible portion of the nails is the nail plate, the transparent layer of epithelial cells covering the nail bed (Fig. 6-2). The vascularity of the nail bed creates the nail's underlying color. The semilunar, whitish area at the base of the nail bed from which the nail plate develops is called the *lunula*.

Two types of hair cover the body: terminal hair (long, coarse, thick hair easily visible on the scalp, axillae, pubic areas, and in the beard of males) and vellus hair (small, soft, tiny hairs covering the whole body except for palms and soles). Assessment of the hair occurs during all portions of the examination.

Rationale

The skin provides a window for the nurse to detect a variety of conditions, including changes in oxygenation, circulation, nutrition, local tissue damage, and hydration. In a hospital setting the majority of clients are older adults, debilitated clients, or young but seriously ill clients. They are at risk for skin lesions resulting from trauma during administration of care, from exposure to pressure of immobilization, or from reaction to medications used in treatment. Clients most at risk for integumentary injury are the neurologically impaired; chronically ill; orthopedic clients; and clients with diminished mental status, poor tissue oxygenation, low cardiac output, and inadequate nutrition. In nursing homes and extended care facilities, clients may be at risk for many of the same problems depending on their level of mobility and presence of chronic illness. Nurses must routinely assess the skin to look for primary or initial lesions that may develop. Without proper care, primary lesions can quickly deteriorate to become secondary lesions that require more extensive nursing care.

The condition of the nails and hair can reflect a person's general health, state of nutrition, occupation, and level of self-care. Even a person's psychologic state may be revealed by evidence of conditions such as nail biting.

Critical Thinking

Knowledge

During assessment of the skin, recall your knowledge of the risk of infection posed by any break or disruption of the skin. This may require you to take steps to prevent further tissue injury while the remainder of the examination is performed.

Be familiar with common pathologic conditions that may be reflected by changes in the integument, such as anemia (generalized pallor), arterial insufficiency (marked localized pallor), liver disease (jaundice of the skin, especially the palms), renal failure (orange-green or gray color in light-skinned clients), and hyperemia associated with inflammation or fever.

Experience

There are wide variations in the condition of clients' integument. Recall previous clients who presented with lesions or changes in the condition of the skin. This may help you to locate sites where problems commonly develop (e.g., basal cell cancers occurring over sun-exposed areas).

Standards

Apply the following principles when examining the integument:

- Begin with a brief but careful overall visual sweep of the entire body.
- Do not ignore "hard-to-see" locations such as under the female client's breasts, under the arms, or in the pubic area.
- Skin temperature changes can reflect alterations in blood flow and may require attention to vascular assessment (see Chapter 13).
- Use the client as a resource. He or she will be best informed as to whether skin lesions are newly developed or old.
- Measure any skin lesions accurately, using a centimeter ruler.

Delegation Considerations

The examination of the integument requires problem solving and knowledge application unique to a professional nurse. However, unlicensed assistive personnel can learn to observe for changes in the client's skin, especially areas of hyperemia, actual breakdown, rashes, and lesions. When delegated to assist in the care of dependent clients, instruct staff to be especially observant of signs of pressure sores or tears to the skin. Have staff report any observations immediately.

Equipment

Adequate lighting
Disposable gloves (for broken skin or moist or draining lesions and for presence of lice or lesions of the scalp)
Centimeter ruler

Skin Assessment

Client Preparation

- For a total assessment of all skin surfaces the client must assume several positions.
- The area to be examined must be fully exposed.
- If an area is not clean or is covered with cosmetics, it may be necessary

to cleanse the skin for adequate inspection.

History

- Ask the client about history of changes in the skin, such as dryness, pruritus, sores, rashes, lumps, color, texture, odor, and lesions that do not heal. Consider if alterations are caused by heat, cold, stress, exposure to toxic material, travel to exotic places, or skin care products.
- Consider if the client has the following history: age over 50; male; fair, freckles, ruddy complexion; light-colored hair or eyes; tendency to burn easily.

! ***Nurse Alert*** *These are risk factors for skin cancer.*

- Determine if client works or spends excessive time outside. If so, ask whether a sunscreen is worn and the level of protection.
- Question client about frequency of bathing and type of soap used. Excessive bathing or harsh soaps can dry the skin.
- Ask if client has had recent trauma to the skin.
- Does client have a history of allergies? If so, what skin changes, if any, normally occur?
- Ask if client uses topical medications or home remedies on the skin.
- Ask if client goes to tanning parlors, uses sun lamps, or takes tanning pills.
- Does client have family history of serious skin disorders such as skin cancer or psoriasis?
- Does client work with creosote, coal tar, and/or petroleum products?

Assessment	Normal Findings	Deviations From Normal
Standard Precautions Alert *If client has moist or open lesions, wash hands and apply gloves.*		
Inspect the skin for color and pigmentation. Inspect sites where abnormalities are more easily identified on skin surfaces with the least amount of pigmentation. For example, inspect color of volar aspect of forearms, palms of hands, soles of feet, buccal (mouth) mucosa, abdomen, nail beds, and conjunctivae. Compare color of symmetric body parts.	Usually there is an underlying red tone in these areas (Giger and Davidhizar, 1995). Dark-skinned clients have lighter-colored palms, soles, lips, and nail beds. Skin color is usually uniform over the body. Normal pigmentation ranges in tone from ivory to light pink to ruddy pink in white skin and light to deep brown or olive in dark skin. Areas exposed to the sun, such as the face and arms, will be darker. Sun-darkened skin is common around knees and elbows.	Pallor can be seen in the face, buccal mucosa, conjunctivae, and nail beds. Cyanosis is best observed in the lips, nail beds, and palms. Jaundice appears in the client's sclera. Increased vascularity of the face is common from chronic alcohol ingestion. Basal cell carcinomas (see Appendix G) are most commonly seen in sun-exposed areas and frequently occur in a background of sun-damaged skin (Smoller and Smoller, 1992). See Table 6-1 for skin color abnormalities.

Table 6-1 Skin color variations

Color	Condition	Causes	Assessment Locations
Bluish (cyanosis)	Increased amount of deoxygenated hemoglobin (associated with hypoxia)	Heart or lung disease, cold environment	Nail beds, lips, mouth, skin (severe cases)
Pallor (decrease in color)	Reduced amount of oxyhemoglobin	Anemia	Face, conjunctivae, nail beds, palms of hands
	Reduced visibility of oxyhemoglobin resulting from decreased blood flow	Shock	Skin, nail beds, conjunctivae, lips
Loss of pigmentation	Vitiligo	Congenital or autoimmune condition causing lack of pigment	Patchy areas on skin over face, hands, arms
Yellow-orange (jaundice)	Increased deposit of bilirubin in tissues	Liver disease, destruction of red blood cells	Sclera, mucous membranes, skin
Red (erythema)	Increased visibility of oxyhemoglobin caused by dilation or increased blood flow	Fever, direct trauma, blushing, alcohol intake	Face, area of trauma, sacrum, shoulders, other common sites for pressure ulcers
Tan-brown	Increased amount of melanin	Suntan, pregnancy	Areas exposed to sun: face, arms; areolae, nipples

Assessment	Normal Findings	Deviations From Normal
Inspect hard-to-see areas such as those around casts, traction, splints, or dressings.	Skin should be intact, with absence of inflammation.	Skin will become reddened and excoriated from friction.
Note any patches or areas of skin with color variations.	Variations are absent.	Localized skin changes, such as pallor or erythema, may indicate circulatory changes. Petechiae are tiny, pinpoint-size red or purple spots on the skin caused by small hemorrhages (may indicate blood clotting disorders, drug reactions, or liver disease). Localized changes such as rash, inflammation, or swelling may result from an allergic reaction to cosmetics.
Pay close attention along arms and legs where major veins are distributed, looking for presence of injection sites.	Skin overlying major veins is intact and clear.	Reddened, edematous, and warm areas are found along the arms and legs, suggesting recent injections. Hyperpigmented and shiny areas are evidence of old injection sites (Caulker-Burnett, 1994).

Assessment	Normal Findings	Deviations From Normal
Inspect condition of skin over regions exposed to pressure (Fig. 6-3).	Normal reactive hyperemia (redness) is a visible effect of localized vasodilation, the body's normal response to lack of blood flow to underlying tissue. Normal hyperemia over pressure area lasts less than 1 hour after client repositions (Pires and Muller, 1991).	Pallor and mottling represent persistent hypoxia in tissues. Absence of superficial skin layers represents early pressure ulcer formation. **! *Nurse Alert*** *Never massage reddened areas. Massage increases breaks in capillaries in underlying tissues and increases risk of pressure ulcer formation (AHCPR, 1992; Maklebust, 1991).*
Assess additional areas of potential pressure: skin of nares around nasogastric tubes, intravenous sites, drainage tube sites, and where Foley catheters exit the meatus.	Skin and mucosa are intact, with minimal redness.	Stress at catheter or tube exit sites causes redness and excoriation.

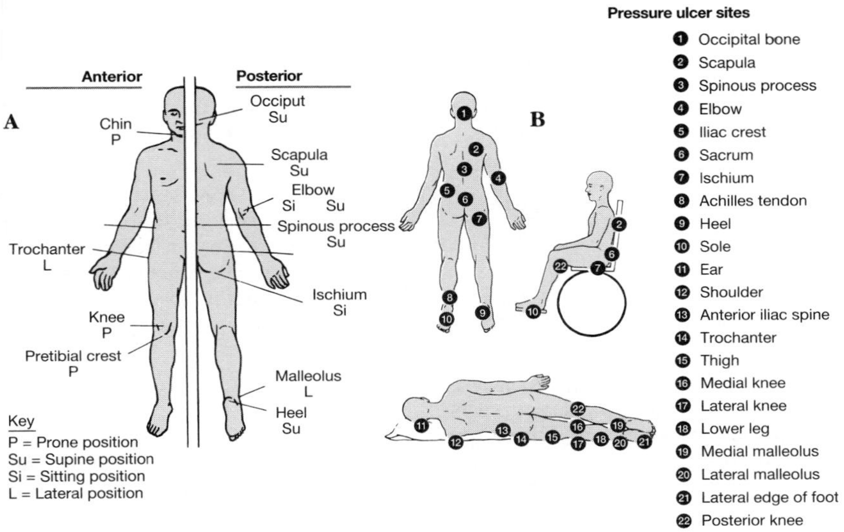

Fig. 6-3
A, Bony prominences most frequently underlying pressure ulcer. **B,** Pressure ulcer sites.
(From Trelease CC: *Ostomy/Wound Manage* 20:46, 1988.)

Assessment	Normal Findings	Deviations From Normal
Using ungloved fingertips, palpate skin surfaces to feel the skin's moisture and observe mucous membranes (see Chapter 11) for dullness, dryness, and flaking.	Skin is normally smooth and dry. Minimal perspiration or oiliness should be present (Seidel et al., 1995). Skin folds such as the axillae are normally moist. Increased perspiration may be associated with activity, warm environment, obesity, anxiety, or excitement.	Flaking (appearance of dandrufflike flakes when the skin is rubbed) and scaling (fishlike scales easily rubbed off the skin) are indicators of abnormally dry skin (Hardy, 1990).
Palpate skin temperature with the dorsum or the back of the hand. Compare symmetric body parts. Compare upper and lower body parts. Palpate over pressure sites.	Skin is normally cool or warm to the touch.	Variation of temperature in an area of the body may reveal an abnormality such as localized warmth at an infected wound site or coldness resulting from reduced blood flow. A stage I pressure ulcer will feel warm to the touch.
Stroke skin lightly with fingertips and gently palpate to determine texture. Note if skin is smooth or rough, thin or thick, tight or supple, and indurated (hardened) or soft.	Skin texture is normally smooth, soft, even, and flexible in children and adults. However, texture is usually not uniform throughout body. Palms of hands and soles of feet are thicker.	Localized changes may result from trauma, surgical wounds, or lesions. With irregular findings in texture ask client about changes.

Palpate the skin lightly to check the tenderness, firmness, and depth of surface lesions. Palpate more deeply with fingertips for areas that appear irregular.

Localized areas of hardness may be the result of repeated intramuscular or subcutaneous injections (e.g., insulin, B_{12}).

Assess turgor by grasping a skin fold on the back of the forearm or sternal area and releasing (Fig. 6-4). Note how easily the skin moves and snaps back into place.

Normally the skin snaps back immediately to resting position in a person under 65 years of age.

Skin stays pinched, indicating dehydration.

If areas of redness over the skin are noted, place fingertip over area and apply gentle pressure, then release.

Normal reactive hyperemia (redness) is the visible effect of localized vasodilation. Affected areas of skin will blanch with fingertip pressure.

Inspect and palpate any edematous areas of the skin. Note location, color, and shape. Palpate for mobility, consistency, and tenderness. To assess pitting edema, press the area firmly with thumb for 5 seconds and release; record depth of pitting in millimeters (Seidel et al., 1995).

Dependent areas such as feet, ankles, and sacrum should be free of edema.

Dependent areas look stretched, swollen, and shiny. Palpation leaves indentation (pitting edema) (Fig. 6-5). Dependent edema may indicate poor venous return. Direct trauma will also cause edema.

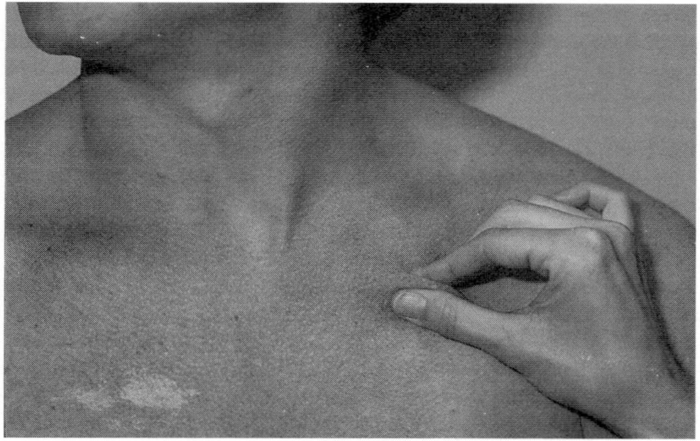

Fig. 6-4
Assessment for skin turgor.
(From Seidel HM et al: *Mosby's guide to physical examination,* ed 3, St Louis, 1995, Mosby.)

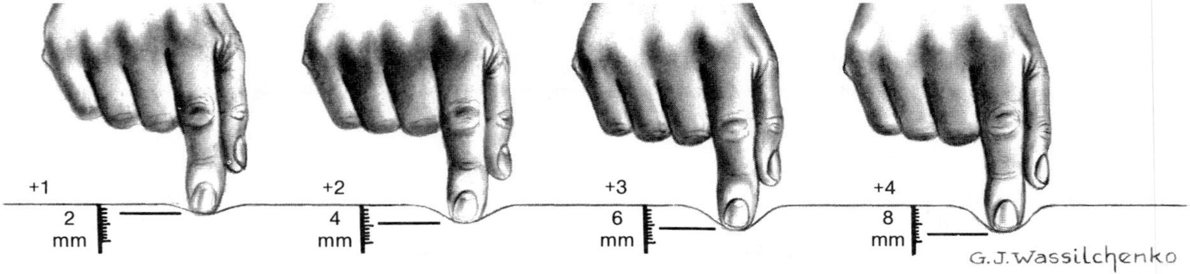

Fig. 6-5
Assessing for pitting edema.
(From Seidel HM et al: *Mosby's guide to physical examination,* ed 3, St Louis, 1995, Mosby.)

Assessment	Normal Findings	Deviations From Normal
Inspect any lesion for color, location, texture, size, shape, type, grouping (clustered or linear), and distribution (localized or generalized). Observe exudate for color, odor, amount, and consistency.	Skin should be free of lesions, except common freckles or age-related changes such as skin tags, senile keratosis (thickening of skin), cherry angiomas (ruby red papules), and atrophic warts.	If findings indicate lesions, ask client about changes. Is a mole asymmetric? Are the borders irregular? Is the color uneven or irregular? Has the mole's diameter changed, and is it bigger than a pencil eraser (Flory, 1992)? See Appendix G for abnormal lesions.
Gently palpate any lesion to determine mobility, contour (flat, raised, or depressed), and consistency (soft or hard). Note if client complains of tenderness during palpation. Measure size of a lesion using a centimeter ruler. Measure height, width, and depth when possible.	Skin is free of lesions.	Tumors are elevated and solid. Scabs, blisters, or pimples are early signs of skin damage from pressure, but damage to underlying tissue may be more progressive (Pires and Muller, 1991).

Nail Assessment

Client Preparation

- Performed during skin assessment; the client is usually lying or sitting.

History

- Ask whether the client has experienced recent trauma or changes to the nails (e.g., splitting, breaking, discoloration, thickening).
- Determine the client's nail care practices and occupation.
- Has the client had other symptoms of pain, swelling, presence of systemic disease with fever, or psychologic or physical stress?
- Ask the parents whether a pediatric client bites the nails.
- Determine if client has risks for nail or foot problems (e.g., diabetes, older adulthood, obesity).

Assessment Techniques

Assessment	Normal Findings	Deviations From Normal
Inspect the nail bed color, cleanliness, length, thickness and shape of the nail plate, texture of the nail, and condition of tissue around the nail.	Nails normally are transparent, smooth, well rounded, and convex, with surrounding cuticles smooth, intact, and without inflammation.	Nails are ragged, dirty, and poorly kept. Erythema around cuticles. Nail growth may be impaired by direct injury or generalized disease. Changes in shape or curvature of nail body can indicate systemic disease. Bluish-black discoloration usually indicates hemorrhage under the nail from trauma. See Box 6-1 for abnormalities of the nail bed.

BOX 6-1 Abnormalities of the Nail Bed

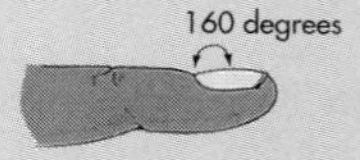

Normal nail: Approximately 160-degree angle between nail plate and nail

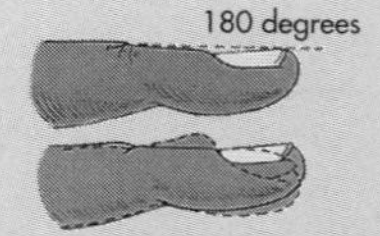

Clubbing: Change in angle between nail and nail base (eventually larger than 180 degrees); nail bed softening, with nail flattening; often, enlargement of fingertips

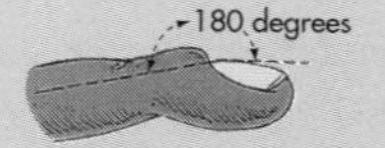

Causes: Chronic lack of oxygen: heart or pulmonary disease

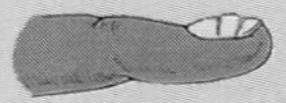

Beau's lines: Transverse depressions in nails indicating temporary disturbance of nail growth (nail grows out over several months)
Causes: Systemic illness such as severe infection, nail injury

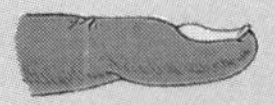

Koilonychia (spoon nail): Concave curves
Causes: Iron-deficiency anemia, syphilis, use of strong detergents

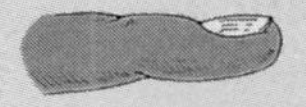

Splinter hemorrhages: Red or brown linear streaks in nail bed
Causes: Minor trauma, subacute bacterial endocarditis, trichinosis

Paronychia: Inflammation of skin at base of nail
Causes: Local infection, trauma

Assessment	Normal Findings	Deviations From Normal
Inspect the angle between the nail and nail bed. Have client place together the nail (dorsal) surfaces of the fingertips of corresponding fingers of the right and left hand. If nails are clubbed, diamond-shaped window at base of the nails disappears and angle between distal tips increases.	Nail bed angle is 160 degrees.	Change in angle between nail and nail base larger than 180 degrees may suggest chronic oxygenation deficiency.
Inspect the lateral and proximal nail folds around the nail. Are they bitten to the quick?	Nail folds are smooth and intact.	Nail folds are inflamed, rough, with torn edges.

Assessment	Normal Findings	Deviations From Normal
Inspect the nail plate. Look for ridging, grooves, depressions, and pitting.	Nail plate is smooth; longitudinal ridging and beading are common.	
Palpate the nail base for firmness by gently squeezing the nail between your thumb and the pad of your finger. Does nail adhere to nail bed?	Nail bed is normally firm and adherent.	Softening and flattening of nail caused by clubbing. Inflamed, swollen nail bed can indicate paronychia, caused by infection and trauma. A mass or hardening in area just below nail bed in interphalangeal joint can be from traumatic injury to interphalangeal joint capsule from repetitive striking of finger.
Assess adequacy of circulation and capillary refill by palpation: grasp the client's finger and observe the color of the nail bed. Next, apply gentle, firm pressure with thumb to nail bed. As pressure is applied, the nail bed appears white or blanched. Release pressure quickly for return of pink color.	White color of nail bed under pressure should return to pink within 2 or 3 seconds, or the time it takes to say "capillary refill."	Circulatory insufficiency, indicated by failure of pinkness to return promptly.

Inspect surfaces of sides and bottoms of toes and sides of fingers.	Skin is smooth and not swollen.	Calluses and corns are flat and painless, resulting from thickening of epidermis caused by friction. Changes are harmless but may be a source of discomfort from eventual pressure against shoes.

Hair and Scalp Assessment

Client Preparation

- Assessment occurs during all portions of the examination.
- Explain the need to separate parts of hair to detect obvious problems. Clients may be sensitive to having hair examined.

History

- Ask whether the client is wearing a wig or hairpiece and request that it be removed.
- Determine whether the client has noted a change in growth or loss of hair or lesions of scalp.
- Identify type of shampoo, other hair care products, and curling irons used for grooming. Does client use a rinse or dye in hair?
- Has client had recent trauma to the scalp?
- Determine if client has recently taken chemotherapy (if hair loss is noted) or vasodilators (minoxidil) if hair growth is noted.
- To rule out risk of ticks, ask if client recently spent time outdoors (e.g., camping).
- Ask if client has noted changes in diet or appetite (see Chapter 5).

Assessment Techniques

Assessment	Normal Findings	Deviations From Normal
◉ ***Standard Precautions Alert*** *Apply gloves if lice are suspected.* Inspect the color, distribution, quantity, thickness, texture, and lubrication of body hair.	Hair is normally distributed evenly, is neither excessively dry nor oily, and is pliant. Balding is common in men, occurring first toward the front of the scalp.	In women, hirsutism results in hair growth on the upper lip, chin, and cheeks, with vellus hair becoming coarser over the body. Reduction of hair covering the extremities may be from arterial insufficiency, but do not confuse this with loss of hair from shaven legs or chronic rubbing of calves from men's pant legs. Hair loss can be related to endocrine disorders such as diabetes, thyroiditis, and even menopause.
Separate sections of scalp hair to observe characteristics of color, texture, and coarseness.	Scalp hair may be coarse or fine, curly or straight, and it should be shiny, smooth, and pliant. It is not excessively oily or dry. Color varies	Excessively oily hair may result from androgen hormone stimulation. Dry, coarse, or discolored hair may result from poor nutrition. Brittle hair

from very light blond to black to gray and may show alterations from rinses or dyes.

may be caused by excessive use of shampoo or chemical agents.

Inspect the scalp for lesions, which easily go unnoticed in thick hair; separate hair for thorough examination.

Scalp is smooth and inelastic, with even coloration. Moles are common.

Lumps or bruises may indicate trauma. Scaliness or dryness of scalp is frequently caused by dandruff or psoriasis.

Inspect hair follicles on the scalp and pubic areas for lice or other parasites. Lice attach their eggs to hair. Avoid close contact of your clothing to prevent transmission of lice.

Lice are difficult to see. The tiny eggs look like oval particles of dandruff. Head and body lice are very small with grayish-white bodies. Crab lice have a red appearance. Lice leave bites or pustular eruptions in the hair follicles and in areas where skin surfaces meet (e.g., behind the ears).

Standard Precautions Alert *After inspecting for lice, discard gloves in appropriate container and wash hands thoroughly before continuing examination.*

Nursing Diagnoses

Assessment data may reveal defining characteristics for the following nursing diagnoses:

- Impaired skin integrity
- Risk for impaired skin integrity
- Fluid volume deficit
- Risk for infection
- Body image disturbance
- Self-care deficit

Pediatric Considerations

- When exposing an infant to an examination of the skin be sure the room is comfortably warm, because air conditioning can cause a cold-induced cyanosis and excessive heat can produce flushing.
- Skin color of light-skinned children varies from a milky-white and rosy color to a more deeply hued pink color. Dark-skinned children, such as Hispanic, African American, Latin, or Mediterranean, have inherited various brown, red, yellow, olive-green, and bluish tones in their skin, which can falsely alter assessment.
- Common changes in texture may indicate cradle cap, eczema, diaper rash, or excessive dryness (xeroderma) (Wong, 1995).
- Skin rashes are common in infants because of food allergies.
- Periorbital edema may normally be evident in children who have been crying, sleeping, or who have allergies.
- Developmental changes may cause skin changes such as facial acne in adolescents.
- In children assess the dermatoglyphics, or pattern of handprint. Note the flexion creases in the palm of the hand (they also can be seen in the sole of the foot). Normally there are three flexion creases. When the two distal creases are fused to form a single horizontal crease (simian crease), this may indicate Down syndrome.
- Localized loss of hair such as on the back of the head may indicate that the infant lies too frequently in one position and may have unmet stimulation needs.
- Tufts of hair anywhere along the spine, especially over the sacrum, can indicate the site of spina bifida occulta.
- During adolescence a change in the amount and distribution of hair growth occurs.
- Be familiar with skin changes that occur in common communicable diseases:

  Chickenpox (varicella)—Rash highly pruritic, begins as macule rapidly progresses to papule and then vesicle (surrounded by erythematous base) becomes cloudy, breaks easily, and forms crusts; all three stages (papule, vesicle, crust) are present in varying degrees at one time. Rash is distributed centripetally, spreading to face and proximal extremities but sparse on distal limbs and less on areas not exposed to heat (Wong, 1995).

Measles (rubeola)—Stages of rash development: appears 3 to 4 days after onset of prodromal stage; begins as erythematous maculopapular eruption on face and gradually spreads downward; more severe in earlier sites and less intense in later sites. After 3 to 4 days it assumes a brownish appearance, and fine desquamation occurs over areas of extensive involvement (Wong, 1995).

German measles (rubella)—Rash first appears on face and rapidly spreads downward to neck, arms, trunk, and legs; after first day body is covered with a discrete, pinkish-red maculopapular exanthema. The rash disappears in same order it began and is gone by third day. Communicable 7 days before to about 5 days after appearance of rash (Wong, 1995).

Scarlet fever—Rash appears within 12 hours after onset of fever, chills, and abdominal pain. Red pin-head–size punctate lesions rapidly become generalized but are absent on the face, which becomes flushed with striking circumoral pallor. Rash is more intense in folds of joints, and by end of first week desquamation begins (fine, sandpaper-like on torso; sloughing on palms and soles). Communicable during incubation period and clinical illness approximately 10 days and during first 2 weeks of carrier phase (Wong, 1995).

Exanthema subitum (roseola)—Rash is discrete rose-pink macules or maculopapules appearing first on trunk, then spreading to neck, face, and extremities; nonpruritic, fades on pressure, lasts 1 to 2 days (Wong, 1995).

Gerontologic Considerations

- Older adults may have difficulty reaching all body parts for cleansing. Difficult-to-reach areas may have body odor.
- Pigmentation of the skin increases

unevenly, causing discolored skin.

- With increasing age, the skin becomes wrinkled and leathery, with decreased turgor. Overall there is an increase in skin folds and laxness in the skin's ability to return to normal position. Skin turgor is best checked in older adults over the sternum, forehead, or abdomen.
- Skin may be drier because of diminished sebaceous and sweat gland activity.
- A common skin lesion that develops with aging is seborrheic or senile keratosis. This is a benign wartlike growth appearing on the trunk, face, and scalp as single or multiple lesions. It is a superficial, circumscribed, raised area that thickens and darkens over time.
- Actinic keratosis, common in men past middle age, is a lesion that can become cancerous. It appears in areas exposed to the sun, such as bald heads, hands, and faces. The lesion is a localized thickening of the skin that begins as a reddish, scaly, superficial area.
- It is normal to have evidence of delayed healing of bruises, lacerations, and excoriations.
- Older adults' hair becomes dry, brittle, dull gray, white, or yellow. It also thins over the scalp, axillae, and pubic areas.
- Older men lose facial hair.
- With aging, the nails of the fingers and toes develop longitudinal striations and grow at a slower rate.
- Because of insufficient calcium, nails may turn yellow in older adults.
- The cuticle also becomes less thick and wide.

Cultural Considerations

- Cultural variations in skin color influence ability to detect abnormalities; in white skin, pallor may be an extreme paleness of the skin, whereas in dark skin there is a loss of red tones. Erythema is noted by palpation of increased warmth in dark-skinned clients. It is easier to detect cyanosis in the lips and tongue of dark-skinned clients, where cyanosis is an ashen gray.
- White and African-American adolescents and adults generally have body odor, but Oriental and Native-American adolescents and adults generally do not. The difference is caused by few functioning apocrine glands and a difference in the glands' secretions (Seidel et al., 1995).
- It may be necessary to palpate rashes in dark-skinned clients,

because rashes may not be readily visible to the eye (Giger and Davidhizar, 1995). Note induration and warmth of the area.

- African Americans often develop keloids, ropelike scars that occur as a result of an exaggeration of the wound-healing process following trauma or inflammation to the skin.
- When assessing the darkly pigmented client for specific color changes such as pallor or jaundice, inspect the conjunctivae and oral membranes of the buccal mucosa (see Chapter 11).
- Mongolian spots (bluish pigment from fetal migratory melanocytes) found generally in the lumbosacral region are present in 80% of Orientals at birth (Giger and Davidhizar, 1995). They can be mistaken for bruises.
- In whites, nail beds are pink with translucent white tips. In African Americans, a brown or black pigmentation is normally present in longitudinal streaks.
- Asian and African Americans have less hair over the chest and legs than do whites, and Native Americans have little or no hair on their bodies.
- The hair of African Americans is usually thicker and drier than the hair of whites. Hispanics have hair that is usually dark and may be curly and wooly, straight, or wavy (Monrroy, 1983).

Client Teaching

Skin

- Instruct client to conduct a complete monthly self-examination of the skin, noting moles, blemishes, and birthmarks. Tell client to inspect all skin surfaces. Cancerous melanomas start as small, molelike growths that increase in size, change color, become ulcerated, and bleed. Follow the ABCD rule (American Cancer Society, 1996b):
  - **A** is for **A**symmetry
  - **B** is for **B**order irregularity; edges are ragged, notched, or blurred
  - **C** is for **C**olor; pigmentation is not uniform
  - **D** is for **D**iameter; greater than 6 mm
- Tell client to report to a physician or care provider any change in skin lesions or a sore that bleeds or does not heal. Especially instruct older adults, who tend to have delayed wound healing.
- Instruct client to reduce risk of skin cancer by avoiding overexposure to the sun: wear wide-brimmed hats

and long sleeves; use sunscreens with SPF greater than or equal to 15 approximately 20 minutes before going into sun and after swimming or perspiring; avoid tanning at midday (10 AM to 3 PM); and do not use indoor sunlamps, tanning parlors, or tanning pills. Medications such as oral contraceptives and antibiotics can make skin more sensitive to the sun. Children require special protection from the sun (keep clothed and in the shade).
- To treat "winter itch" tell client to avoid hot water, harsh soaps, and drying agents such as rubbing alcohol. Use a superfatted soap (e.g., Dove), and pat rather than rub the skin dry.
- Tell the client to apply alcohol-free lotion and moisturizer regularly to the skin to reduce itching and drying.
- Inform the client that baths need not be taken daily.
- Instruct adolescents on proper skin cleansing and the importance of a balanced diet and adequate rest.

Nails

- Instruct client to cut nails only after soaking them at least 10 minutes in warm water. (EXCEPTION: Diabetics should not soak nails.)
- Caution client against use of over-the-counter preparations to treat corns, calluses, or ingrown toenails.
- Tell client to cut nails straight across and even with tops of fingers and toes. If client has diabetes, tell client to file, not cut, nails.
- Instruct client to shape nails with a file or emery board.
- If client is a diabetic: wash feet daily in warm water. Inspect the feet each day in a place with good lighting, looking for dry places and cracks in the skin. Soften dry feet by applying a cream or lotion such as Nivea, Eucerin, or Alpha Keri. Do not put lotion between the toes. Caution against using sharp objects to poke or dig under the toenail or around the cuticle. Have client see a podiatrist for treatment of ingrown toenails and nails that are thick or tend to split.

Hair and scalp

- Clients may require instruction about basic hygiene measures, including shampooing and combing the hair.
- Instruct clients who have head lice to shampoo thoroughly with a pediculicide (shampoo available at drug stores) in cold water, comb

thoroughly with fine-tooth comb, and discard comb. After combing, remove any detectable nits or nit cases with tweezers or between the fingernails. A dilute solution of vinegar and water may help loosen nits.

- Ways to reduce transmission of lice include the following:
  - Do not share personal care items with others.
  - Vacuum all rugs, car seats, pillows, furniture, and flooring thoroughly and discard vacuum bag.
  - Seal nonwashable items in plastic bags for 14 days if parents cannot afford dry-cleaning (Clore, 1989).
  - Use thorough hand washing.
  - Launder all clothing, linen, and bedding in hot soap and water and dry in hot dryer for at least 20 minutes. Dry-clean nonwashables.
  - Instruct client that his or her partner must be notified if lice were sexually transmitted.

7 Head and Neck

Assessment of the head and neck includes assessing the general appearance of the head and then focusing on neck structures, including neck muscles, lymph nodes, carotid arteries and jugular veins, thyroid gland, and trachea. The assessment of the carotid arteries and jugular veins can be deferred until conducting assessment of the vascular system (see Chapter 13).

Anatomy and Physiology

The head provides a protective cover for the brain and special sensory organs. The skull consists of seven bones (two frontal, two parietal, two temporal, and one occipital) that are fused together and covered by the scalp. The nurse describes assessment findings by bone location.

The facial skull contains cavities for the eyes, nose, and mouth. The bony structure of the face is formed from the fused frontal, nasal, zygomatic, ethmoid, lacrimal, sphenoid, and maxillary bones, which serve as additional landmarks (Fig. 7-1).

The structure of the neck is formed by the cervical vertebrae, the ligaments, and the sternocleidomastoid and trapezius muscles. The two sets of muscles divide each side of the neck into two triangles (Fig. 7-2). The ante-

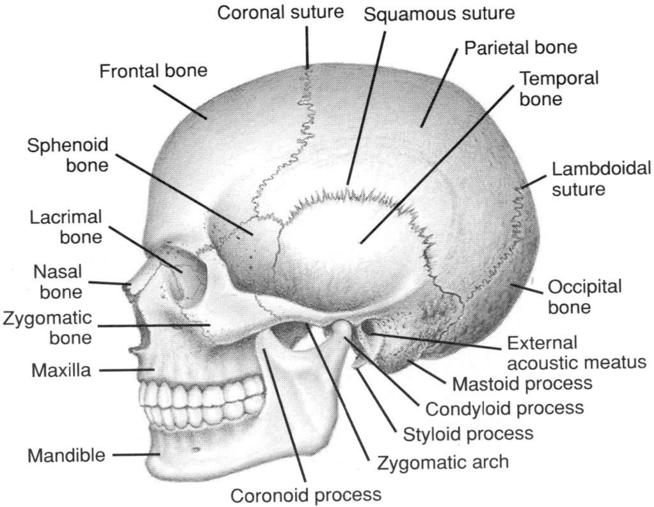

Fig. 7-1
Bones of the skull.

rior triangle contains the trachea, thyroid gland, carotid artery, and anterior cervical lymph nodes. The posterior triangle contains the posterior lymph nodes. The lymph nodes collect drainage of lymphatic fluid from the head and neck areas. The immune system protects the body from foreign antigens, removes damaged cells from the circulation, and provides a partial barrier to growth of malignant cells within the body. Fig. 7-3 shows the location of major lymphatic chains in the head and neck.

The thyroid gland lies in the anterior lower neck on both sides of the trachea, with the isthmus of the gland overlying the trachea (Fig. 7-4). Its two lateral lobes are butterfly shaped and joined by the isthmus at their lower aspect. The lobes curve posteriorly around the cartilages and are in large part covered by the sternocleido-

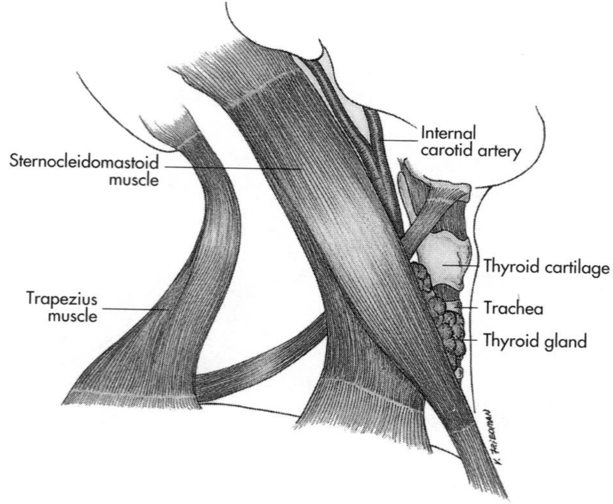

Fig. 7-2
Anatomic position of major neck structures.

mastoid muscles. The trachea is located midline above the suprasternal notch.

Rationale

The nurse inspects the head to determine presence of any obvious deformities or indication of trauma. Examination of the neck determines the integrity of neck structures and the lymphatic system. Remember that the lymphatic system is examined region by region during the assessment of other body systems (e.g., breast, genitalia, extremities). An assessment of superficial lymph nodes helps to reveal the presence of infection or malignancy throughout the lymphatic system. The examination of the thyroid and trachea can also alert the nurse to potential malignancies.

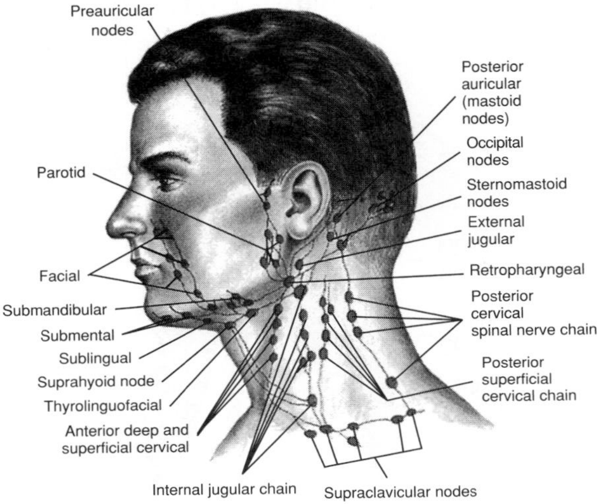

Fig. 7-3
Head and neck lymphatic system.
(From Seidel HM et al: *Mosby's guide to physical examination,* ed 3, St Louis, 1995, Mosby.)

Critical Thinking

Knowledge

It is helpful to refer to previous knowledge regarding infectious disease and the immune system. Clients with suspected immunoincompetence may have involvement of the lymphatic system. Knowledge of neurologic function must be applied when examining the head, because the presence of trauma poses risk for neurologic injury. Serious head trauma would cause you to defer the examination to a thorough neurologic assessment (see Chapter 19). Be alert for indication of possible cervical neck injury with head trauma. This is a life-threatening injury and requires immediate immobilization of cervical vertebrae.

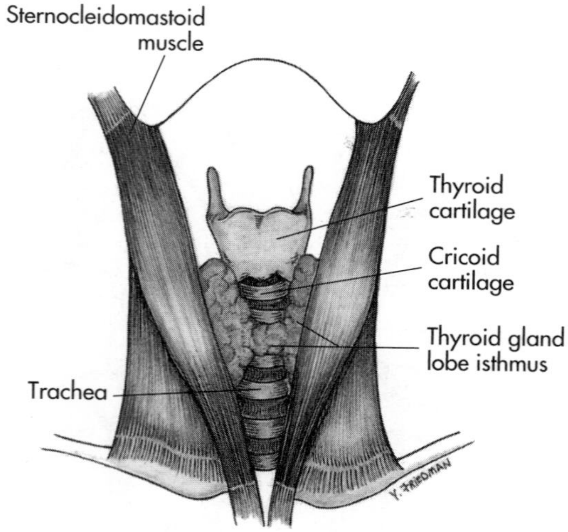

Fig. 7-4
Anatomic position of the thyroid gland.

Experience

Gaining expertise in palpation of lymph nodes and the thyroid gland takes considerable practice. Have a more experienced clinician confirm any findings you make. Over time you will find that a certain positioning technique works best for you to palpate structures successfully.

Standards

During examination of the head and neck, be methodical in examining each lymph node chain on both sides of the neck.

Equipment

Stethoscope
Cup of water

Delegation Considerations

Physical examination of the head and neck requires problem solving and knowledge application unique to a professional nurse. The examination should not be delegated to unlicensed assistive personnel. Staff should know to report any instances of clients noting reduced range of motion (ROM) in the neck or lumps in their neck.

Head and Neck Assessment

Client Preparation

- Client assumes a sitting position, with head upright and still during examination. Be sure clothing is loosened or removed so neck is fully exposed. Palpate the lymph nodes from behind the client or to the client's side. Palpate the thyroid gland from either the front or behind the client.

History

- Determine if client experienced recent trauma to the head. If so, assess state of consciousness after injury (immediately upon return of consciousness, 5 minutes later, and duration of unconsciousness). Also note any predisposing factors (e.g., seizure, blackout).
- Ask if client has history of headache; note location, onset, duration, character, pattern, associated symptoms, and precipitating factors.
- If the client has experienced trauma, does he or she have neck pain?

! ***Nurse Alert*** *Immobilization of cervical vertebrae may be necessary.*

- Determine length of time client has experienced neurologic symptoms.
- Review client's occupational history for use of safety helmets (if appropriate).
- Ask if the client participates in contact sports, cycling, roller blading, or skateboarding.
- For infants, assess birth history and shape of head on delivery.
- Has the client had a recent cold or infection? Does the client feel fatigued or weak?
- If there is an enlarged lymph node, consider several factors (e.g., infection, malignancy). If client has risk factors for human immunodeficiency virus (HIV) infection, review for history of intravenous (IV) drug use, hemophilia, sexual contact with persons infected with HIV, history of blood transfusion, multiple sexual contacts, or male with homosexual or bisexual tendencies.
- Has the client been exposed to ra-

diation, toxic chemicals, or infection?

- To rule out thyroid problems, ask if client has had change in temperature preference (more or less clothing); swelling in neck; change in hair texture, skin, or nails; or change in emotional stability.
- Does client have history of thyroid disease? Are thyroid medications taken?
- Review medical history of pneumothorax (collapsed lung) or bronchial tumor.

Assessment Techniques

Assessment	Normal Findings	Deviations From Normal
Note position of head in relation to shoulders and trunk.	Head is normally held upright, still, and midline to trunk.	Tilting of head to one side may indicate unilateral hearing or visual loss. Horizontal jerking may be associated with tremor.
Inspect client's facial features (eyelids, eyebrows, palpebral fissures, nasolabial folds, and mouth) for symmetry at rest, shape, movement, and expression.	Some slight asymmetry is common. Characteristics vary with race, sex, and body build.	Facial asymmetry on an entire side of the face may indicate facial nerve paralysis. Facial nerve weakness causes asymmetry of the lower face. Asymmetry of the mouth may result from trigeminal nerve injury. A rounded or "moon-shaped" face may indicate Cushing's syndrome or

obesity. Myxedema or hypothyroidism is characterized by dull, puffy, yellow skin with perioribital edema and temporal loss of eyebrows.

Inspect the head for size, shape, and contour.

The skull is generally round, with prominence in the frontal area anteriorly and occipital area posteriorly.

Local skull deformities are typically caused by trauma. A large head in adults may result from excessive growth hormone (acromegaly).

Palpate the skull for nodules or masses by gently rotating fingertips down the midline of the scalp and then along the sides of the head.

Skull is symmetric and smooth. Bones are not distinguishable.

Indentation or depression of skull may indicate fracture. Tenderness or swelling may indicate hematoma.

For neonate, palpate anterior and posterior fontanels for size, shape, and texture.

Fontanels are normally flat, smooth, and well demarcated.

In infants, a large head may result from congenital anomalies. Hydrocephalus (cerebrospinal fluid in the ventricles) is indicated by an enlarged head, bulging fontanels, dilated scalp veins, and sclerae visible above the iris (Seidel et al., 1995).

Assessment	Normal Findings	Deviations From Normal
Palpate the temporal arteries along the temporal-sphenoid bones; note course, elasticity, and presence of tenderness.	Pulse palpable; vessel easily distensible.	Thickening, hardening, and tenderness of artery may indicate temporal arteritis.
To examine the neck, have client sit facing you. Begin by inspecting the neck in the usual anatomic position, in slight hyperextension. Observe for symmetry of the neck muscles, alignment of the trachea, and any subtle fullness at base of neck. Note any distention or prominence of jugular veins and carotid arteries. During inspection ask the client to swallow a drink of water.	Neck is slightly hyperextended, without masses or asymmetry. Veins and arteries are flat. Thyroid gland cannot be visualized.	Edema of neck may be caused by local infections. A mass at the base of the neck, visible as the client swallows, may indicate an enlarged thyroid.
Ask the client to flex the neck with the chin to the chest, then hyperextend the neck backward, and move the head laterally to each side and then sideways so that the ear moves toward the	Moves freely; full range without discomfort or dizziness: Flexion = 45 degrees Extension = 55 degrees Lateral abduction = 40 degrees	Limited ROM may indicate cranial nerve injury, muscular spasm, or trauma.

shoulder. This tests the sternocleidomastoid and trapezius muscles.

With the client's chin raised and head tilted slightly back, carefully inspect the area of the neck where lymph nodes are distributed. Compare both sides and look for apparent enlargement, erythema, or red streaks.

Nodes are not visible and are without inflammation.

Enlarged mass is noted; may indicate infection, malignancy, or benign mass (e.g., cyst).

To examine lymph nodes, have the client relax with neck flexed slightly forward or toward side of the examiner to relax tissues and muscles. Examine both sides of the neck.

Assessment	Normal Findings	Deviations From Normal
Use the pads of the middle three fingers and gently palpate in a rotary motion for superficial and deep lymph nodes (see Fig. 7-3). Check nodes in the following sequence: Occipital nodes at base of skull Postauricular nodes over mastoid Preauricular nodes just in front of ear Parotid and retropharyngeal nodes at angle of mandible Submaxillary nodes Submental nodes in midline behind mandibular tip Superficial cervical nodes Posterior cervical nodes along border of trapezius Where the skin is more mobile, press lightly at first, then increase pressure gradually	Lymph nodes are not easily palpable. Superficial nodes that are palpable but not firm or large enough to be felt are common.	! ***Nurse Alert*** *A palpable fixed node may indicate a cancerous tumor.*

For any palpable node, note location, size, shape, tenderness, consistency, movability or fixation, and discreteness. **!** ***Nurse Alert*** *Do not use excessive pressure to palpate, because small nodes may be missed.*	Small (less than 1 cm), mobile, soft, nontender nodes are not uncommon.	Tender nodes that are warm to the touch indicate inflammation or infection. Cancerous nodes are usually nontender, hard, and more discrete with unilateral enlargement. Tuberculosis is indicated by soft, matted, nontender, and cool-to-touch nodes.
Palpate supraclavicular nodes by asking the client to bend the head forward and relax the shoulders (Fig. 7-5). It may be necessary to hook the index and third finger over the clavicle, lateral to the sternocleidomastoid muscle, to palpate the nodes.	Nodes are not palpable.	Supraclavicular enlarged nodes are frequently sites of metastatic disease (Seidel et al., 1995).
Palpate the trachea for midline position by slipping thumb and index finger to each side at the suprasternal notch. Compare the space between the trachea and the sternocleidomastoid muscle on each side.	The trachea is midline at the suprasternal notch.	Lateral displacement of the trachea may result from a mass in the neck or mediastinum or pulmonary abnormality.

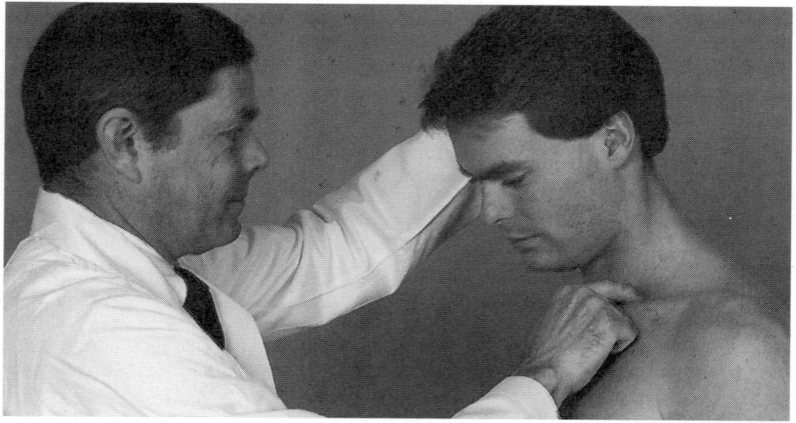

Fig. 7-5
Palpation for supraclavicular lymph nodes.
(From Seidel HM et al: *Mosby's guide to physical examination*, ed 3, St Louis, 1995, Mosby.)

Assessment	Normal Findings	Deviations From Normal
To palpate the thyroid gland posteriorly, stand behind the client. Have the client flex the neck forward slightly and relax the neck muscles. Give the client a glass of water to use when swallowing is required.		
Place both of your hands around the client's neck, with two fingers of each hand on the sides of the trachea just beneath the cricoid cartilage. As the client swallows, feel for movement of the thyroid isthmus.	Thyroid moves beneath fingers as client swallows.	Isthmus is enlarged.

Assessment	Normal Findings	Deviations From Normal
To examine each lobe, have the client swallow while displacing the trachea to the right or left. Palpate the main body of each lobe (Fig. 7-6). For example, while examining the right lobe, move the fingers of the left hand between the trachea and the right sternocleidomastoid muscle. Then place fingers of the right hand behind the right sternocleidomastoid muscle and gently press the hands together to palpate the lobe as the client swallows. Repeat for left lobe.	Thyroid is small, smooth, and free of nodules. In thin clients, gland is more easily palpable.	Enlargement of the thyroid gland may indicate thyroid dysfunction or tumor. Thyroid at its broadest base is approximately 1½ to 2 inches (4 cm) (Seidel et al., 1995). Masses or nodules may indicate Hashimoto's disease or malignancy. An enlarged, tender thyroid usually indicates thyroiditis.
To palpate the thyroid anteriorly, stand to the client's side. Use the pads of the index and middle finger and palpate the left lobe with the right hand and the right lobe with the left hand as the client swallows. Gently displace the trachea during palpation.	No palpable nodes.	

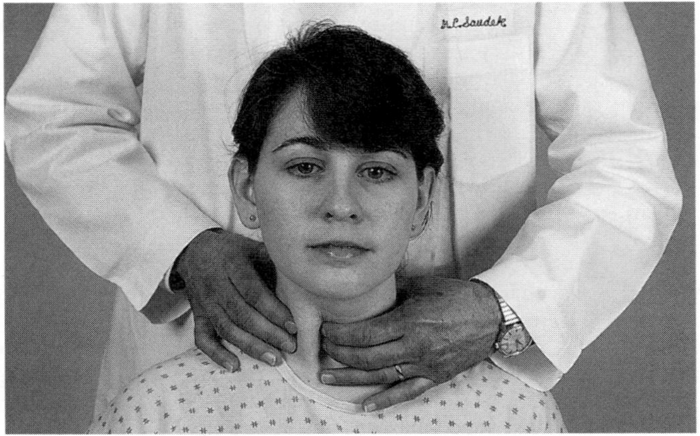

Fig. 7-6
Palpation of the right thyroid lobe from behind the client.
(From Seidel HM et al: *Mosby's guide to physical examination,* ed 3, St Louis, 1995, Mosby.)

Assessment	Normal Findings	Deviations From Normal
When gland appears enlarged, place diaphragm of stethoscope over thyroid.	No sound audible.	Enlarged gland causes increase in arterial flow, resulting in fine vibration auscultated as a soft bruit.

Nursing Diagnoses

Assessment data may reveal defining characteristics for the following nursing diagnoses:

- Impaired physical mobility
- Fatigue
- Risk for infection

Pediatric Considerations

- The posterior fontanel normally closes by the second month, and the anterior fontanel closes at 12 to 18 months of age.
- Avoid applying pressure directly over fontanels because of potential for intracranial damage.
- In a child, Down syndrome is characterized by depressed nasal bridge, epicanthal folds, mongoloid slant of eyes, low-set ears, and large tongue.
- Presence of small, firm, discrete, and movable lymph nodes that are neither warm nor tender are not uncommon. These can be found in the occipital, postauricular, and cervical chains (Seidel et al., 1995).
- Do not confuse lymph node enlargement with mumps. Mumps is a painful swelling of the parotid glands, unilateral or bilateral. Swelling can obscure the angle of the jaw.
- Mononucleosis (Epstein-Barr virus) occurs commonly in adolescents and young adults. Affected nodes are generalized but are more commonly felt in the anterior and posterior cervical chains. The client will have fever, acute pharyngitis, fatigue, and malaise.
- The thyroid is difficult to palpate in infants unless it is enlarged. In children, the thyroid may be palpable.

Gerontologic Considerations

- Size of head is proportional to overall body size. Head may be tilted backward slightly.
- Older adults may have reduced neck ROM resulting from arthritic changes. Proceed slowly when evaluating ROM.
- Older adults typically have two prominent wrinkle lines appearing on either side of the midline of the neck. Sagging of surrounding tissue and deposition of fat create a double chin.
- The thyroid may move to a lower position in relation to the clavicles. The gland itself becomes more flexible, which may increase its nodularity on palpation (Lueckenotte, 1994).
- Size of lymph nodes decreases with advancing age because of loss of some lymphoid elements. Nodes become fibrotic and fatty.

Cultural Considerations

- Thyroid disease is common in Vietnamese clients.
- Filipinos living in Hawaii have been found to have high incidence rates for thyroid cancer (Kolonel, 1985).

Client Teaching

- Assure parents or caregivers that open fontanels in newborns are normal, and caution them to protect the neonate's skull from pressure and potential trauma.
- Teach client about the lymph nodes and how infection can commonly cause node tenderness.
- Instruct client to call physician or care provider when an enlarged lump or mass is noted in the neck.
- Teach client risk factors for HIV infection.
- Stress the importance of regular compliance with medication schedule to clients with thyroid disease.

Eyes

8

Anatomy and Physiology

The organs of sight are contained in a bony orbit at the front of the skull, embedded in orbital fat, and innervated by one of a pair of optic nerves from the brain's occipital lobes. Light enters the eye through the transparent cornea (Fig. 8-1). The iris changes the size of the pupil to control the brightness of light entering. The lens changes shape to focus light on a layer of rods and cones constituting the retina. Impulses created by the retina's specialized nerve cells transmit a visual image along the optic nerve to the brain.

The external eyelids protect the eyes from dust and other foreign objects, injury, and strong light. The exposed part of the eye has the transparent conjunctiva for protection. The transparent cornea protects the iris.

Rationale

Examination of the eye involves the assessment of four areas: visual acuity, visual fields, extraocular movements, and external structures. It also includes an ophthalmoscopic examination. The nurse determines the presence of visual symptoms that may indicate the presence of specific eye disorders. Any visual alterations can significantly affect a client's ability to ambulate

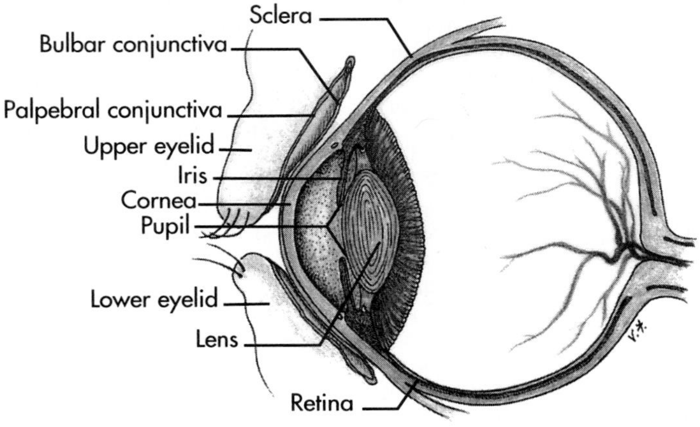

Fig. 8-1
Cross-section of the eye.

safely and to remain independent in performing self-care activities.

Critical Thinking

Knowledge

Signs and symptoms of eye disorders may represent injury or pathology affecting the visual structures, or they can indicate neurologic injury to the second cranial nerve, anywhere along its course from the retina to the occipital lobe of the brain. Involvement of the nerve creates changes in a client's visual fields. Consider knowledge of eye and neurologic anatomy when conducting an assessment.

Experience

After caring for clients with eye disorders, you will learn that most clients become very independent in the instillation of eye drops, cleansing and insertion of contact lenses, and managing any self-care limitations. Learn how to use this to your advantage while conducting an examination. Also learn how your clients adapt to visual alterations in the home. There are many useful tips about which you can instruct clients, but often they have devised unique approaches to self-care management.

Standards

During an eye examination, apply the following principles:

- Be very gentle during an eye examination. External and internal eye structures can easily be injured.
- Clients are very fearful of loss of vision. Take extra time to explain what will be done during an examination, and explain your findings.

Equipment

Newspaper or magazine
Index card or plastic eye shield
Snellen eye chart or lighted screen with chart
Cotton-tipped applicator
Penlight
Ophthalmoscope
Small ruler
Disposable gloves (if drainage is present)

Delegation Considerations

The physical examination of the eyes requires problem solving and knowledge application unique to a professional nurse. The examination should not be delegated to unlicensed assistive personnel. However, staff can learn the common symptoms of eye disease (see history) and know to report their occurrence. In addition, when administering clients' care, unlicensed personnel may become aware of subtle changes such as clients repositioning items within their visual field, being unable to read a diet menu, or continually stumbling over objects in their walking path that may indicate visual disorders. Any such changes should be reported to the RN immediately.

Eye Assessment

Client Preparation

- Throughout the examination the client is asked to sit or stand.
- The room may be darkened during

the corneal reflex and ophthalmoscopic examination.

History

- Determine if the client has history of eye disease and/or surgery, eye trauma, diabetes, or hypertension.
- Determine problem that prompted client to seek health care. Ask the client about eye pain, photophobia (sensitivity to light), burning, itching, excess tearing or crusting, diplopia (double vision), blurred vision, awareness of a "film" over the field of vision, floaters (small black spots that seem to cross the field of vision), flashing lights, or halos around lights.
- Determine whether there is a family history of eye disorders, including glaucoma or retinitis pigmentosa.
- Assess client's occupational history for activities requiring close, intricate work; work involving computers; or activities such as welding and exposure to chemicals that create risk for eye injury. Are safety glasses worn?
- Ask the client whether glasses or contacts are normally worn, and how often.
- Determine date of the client's last eye examination.
- Assess medications client is taking, including eye drops or ointment.

Assessment Techniques

Assessment	Normal Findings	Deviations From Normal
Visual Acuity Testing progresses in stages, depending on the response in each stage and the reason for the assessment.		

Assessment	Normal Findings	Deviations From Normal
Stage I: Ask the client to read newspaper or magazine print under adequate lighting. A client who wears glasses should wear them during this stage of assessment. Note distance from eyes where the client holds the print. **!** ***Nurse Alert*** *Know if the client speaks a language other than English and whether the client is literate. (Literacy can be difficult to detect; asking the client to read aloud can be effective.)* Stage II: For accurate assessment, use a Snellen eye chart (available in many offices as a chart or a projected light screen). Be sure a paper chart is well lighted. Always test vision without corrective lenses first. Have the client sit or stand 20 feet (6.1 m) away from the chart or sit in an ex-		

amination chair specially positioned across from the screen. Ask the client to read all of the letters beginning at any line—once with both eyes open and then with each eye separately (with the opposite eye covered by index card or eye cover). Have the client avoid applying pressure to the eye. Repeat test with client wearing corrective lenses. If client is unable to read, use an "E" chart or one with pictures of familiar objects. Have client describe which direction the "E" is pointing or the name of the object.

Record visual acuity score for each eye and both eyes as two numbers:

Numerator is the distance from the chart in feet.

Assessment	Normal Findings	Deviations From Normal
Denominator is the standardized number for the last line read on the chart (e.g., 20/80). This standardized number is the distance from which the normal eye can read the line.		
Stage III: If clients cannot read even the largest letters or figures of a Snellen chart, test their ability to count upraised fingers or distinguish light. Hold a hand 30 cm (1 foot) from the face and ask client to count the upraised fingers. To check light perception, shine a penlight into the eye and then turn the light off. Ask if the client sees the light.	Normal visual acuity is 20/20. Note if visual acuity is measured with correction of glasses or contacts (cc) or without correction (sc).	In the United States, a person is usually considered legally blind when vision in the better eye, corrected by lenses, is 20/200 or less (Bates, 1990). The inability to perceive light is indicative of blindness. Blurred vision may be caused by ingestion of clomiphene citrate, guanethidine, hydralazine, ibuprofen, or quinine or by use of marijuana (McKenry and Salerno, 1995).
Extraocular Movements		
Have the client sit or stand 2 feet (60 cm) away, facing you at eye level.		

Hold a finger at a comfortable distance (6 to 12 inches, or 15 to 30 cm) in front of the client's eyes. Hold the client's chin to prevent movement, or ask the client to keep the head in a fixed position facing you and follow the movement of the finger with the eyes only.

Assessment	Normal Findings	Deviations From Normal
The client watches your finger as it moves through the six cardinal fields of gaze (Fig. 8-2). Periodically stop movement of the finger and note if the eye begins to oscillate. Note parallel eye movement and presence of abnormal movements.	Eyes follow fields of gaze smoothly with the upper eyelid only covering the iris slightly. A few horizontal nystagmic beats (rhythmic movement of eye) are common in a lateral gaze.	Strabismus is a condition in which both eyes do not focus on an object simultaneously because of impairment of muscles or their nerve supply. Nystagmus is an involuntary, jerking movement of the eye. Jerking nystagmus, faster movement of the eye in one direction, is identified by its rapid phase. If eye moves rapidly to the right and then slowly drifts to the left, the client has nystagmus to the right. Pendular nystagmus is oscillations equal in both directions. Jerking nystagmus can indicate barbiturate intoxication or vestibular, vascular, or neurologic disease. Pendular nystagmus occurs in various diseases of the retina and in miners who have worked in darkness.

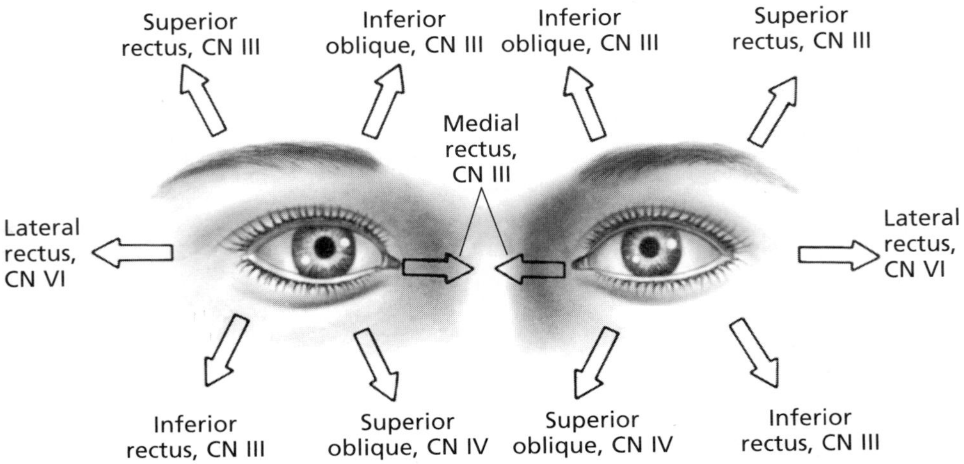

Fig. 8-2
Six directions of gaze.
(From Seidel HM et al: *Mosby's guide to physical examination,* ed 3, St Louis, 1995, Mosby.)

Assessment	Normal Findings	Deviations From Normal
Have client follow your finger in the vertical plane, going from ceiling to floor. Observe the coordinated movement of the globes and the upper eyelid.	Movement is smooth and without exposure of sclera.	Lid lag, exposure of the sclera above the iris, may indicate hyperthyroidism. The upper eyelid covers much of the iris, indicating possible edema or cranial nerve involvement.
Check the alignment of the eyes (balance of extraocular muscles) by shining a penlight onto the bridge of the client's nose from about 12 inches (30 cm) away in a darkened room. Have the client look at a nearby object but not at the light.	Light reflects on the cornea in the same spot on both eyes.	Light shines on a different spot on each eye.
Perform the cover test. Have the client stare ahead at a near fixed point (30 cm, or 12 inches, away). Cover one eye and observe for movement of the uncovered eye while the client gazes ahead. Remove the cover and watch for movement of the newly un-	Uncovered eye does not move and is thus aligned.	Uncovered eye moves, revealing a misalignment. When the stronger eye is temporarily covered, the weaker eye attempts to fixate on the object.

covered eye as it fixes on the object. Repeat with the other eye.

Visual Fields

Have the client sit or stand 3 feet (1 m) away, facing you at eye level. Ask the client to gently close or cover one eye with index card and look at your eye directly opposite (e.g., client's left eye, nurse's right eye).

Close or cover your opposite eye so that your field of vision is superimposed on that of the client. Both you and client should be looking at each other's eye.

Assessment	Normal Findings	Deviations From Normal
Fully extend your arm midway between the client and yourself. Then move the arm centrally with fingers moving. Ask the client to tell you when the moving fingers are first seen. Compare the client's response to the time you first noted the fingers. Move the arm nasally, temporally, superiorly, and inferiorly from outside the field of vision and then slowly back into the visual field. Repeat procedure on the other side, for each field, always comparing the point at which you see the finger coming into your field of vision and the point at which the client sees it.	Both you and the client should see your finger entering the field of vision at about the same time. All objects in the periphery can normally be seen.	If you see the finger before the client does, a portion of the client's visual field is reduced. May indicate degenerative cataract changes, optic nerve injury, or retinal disease. **!** ***Nurse Alert*** *A sudden reduction in visual fields requires referral to an ophthalmologist. Clients with visual field alterations may be at risk for injury, because they cannot see all objects in front of them.* Presence of abnormal eye movements such as nystagmus (rhythmic, involuntary oscillation of the eyes) is often elicited by a gaze to the far left or right. Altered eye movements can reflect injury or disease of eye muscles, supporting structures, or cranial nerves.

External Eye Structures

Stand or sit directly in front of client at eye level and ask the client to look at your face. Inspect the position of the eyes in relation to one another.

Eyes are normally parallel to each other.

Bulging (exophthalmos) is usually caused by hyperthyroidism when both eyes are involved. Tumors or inflammation of the orbit can cause unilateral abnormal eye protrusion.

For the remainder of the examination, the client's contact lenses should be removed.

Inspect the eyebrows for size, extension, hair texture, and alignment. Note whether eyebrows extend beyond the eye itself or end short of it. If eyebrows are sparse or absent, ask client if voluntary removal was done.

Eyebrows are normally symmetric.

Asymmetry. Coarseness of hair and failure to extend beyond the temporal canthus may indicate hypothyroidism. Loss or absence of hair may indicate a hormonal disturbance or may be a result of waxing or plucking.

Have the client raise and lower the eyebrows.

Brows raise and lower symmetrically. Some clients are able to move one brow at a time.

Paralysis of the facial nerve causes impaired movement of the eyebrow.

Inspect the orbital area for edema, puffiness, or sagging tissue below the orbital ridge.

Orbital area is relatively flat with eyes closed. Excess skin folds may appear as eyes open.

Assessment	Normal Findings	Deviations From Normal
Inspect the eyelids for position. Ask the client to relax with eyes open.	Lids do not cover the pupil. The sclera cannot be seen above the iris.	Abnormal drooping of the lid over the pupil is ptosis, caused by edema or impairment of the third cranial nerve.
Inspect lid margins (upper and lower). Note blink reflex.	Lids are close to the eyeball. The client blinks involuntarily and bilaterally up to 20 times a minute.	Older adults frequently have lid margins that turn out (ectropion) or in (entropion). This can cause irritation to the conjunctiva and cornea. ! ***Nurse Alert*** *Absent or infrequent blinking should be reported.*
Note condition and direction of eyelashes.	Eyelashes are normally distributed evenly and curved outward away from the eye.	Inward turn of lashes (see entropion, mentioned previously) can cause chronic irritation.
Inspect surface of upper eyelids by asking client to close the eyes as you raise both eyebrows gently with the thumb and index finger to stretch the skin.	Lids are normally smooth and the same color as the skin.	Redness indicates inflammation or infection. Lid edema may be from allergies or heart or kidney failure.

If lesions are present, note size, shape, distribution, and presence of discomfort and drainage.

◉ *Standard Precautions Alert* *Apply gloves if drainage is present.*

An acute inflammation of the follicle of an eyelash can cause an erythematous or yellow lump. This is called a *hordeolum* or *sty.*

Ask client to relax and close eyes gently.

Lids close symmetrically.

Unconscious clients or those with facial nerve paralysis have lids that only partially close, increasing risk of corneal drying and irritation.

Inspect lacrimal gland area in upper outer wall of anterior part of orbit for edema and redness (Fig. 8-3). Inspect lacrimal duct at the nasal corner (inner canthus) for edema or excess tearing.

Tears flow from the gland across the eye's surface to the lacrimal duct, located in the nasal corner or inner canthus of the eye.

Edema of gland may indicate infection or tumor. Excess tearing may be caused by blockage in nasolacrimal duct.

Palpate gland area gently to detect any tenderness.

The lacrimal gland area is nontender. The gland cannot usually be palpated.

If excess tearing is noted, gently palpate nasolacrimal duct at the lower eyelid just inside the lower orbital rim, not on the side of the nose.

Regurgitation of tears suggests a blockage.

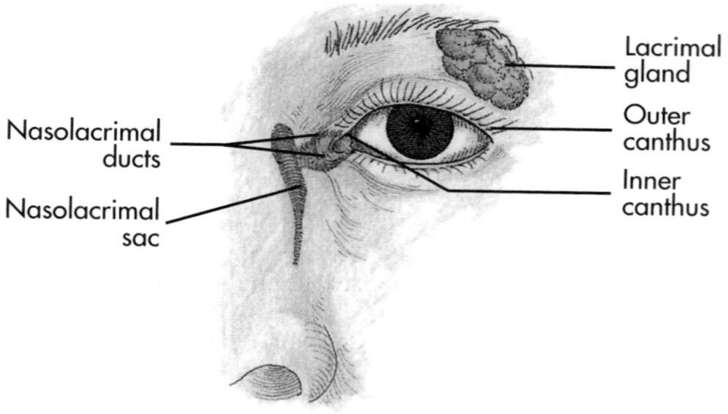

Fig. 8-3
The lacrimal apparatus.

Assessment	Normal Findings	Deviations From Normal
Gently retract eyelids to inspect the bulbar conjunctiva that covers the exposed surface of the eyeball up to the edge of the cornea. Avoid applying pressure directly on eyeball. Retract both lids gently, with the thumb and index finger pressed against the lower and upper bony orbits. Have client look up, down, and side to side. Inspect for color, edema, and lesions. ***Standard Precautions Alert*** *If there is crusty drainage on eyelid margins, apply gloves. Drainage can be infectious and easily spread from one eye to the other. Change gloves from one eye to the other.*	Conjunctiva is transparent with light pink color and free of erythema. Tiny underlying blood vessels can be seen.	Redness may indicate an allergic or infectious conjunctivitis. Drainage from the eye, if yellowish, is likely bacterial in nature. An allergy may cause whitish drainage. Conjunctivitis can also be caused from ingestion of excess amounts of aspirin and use of marijuana (McKenry and Salerno, 1995). Bright red blood in a localized area surrounded by normal-appearing conjunctiva usually indicates subconjunctival hemorrhage.

Assessment	Normal Findings	Deviations From Normal
Gently retract lower eyelid with thumb or index finger to examine the palpebral conjunctiva that lines the eyelids (Fig. 8-4). At times the client can depress the eyelid for you. Note the conjunctiva's color, presence of edema, or lesions.	Conjunctiva is clear and free from erythema.	Pale conjunctiva results from anemia. Fiery red appearance is result of inflammation (conjunctivitis). ❗ ***Nurse Alert*** *Conjunctivitis is a highly contagious infection. Crusty drainage that collects on eyelid margins can easily spread from one eye to the other. Wear gloves during an examination. Wash hands thoroughly before proceeding.*
Inspect upper palpebral conjunctiva lining the upper eyelids by inverting the lid. Do not perform the first time without qualified assistance. *This technique is used only if you suspect a foreign body under the lid.*	Conjunctiva is clear.	Foreign object can be seen, embedded in eye. ❗ ***Nurse Alert*** *Do not attempt to remove foreign object. Notify a physician immediately and apply an eye shield.*

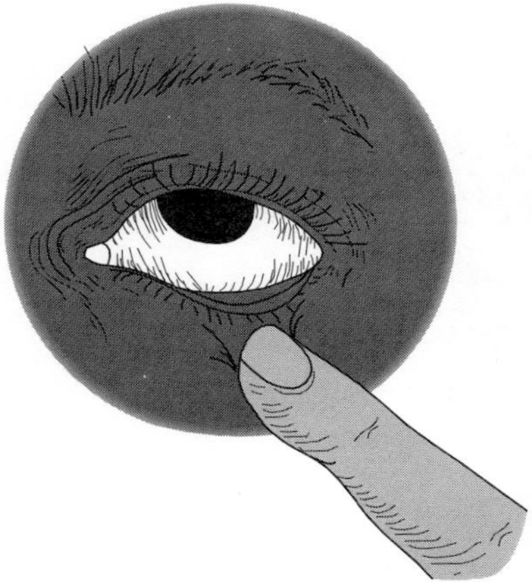

Fig. 8-4
Retraction of the lower eyelid.

Assessment	Normal Findings	Deviations From Normal
Ask the client to look down, relax eyes, and avoid sudden movements. Gently grasp upper lid, pulling lashes down and forward (Fig. 8-5). Place tip of cotton-tipped applicator ½ inch (1 cm) above lid margin. Push down on upper eyelid to turn it inside out; keep lid inverted by careful grasp of upper lashes.		
Inspect conjunctiva for edema, lesions, or presence of foreign bodies. After inspection, return lid to normal position by gently pulling lashes forward and asking client to look up. Eyelid will return to normal position.		

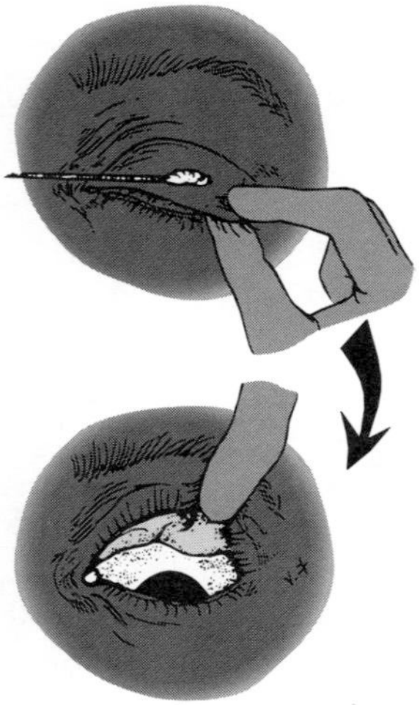

Fig. 8-5
Technique for inspecting the upper palpebral conjunctiva.

Standing at client's side, using oblique lighting, inspect the cornea for clarity and texture.	Cornea is normally shiny, transparent, and smooth.	Irregularity in the surface may indicate an abrasian or tear. Condition is very painful and requires medical intervention. Appearance of what looks like blood vessels is a pterygium.
Test corneal sensitivity by barely touching a wisp of sterile cotton to the cornea.	Normal response is a blink.	Absence of blink reflex indicates involvement of either cranial nerve V or VII.
Inspect appearance of iris and note any margin defects.	Iris pattern should be clearly visible, with the irides the same color.	A section of the iris missing can result from corrective surgery for glaucoma.

Assessment	Normal Findings	Deviations From Normal
Inspect pupil for size, shape, and equality.	Pupils are normally black, round, regular, and equal in size (3 to 7 mm in diameter) (Fig. 8-6). Approximately 20% of healthy people have minor or noticeable differences in pupil size, but reflexes are normal (Seidel et al., 1995).	Bilateral miosis (pupil constriction in both eyes with pupil less than 2 mm in diameter) is the result of miotic eye drops and systemic drugs (e.g., chloral hydrate, clinidine, guanethidine, opiates). Bilateral mydriasis (dilation usually greater than 6 mm) is caused by use of cycloplegic drops (e.g., atropine) and systemic drugs (e.g., indomethacin) (McKenry and Salerno, 1995; Seidel et al., 1995). Mydriasis is also caused by midbrain lesions; acute angle glaucoma; and coma resulting from alcohol, uremia, diabetes, and epilepsy. Cloudy pupil indicates a cataract.

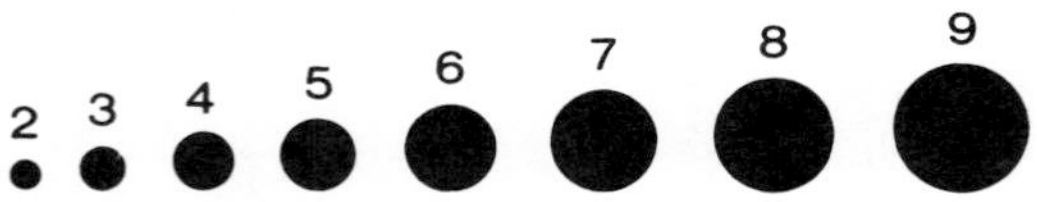

Fig. 8-6
Chart depicting pupillary size in millimeters.

Test pupils' response to light both directly and consensually. Dim the light in the room to dilate the pupils.		
As the client looks straight ahead, bring penlight from side of client's face and direct light onto pupil. Observe the illuminated pupil for quickness of reflex. Also observe opposite pupil for equality of reflex.	The illuminated pupil should constrict briskly (Fig. 8-7). The opposite pupil constricts consensually.	Delay in pupil response to light can indicate increased intracranial pressure.
Repeat examination for opposite eye.		
Test for the accommodation reflex by asking client to gaze at a distant object (far wall) and then at a test object (finger or pencil) held 4 inches (10 cm) from the bridge of the client's nose.	Pupils converge and accommodate by constricting when looking at close objects. Pupil responses are equal.	Test is significant only if there is a defect in the pupillary response to light (Seidel et al., 1995). Delayed or absent light or accommodation reflex may indicate changes in intracranial pressure, nerve lesions, or direct trauma to eye.

A

B

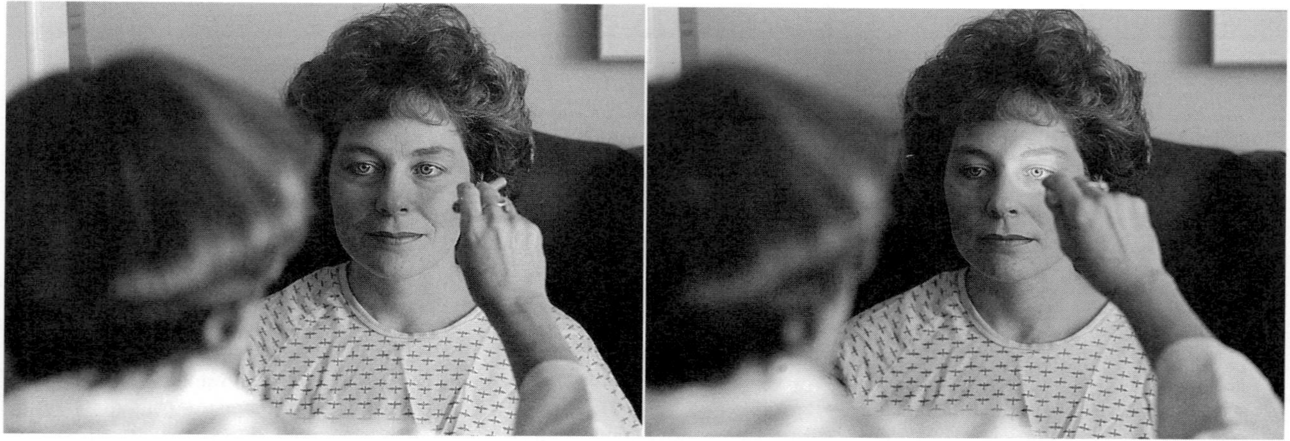

Fig. 8-7

A, Check pupil reflexes by first holding the penlight to the side of the client's face. **B,** Illumination of the pupil causes pupillary constriction.

Internal Eye Structure Examination (Ophthalmoscopic Examination)

Ophthalmoscopic examination is particularly important for clients with diabetes, hypertension, or intracranial pathologic conditions. The examination can detect early stages of disease.

Client Preparation

- Have client remove glasses. Contact lenses may remain in place. (Examiner should remove glasses too.)
- Conduct examination in a darkened room.
- Avoid prolonging the examination without giving the client brief intervals for rest. The light is very bright and can cause discomfort.

Assessment Techniques

Assessment	Normal Findings	Deviations From Normal
Be familiar with how to handle the ophthalmoscope correctly. Practice holding it in each hand, using the index finger to rotate the lens dial. Turn the white light on; rotate the lens dial to 0; and look through the keyhole, focusing first on a near object such as the palm of the hand. Reading the newspaper is good practice. In a darkened room, be sure that both you and the client are in comfortable positions, facing each other with eyes at the same height (e.g., both sitting, or client sitting on examination table and you standing).		

Turn ophthalmoscope light on and rotate lens to clear adjustment to 0. Keep index finger on lens dial to refocus during examination.

Face the client with your eyes at the client's eye level. Ask the client to gaze straight ahead at an object slightly upward, keeping both eyes open. Keep both of your eyes open as well.

Use right hand and eye to inspect the client's right eye and left hand and eye to inspect the client's left eye. From a distance of approximately 25 cm (10 inches) from the client and 25 degrees lateral to the client's central line of vision, shine the light on the pupil (Fig. 8-8).

Bright, orange glow in the pupil, called the *red reflex,* can be seen. The pupil will constrict.

Absence of red reflex is usually caused by an improperly positioned ophthalmoscope. A total opacity of the lens from a cataract or hemorrhage into the vitreous humor can also block the light.

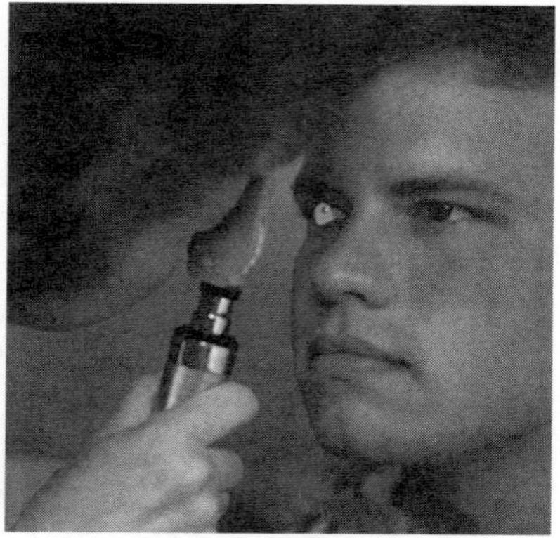

Fig. 8-8
Visualize internal eye structures by moving in toward the pupil with the ophthalmoscope's light focused on the red reflex.

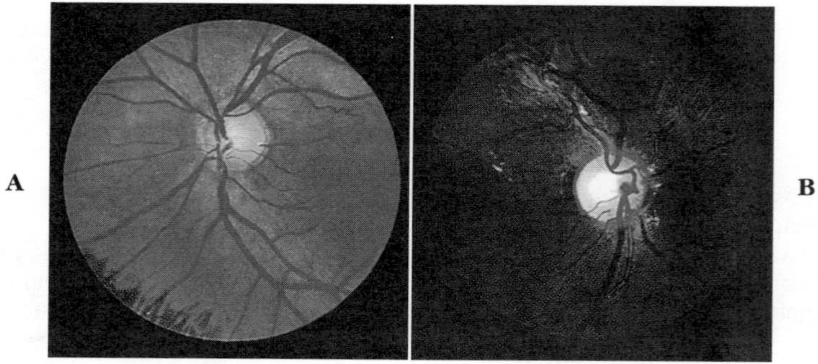

Fig. 8-9
Normal fundus. **A,** White adult. **B,** African American.

Assessment	Normal Findings	Deviations From Normal
Move the light slowly toward the pupil while the nurse keeps it focused on the red reflex. Remember to stay relaxed and keep both of your eyes open. At any one time you will only see a small portion of the retina or fundus (Fig. 8-9). Rotate the lens dial to bring the internal structures into focus.		
The first structures commonly seen are blood vessels. Note how they branch. The vessels always branch away from the optic disc and thus can be used as landmarks to locate the disc.		
Inspect the vascular supply of the retina. Follow the vessels distally as far as you can see them in each of the four quadrants of the fundus. Note the sites where arterioles and venules cross.	Arterioles are smaller than venules; 3:5 or 2:3 ratio. Light reflected from arterioles is brighter, and oxygenated blood is brighter.	With hypertension arterioles become smaller. Thickening of the arteriolar coat causes a nicking of the venule where the venule passes beneath the arteriole.

Assessment	Normal Findings	Deviations From Normal
Examine the size, color, and clarity of the disc; integrity of vessels; and presence of retinal lesions (Fig. 8-10). Use the diameter of the disc to estimate size of any lesions you observe (e.g., an abnormality of an artery may occur 2 disc diameters from the optic nerve and is 1 disc diameter long, 0.5 diameter wide).	Clear, yellow, sharply well-defined optic disc (reddish-pink in light-skinned clients; darkened retina in dark-skinned clients). Light red arteries and dark red veins. Disc is about 1.5 mm in diameter.	Papilledema, caused by increased intracranial pressure, is loss of definition of the disc. Central vessels may bulge forward, and veins are dilated. In glaucoma, there may be cupping of the disc. Chronic loss of blood supply causes vessels to disappear over the edge of the disc and can be seen again deep within the disc. Disc may also appear whiter.
Examine the macula or fovea centralis. This is the site of central vision, located about 2 disc diameters temporal to the optic disc. To see the macula, it helps to ask the client to look directly at the light.	No blood vessels enter the fovea; it appears as a yellow dot surrounded by a deep-pink periphery.	

Because the bright light of the ophthalmoscope is irritating and can cause tearing, do not illuminate the fundus too long. Ask clients to tell you if they become uncomfortable.

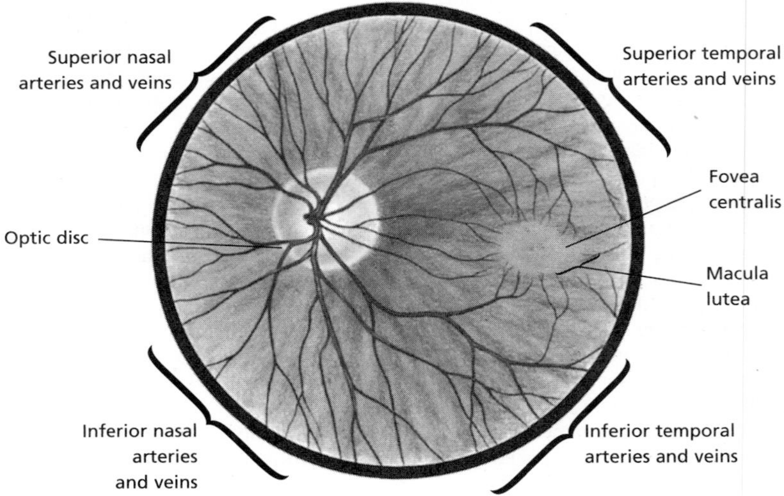

Fig. 8-10

Retinal structures of the eye.

(From Seidel HM et al: *Mosby's guide to physical examination,* ed 3, St Louis, 1995, Mosby.)

Nursing Diagnoses

Assessment data may reveal defining characteristics for the following nursing diagnoses:

- Risk for injury
- Sensory/perceptual alteration (visual)
- Pain
- Knowledge deficit
- Self-care deficit
- Impaired physical mobility

Pediatric Considerations

- Infants shut their eyes tightly during an eye examination. A dimly lit room may encourage the infant to open the eyes. Holding an infant upright, suspended under the arms, also encourages the eyes to open (Seidel et al., 1995).
- The Snellen symbol chart and the Blackbird Preschool Vision Screening System are used to assess visual acuity in children (Wong, 1995).
- Abnormalities in placement or position of the eyes may indicate congenital alterations. Look for an epicanthal fold, a vertical fold of skin nasally that covers the lacrimal duct area. This fold is common in Asian children but may suggest Down syndrome. Draw an imaginary line through the medial canthus of each eye and extend the line past the outer canthus. The medial and outer canthus should be horizontal.
- Widely spaced eyes, or hypertelorism, is a finding associated with mental retardation. The distance between the inner canthus of each eye is normally 1.2 inches (3 cm).
- Lacrimal apparatus may not function properly until 3 months of age.
- The National Society for the Prevention of Blindness recommends the following criteria for referring children with visual acuity problems: 3-year-old child with vision in either eye of 20/50 or less; all other ages with vision in either eye of 20/40 or less; a two-line difference in visual acuity between the eyes in the passing range (e.g., 20/20 in one eye and 20/40 in the other).
- Because a child may be fearful of the equipment and the dark, the nurse should show the ophthalmoscope to the child and explain the procedure before beginning.
- It is helpful to screen children for color blindness. School-age children can have performance of academic skills affected by being unable to detect color variations in instructional materials.

Gerontologic Considerations

- Eyebrows may become more coarse in males and thin at the temporal sides in males and females (Lueckenotte, 1994).
- With aging, the lacrimal glands decrease their production of tears. Tears also evaporate quickly, causing the conjunctivae to be drier.
- A common change of aging is the presence of arcus senilis, a white ring that appears around the iris. It is caused by the deposit of lipids in the periphery of the cornea. If present in clients under age 40, the condition may indicate hyperlipidemia.
- Other changes include scleral discolorations, decrease in pupil size and the ability to constrict in response to light, decrease in peripheral vision, and an increase in the rate of dark adaptation. The lens yellows and becomes opaque, resulting in cataract formation. The pupil may have an irregular shape unilaterally or bilaterally in older adults.
- With aging the conjunctiva thins and takes on a yellowish appearance.
- With aging the retinal vessels become narrowed and straighter. Arteries may appear more opaque and somewhat gray in color (Lueckenotte, 1994). The red or orange glow of the red reflex may be interrupted by dark spots or black shadows indicating opacities.
- The fovea centralis is less bright with advanced age.

Cultural Considerations

- The sclera has color of white porcelain in white clients and is light yellow in African-American clients.
- Clients at risk for hypertension include African Americans, Russian Americans, and Filipino Americans (Giger and Davidhizar, 1995). Screening for retinal changes is important.
- American Eskimos are susceptible to primary narrow-angle glaucoma (Giger and Davidhizar, 1995).

Client Teaching

- School-age children require visual screening by age 3 or 4 and every 2 years thereafter.
- Inform adult clients that persons younger than 40 years of age should

have complete eye examinations every 3 to 5 years (or more often, if family history reveals risks such as diabetes or hypertension).

- Instruct clients older than 40 years of age to have eye examinations every 2 years to screen for glaucoma. Screening should also be done for presbyopia.
- Persons older than 65 years of age should have yearly eye examinations.
- Instruct clients on the typical warning signs of eye disease (see history).
- Clients with burning or itching of the eyes should avoid rubbing them to prevent transmitting infection from one eye to the other.
- Instruct clients on proper administration of eye drops and ointments. Instruct clients never to share medications with another person. Cleanse the eye by wiping from the inner to the outer canthus.
- Instruct older adults to take the following precautions because of normal visual changes: avoid night driving or use caution when driving at night; increase nonglare lighting in the home to reduce risk of falls; paint the first and last steps of a staircase and the edge of each step in between in a bright color to aid depth perception; and look to the sides before crossing streets.

Ears

9

Anatomy and Physiology

The organ of hearing consists of the external, middle, and inner ear (Fig. 9-1). External ear structures consist of the auricle, outer ear canal, and tympanic membrane (eardrum). The ear canal is normally curved and about 1 inch (2.5 cm) long in an adult. It is lined with skin containing fine hairs, nerve endings, and glands secreting cerumen. The middle ear is an air-filled cavity containing the three bony ossicles (malleus, incus, and stapes). The eustachian tube connects the middle ear to the nasopharynx. Pressure between the outer atmosphere and middle ear is stabilized through the eustachian tube.

Sound waves transmitted by way of the external auditory canal cause the sensitive tympanic membrane to vibrate and conduct sound waves through the bony ossicles of the middle ear to the sensory organs of the inner ear. The semicircular canals, vestibule, and cochlea within the inner ear are the sensory structures for hearing and balance. Sound waves are transduced into nerve impulses, which travel from the inner ear along the eighth cranial nerve to the brain.

Clients may experience three types of hearing loss: conduction, sensorineural, and mixed. A conduction loss interrupts sound waves as they travel from the outer ear to the cochlea of

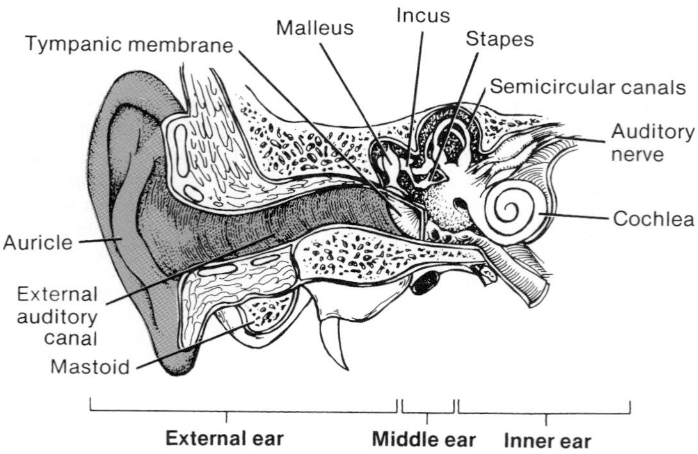

Fig. 9-1
Structures of the external, middle, and inner ear.

the inner ear, because the sound waves are not transmitted through the outer and middle ear structures. Swelling of the auditory canal or tears in the tympanic membrane can be causes. A sensorineural loss involves the inner ear, auditory nerve, or hearing center of the brain. Sound is conducted through the outer and middle ear, but the continued transmission of sound becomes interrupted at some point past the bony ossicles. A mixed loss involves a combination of conduction and sensorineural loss.

Rationale

The nurse assesses the ears to determine the integrity of ear structures and the condition of hearing. Ear disorders may result from mechanical dysfunction (blockage by ear wax or foreign body), trauma (foreign bodies or noise exposure), neurologic disorders (auditory nerve damage), acute illnesses (viral infections), or toxic effects of medications.

Critical Thinking

Knowledge

Hearing is critical for a person to interact successfully within the environment. Refer to the knowledge you have regarding communication techniques for clients with hearing deficits to assess the client accurately. Clients with existing hearing deficits may not always acknowledge a hearing problem.

Also be aware that hearing deficits may result from localized problems of the ear itself or neurologic abnormalities affecting the course of the eighth cranial nerve to the pons and medulla.

Experience

Caring for clients with hearing deficits in the home environment will allow you to learn how these clients adapt to their sensory losses. Use this experience when teaching clients with relatively recent deficits.

Standards

During an ear examination apply the following principles:

- The external auditory canal is very sensitive, because little subcutaneous tissue is present between skin and underlying cartilage. Use care when palpating or inserting the otoscope.
- Speak to the client in a normal tone of voice.

Equipment

Otoscope
Ear speculum (choose largest one that fits comfortably into ear canal)
Tuning fork (256, 512, or 1024 Hz)
Disposable gloves (if drainage is present)

Delegation Considerations

The examination of the ear requires problem solving and knowledge application unique to a professional nurse. The examination should not be delegated to unlicensed assistive personnel. Be sure staff who care for clients with hearing deficits are familiarized with appropriate communication techniques.

Ear Assessment

Client Preparation

- Have the adult client sit during the examination.
- Explain steps of the procedure, particularly when the otoscope is inserted, and assure client that procedure is normally painless.

History

- Has the client experienced an earache, itching, discharge, tinnitus (ringing in ears), vertigo (sensation of spinning), or change in hearing? Note onset and duration.
- Assess risks for hearing problem:
  - Infants/children: Hypoxia at birth, meningitis, birth weight less than 1500 g, family history of hearing loss, congenital anomalies of skull or face, nonbacterial intrauterine infections (e.g., rubella, herpes), maternal drug use, excessively high bilirubin, head trauma.
  - Adults: Exposure to industrial or recreational noise, genetic disease (Meniere's disease), neurodegenerative disorders. For armed service veterans, exposure to explosions during wartime.
- If client has had recent hearing loss, note affected ear, onset, contributing factors (e.g., repeated history of cerumen impaction), and effect on activities of daily living.
- Determine whether the client uses a hearing aid.
- Determine the client's exposure to loud noises at work and the availability of protective devices.
- Note behaviors indicative of hearing loss, including failure to respond when spoken to; repetition of the question, "What did you say?"; leaning forward to hear; inattentiveness in children; or use of monotonous or loud voice tone.
- Ask whether the client takes large doses of aspirin or other ototoxic medications such as aminoglycosides, furosemide, streptomycin, cisplatin, and ethacrynic acid.
- Ask how the client normally cleans the ears.

Assessment	Normal Findings	Deviations From Normal
Inspection of Auricle ***External Ear*** Inspect the auricle's position, color, size, shape, symmetry, and landmarks and compare with normal findings. Be sure to examine lateral and medial surfaces and the surrounding tissue.	Auricles are of equal size and level with each other with the upper point of attachment in a straight line with the lateral canthus or corner of the eye. The auricle also sits vertically. Color is same as the face, without cysts, moles, deformities, or nodules.	Ears that are low set or at an unusual angle are a sign of chromosome abnormality (e.g., Down syndrome). Redness is a sign of inflammation or fever. Extreme pallor indicates frostbite.
Gently palpate the auricle for texture, tenderness, swelling, and lesions (Fig. 9-2).	The auricle is smooth, firm, mobile, and without nodules. If folded forward, the auricle returns to its normal position upon release. A Darwin tubercle (thickening along the upper ridge of the helix) is a normal variation (Seidel et al., 1995).	A cauliflower ear (multiple enlarged cartilaginous nodules along the helix) is a sign of blunt trauma and necrosis of the underlying cartilage.

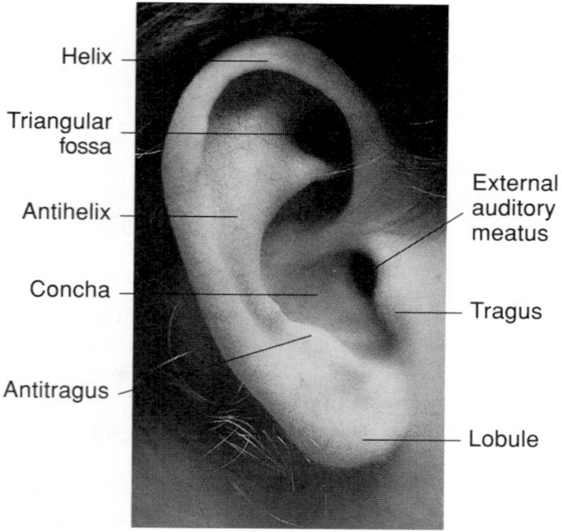

Fig. 9-2
Anatomic structures of the auricle.
(From Seidel HM et al: *Mosby's guide to physical examination*, ed 3, St Louis, 1995, Mosby.)

Assessment	Normal Findings	Deviations From Normal
If the client complains of pain, gently pull the auricle; press on the tragus; and palpate behind the ear over the mastoid process for tenderness, swelling, and nodules.	Tragus and mastoid are smooth, without nodules, and nontender.	If palpation of the auricle and tragus does not increase the pain, client may have a middle ear infection. If there is an increase in pain, client likely has an outer ear infection. Tenderness in mastoid area can indicate mastoiditis.
Inspect opening of the ear canal for size and discharge.	Absence of swelling at meatus; no discharge. A small amount of ear wax (cerumen) is normal.	Yellow or green, foul-smelling discharge may indicate infection or a foreign body. If the client has a history of head trauma, bloody or serous drainage in the external canal suggests a skull fracture.
Ear Canals and Eardrums The otoscope is used to examine deeper ear structures. Specula come in different sizes to conform to the size of ear canals.		

Assessment	Normal Findings	Deviations From Normal
Before inserting the speculum, check for foreign bodies in the opening of the canal.	Canal is clear.	
Instruct client to not move the head during the otoscopic examination. Turn on the otoscope by rotating the dial at the top of the battery tube. Have the client tip the head slightly toward the opposite shoulder. Hold the handle of the otoscope in the space between the thumb and index finger, supported on the middle finger (right hand for right ear; left hand for left ear). Use the ulnar side of the hand to rest against the side of the client's head to stabilize the otoscope.		
Pull the auricle upward, backward, and slightly out to straighten the ear canal (Fig. 9-3). Insert the speculum		

slightly down and forward 1.0 or 1.5 cm (½ inch) into the ear canal. Do not abrade the lining of the ear canal. Avoid any sudden movement.

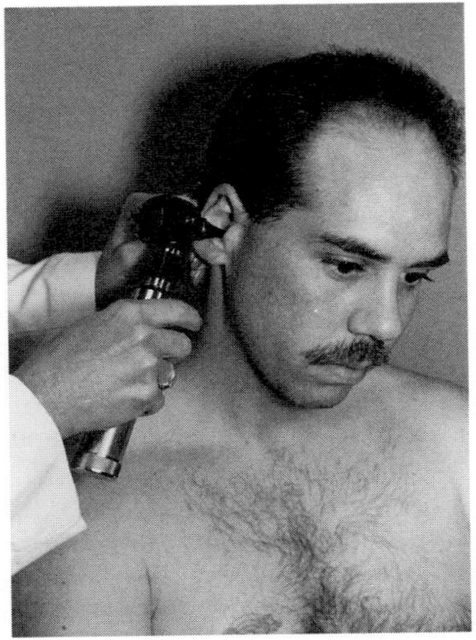

Fig. 9-3
Insertion of the otoscope.

Assessment	Normal Findings	Deviations From Normal
Inspect auditory canal from meatus to tympanic membrane for color, lesions, scaling, foreign bodies, and cerumen or discharge.	Canal has little cerumen and is uniformly pink with tiny hairs in the outer third of the canal. Cerumen is dry (light brown to gray and flaky) or moist (dark yellow or brown) and sticky. Cerumen is odorless. Absence of lesions, discharge, or foreign body.	A reddened canal with discharge is a sign of inflammation or infection. **!** ***Nurse Alert*** *If the otoscope touches the bony walls of the auditory canal (inner two thirds), the client will sense pain.*
Inspect eardrum (tympanic membrane) by slowly moving the otoscope to see the entire drum and its periphery. It helps to vary the direction of the otoscope light. Know the anatomic landmarks (Fig. 9-4, *A*). Inspect the color, integrity, position of bony ossicles, and presence of cone of light.	The eardrum is translucent, shiny, and pearly gray. It is free from tears or breaks (Fig. 9-4, *B*). A ring of fibrous cartilage surrounds the oval membrane. The umbo is near the center of the membrane, and the attachment of the malleus is behind it. A cone of light appears on the membrane. The membrane may move during swallowing.	A pink or red bulging membrane indicates inflammation. Blood may be behind the eardrum if it appears dull with a bluish color or if the cone of light is distorted. A white color reveals pus behind it. Perforations or scarring is abnormal. **!** ***Nurse Alert*** *If a foreign body is present in the ear canal, be careful not to impact the body farther into the ear canal with the otoscope. With impacted foreign bodies, a physician or other specialist should perform the removal. If tympanic membrane is blocked by cerumen, a warm-water irrigation will safely remove the wax.*

A

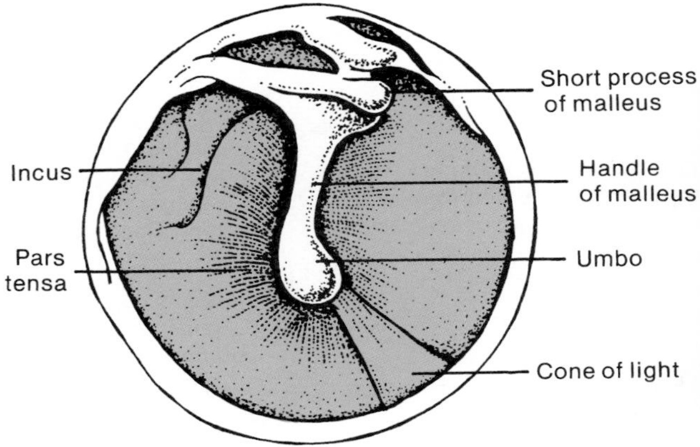

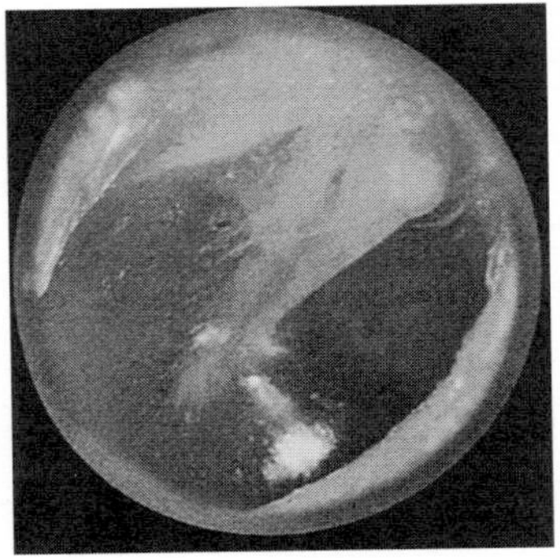

B

Fig. 9-4
A, Anatomic landmarks of tympanic membrane. **B,** Normal tympanic membrane.

Assessment	Normal Findings	Deviations From Normal
Hearing Acuity		
Have the client remove hearing aid if worn. Note the client's response to questions during normal conversation.	Client responds without excessive requests to have you repeat questions.	Client frequently asks you to repeat questions.
If you suspect a hearing loss, check the client's response to the whispered voice. Test one ear at a time while the client occludes the other ear with his or her finger. Have the client gently move the finger up and down during the test.		
While standing 1 to 2 feet (30 to 60 cm) from the ear being tested, cover your mouth so that the client is unable to read lips. After exhaling fully, whisper softly toward the unoccluded ear, reciting random numbers (e.g., "nine-four-ten") with equally accented syllables.	Client correctly repeats the numbers. Responds correctly at least 50% of the time (Seidel et al., 1995).	Client is unable to repeat numbers.

If necessary, gradually increase the loudness of the whisper. Test other ear and note any difference.

If a client has difficulty hearing, test further with tuning fork tests:

Weber's test (Fig. 9-5): Hold tuning fork at its base and tap it lightly against heel of palm. Place base of vibrating fork on midline vertex of client's head or middle of forehead. Ask client if sound is heard equally in both ears or better in one ear.

Client hears sound equally in both ears or in midline of head.

Conduction deafness: sound is heard best in impaired ear. Unilateral sensorineural loss: sound is identified only in normal ear.

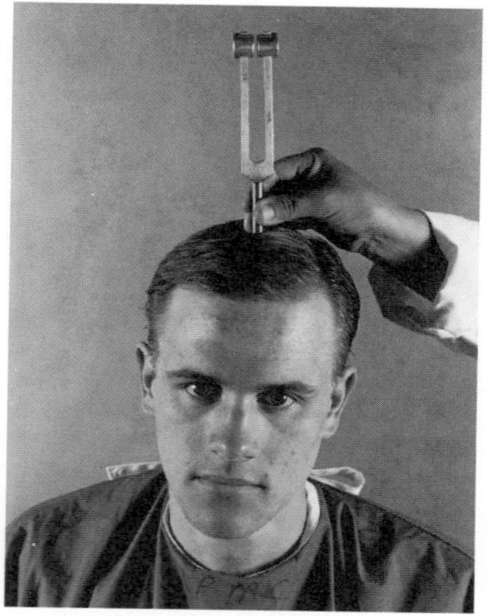

Fig. 9-5
Weber's test.

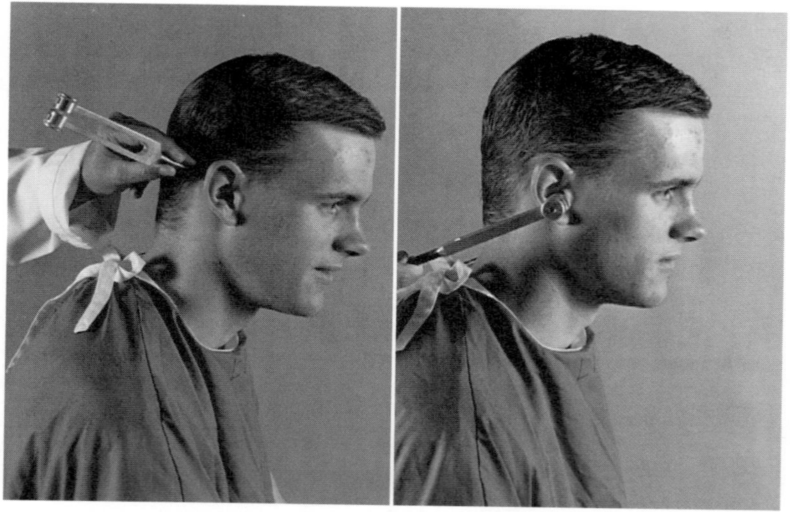

Fig. 9-6
Rinne test.

Assessment	Normal Findings	Deviations From Normal
Rinne test (Fig. 9-6): Place stem of vibrating tuning fork against client's mastoid process. Begin counting the interval with your watch. Ask client to tell you when sound is no longer heard; note number of seconds. Quickly place the still-vibrating tines 1 to 2 cm (½ to 1 inch) from the ear canal, and ask client to tell you when the sound is no longer heard. Continue counting time the sound is heard by air conduction. Compare number of seconds sound is heard by bone versus air conduction.	Air-conducted sound is heard twice as long as bone-conducted sound.	Conduction deafness: bone-conducted sound can be heard longer. Sensorineural loss: sound is reduced and heard longer through air. ! ***Nurse Alert*** *Clients with impaired hearing should be referred to their physician for further evaluation. To minimize communication problems, stand to the side of the client's better ear; speak in a clear, normal tone of voice; and face the client so that your lips and face can be seen.*

Nursing Diagnoses

Assessment data may reveal defining characteristics for the following nursing diagnoses:

- Sensory/perceptual alterations (auditory)
- Knowledge deficit regarding ear care
- Risk for injury
- Pain
- Risk for infection

BOX 9-1 Expected Hearing Response (Newborn to 1 Year)

Birth to 3 months: Startle reflex, crying, cessation of breathing in response to sudden noise
4 to 6 Months: Turns head toward source of sound but may not locate sound; responds to parents' voice
6 to 10 Months: Responds to own name, telephone ringing, person's voice; begins to localize sound above and below
10 to 12 Months: Recognizes and lateralizes sources of sound

Modified from Seidel HM et al: *Mosby's guide to physical examination*, ed 2, St Louis, 1991, Mosby.

Pediatric Considerations

- Infant's ability to hear is assessed by noting behaviors and responses to sound (Box 9-1).
- Before otoscopic examination, be sure the child has not placed a foreign body in the ear. Young children may need to be restrained or held by the parent, with head immobile. Infants should lie supine with the head turned to one side and arms held securely at the sides.
- Invert the otoscope and brace it against the side of the child's head or cheek to prevent accidental movement when the scope is in the ear canal.
- When inserting the scope into the meatus, move it around the outer rim to accustom the child to the feel of something in the ear. If the ear is painful, touch a nonpainful part first, then examine the unaffected ear, and finally return to the painful ear (Wong, 1995).
- In children under 3 years of age, pull the pinna down and back to straighten the ear canal. Introduce the speculum into the meatus in a downward and forward position.
- Allow older children to play with the otoscope before insertion. This lessens their anxiety.

Gerontologic Considerations

- Because of changes in sebaceous glands, itching of the ear canal may be a problem for some older adults. Excessive scratching or rubbing, which may lead to inflammation, should be avoided.

- The lobule of the external ear may become elongated with creases.
- With aging the external ear canal narrows as a result of inward collapsing of the canal wall. Cilia become coarser and stiffer (Lueckenotte, 1994).
- Tympanic membrane may have a dull, retracted, white or gray appearance.
- Degenerative changes in the cochlea and neurons of higher auditory pathways result in presbycusis, a bilateral, progressive, sensorineural hearing loss that begins in middle age.
- Older adults often have a reduced ability to hear high-frequency sounds and consonant sounds such as *S, Z, T,* and *G*. In addition, they typically are able to hear softly whispered words with 50% accuracy at distance of 1 to 2 feet (Lueckenotte, 1990).

Cultural Considerations

- Whites have earlobe creases much earlier than Navajo Indians (Giger and Davidhizar, 1995).
- Mexican Americans believe that certain diseases are caused by a hot and cold imbalance, in which illness is thought to be caused by prolonged exposure to hot or cold. Earaches are thought to be caused when cold air enters the body. When a person has an earache with a fever, a hot poultice is administered to the legs to draw the fever out of the head to the cool legs (Giger and Davidhizar, 1995).

Client Teaching

- Instruct the client about the proper way to clean the outer ear with a damp cloth and to avoid the use of cotton-tipped applicators and sharp objects such as hair pins.
- Tell the client to avoid inserting pointed objects into the ear canal. Parents should caution children against placing any kind of object into the ears.
- Children should have routine ear screenings. Clients over 65 years of age should have their hearing checked regularly. Explain that a reduction in hearing is a normal part of aging.
- Instruct family members of clients with hearing losses to speak in normal lower tones, to not shout,

and to face the client while speaking.

- Instruct hearing-impaired clients to get safety measures such as wake-up and burglar alarms, doorbells, smoke detectors, or telephones connected to a flashing light.
- Explore use of a hearing aid with the client. If the client has an aid, explain how to care for the device: routine cleansing, proper storage, and care of batteries.

Nose and Sinuses

10

Anatomy and Physiology

The nose consists of an internal and an external portion. The external portion, formed by bone and cartilage and covered with skin, is considerably smaller than the internal portion, which lies over the roof of the mouth. The interior of the nose is hollow and is separated by a partition, the septum, into a right and a left cavity. Each nasal cavity is divided into three passageways (superior, middle, and inferior meatus) by the projection of the turbinates (conchae) from the lateral walls of the internal portion of the nose. The technical name for the external openings into the nasal cavities (nostrils) is *anterior nares*. The posterior nares (choanae) are openings from an area of the internal nasal cavity above the superior meatus, called the *sphenoethmoidal recess*, into the nasopharynx (Fig. 10-1).

The internal nose is covered by a vascular mucous membrane lined with small hairs and mucous secretions. The membrane collects and carries debris and bacteria from inspired air to the nasopharynx for swallowing or expectoration.

The nose serves as a passageway for air going to and from the lungs. It filters air of impurities and warms, moistens, and chemically examines air for substances that might prove irritating to the mucous lining of the respiratory tract. The nose is the organ of smell, because olfactory receptors are located in the nasal mucosa, and it aids in phonation.

The paranasal sinuses are air-filled extensions of the nasal cavities. They are lined by mucosa and cilia that move secretions through the nasal cavity and nasopharynx.

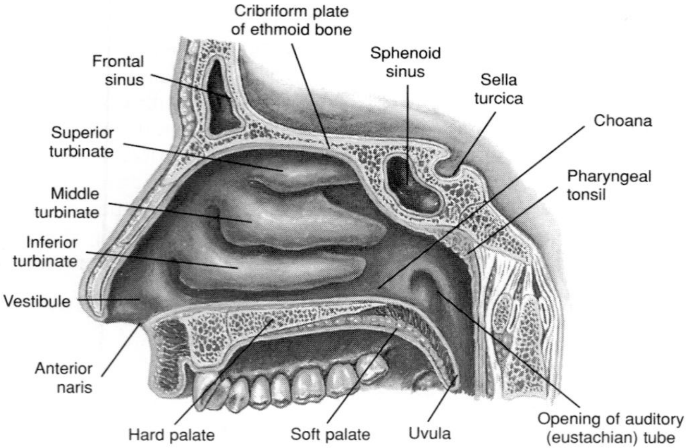

Fig. 10-1
Cross-section of nose and nasopharynx.
(From Seidel HM et al: *Mosby's guide to physical examination*, ed 3, St Louis, 1995, Mosby.)

Rationale

The nurse inspects the nose to determine symmetry of structures and the presence of trauma, inflammation, or infection.

Critical Thinking

Knowledge

Be familiar with what the chronic use of nasal decongestants and drugs such as intranasal cocaine and opioids can do to the nasal mucosa. Habitual use of these drugs is a common health problem.

Standards

During examination of the nose and pharynx apply the following principles:

- Remember that the nasal mucosa is sensitive tissue.
- For any client with a nasally introduced tube (e.g., nasogastric tube, nasotracheal tube), frequent inspection is necessary to recognize early signs of tissue irritation.

Equipment

Nasal speculum
Examination light
Penlight
Gloves (optional; if drainage is present)

Delegation Considerations

Examination of the nose and sinuses requires problem solving and knowledge application unique to a professional nurse. The examination should not be delegated to unlicensed assistive personnel. Do instruct staff to observe for nasal irritation in clients with nasogastric or intestinal tubes and to report such changes immediately.

Nose and Sinus Assessment

Client Preparation

- The client may sit.

History

- Ask whether the client experienced recent trauma or surgery to the nose.
- Ask whether the client has a history of allergies, nasal discharge (character, odor, amount, duration), epistaxis (nosebleeds), or postnasal drip.
- If there is a history of nasal discharge, assess character, amount, odor, duration, and associated symptoms (e.g., sneezing, nasal congestion, obstruction or mouth breathing).
- If there is a history of nosebleed (epistaxis), assess site, frequency, amount of bleeding, treatment, and difficulty stopping bleeding. Trauma, medication use, and excessive dryness are most common causes.
- Ask whether the client uses a nasal spray or drops (type, amount, frequency, duration).
- Ask whether the client snores at night or has difficulty breathing.
- Determine if client has a history of cocaine use or inhalation of aerosol fumes.

Assessment Techniques

Assessment	Normal Findings	Deviations From Normal
Nose		
Inspect external nose for shape, size, skin color, and presence of deformity or inflammation.	Nose is smooth and symmetric with same color as face. Columella is directly midline, and its width does not exceed diameter of a naris. Nares are oval and symmetrically positioned.	Recent trauma may cause edema and discoloration.
If swelling or deformities exist, gently palpate the ridge and soft tissue of the nose by placing one finger on each side of the nasal arch and gently moving fingers from the nasal bridge to the tip. Note any tenderness, masses, and underlying deviations.	Nasal structures are firm and stable.	Localized tenderness is a result of trauma or inflammation.
Observe nares for discharge and flaring.	Nares are without discharge or flaring.	
If discharge is present, describe its character (watery, mucoid, purulent,		Bilateral watery discharge, associated with sneezing and congestion, is

crusty, or bloody), amount, color, and whether unilateral or bilateral.

Standard Precautions Alert If discharge is present, apply gloves for remainder of examination.

from an allergy. Unilateral watery discharge in a client with head trauma may be caused by spinal fluid leaking from a fracture. Bloody discharge results from epistaxis or trauma. Bilateral purulent discharge is from upper respiratory infection.

Assess patency of nares by placing a finger on side of the nose and occluding one naris. Ask the client to breathe with mouth closed. Repeat for other naris.

Nasal breathing is noiseless and equal bilaterally, free for the exchange of air.

Nasal breathing is noisy; client has difficulty with air exchange, indicating blockage.

Use examination light to illuminate nares. Inspect visible mucosa for color, lesions, discharge, swelling, and evidence of bleeding.

Mucosa is pink and moist, without lesions.

Pale mucosa with clear discharge indicates allergy. Habitual use of intranasal cocaine and opioids can cause puffiness and increased vascularity of mucosa (Master and Terpstra, 1992).

Assessment	Normal Findings	Deviations From Normal
For client with nasogastric, nasopharyngeal, or nasointestinal tube routinely check for local skin breakdown (excoriation) of the naris.	Naris is clear, without inflammation.	Mucosa of naris is inflamed, with sloughing skin and tenderness. **! *Nurse Alert*** *Sloughing of tissue requires immediate removal and replacement of tube, either in opposite naris or via a different route. This is sometimes impossible because of the critical nature of client's condition. Family should be aware of possible tissue damage, because permanent scarring can occur.*
To view the septum and turbinates have the client tip the head back slightly for a clear view. Inspect for alignment, perforation, or bleeding.	Septum is close to midline and is thicker anteriorly than posteriorly. Turbinates are covered with mucus that is pink, moist, and clear.	Deviated septum can obstruct breathing and interfere with passage of nasogastric or other tubes. Perforation of septum can occur after repeated use of intranasal cocaine. Polyps may form intranasally.
For a more thorough examination of the nasal cavity use a nasal speculum. Hold the speculum (connected to otoscope) in the palm of the hand and		

use the index finger for stabilization. Use the other hand to change the client's head position.

Have the client tip the head backward. Insert the speculum gently and carefully about ½ inch (1 cm) to dilate naris. Do not overdilate the naris. Inspect for color, discharge, masses, lesions, and edema. Keep client's head erect to see the vestibule and inferior nasal turbinate. Tilt the client's head back to see the middle meatus and middle turbinate. Move the speculum tip midline to view the septum. Repeat for other naris.

Nasal mucosa is deep pink and glistening. Clear discharge is present on septum. Turbinates have same color as surrounding area and are firm.

Erythema of mucosa indicates infection. Turbinates that are bluish-gray or pale pink with swelling may indicate allergy.

Assessment	Normal Findings	Deviations From Normal
Sinus Palpation		
Palpate externally the frontal and maxillary facial areas to detect tenderness of sinuses. Palpate frontal sinus by exerting pressure with the thumb up and under the client's eyebrow. Palpate maxillary sinuses by pressing thumb up under the zygomatic process (Fig. 10-2). **!** *Nurse Alert Avoid applying pressure to the eyes.*	Sinuses are nontender.	Tenderness indicates inflammation from infection and/or allergy.
If sinus tenderness is present or infection is suspected, transilluminate the sinuses. Conduct examination in a darkened room using a sinus transilluminator or small bright penlight. To view the frontal sinuses, place the light against the medial aspect of each supraorbital rim. Look for a dim red glow of light just above the eyebrow (Fig. 10-3, *A*).	Light is transmitted through tissues.	Absence of glow in sinus indicates sinus either contains secretions or is underdeveloped.

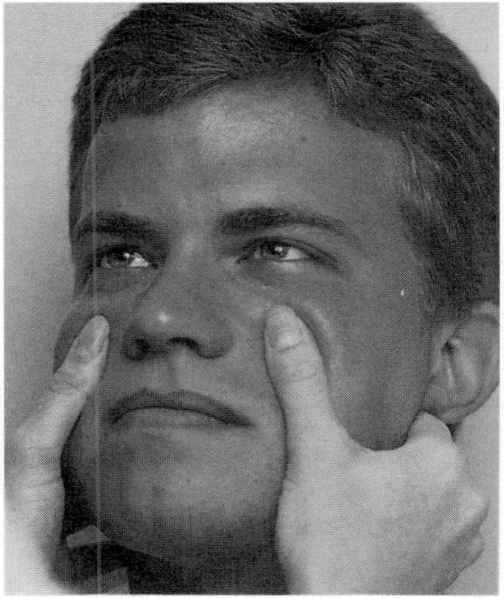

Fig. 10-2
Palpation of maxillary sinus.

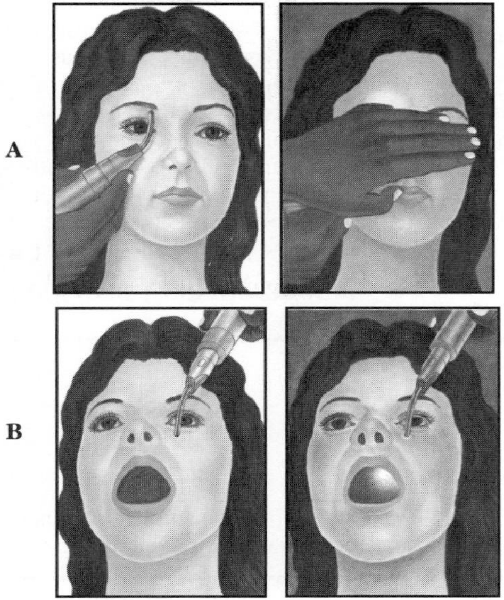

Fig. 10-3
A, Transillumination of frontal sinus. **B,** Transillumination of maxillary sinus.
(From Seidel HM et al: *Mosby's guide to physical examination,* ed 3, St Louis, 1995, Mosby.)

Assessment	Normal Findings	Deviations From Normal
To view the maxillary sinuses, place the light lateral to the client's nose, just beneath the medial aspect of the eye (Seidel et al., 1995). Have the client open the mouth and look to see if the hard palate is illuminated (Fig. 10-3, *B*). Notice the outline of the sinus, and observe for color variations.	Air, normally found within the sinuses, is outlined by a dim red glow.	

Nursing Diagnoses

Assessment data may reveal defining characteristics for the following nursing diagnoses:

- Knowledge deficit regarding use of over-the-counter nasal sprays
- Pain
- Risk for infection

Pediatric Considerations

- External nose should be symmetric and positioned in vertical midline of the face. The nares should move minimally with breathing.
- Congenital anomalies may be revealed through a saddle-shaped nose with a low bridge and broad base or a short, small nose (Seidel et al., 1995).
- Flaring of nostrils is a sign of respiratory difficulty in children.
- While examining infants or young children, it is usually adequate to tilt the nose tip upward with a thumb to view internal nose structures. Use a speculum only if closer examination of the nasal membranes is necessary.
- If a child has been crying, a watery nasal discharge is normal.
- Discharge from one nostril and a foul odor may be caused by a foreign body.

- Examination of the maxillary and ethmoid sinuses is unnecessary.

Gerontologic Considerations

- Nasal mucosa may appear drier.

Cultural Considerations

- Bridge of the nose is sometimes flat in Oriental and African-American children.

Client Teaching

- Caution clients against overuse of over-the-counter nasal sprays, which can lead to rebound effect, causing excess nasal congestion.
- Instruct parents on care of children with nosebleeds: have the child sit up and lean forward to avoid aspiration of blood; apply pressure to the anterior of nose with thumb and forefinger as the child breathes through mouth; apply ice or cold cloth over bridge of nose if pressure fails to stop bleeding, and notify a physician.
- Instruct older adults with reduced sense of smell to always check dated labels on food to ensure against spoilage.

Mouth and Pharynx

11

Anatomy and Physiology

The mouth, containing the tongue, teeth, and gums, is the anterior opening of the oropharynx (Fig. 11-1). The roof of the mouth is formed by the bony arch of the hard palate and the fibrous soft palate. The floor of the mouth consists of loose, mobile tissue. The tongue is anchored to the back of the oral cavity at its base and to the floor of the mouth by the frenulum.

Salivary glands are located in tissues surrounding the oral cavity. Saliva initiates digestion and moistens the oral mucosa. The gingivae or gums are fibrous tissue covered by mucous membrane. The roots of the teeth are anchored to alveolar ridges, and the gingivae cover the neck and roots of each tooth. Adults have 32 permanent teeth.

The mouth and oropharynx provide a passageway for food, liquid, and saliva; initiate digestion through mastication and salivary secretion; detect the sense of taste; and emit air for vocalization and nonnasal expiration. The oropharynx is continuous with the nasopharynx and separated from the mouth by the anterior and posterior tonsils.

Rationale

The nurse's assessment of the oral cavity determines the client's ability to enunciate words, masticate, salivate, swallow, and taste. The nurse exam-

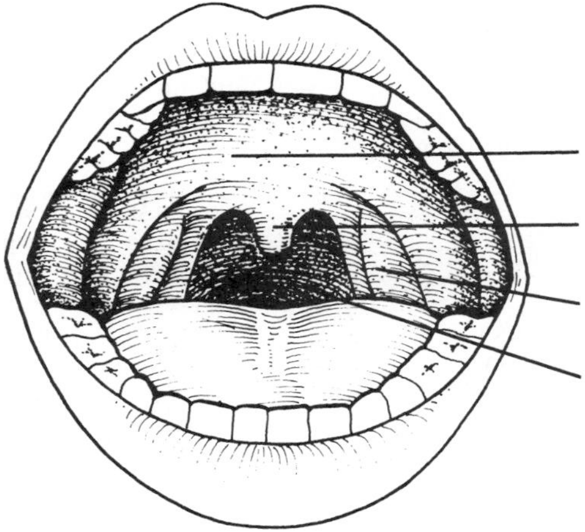

Fig. 11-1
Oral cavity.

ines the oral cavity for the presence of local or systemic changes that can interfere with a client's nutritional intake and predispose the client to more serious health alterations. Assessment may be done during participation in clients' oral hygiene. The nurse also inspects the mouth and pharynx to determine oral hygiene needs and develop a plan of care for clients with dehydration, restricted intake, oral trauma, or oral airway obstruction or clients who will undergo or have recently undergone surgery.

Critical Thinking

Knowledge

Apply what you know regarding oral hygiene principles. The assessment will reveal a great deal about the client's hygiene habits and pattern of routine dental visits. Also recognize that changes in oral mucosa can be associated with alcohol and tobacco abuse.

Experience

This type of examination is easily integrated into routine nursing care. Whenever a client receives oral hygiene, use the time to conduct a thorough oral examination.

Clients at high risk for mucosal dehydration include those who are NPO and who have intranasal or interoral tubes that cause air breathing and/or irritation to oral mucosa.

Standards

During an oral and pharyngeal examination, apply the following principles:

- Oral lesions can be very uncomfortable; use care when examining tissues.
- Clients become very self-conscious during removal of dentures. Conduct the examination as quickly as possible.
- Be thorough in examining all surfaces of the oral cavity.
- Unconscious clients may have a bite reflex elicited during stimulation of the mouth. Use a padded tongue blade to keep the mouth open and to prevent injury to your hands.

Equipment

Penlight
Tongue depressor
Gauze square
Clean gloves

Delegation Considerations

The examination of the mouth and pharynx requires problem solving and knowledge application unique to a professional nurse. The examination should not be delegated to unlicensed assistive personnel. However, staff will be involved in administering oral hygiene and in assisting with feeding. Instruct them on types of abnormalities to report (e.g., lesions, bleeding, difficulty swallowing, pain).

Mouth and Pharynx Assessment

Client Preparation

- Client may sit or lie.
- Ask the client to remove dentures and retainers.

History

- Determine whether dentures or retainers the client wears are comfortable and snug. What is the condition of braces, dentures, bridges, or crowns?
- Has the client had a recent change in appetite or weight?
- Assess the client's dental hygiene practices, including use of fluoride toothpaste, frequency of brushing and flossing, and frequency of dental visits.
- Does the client have risks for oral or pharyngeal cancer, including cigarette, cigar, or pipe smoking; use of smokeless tobacco; or excessive consumption of alcohol?
- Does the client have any pain or lesions of the mouth; a lump or thickening; a red or white patch that persists; or difficulty chewing, swallowing, or moving the tongue or jaws? These are signs and symptoms of oral and pharyngeal cancer (American Cancer Society, 1996b).
- Does the client have history of streptococcal infection, tonsillectomy, or adenoidectomy?

Assessment Techniques

Assessment	Normal Findings	Deviations From Normal
Inspection and Palpation		
◙ ***Standard Precautions Alert*** *Apply gloves for the examination.*		
Begin by inspecting the lips for color, texture, hydration, contour, and lesions. Have client close mouth, and view the lips end to end. Female clients should remove lipstick before the examination.	Lips are pink, moist, symmetric, and smooth, with surface free from lesions.	Pallor can be caused by anemia. Cyanosis is the result of respiratory or cardiovascular problems. A cherry red color is caused by acidosis and carbon monoxide poisoning (Seidel et al., 1995). Lesions such as nodules or ulcerations can be related to infection, irritation, or skin cancer. Dry, cracked lips can result from dehydration, wind chapping, or excessive lip licking.
Ask client to clench the teeth and smile. Assess for teeth occlusion.	Upper molars rest directly on the lower molars with the upper incisors slightly overriding the lower incisors. Symmetric smile reveals normal facial nerve function.	Droop in smile indicates facial nerve paralysis. Malocclusion is evidenced by protrusion of the upper or lower incisors, failure of upper incisors to overlap with lower teeth, and

failure of back teeth to meet (Seidel et al., 1995).

Inspect the condition of teeth, including posterior surfaces. Ask client to open and relax mouth slightly. A tongue depressor may be needed to retract the lips and cheeks to view the molars.

Teeth are smooth, white, and shiny. Yellow or darkened teeth may result from stains caused by coffee and tea or smokeless tobacco.

Chalky, white discoloration of the enamel is an early indication of dental caries. Tartar along the base of the teeth, extraction sites, and blackened spots on teeth (caries) may indicate poor pattern of hygiene.

Count the number of teeth.

Normal adult has 32 teeth.

To view the anterior mucosa and gums, ask the client to open and relax the mouth slightly and then gently retract the client's lower lip away from the teeth (Fig. 11-2). Repeat process for upper lip. Inspect mucosa for color, texture, hydration, and lesions.

Mucosa is pinkish-red, smooth, and moist. Small yellow-white raised lesions commonly seen on the buccal mucosa and lips are Fordyce's spots, ectopic sebaceous glands (Seidel et al., 1995).

Stomatitis or inflammation of buccal mucosa may be caused by bacterial infection, herpes virus, vitamin deficiency, and side effect of chemotherapeutic drugs. Gingivitis, inflammation of the gums, is caused by poor oral hygiene and infection.

If lesions are present, palpate them gently with a gloved hand for tenderness, size, and consistency.

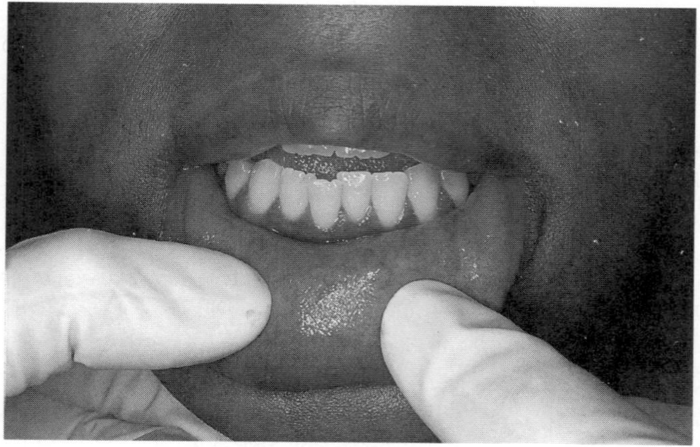

Fig. 11-2
Inspection of inner oral mucosa.

Assessment	Normal Findings	Deviations From Normal
Inspect buccal mucosa by asking client to open mouth; retract cheek with a gloved finger covered with gauze or a tongue depressor (Fig. 11-3). View the surface of the mucosa from right to left and top to bottom. Use a penlight to view posterior mucosa.	Mucosa is glistening pink, soft, smooth, and moist.	Buccal mucosa is good site to inspect for jaundice and pallor. Thick white patches (leukoplakia) can be seen in heavy smokers and alcoholics. **! *Nurse Alert*** *Leukoplakia should be reported, because it is a precancerous lesion.*
Palpate the cheek with one finger along the inner mucosa and the thumb along the outside cheek to check for deep-seated lumps or ulcerations.	Mucosa is smooth, without lesions.	
Retract the cheeks to inspect the gums or gingivae. Inspect for color, edema, retraction, bleeding, and lesions. Take care to view the gums around the back molars.	Gums are a slightly stippled pink color, moist, and smooth, with a tight margin at each tooth.	Gums are swollen, tender, and separated from teeth, indicating that gingivitis is present.
Palpate the gums to assess for lesions, thickening, or masses.	No tenderness on palpation.	Spongy gums that bleed easily indicate periodontal disease and vitamin C deficiency.

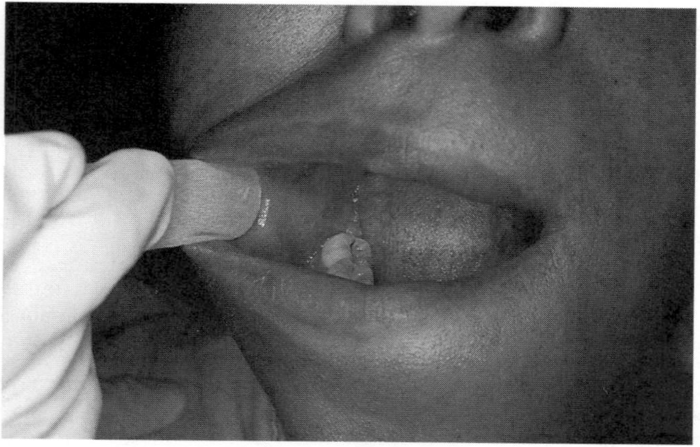

Fig. 11-3
Retraction of the buccal mucosa.

Assessment	Normal Findings	Deviations From Normal
Probe each tooth gently with a tongue blade.	Teeth are firmly set.	Loose or mobile teeth, swollen gums, or pockets containing debris at tooth margins indicate periodontal disease.
Have the client relax mouth and protrude tongue halfway. Note any deviation, tremor, or limitation in movement. Then ask client to raise the tongue up and move it side to side.	Tongue protrudes midline, without fasciculation. Tongue moves freely. Tests function of cranial nerves IX and XII (see Chapter 19).	Deviation or limitation of movement may indicate involvement of hypoglossal nerve.
Use a penlight to illuminate the tongue. Inspect the tongue for color, size, hydration, texture, position, and coating or lesions.	Medium or dull red in color, moist, slightly rough on top surface and smooth along lateral margins.	Presence of thickened secretions or coating may indicate dehydration. A smooth tongue results from vitamin deficiency. Glossitis or swelling and inflammation of the tongue may result from an infectious disease, burn, bite, or other injury.

Assessment	Normal Findings	Deviations From Normal
To view the undersurface of the tongue and floor of the mouth, ask the client to lift the tongue by placing its tip on the palate behind the upper incisors (Fig. 11-4). Inspect for color, swelling, and lesions such as nodules or cysts.	Ventral surface of tongue is pink and smooth, with large veins between frenulum and folds.	Swollen mass the color of the mucosa in the floor of the mouth may indicate oral cancer. A swollen, bluish or blackened mass may be a varicosity.
Palpate the tongue by asking the client to protrude the tongue halfway out. Grasp the tip gently with a gauze square. Gently pull the tongue to one side. Palpate the full length of the tongue and the base for any areas of hardening or ulceration.	Varicosities (swollen, torturous veins) are not uncommon. Tongue has smooth, even texture and is firm and without lesions.	
Have the client tip head back and hold mouth open as you inspect the hard and soft palates for color, shape, texture, and extra bony prominences or defects (Fig. 11-5).	Hard palate or roof of mouth is located anteriorly. The whitish hard palate is dome shaped. The soft palate, best seen while depressing the tongue with a tongue blade, extends posteriorly toward the pharynx. It is light pink and smooth.	Bony growth (exostosis) between the two palates is common.

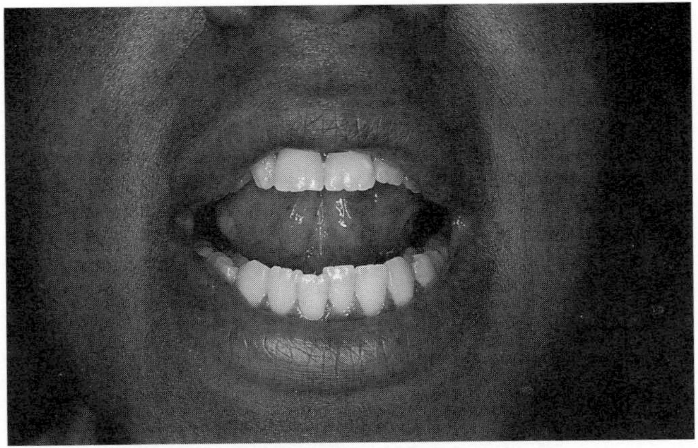

Fig. 11-4
Undersurface of the tongue.

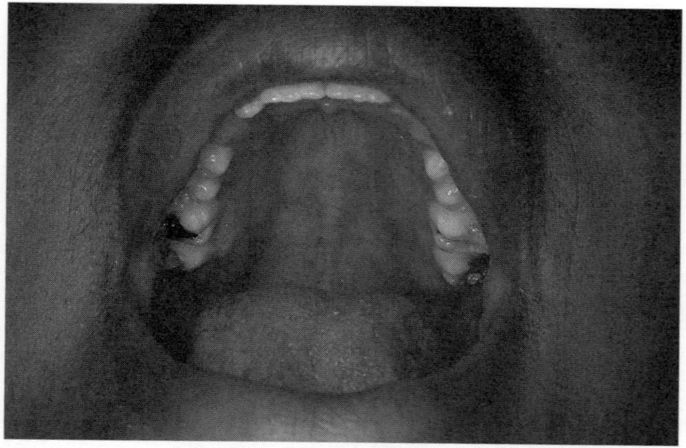

Fig. 11-5
Soft and hard palates.

Assessment	Normal Findings	Deviations From Normal
Explain the pharyngeal examination to client. Ask client to tip head back, open mouth, and say "Ah." Have tongue depressor on middle third of tongue. Use penlight to inspect pharynx.		
Inspect the uvula and soft palate as the client says "Ah." **!** ***Nurse Alert*** *Do not place tongue depressor too far anteriorly, or posterior tongue will mound up to obstruct view. Do not place depressor too far posteriorly, or gag reflex will be elicited.*	Both structures rise centrally. Uvula varies in length and thickness.	Deviation or immobility may indicate involvement of the vagus nerve (cranial nerve X).
Inspect the arch formed by the anterior and posterior pillars, soft palate, and uvula. The tonsils can be seen in the cavities between the pillars.	Tonsils are oval with infoldings of tissue. Pharyngeal tissues are pink and smooth.	Edema, ulceration, or inflammation indicates infection or abnormal lesions. Absence of tonsils indicates previous surgical removal.

Assessment	Normal Findings	Deviations From Normal
View the posterior pharynx behind the pillars.	Tissues are smooth, glistening pink, and well hydrated. Small irregular spots of lymphatic tissue and small blood vessels are normal.	Clear exudate may be found with chronic sinus problems. Yellow or green exudate indicates an infection. A typical sore throat is evidenced by reddened and swollen uvula and tonsillar pillars with possible exudate. Client will express discomfort.

Nursing Diagnoses

Assessment data may reveal defining characteristics for the following nursing diagnoses:

- Altered oral mucous membrane
- Pain
- Knowledge deficit regarding oral hygiene
- Risk for infection
- Impaired swallowing
- Altered nutrition: less than body requirements
- Altered health maintenance

Pediatric Considerations

- Children have 20 deciduous teeth that erupt between 8 and 30 months of age depending on the tooth. Permanent teeth begin to appear around 6 years of age, with final molars in place at 12 to 17 years of age.
- It is easier to inspect the oral cavity while an infant is crying.
- Nonadherent white patches on the tongue or buccal mucosa are usually milk deposits. Adherent patches may indicate candidiasis (thrush).
- Drooling is common in infants up to 6 months of age but may indicate neurologic disorder after 12 months of age.
- Inspect infant's hard and soft palates carefully for presence of clefts.
- Children may need to be gently re-

strained in a parent's lap during the examination. The parent reaches around to restrain the child's arms with one arm and controls the child's head with the other.

Gerontologic Considerations

- In older adults, the mucosa is normally dry because of reduced salivation, and the gums are pale.
- The tongue may appear more fissured.
- Loose or missing teeth are common, because bone resorption increases.
- An older adult's teeth often feel rough when tooth enamel calcifies. Yellow or darkened teeth are also common because of the general wear and tear that exposes the darker, underlying dentin.
- The teeth may appear longer because of resorption of the gum and bone underneath.

Cultural Considerations

- Dark-skinned clients will have increased pigmentation on the buccal mucosa and gums.
- When comparing clients from different cultures, whites have the smallest teeth, African Americans have somewhat larger teeth, and Orientals and Native Americans have even larger teeth. The Australian Aborigines have the largest teeth in the world, as well as extra molars (Giger and Davidhizar, 1995; Merz et al., 1991).
- Hyperpigmentation of the buccal mucosa is normal in 10% of whites and 90% of African Americans over 50 years of age.

Client Teaching

- Discuss proper techniques for oral hygiene, including brushing and flossing.
- Warn parents not to take a child to bed with a bottle containing formula, milk, or juice, because these liquids may pool and cause tooth decay.
- Explain early warning signs of oral cancer, including a sore in the mouth that bleeds easily and does not heal in 2 to 3 weeks, a lump or thickening in the mouth, numbness or pain in mouth and throat, and red or white patches on mucosa that persist (American Cancer Society, 1996b).
- The use of smokeless tobacco (plug, leaf, and snuff) is on the increase in the United States. The 1993 Youth Risk Behavior Survey by the Cen-

ters for Disease Control and Prevention (CDC) reported that 20% of male high-school students used smokeless tobacco (American Cancer Society, 1996b). Caution clients against the risk for cheek and gum cancer.

- Explain warning signs of gum (periodontal) disease, including gums that bleed easily; red, swollen gums that pull away from teeth; and pus between teeth or around a loose tooth.
- Encourage yearly dental examinations for children and adults.
- Older adults should visit a dentist every 6 months.
- Older adults should eat soft foods and cut food into small pieces because of difficulty in chewing.

Thorax and Lungs

12

Examination of the thorax and lungs involves the assessment of three areas: the posterior thorax, the lateral thorax, and the anterior thorax. These are described separately in the following sections.

Anatomy and Physiology

The two primary physiologic functions of the lungs are the exchange of respiratory gases and maintenance of acid-base balance. There are three steps in the process of oxygenation: ventilation, perfusion, and diffusion. For the exchange of gases to occur, the organs, nerves, and muscles of respiration must be intact.

The thorax is a cage of bone, cartilage, and muscle that moves as the lungs expand. The anterior thorax consists of the sternum, manubrium, xiphoid process, and costal cartilages. The lateral chest is formed by the 12 pairs of ribs. Posteriorly, the thorax consists of the 12 thoracic vertebrae, eight of which extend behind the bony scapulae. All of the ribs connect to the thoracic vertebrae; the upper seven attach to the sternum by the costal cartilages.

The primary muscles of respiration are the diaphragm and intercostal muscles. During inspiration the diaphragm contracts and moves downward, lowering the abdominal contents to increase intrathoracic space. The external intercostal muscles increase the anteroposterior chest diameter during inspiration. The internal intercostals decrease the transverse diameter during expiration.

The interior chest contains the right and left pleural cavities and the mediastinum. The mediastinum, situated between the lungs, contains all of the thoracic organs except the lungs. The pleural cavities are lined with parietal and visceral pleura, serous membranes that enclose the lungs. The elastic, spongy lungs are paired, asymmetric organs located within the pleural cavities. The right lung has three lobes, and the left has two. Each lung is cone shaped with the rounded apex extending about 1½ inches (4 cm) above the first rib. The base of each lung is broad and concave. Each lobe contains blood vessels, lymphatics, nerves, and an alveolar duct connecting with the alveoli.

The tracheobronchial tree is a tubular system that forms a pathway for air to travel from the upper airway to the alveoli. The trachea is 10 to 11 cm (4 to 4½ inches) long and about 2 cm (¾ inch) in diameter. It lies anterior to the esophagus and posterior to the thyroid isthmus. The trachea divides into the right and left main bronchi at the level of thoracic vertebra T4 or T5.

During assessment, it is important to use key landmarks in describing findings (Fig. 12-1). The angle of Louis (manubriosternal junction), suprasternal notch, costal angle, clavicles, and vertebral prominens (spinous process of C7) are key landmarks for chest assessment. An examiner keeps in mind the underlying position of the lungs and the position of each rib. Anteriorly (Fig. 12-2), locate the angle of Louis at the manubriosternal junction. The angle is a visible and palpable angulation of the sternum below the suprasternal notch, at the point at which the second rib articulates with the sternum. Count the ribs and the intercostal spaces (between the ribs) from this point to locate findings. The number of each intercostal space corresponds to that of the rib just above it. The spinous process of the third thoracic vertebra and the fourth, fifth, and sixth ribs help to locate the lung's lobes laterally (Fig. 12-3). The lower lobes project laterally and anteriorly. Posteriorly, the tip or inferior margin of the scapula lies approximately at the level of the seventh rib (Fig. 12-4). By identifying the seventh rib the examiner can count upward to locate the third thoracic vertebra and align it with the inner

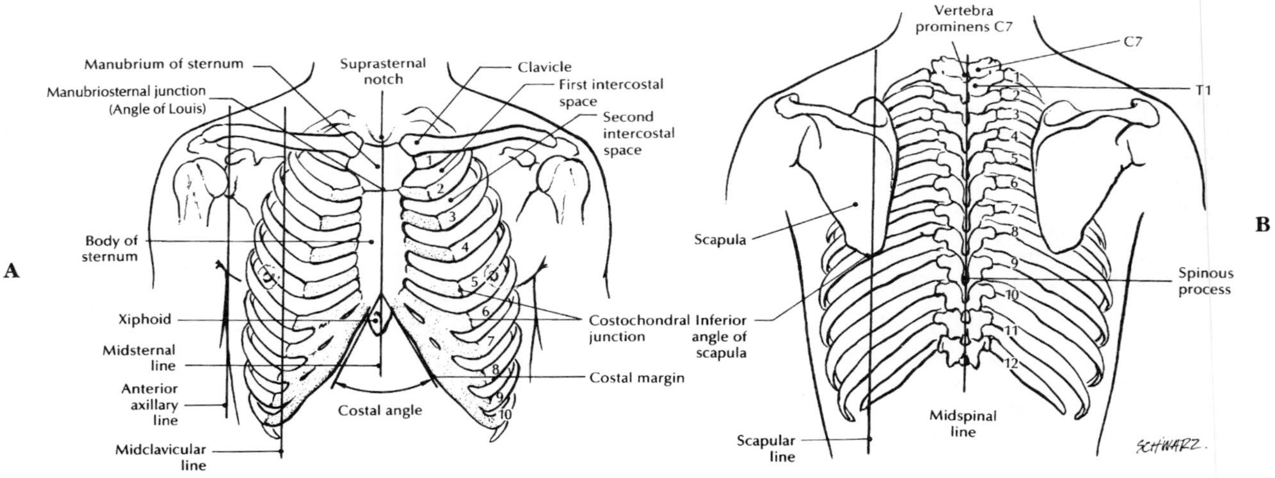

Fig. 12-1
Topographic landmarks. A, Anterior thorax. B, Posterior thorax.
(From Malasanos L et al: *Health assessment,* ed 4, St Louis, 1990, Mosby.)

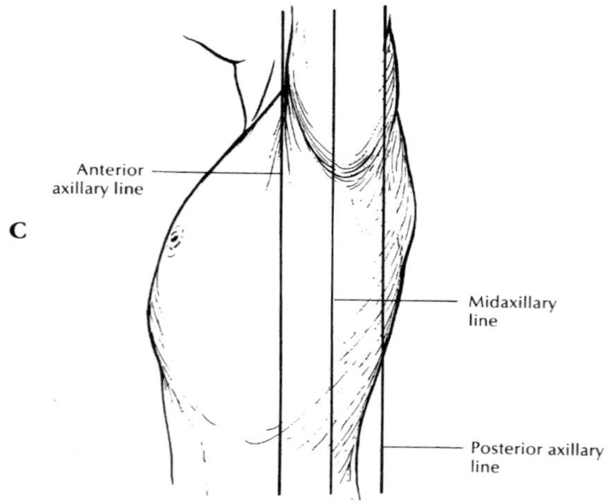

Fig. 12-1, cont'd
C, Lateral thorax.

borders of the scapula to locate the posterior lobes. The vertebral prominens can be more readily seen and felt when the client bends the head forward. If two prominences are felt, the upper is that of the spinous process of C7 and the lower is that of T1.

Rationale

Oxygen is a basic human need required to sustain life. Pulmonary disease can be acute or chronic, and nurses in all settings can screen clients early for disorders and assess long-term disabilities. If the lungs are affected by disease, other body systems will reflect alterations. For example, reduced oxygenation can cause changes in mental alertness because of the brain's sensitivity to lowered oxygen levels. This assessment is particularly important for clients at risk

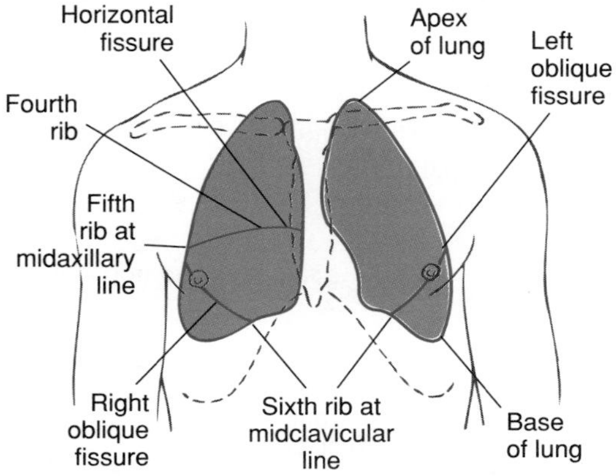

Fig. 12-2
Anterior position of lung lobes.

for developing pulmonary complications, including clients who are immobilized or clients with chest or abdominal pain impairing normal ventilation.

Critical Thinking

Knowledge

Refer to the knowledge you have regarding the physiology of respiratory control. Chemoreceptors respond to changes in hydrogen ion concentration and send signals to the respiratory center in the medulla to control respiration.

Refer to the knowledge you have regarding possible pulmonary pathologies. Physical assessment findings may be caused by abnormal collections of air or fluid or by solid tumors within the pleural space.

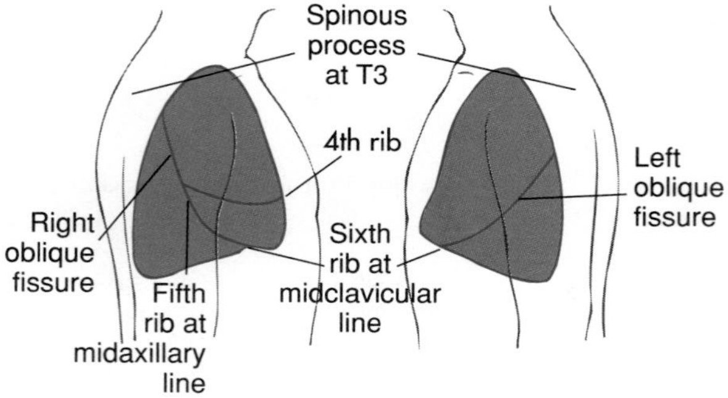

Fig. 12-3
Lateral position of lung lobes.

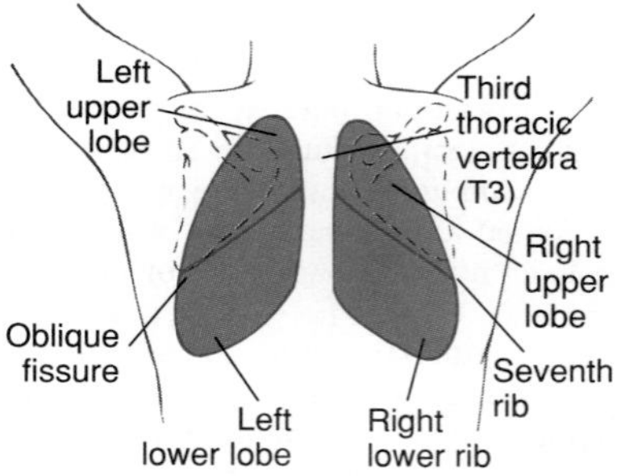

Fig. 12-4
Posterior position of lung lobes.

Experience

To accurately assess the lungs and thorax it is important to feel comfortable using the stethoscope. See Chapter 3 for exercises on use of the stethoscope.

Standards

During the examination of the lungs and thorax apply the following principles:

- Be sure the client is in as comfortable a position as possible to allow for full chest expansion.
- Clients in respiratory distress are anxious and restless. Keep the history brief and use simple "Yes" and "No" questions.

- Be systematic in the examination. Examine all lung lobes bilaterally (anteriorly, laterally, and posteriorly).

Equipment

Stethoscope
Centimeter ruler and tape measure
Marking pencil

Delegation Considerations

The examination of the lungs and thorax requires problem solving and knowledge application unique to a professional nurse. Delegation of the examination is inappropriate. However, unlicensed personnel can learn to monitor respirations and report any abnormalities to the RN. In addition, instruct staff to report any changes in character of sputum.

Thorax and Lung Assessment

Client Preparation

- Client must be undressed to the waist.
- Make sure lighting is good.
- Client sits (when possible) for assessment of posterior and lateral chest. Assessment in the side-lying position is possible but not desirable. Client may sit or lie with head of bed raised for assessment of anterior chest (if client cannot sit up alone, provide assistance).

History

- Assess history of tobacco or marijuana use, including type of tobacco, duration, and amount (pack years = number of years smoking × number of packs per day), age started, and efforts to quit. Be sure to include cigar or pipe smoking.
- Does the client have a *persistent cough* (productive or nonproductive), *sputum production, chest pain,* shortness of breath, orthopnea, dyspnea during exertion or at rest, poor activity tolerance, or *recurrent attacks of pneumonia or bronchitis?* (Italic symptoms are warning signals for lung cancer.)
- Does the client have a history of chronic pulmonary disease (tuberculosis [date, treatment, compliance], asthma, emphysema, bronchitis, cystic fibrosis)?
- Does the client work in an environment that contains pollutants (e.g., asbestos, arsenic, coal dust, exhaust fumes, chemical irritants)? Does the client use protective devices?
- What is the extent of smoking by others at work or home (passive smoking)?
- To rule out risk for tuberculosis,

determine if client has history of known or suspected human immunodeficiency virus (HIV) infection, substance abuse, low income, and/or residence in a nursing home (American Thoracic Society, 1992). Does client have history of cough, hemoptysis, weight loss, fatigue, night sweats, and fever?

- Assess history of allergies to pollens, dust, or other airborne irritants, as well as to foods, drugs, or chemical substances.
- If a client, especially a young adult, complains of acute chest pain, consider drug use, particularly cocaine. Cocaine can cause pneumothorax with severe acute chest pain (Seidel et al., 1995).
- What is client's exercise tolerance?
- Does client have history of chronic hoarseness (indicative of laryngeal disorder or abuse of cocaine and opioids from sniffing)?
- Review the client's family history for cancer, tuberculosis, cystic fibrosis, allergies, and chronic obstructive pulmonary disease (e.g., asthma, emphysema).
- Has the client had the pneumonia or influenza vaccine? When did the client last have a chest x-ray examination or tuberculosis test?

Assessment Techniques

Assessment	Normal Findings	Deviations From Normal

Posterior Thorax

This is a time to compare findings from assessment of the skin, nails, and oral mucosa, noting if cyanosis or pallor is present. Reduced oxygenation can cause reduced mental alertness, clubbing of the nails, or signs of cyanosis in the skin or mucous membranes. Note the client's breath. Malodorous breath can indicate pulmonary infection.

Observe the shape and symmetry of the chest from the back and front. Note the anteroposterior diameter.

Chest contour is relatively symmetric. The bony framework is obvious, the clavicles are prominent, and the sternum is rather flat. The anteroposterior diameter (front to back) is normally one third to one half of the transverse or side-to-side diameter.

Chronic lung disease is characterized by a barrel-shaped chest (anterior-posterior diameter equals transverse; ribs are more horizontal). Abnormal contours are caused by congenital and postural alterations. Client may lean over a table or splint side of the chest as a result of a breathing problem. Splinting or holding the chest wall as a result of localized pain causes a client to bend toward the affected side.

Observe for bulging of the intercostal spaces on expiration.

No bulging or active movement should occur in the intercostal spaces with breathing.

Bulging indicates great effort to breathe.

Assessment	Normal Findings	Deviations From Normal
Standing at a midline position behind the client, look for deformities, position of the spine, slope of ribs, and symmetry of scapulae.	Spine is normally straight without lateral deviation. Posteriorly the ribs tend to slope across and down. Scapulae are symmetric and closely attached to the chest wall.	Spine may be deviated posteriorly (kyphosis) or laterally (scoliosis). A pigeon chest (pectus carinatum) is a prominent sternal protrusion. A funnel chest (pectus excavatum) is an indentation of the lower sternum above the xiphoid process.
Observe the thorax as a whole. Determine the respiratory rate and rhythm (see Chapter 5). Do not let client know you are counting respirations if possible.	The thorax expands and relaxes with equality of movement bilaterally. The client breathes easily and regularly. Respiratory rate should be 12 to 20 per minute.	See Chapter 5 for alterations in breathing patterns.
Inspect the chest wall movement during respiration.	Expansion is symmetric.	Chest asymmetry can be from unequal expansion of the lungs. Unilateral or bilateral bulging can be a reaction of the ribs and interspaces to respiratory obstruction (Seidel et al., 1995).

Palpate the posterior thoracic muscles and skeleton for lumps, masses, pulsations, tenderness, bulges, and unusual movement or position; with pain or tenderness, avoid deep palpation because fractured rib fragments may displace against vital organs.

Chest wall is not tender. Rib cage is somewhat elastic, whereas thoracic spine is rigid.

Localized pain can indicate fractured rib. Crepitus is a crackly sensation that can be palpated and feels like cellophane under the skin. It is the result of air in the subcutaneous tissues from a rupture in the respiratory system. This is a sign requiring immediate medical attention (Seidel et al., 1995).

If a suspicious mass or swollen area is detected, lightly palpate for size, shape, and typical qualities of a lesion.

Measure posterior chest excursion:

Stand behind the client and place the thumbs along the spinal processes at the level of the tenth rib (Fig. 12-5, *A*), with the palms lightly in contact with the posterolateral surfaces.

A

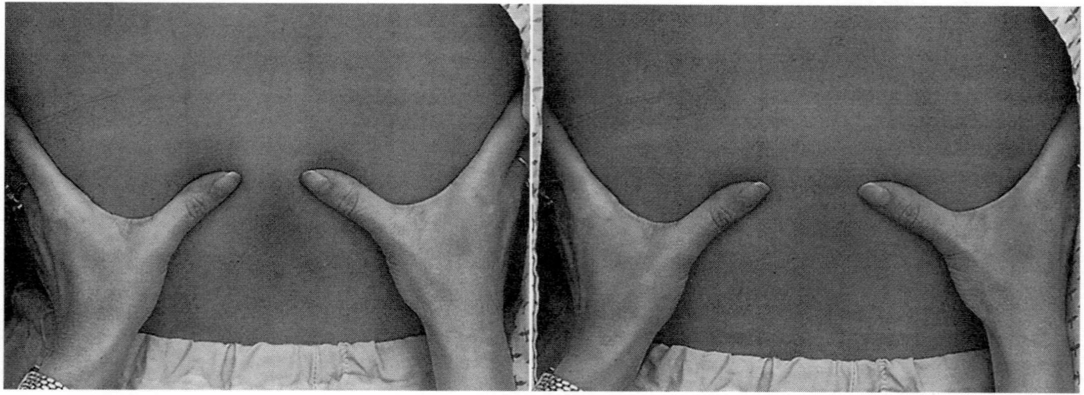

B

Fig. 12-5
Position of nurse's hands for palpation of excursion. **A,** Before client inhales. **B,** After client inhales.

Assessment	Normal Findings	Deviations From Normal
The thumbs should be about 2 inches (5 cm) apart, pointing toward the spine and fingers pointing laterally.		
Press hands (do not slide) toward spine to create a small skin fold between the thumbs.		
Ask the client to take a deep breath after first exhaling; observe the movement of your thumbs (Fig. 12-5, *B*). Palpate for symmetry of respiration.	Chest excursion should be symmetric, separating the thumbs 1¼ to 2 inches (3 to 5 cm).	Reduced chest excursion can be caused by pain, postural deformity, or fatigue.
Palpate for tactile (vocal) fremitus (the palpable vibration of the chest wall during speech):		
Place the ball or lower palm of hand over symmetric intercostal spaces, beginning at the lung apex (Fig. 12-6).		

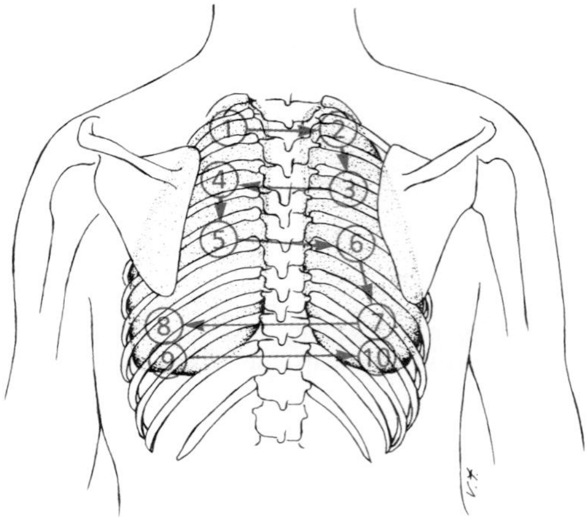

Fig. 12-6
Nurse follows a systematic pattern when comparing fremitus, percussion, and auscultation. Posterior thorax.

Assessment	Normal Findings	Deviations From Normal
At each position ask client to say "99." Use a firm, light touch. For comparison, palpate both sides simultaneously and symmetrically, or use one hand very quickly while alternating sides.		
If fremitus is faint, ask client to speak louder or in a lower tone.	There is a faint vibration as the client speaks. Tactile fremitus is symmetric and strongest at top near the tracheal bifurcation and decreases over periphery of chest. It may be difficult to palpate posteriorly, because the scapula can obscure fremitus.	Decreased fremitus is from excess air in the lungs (emphysema, pleural effusion, pulmonary edema). Increased fremitus feels rougher and occurs in the presence of fluids or a solid mass within the lungs (Seidel et al., 1995).

Assessment	Normal Findings	Deviations From Normal
Percuss the chest wall to determine whether lung tissue is air filled, fluid filled, or solid:		
Ask the client to fold arms across chest with head bent forward.		
With indirect percussion technique, percuss intercostal spaces at 1½- to 2-inch (4- to 5-cm) intervals, following a systematic pattern to compare both sides (see Fig. 12-6).	The posterior thorax is normally resonant on percussion. Percussion over scapula, ribs, or spine is dull.	A lung mass causes a flat sound. Hyperresonance may be from emphysema, pneumothorax, or asthma. Dullness may be caused by atelectasis, pleural effusion, or asthma.
Measure the diaphragmatic excursion (Seidel et al., 1995):		
Have client breathe deeply and hold.		
Percuss along the scapular line until you locate the lower border where resonance turns to dullness.		

Mark the point with the skin pencil at the scapular line.

Allow client to breathe and repeat on the other side.

Have client take several breaths and then exhale as much as possible and hold.

On each side, percuss up from the marked point and make a mark at the change from dullness to resonance. Have client resume breathing.

Measure with the ruler and record distance in centimeters between the marks on each side.

Normal excursion distance is 1¼ to 2 inches (3 to 5 cm). The diaphragm is normally higher on the right than the left.

Diaphragmatic descent may be limited by pulmonary lesions (emphysema), abdominal lesions (tumor or ascites), or superficial pain.

Auscultate lung sounds to detect mucus or obstructed airways and lung condition:

Use the stethoscope diaphragm for adults and the bell for children.

Assessment	Normal Findings	Deviations From Normal
Have client again fold arms in front, with head bent forward.		
Place stethoscope firmly on skin over intercostal spaces.		
Ask the client to breathe slowly and deeply with the mouth slightly open.		
Listen to an entire inspiration and expiration at each stethoscope position.		
If sounds are faint, as in the obese client, ask the client to breathe harder and faster.		
Follow the same systematic pattern as with percussion to compare both sides (see Fig. 12-6).	Normal breath sounds (Table 12-1) include bronchovesicular sounds between the scapulae (a blowing sound with equal inspiratory and expiratory phases) and vesicular sounds at the	Abnormal sounds result from air passing through moisture, mucus, or narrowed airways; from alveoli suddenly reinflating; or from an inflammation between the lung's pleural

lungs' periphery (soft, breezy, low-pitched sounds, with the inspiratory phase lasting about three times longer than the expiratory phase).

linings. See Table 12-2 for adventitious sounds. The absence of lung sounds may indicate collapsed lung or surgically removed lobes.

If client has history of heart failure, begin auscultation at the bases to detect crackles that may disappear with continued, exaggerated respiration.

If tactile fremitus, percussion, or auscultation reveals abnormalities, auscultate for altered voice sounds:

Place stethoscope over same locations to hear breath sounds.

Have the client say "99" or whisper "One, two, three."

In bronchophony the "99" is normally muffled, and whispered pectoriloquy sounds are faint and indistinct.

Lateral Thorax

With client remaining seated and arms raised above the head, extend assessment to lateral thorax.

Table 12-1 Normal breath sounds

Description	Location	Origin
Vesicular		
Vesicular sounds are soft, breezy, and low pitched. Inspiratory phase is three times longer than expiratory phase.	Best heard over lung's periphery (except over scapula)	Created by air moving through smaller airways
Bronchovesicular		
Bronchovesicular sounds are medium-pitched and blowing sounds of medium intensity. Inspiratory phase is equal to expiratory phase.	Best heard posteriorly between scapulae and anteriorly over bronchioles lateral to sternum at first and second intercostal spaces	Created by air moving through large airways
Bronchial		
Bronchial sounds are loud and high pitched with hollow quality. Expiration lasts longer than inspiration (3:2 ratio).	Best heard over trachea	Created by air moving through trachea to chest wall

Table 12-2 Adventitious sounds

Sound	Site Auscultated	Cause	Character
Crackles (previously called *rales*)	Are most commonly heard in dependent lobes: right and left lung bases	Random, sudden reinflation of groups of alveoli*; disruptive passage of air	Fine crackles are high-pitched, fine, short interrupted crackling sounds heard during end of inspiration, usually not cleared with coughing* Moist crackles are lower, more moist sounds heard during middle of inspiration; not cleared with coughing
Rhonchi	Are primarily heard over trachea and bronchi; if loud enough, can be heard over most lung fields	Muscular spasm, fluid, or mucus in larger airways, causing turbulence	Are loud, low-pitched, rumbling, coarse sounds heard most often during inspiration or expiration; may be cleared by coughing
Wheezes	Can be heard over all lung fields	High-velocity air flow through severely narrowed bronchus	Are high-pitched, continuous musical sounds like a squeak heard continuously during inspiration or expiration; usually louder on expiration, do not clear with coughing†
Pleural friction rub	Is heard over anterior lateral lung field (if client is sitting upright)	Inflamed pleura, parietal pleura rubbing against visceral pleura	Has dry, grating quality heard best during inspiration; does not clear with coughing, heard loudest over lower lateral anterior surface

*Data from Forgacs P: The functional basis of pulmonary sounds, *Chest* 73:399, 1978.
†Data from Wilkins RL, Hodgkin JE, Lopez B: *Lung sounds: a practical guide,* St Louis, 1988, Mosby.

Assessment	Normal Findings	Deviations From Normal
Inspect, palpate, percuss, and auscultate lateral thorax in same manner as with posterior thorax. Use a systematic method to compare both sides (Fig. 12-7). Excursion cannot be assessed laterally.	Percussion notes are resonant. Breath sounds are vesicular.	Deviations are same as with posterior thorax.
Anterior Thorax		
Have client sit or lie down with head elevated.		
Observe the accessory muscles of breathing: trapezius, sternocleidomastoid, and abdominal muscles.	The accessory muscles move little with normal passive breathing.	Straining of accessory muscles indicates an effort to breathe. May be caused by chronic obstructive pulmonary disease. Some clients produce a grunting sound.
Observe the width of the costal angle.	The angle is usually larger than 90 degrees between the two costal margins.	

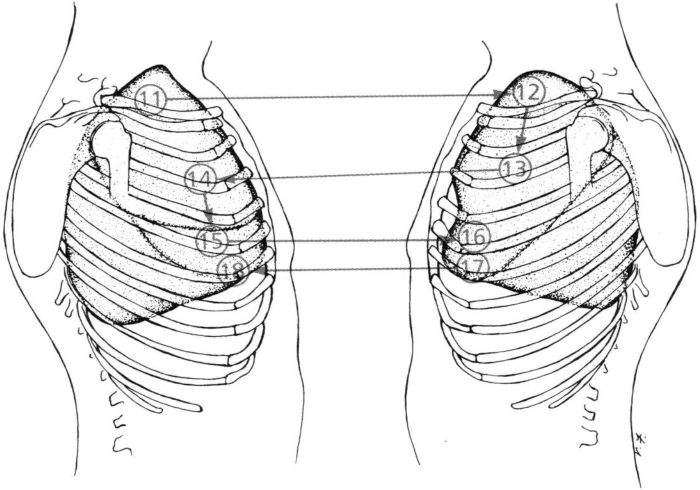

Fig. 12-7
Lateral thorax.

Assessment	Normal Findings	Deviations From Normal
Observe the client's breathing pattern.	Normal breathing is quiet and barely audible near the open mouth. Respiration of males is more diaphragmatic (more movement of abdominal muscles), and respiration of females is more costal (more movement of ribs).	
Palpate anterior thoracic muscles and skeleton (see *Posterior Thorax*).	Sternum and xiphoid are relatively inflexible.	
Measure anterior chest excursion:		
Place hands over each lateral rib cage along the costal margin.		
Place thumbs parallel 2½ inches (6 cm) apart and angled along the costal margins.		
Push thumbs toward midline to create a skin fold.		
Ask client to inhale deeply.		

Observe separation of thumbs.

Chest excursion should separate the thumbs 1¼ to 2 inches (3 to 5 cm).

See *Posterior Thorax* for abnormalities in chest excursion.

Palpate for tactile fremitus (Fig. 12-8), with the same technique used for the posterior thorax. Fremitus is best felt next to the sternum at the second intercostal space, at the level of the bifurcation of the bronchi (Seidel et al., 1995).

! ***Nurse Alert*** *You will not be able to sense vibrations over breast tissue and thus must retract the breasts gently.*

Fremitus is normally decreased over the heart, lower thorax, and breast tissue.

See *Posterior Thorax* for abnormalities.

With client sitting or supine, percuss the anterior thorax and compare both sides (see Fig. 12-8), considering the locations of the underlying liver, heart, and stomach (Fig. 12-9).

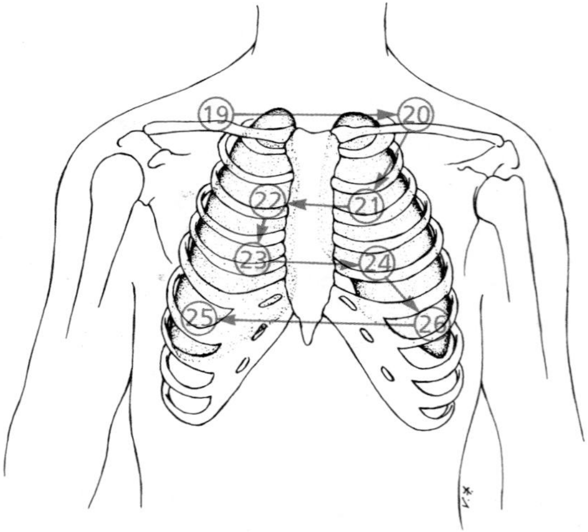

Fig. 12-8
Anterior thorax.

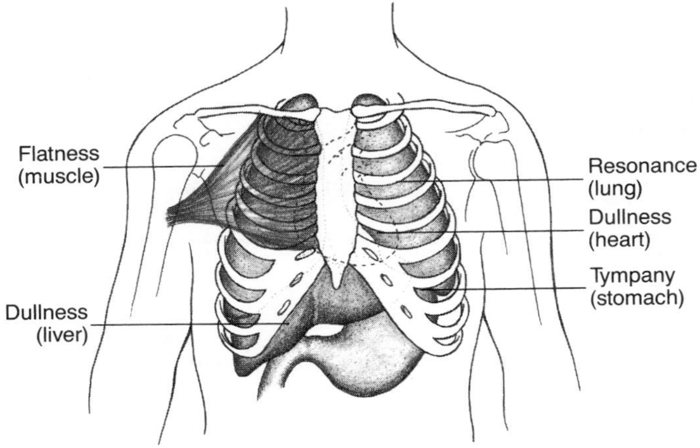

Fig. 12-9
Variations in percussion notes in the normal thorax and upper abdomen.

Assessment	Normal Findings	Deviations From Normal
Percuss in a systematic pattern from above the clavicles, moving across and down; displace female breasts as needed.	Percussion notes over the heart and liver are dull. The gastric air bubble is percussed as a tympanic sound.	
With client sitting erect and shoulders held back, auscultate the anterior thorax using the same pattern as with percussion (see Fig. 12-8).	Pay particular attention during auscultation of the lower lobes, where mucous secretions commonly accumulate.	Bronchovesicular and vesicular sounds are heard above and below the clavicles and along the lung periphery. Bronchial sounds are normal over the trachea: loud, high-pitched, and hollow sounding, with expiration lasting longer than inspiration.

Nursing Diagnoses

Assessment data may reveal defining characteristics for the following nursing diagnoses:

- Ineffective airway clearance
- Ineffective breathing pattern
- Impaired gas exchange
- Pain
- Impaired mobility
- Knowledge deficit regarding risks for lung disease
- Risk for infection

Pediatric Considerations

- The chest circumference is almost round in infants.
- In newborns, try to conduct the examination without disturbing the baby. Percussion is usually unreliable (Seidel et al., 1995).

- Measure an infant's chest circumference; it is normally 11¾ to 14¼ inches (30 to 36 cm) in a healthy full-term infant.
- Irregular respirations are common among preterm infants at birth.
- In children younger than 6 years of age, ventilatory movement is mainly abdominal or diaphragmatic rather than costal. Infants have a thin chest wall with a bony and cartilaginous rib cage that is soft and pliant. Lungs are usually hyperresonant throughout in infants and young children. Breath sounds are louder and harsher.
- For normal respiratory rates for children, see Chapter 5.

Gerontologic Considerations

- Because of calcification of the vertebral cartilages, reduced mobility of the ribs, partial contraction of the intercostal muscles, and kyphosis that frequently occurs with aging, older adults do not breathe as deeply as younger adults.
- An older client is not able to cough as effectively because of a more rigid thoracic wall and weaker respiratory muscles.
- Loss of lung resiliency, coupled with the loss of skeletal muscle strength in the thorax and diaphragm, results in a characteristic barrel chest (Leuckenotte, 1994).
- Older adults have difficulty breathing deeply and holding their breath.
- Alveoli become less elastic and more fibrous, which decreases the body's exertional capacity (Lueckenotte, 1994).
- Drier mucous membranes impede removal of secretions and pose a risk for respiratory infection (Lueckenotte, 1994).

Cultural Considerations

- There are many countries in which tuberculosis is endemic. Ethnic minorities account for more than two thirds of all of the reported cases of tuberculosis in the United States. This is partly because of an increased incidence of HIV (CDC, 1989).
- American Indians have had a tuberculosis incidence as much as 7 to 15 times that of non-Indians, whereas African Americans have had a tuberculosis incidence three times higher

than whites. Tuberculosis is also five times more prevalent among American Eskimos than in the general U.S. population (Giger and Davidhizar, 1995).

- Immigrants from Haiti and Mexico have a high incidence of tuberculosis (Giger and Davidhizar, 1995).
- Russians typically receive an immunization of bacillus Calmette-Guérin (BCG) 2 days after birth. The bacillus is an effective treatment when a high prevalence of tuberculosis exists. The immunization causes tuberculin reactions to read positive and makes tuberculin readings unclear (Giger and Davidhizar, 1995).
- The highest death rates per 100,000 population from lung cancer occur in Hungary, the Czech Republic, the Russian federation, Poland, and Estonia (American Cancer Society, 1996b).

Client Teaching

- Explain risk factors for chronic obstructive lung disease and lung cancer, including cigarette smoking; history of cigarette smoking for over 20 years; exposure to environmental pollution (e.g., arsenic, asbestos); and radiation exposure from occupational, medical, and environmental sources. Residential radon exposure may increase risk for lung cancer, especially in cigarette smokers (American Cancer Society, 1996b).
- Clients who are overweight will experience an exacerbation of pulmonary symptoms. The extra weight impairs normal ventilatory movement.
- Discuss warning signs of lung cancer, including persistent cough, sputum streaked with blood, chest pains, and recurrent attacks of pneumonia or bronchitis.
- Instruct clients with excessive mucus about the need for deep-breathing exercises, coughing, intake of fluids, postural drainage, and chest percussion.
- Instruct older adults regarding benefits of annual influenza and pneumonia vaccinations to reduce chances of respiratory infection.
- Refer interested clients to smoking-cessation programs.
- Nonsmokers may be more at risk for lung cancer from exposure to passive smoke.

Heart and Vascular System

13

Assessment of the heart and vascular system should be performed together, because alterations in either system may be manifested as changes in the other. If the nursing history reveals heart disease or the presence of risk factors, observe carefully for abnormalities. Assessment of the heart includes inspection, palpation, and auscultation of heart sounds. Assessment of the vascular system includes measuring blood pressure (see Chapter 5) and assessing integrity of accessible arteries and veins.

Anatomy and Physiology

Heart

The heart is located in the thoracic cavity toward the middle of the mediastinum, left of the midline, just above the diaphragm and bounded on both sides by the lungs (Fig. 13-1). It lies behind the sternum and the contiguous parts of the third to the sixth costal cartilages. The base of the heart is the upper portion, and the apex is the bottom tip. The apex actually touches the anterior chest wall at approximately the fourth to fifth intercostal space just medial to the left midclavicular line. This point is known as the apical impulse or point of maximal impulse (PMI). The area of the chest overlying the heart is the precordium.

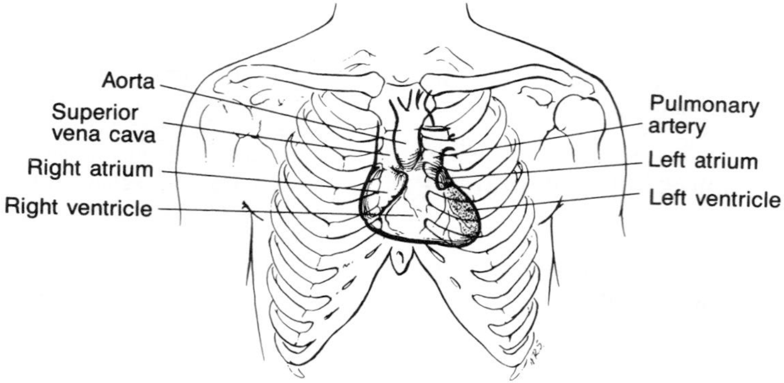

Fig. 13-1
Chest wall landmarks.
(Modified from Malasanos L et al: *Health assessment,* ed 4, St Louis, 1990, Mosby.)

The heart has the shape of a blunt cone and is about the size of a closed fist.

The heart is a muscular, four-chambered pump that delivers blood to the lungs and the arterial system. The pericardium is a tough, double-walled sac encasing and protecting the heart. The fibrous pericardium is the tough outer layer that prevents overdistention of the heart. The serous pericardium is the thin, transparent inner layer. It forms a space around the heart that is filled with a thin layer of pericardial fluid. The fluid helps reduce friction as the heart moves within the pericardial sac.

The heart is divided into four chambers: two ventricles and two atria. The right atrium and right ventricle form the right heart, which receives blood from the systemic circulation. Blood enters the right atrium and then passes into the right ventricle as the ventricle relaxes following a previous contraction. While the right atrium contracts, the blood is pushed into the ventricle. Contraction of the right ventricle pushes blood against the tricuspid valve, forcing it closed, and against the pulmonary semilunar valve, forcing it open, thus allowing blood to enter the pulmonary trunk. The pulmonary trunk carries the blood to the lungs, where carbon dioxide is released and oxygen is picked up. Blood returning from the lungs enters the left atrium through the pulmonary veins. The blood passes from the left atrium to the left ventricle through the bicuspid valve during atrial contraction. Contraction of the left ventricle then forces blood against the bicuspid valve, closing it, and against the aortic semilunar valve, opening it and allowing blood to enter the aorta. The arterial system is a branching network of blood vessels that maintains a pressure necessary to deliver blood to distant peripheral tissues. The ability of the arterial system to compensate for changes in heart function, blood volume, and blood flow ensures the delivery of oxygen and nutrients to the body's cells.

The heart's unique electrical conduction system relays electrical impulses through the heart. All cardiac muscle cells generate action potentials (electrical impulses), but the sinoatrial (SA) node does so with greater frequency. Impulses originating from the SA node spread through cardiac muscle fibers of the atrium to the atrioventricular (AV) node. A brief delay in conduction occurs at the AV node. This allows atrial contraction to be completed before ventricular contraction begins. After action potentials pass from the AV node they travel to conduction bundles and Purkinje's fibers that penetrate into the myocardium of the ventricles. Ventricular contraction begins at the apex of the heart and progresses throughout the ventricles. Rhythmic contractions maintain an average cardiac output of 5 L of blood per minute.

To assess heart function, the nurse must understand the cardiac cycle and the physiologic signs of each event. Both sides of the heart function in a coordinated fashion. Events occurring on the left side of the heart have the most dramatic effect on assessment findings. Pressure is greatest on the left side, so longer and louder sounds are created. Events on the left side slightly precede those on the right.

There are two phases to the cardiac cycle: systole and diastole. During systole the ventricles contract and eject blood from the left ventricle into the aorta and from the right ventricle into the pulmonary artery. During diastole the ventricles relax and the atria contract to move blood into the ventricles and fill the coronary arteries.

Heart sounds occur as follows in relation to the cardiac cycle:

- As systole begins the ventricles contract and raise pressure that closes the mitral and tricuspid valves. Valve closure causes the first heart sound (S_1), known as "lub."
- The ventricles contract and blood flows through the aortic and pulmonic valves into the aorta and pulmonary circulation. After the ventricles empty, the pressure in the ventricles falls below that in the aorta and pulmonary artery, allowing the aortic and pulmonic valves to close. Valve closure causes the second heart sound (S_2), known as "dub."
- If the mitral and tricuspid valves open for rapid ventricular filling and there are noncompliant ventricles, a third heart sound (S_3) is created. It is abnormal in adults.
- The atria contract to enhance ventricular filling. If they contract against noncompliant ventricles, a fourth heart sound (S_4) is produced, which is not normally heard in adults.

Vascular System

When the left ventricle pumps blood into the aorta, a pressure wave is transmitted throughout the arterial system in the form of the arterial pulse. The arterial blood pressure is the force exerted by the blood against arterial walls. Pressure waves are manifested as pulses that are palpable in arteries close to the skin or that lie over bones. The carotid arteries are the closest to the heart and are useful in reflecting heart function. Pressure within the carotid arteries correlates with that of the aorta. Both carotid arteries supply blood to the brain; however, occlusion of either can cause serious brain damage.

The most accessible veins to assess are the internal and external jugular, which empty into the superior vena cava. The external vein lies superficially and can be seen just above the clavicle. The internal jugular lies deeper, along the carotid artery. Both veins reflect the activity of the right side of the heart. Jugular venous pressure reflects pressure within the right atrium.

The peripheral arteries deliver oxygenated blood to the extremities. Hand function is impaired by reduced circulation in the brachial artery but not necessarily by impairment of the radial or ulnar artery because of its interconnected circulation. Similarly, the foot is protected by interconnections between the posterior tibial and dorsalis pedis arteries.

Rationale

Assessment of cardiovascular function involves a thorough evaluation of apical and peripheral pulses, the events that occur in relation to the cardiac cycle, and the overall integrity of the heart and major arteries. Heart disease is the leading cause of death in the United States and Canada. The nurse's assessment serves not only to detect cardiovascular alterations but also to focus on potential problems the client can be educated to control or prevent.

Critical Thinking

Knowledge

Be very familiar with the anatomy and physiology of the heart, summarized previously. This will be critical for you to be able to interpret assessment findings. Also apply knowledge that you have regarding fluid and electrolyte balance and its effect on myocardial function.

When clients have possible signs and symptoms of heart disease they can experience significant anxiety. Apply good therapeutic communication techniques as you question and examine the client. Do not show concern (nonverbally) if you detect abnormal findings.

Experience

Be comfortable in using the diaphragm and bell of the stethoscope. Refer to Chapter 3 for practice exercises.

As you care for different clients you will find that the position of the heart may vary somewhat. In tall, slender persons the heart tends to hang more vertically and is positioned more centrally. With increased stockiness and shortness, the heart tends to lie more to the left and horizontally.

Standards

As you examine the heart apply the following principles:

- Be methodical in the examination. Follow a sequence to ensure each area of the heart is examined properly.
- If you are uncertain about heart sounds, ask a more experienced

practitioner to confirm your findings.

- Caution against misinterpreting findings in an anxious client who might have mild tachycardia.

Equipment

Stethoscope
Ultrasound stethoscope (optional) or Doppler stethoscope
Conductance gel
Penlight
Two centimeter rulers

Delegation Considerations

The heart examination requires problem solving and knowledge application unique to a professional nurse. Delegation is inappropriate. If an unlicensed staff member is assisting in the care of a client at risk or known to have heart disease, instruct him or her to report any incidence of chest pain, unusual fatigue, or changes in heart rate and blood pressure immediately.

Heart and Vascular Assessment

Client Preparation for Heart Examination

- The client should initially lie supine with the upper body elevated 45 degrees. The client will be asked to change positions during the examination.
- Stand at the client's right side to begin.
- Ask the client not to talk during the assessment, especially during auscultation of heart sounds.
- Be sure the client is relaxed and comfortable.
- Have good lighting in the room, including an examination light.

Client Preparation for Vascular Examination

- Client sits during examination of the carotid arteries.
- Client lies supine during assessment of the jugular veins and peripheral arteries and veins.

History

- Assess history of smoking, alcohol intake, use of drugs (e.g., cocaine, amyl nitrite), exercise habits, and dietary patterns and intake (including fat and sodium intake). All are risk factors for cardiovascular disease.
- Is the client taking medications for

cardiovascular function or hypertension? If so, does the client know their purpose, dosage, and side effects?

- Assess for chest pain (onset and duration, character, location, severity, associated symptoms, treatment); fatigue (effect on activities of daily living, associated symptoms, medications); cough (onset, duration, character); dyspnea (exertional or positional); leg pain or cramps (onset, duration, character); edema of feet; cyanosis; fainting; and orthopnea. Do symptoms occur at rest or during exercise?
- If chest pain is experienced, determine if it is cardiac in nature (Rossi and Leary, 1992).
  - Anginal pain is usually a deep pressure or ache that is substernal and diffuse and radiates to one or both arms.
  - Determine its frequency.
  - Does the pain radiate to the shoulder, neck, or arms?
  - Has the pain been associated with diaphoresis?
- Does the client have a stressful lifestyle? What physical demands or emotional stress exists?
- Does the client participate in any relaxing activities, such as hobbies or recreational exercise (amount, frequency, intensity)?
- Assess the client's family history for heart disease, diabetes, hypertension, stroke, high cholesterol levels, or rheumatic heart disease.
- Does the client have known hypertension; diabetes or heart disease, including congestive heart failure; congenital heart disease; coronary artery disease; or cardiac dysrhythmia or murmurs? What is the client's understanding of the disease?
- Has the client had previous heart surgery? What was the client's age at the time?
- Is the client obese?
- Determine if the client drinks excessive amounts of caffeine-containing soft drinks, coffee, or tea.
- Assess the client's eating habits, including fat and sodium intake.
- Does the client experience leg cramps; numbness or tingling in the extremities; sensation of cold hands or feet; pain in the legs; or swelling or cyanosis of the feet, ankles, or hands?
- If leg pain or cramps are present, are they aggravated by walking or standing for long periods or during sleep?
- Ask whether the client wears tight garters or hosiery or sits or lies in bed with legs crossed.

Assessment Techniques

Assessment	Normal Findings	Deviations From Normal
Heart Perform inspection and palpation together at each of the following six landmarks: Begin with assessment of the base of the heart and then move toward the apex. Inspect the angle of Louis, which lies between the sternal body and manubrium and can be felt as a ridge in the sternum approximately 2 inches below the sternal notch. Slip your fingers along the angle on each side of the sternum to feel adjacent ribs. The intercostal spaces are just below each rib. The second intercostal space allows identification of the first two anatomical landmarks (Fig. 13-2), the *second right and left interspaces.*		

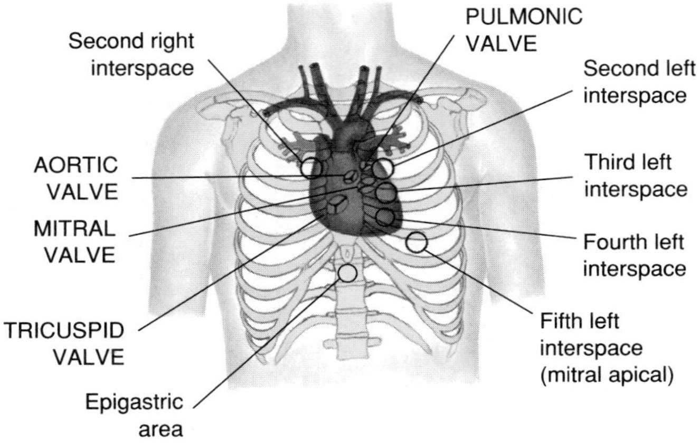

Fig. 13-2
Areas for examination of the heart.
(From Seidel HM et al: *Mosby's guide to physical examination,* ed 3, St Louis, 1995, Mosby.)

Assessment	Normal Findings	Deviations From Normal
The *third and fourth left interspaces* can be found by progressing down along the left side of the sternum, palpating each intercostal space. Deeper palpation is needed to feel the spaces in obese clients or those with well-developed chest muscles. To find the *apical impulse,* locate the fifth intercostal space just to the left of the sternum and move the fingers laterally, just medial to the left midclavicular line. At the apical impulse (PMI) there is a light tap felt in approximately 50% of adult clients in an area 1 to 2 cm (½ inch) in diameter at the apex. The final landmark is the *epigastric area* at the tip of the sternum.		

Look first for the appearance of pulsations or exaggerated lifts, viewing each landmark over the chest at an angle to the side. Use the penlight held at an angle to aid in identifying pulsation.

No pulsations can be seen. Pulsation may be seen at the apical impulse (PMI) or epigastric area in thin clients.

Visible pulsation to the client's left of the midclavicular line may indicate cardiac enlargement. The apical impulse should not be visible in more than one space.

Have client sit up and lean forward.

Causes apical impulse to become visible.

Be sure your hands are warm. Then, with the client supine, palpate each landmark, first using the metacarpophalangeal joints of the four fingers together and then alternating with the ball of the hand. Touch gently and allow movements to lift your hand. Feel for lifts and thrills (fine, palpable, rushing vibrations).

No pulsations, vibrations, or thrills are normally felt in the second, third, or fourth intercostal spaces. Aortic pulsation is palpable at the epigastric area.

Thrill indicates a disruption of blood flow from a defect in closure of one of the semilunar valves (e.g., pulmonary hypertension, atrial septal defect). Usually palpable over base of heart at right or left second intercostal space (Seidel et al., 1995).

Assessment	Normal Findings	Deviations From Normal
Palpate for the apical impulse and identify its location and the distance from the midsternal line. Determine the width of the arc in which it is felt (Fig. 13-3).	Palpable within a small radius, no more than 1 cm (<½ inch). Impulse is gentle and brief. Obesity, muscularity, and large breasts can obscure the apical impulse.	Vigorous pulsation that is forceful and widely distributed is described as a heave or lift and may indicate increased cardiac output or left ventricular hypertrophy. A lift along the left sternal border may be caused by right ventricular hypertrophy.
If the apical impulse cannot be found with the client in the supine position, ask the client to roll onto the left side (left lateral recumbent) (Fig. 13-4) to move the heart closer to the chest wall.	Apical impulse is easily palpable.	Apical impulse to left of midclavicular line indicates enlargement. Absence of apical impulse (in addition to faint heart sounds) indicates pleural or pericardial fluid.
If pulsations or vibrations are palpated, time their occurrence in relation to systole or diastole by auscultation of heart sounds or palpation of the carotid artery simultaneously.	The carotid pulse and S_1 (first heart sound) are practically synchronous.	

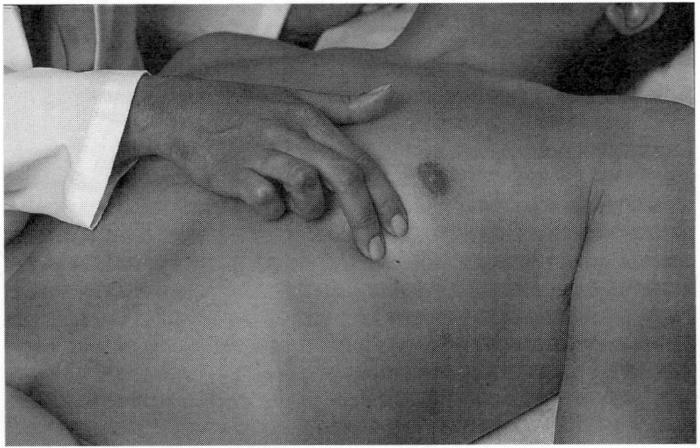

Fig. 13-3
Palpation of PMI.

A

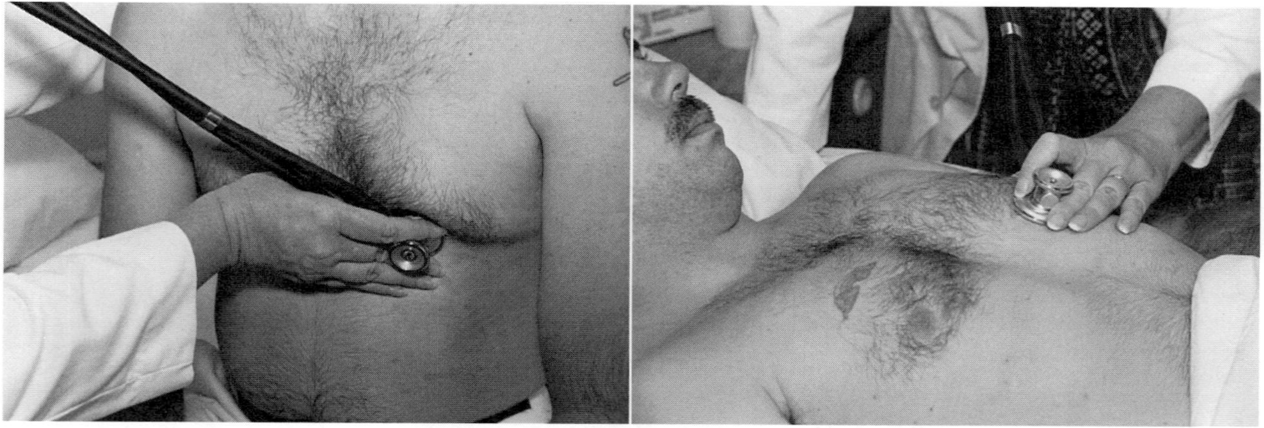

B

Fig. 13-4
Sequence of client positions for heart examination. **A,** Sitting up, leaning slightly. **B,** Supine.

C

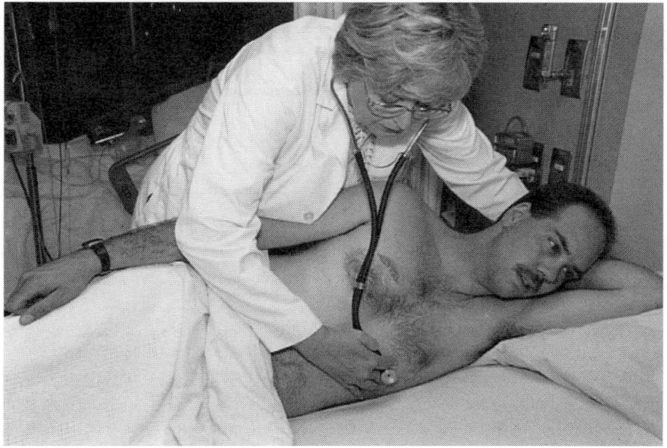

Fig. 13-4, cont'd
C, Left lateral recumbent.

Assessment	Normal Findings	Deviations From Normal
Describe the carotid pulse in relation to the cardiac cycle. While palpating over the heart, use the other hand to palpate the carotid artery.	Carotid pulse and S_1 are almost synchronous.	Lack of synchrony can indicate valvular dysfunction.
Percussion of heart borders to determine heart size is of limited value (x-ray films are preferred).		
To auscultate heart sounds:		
Eliminate any room noise.		
If it takes several seconds to hear heart sounds, explain this to the client to prevent concern.		
Be sure to listen to each sound and each pause in the cardiac cycle.		
Follow a pattern moving systematically and slowly inching the stethoscope across the anatomic sites (see Fig. 13-2).		

After hearing sounds clearly with the diaphragm, repeat sequence using the bell of the stethoscope.

Have client assume three different positions during auscultation: sitting up and leaning forward (good to hear all areas and high-pitched murmurs), supine (good for all areas), and left lateral recumbent (good for all areas and best to hear low-pitched sounds) (see Fig. 13-4).

Lift a female client's left breast to hear over the chest wall better. Begin by using the diaphragm of the stethoscope to hear high-pitched sounds. Listen for the first (S_1) and second (S_2) heart sounds.

Sounds differ in pitch, loudness, and duration depending on the auscultatory site (Table 13-1).

Louder S_1 may be caused by anemia, fever, hyperthyroidism, or effects of vigorous exercise. The intensity of S_1 is decreased with an increase in fat, tissue, or fluid overlying the heart (e.g., obesity, emphysema, pericardial effusion).

Table 13-1 Heart sounds according to auscultatory area

	Aortic	Pulmonic	Second Pulmonic	Mitral	Tricuspid
Pitch	$S_1 < S_2$	$S_1 < S_2$	$S_1 < S_2$	$S_1 < S_2$	$S_1 < S_2$
Loudness	$S_1 < S_2$	$S_1 < S_2$	$S_1 < S_2$*	$S_1 > S_2$†	$S_1 > S_2$
Duration	$S_1 > S_2$	$S_1 > S_2$	$S_1 > S_2$	$S_1 > S_2$	$S_1 > S_2$
S_2 split	>inhale <exhale	>inhale <exhale	>inhale <exhale	>inhale‡ <exhale	>inhale < exhale
A_2	Loudest	Loud	Decreased		
P_2	Decreased	Louder	Loudest		

*S_1 is relatively louder in second pulmonic area than in aortic area.
†S_1 may be louder in mitral area than in tricuspid area.
‡S_2 split may not be audible in mitral area if P_2 is inaudible.

Assessment	Normal Findings	Deviations From Normal
Determine overall rate and rhythm of the heart. Take time to hear each sound and each pause in the cardiac cycle.	S_1 sounds like "lub" and occurs after the long diastolic pause and preceding the short systolic pause. S_1 is high pitched, dull in quality, and heard best at the apex. S_2 sounds like "dub"	Splitting of S_1 (two distinct sound components to S_1) is usually not heard. Splitting of S_2 is expected and best heard on inspiration at the pulmonic area (Lewis et al., 1996). The

and follows the short systolic pause and precedes the long diastolic pause. It is high-pitched and heard best at the aortic area.

usual S_2 will have two audible components. Wide splitting is abnormal and can be caused by delayed activation of contraction or valve stenosis (Seidel et al., 1995).

After both sounds are heard clearly as "lub dub," count each combination of S_1 and S_2 as one heartbeat. Count rate of beats for 1 minute.

Normal rate is 60 to 100 beats/minute in an adult.

Sinus bradycardia: regular rhythm but decreased rate (less than 60 beats/minute); associated with hypothermia, hypothyroidism, and drug intoxication; common in well-conditioned athletes. Sinus tachycardia: regular rhythm but increased rate (more than 100 beats/minute) common after exercise or caffeine or alcohol ingestion; also associated with fever, pain, hyperthyroidism, shock, heart disease, and anxiety.

Assessment	Normal Findings	Deviations From Normal
Assess heart rhythm. Note the time between S_1 and S_2 (systolic pause) and then the time between S_2 and the next S_1 (diastolic pause). Listen to the full cycle at each auscultation area.	Regular rhythm involves regular intervals between each sequence of beats. There is a distinct pause between S_1 and S_2.	Sinus dysrhythmia: pulse rate changes during respiration, increasing at the peak of inspiration and declining during expiration. Ventricular premature contraction: results from abnormal electrical stimulation and conduction in the ventricular tissue. This heartbeat occurs out of rhythm. **!** ***Nurse Alert*** *Ventricular premature contractions can be dangerous and should be reported to the physician. Count and report their frequency per minute.*
If heart rhythm is irregular, compare apical and radial pulse rates to determine whether a pulse deficit exists. Auscultate the apical pulse first and then immediately assess the radial pulse (one examiner). Compare the two rates simultaneously (two examiners).	If a deficit exists, the radial pulse is usually less than the apical pulse.	**!** ***Nurse Alert*** *Presence of a deficit requires further evaluation; usually an electrocardiogram is performed.*

Auscultate for S_3 and S_4 sounds (normal sounds created by vibration of the ventricles during early filling and vibration of the valves and ventricular walls during late filling). They can be heard best with the client lying on the left side and the stethoscope at the apex.

S_3 and S_4 should be quiet and difficult to hear. S_3 sounds like a gallop, occurring just after S_2 at the end of ventricular diastole. The combination of S_1, S_2, and S_3 may sound like "Ken-tuc-*ky*." S_4 is an atrial gallop, occurring just before S_1 or ventricular systole. It may sound like "*Ten*-nes-see."

When S_3 or S_4 becomes easy to hear it may be from increased resistance to filling because of loss of ventricular wall compliance (e.g., hypertension, coronary artery disease) or increased stroke volume (e.g., anemia, pregnancy, thyrotoxicosis). S_3 and S_4 occurring together indicate severe myocardial disease.

Auscultate for extra heart sounds (clicks and rubs). Listen for clicks as short, high-pitched extra sounds. Listen for rubs as squeaky or rubbing sounds.

Extra heart sounds are normally absent with cardiac valves opening noiselessly.

Clicks may be caused by old artificial heart valves inserted during cardiac surgery. Extra heart sounds may also occur with murmurs and usually indicate a pathology such as mitral valve prolapse or aortic stenosis. Rubs result from a rubbing of inflamed pericardial tissues.

Assessment	Normal Findings	Deviations From Normal
Auscultate for murmurs at each auscultatory site: Note timing (in relation to systole or diastole), location heard best, radiation, loudness, pitch, and quality. A murmur is detected by a swishing or blowing sound at the beginning, middle, or end of the systolic or diastolic phase. If a murmur occurs between S_1 and S_2 it is systolic; if it occurs between S_2 and S_1 it is diastolic. To assess for radiation, listen over areas besides where the murmur is heard best, such as the neck or back.		

Note intensity of murmur:

Grade 1	Barely audible
Grade 2	Audible immediately but faint
Grade 3	Loud without thrust or thrill
Grade 4	Loud with thrust or thrill
Grade 5	Very loud, with thrust or thrill; audible with stethoscope only partially applied
Grade 6	Louder; may be heard without stethoscope

Normally no murmurs are heard.

Murmur can be asymptomatic or indicative of heart disease. They usually indicate a disruption of blood flow into, through, or out of the heart.

Vascular System

Auscultate blood pressure at the brachial artery site in both arms.

Readings between the arms may vary by as much as 10 mm Hg and tend to be higher in the right arm (Seidel et al., 1995). The higher reading is accepted as closest to the client's blood pressure.

Systolic reading that differs by 15 mm Hg or more suggests atherosclerosis or aortic disease.

Assessment	Normal Findings	Deviations From Normal
Compare sitting blood pressure with pressures measured while client is in lying and standing positions.	When client changes position from supine or sitting to standing there is a slight or no drop in systolic pressure and a slight rise in diastolic pressure.	Orthostatic hypotension is indicated by a drop in systolic blood pressure of 15 mm Hg or more and a fall in diastolic pressure. ! ***Nurse Alert*** *Clients most at risk are those who have just donated blood, have autonomic nervous system disease, take certain vasodilator medications, or have stayed a prolonged time in a recumbent position.*
Assess the carotid arteries with the client seated: Inspect the neck on both sides for obvious artery pulsation. Ask the client to turn the head slightly away from the side being examined during inspection.		

Examine only one carotid artery at a time.

! *Nurse Alert Do not vigorously palpate artery so as to prevent carotid sinus stimulation, which produces a drop in heart rate and blood pressure.*

During palpation it may help to have the client turn the head slightly toward the side being examined. Palpate gently with index and middle fingers around medial edge of sternocleidomastoid muscle (Fig. 13-5).

Note if pulse changes as client inspires and expires.

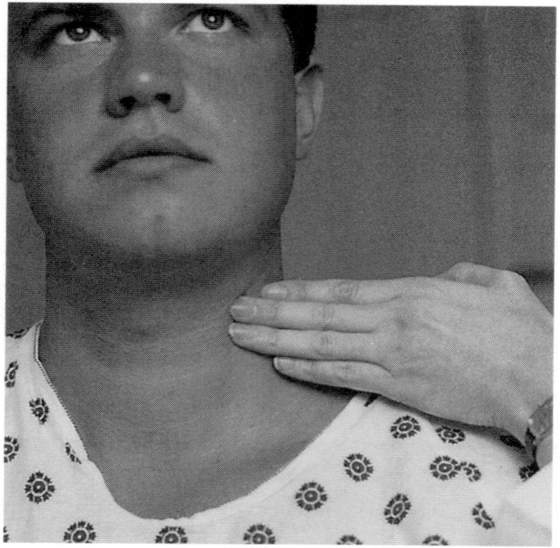

Fig. 13-5
Palpation of internal carotid artery.

Assessment	Normal Findings	Deviations From Normal
Compare rate, rhythm, and strength of pulse on each side.	The carotid pulse is localized, strong, thrusting, and unchanged by inspiration, expiration, or position changes. Rotation of the neck or a shift from a sitting to a supine position does not change the carotid's quality. Both pulses are equal in rate, rhythm, and strength bilaterally. Rate is the same as apical pulse.	Diminished or unequal carotid pulsations can indicate atherosclerosis or aortic arch disease. Change in carotid pulse during inspiration may indicate a sinus dysrhythmia.
Place the bell of the stethoscope over the carotid artery at the lateral end of the clavicle and the posterior margin of the sternocleidomastoid muscle. Have the client turn the head slightly away from the side being examined. Then ask the client to hold the breath for a moment so that breath sounds do not obscure vascular sounds.	No sound is heard over the carotid arteries on auscultation.	A bruit or blowing sound is auscultated, indicating disturbance in blood flow because of arterial narrowing. **!** ***Nurse Alert*** *A bruit should be reported immediately to the client's primary care provider.*

Assessment	Normal Findings	Deviations From Normal
If a bruit is auscultated, palpate the artery lightly for a thrill.	A palpable bruit (thrill) can be felt in severe arterial narrowing.	
Examine the right internal jugular to indirectly determine pressure in the right atrium. Be sure there is no clothing constricting around the client's neck. First, have the client sit upright at a 45- to 90-degree angle. A pillow may be used for client comfort (Fig. 13-6).	Normal veins are flat; pulsations are not evident.	Distended veins while sitting indicates heart disease.
Have the client slowly lean backward into a supine position. Avoid neck hyperextension or flexion. Be sure penlight is tangential to illuminate neck area.	Level of venous pulsations begins to rise above level of manubrium, 1 to 2 cm when client reaches 45-degree angle (Seidel et al., 1995).	

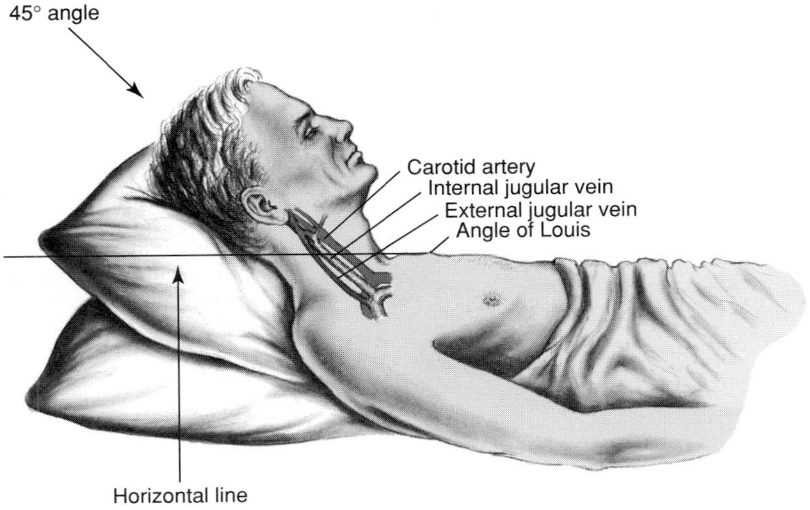

Fig. 13-6
Position of client to assess jugular vein distention.
(From Thompson JM et al: *Mosby's clinical nursing,* ed 3, St Louis, 1993, Mosby.)

Assessment	Normal Findings	Deviations From Normal
Measure venous pressure by measuring the vertical distance between the angle of Louis and the highest level of the visible point of the internal jugular vein pulsation:		
Use two rulers. Line up the bottom edge of a regular ruler with the top of the area of pulsation in the jugular vein. Then take a centimeter ruler and align it perpendicular to the first ruler at the level of the sternal angle. Measure in centimeters the distance between the second ruler and the sternal angle (Fig. 13-7).		
Repeat measurement on the other side.	Measurement of 2 cm or less is considered normal.	Bilateral pressures higher than 2.5 cm (1 inch) are considered elevated and are a sign of right heart failure.

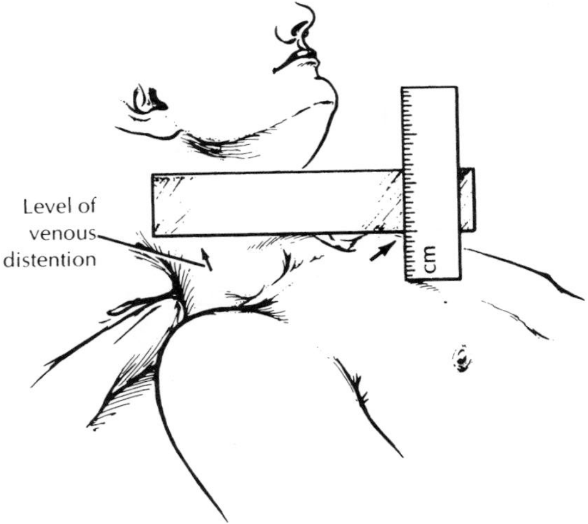

Fig. 13-7
Measurement of jugular vein distention.
(From Seidel HM et al: *Mosby's guide to physical examination,* ed 3, St Louis, 1995, Mosby.)

Assessment	Normal Findings	Deviations From Normal
Observe the right and left jugulars for symmetry.	Equal bilaterally.	Distention on one side suggests a localized abnormality (e.g., obstruction). Bilateral distention suggests an intracardiac problem.
Examine each peripheral artery using the distal pads of the second and third fingers. The thumb may be used to assess larger arteries such as the femoral.		
Apply firm pressure, but do not occlude the pulse. When it is difficult to find a pulse, try to vary pressure and feel all around the pulse site. Be sure you are not palpating your own pulse:		
Temporal artery: see Chapter 7.		
Radial artery: located along the radial side of the forearm, at the wrist. In thin individuals, a groove		

is formed lateral to the flexor tendon of the wrist (Fig. 13-8).

Ulnar artery: located on the opposite side of the wrist from the radial artery. Feels less prominent than the radial (Fig. 13-9).

Brachial artery: located in groove between biceps and triceps muscles above the elbow at the antecubital fossa. The artery runs along the medial side of the extended arm (Fig. 13-10).

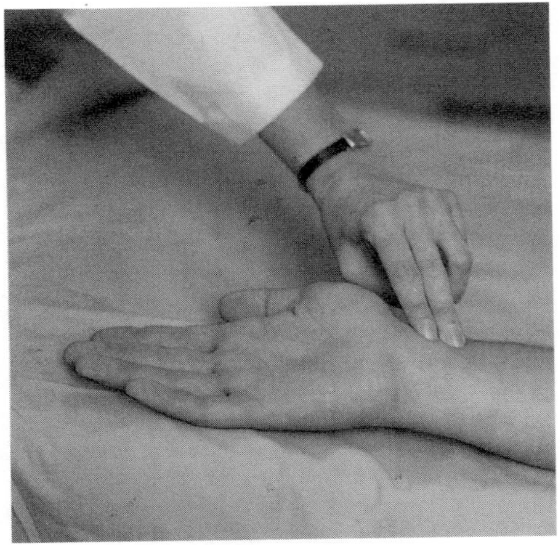

Fig. 13-8
Radial pulse site.

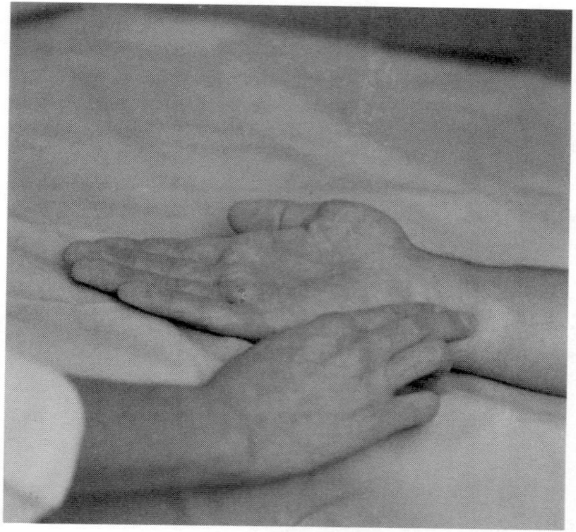

Fig. 13-9
Ulnar pulse site.

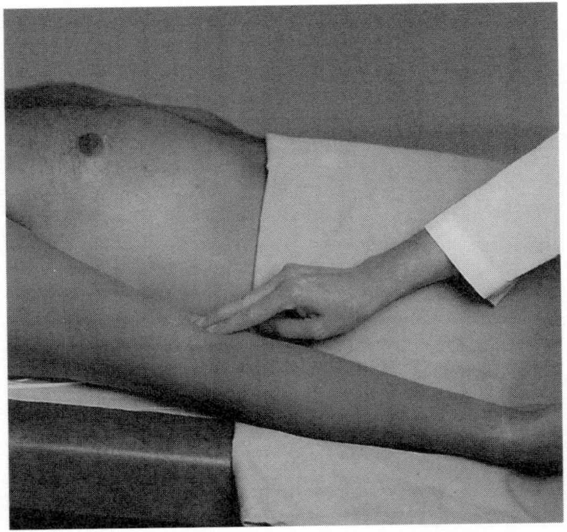

Fig. 13-10
Brachial pulse site.

Assessment	Normal Findings	Deviations From Normal

Femoral artery: primary artery in the leg. Have client lie supine with inguinal area exposed. Artery is located below the inguinal ligament, midway between the symphysis pubis and the anterosuperior iliac spine (Fig. 13-11). Bimanual pulsation, with fingertips of both hands on opposite sides of the pulse site, may be necessary in obese clients.

Popliteal pulse: located behind the knee. Have client flex the knee, with the foot resting on the examination table, or assume a prone position with the knee slightly flexed (Fig. 13-12). Palpate deep into the popliteal fossa, just lateral to the midline.

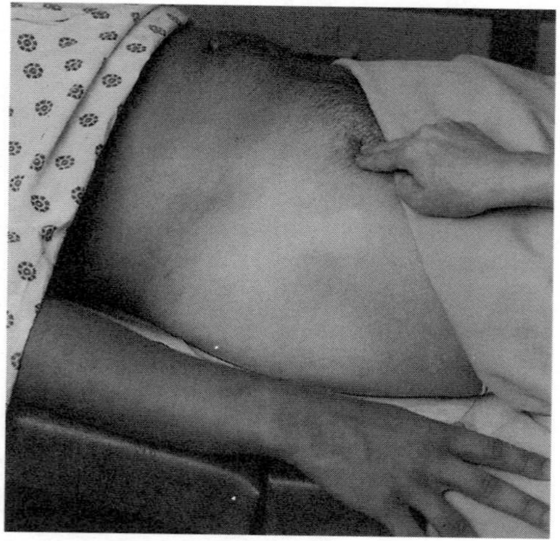

Fig. 13-11
Femoral pulse site.

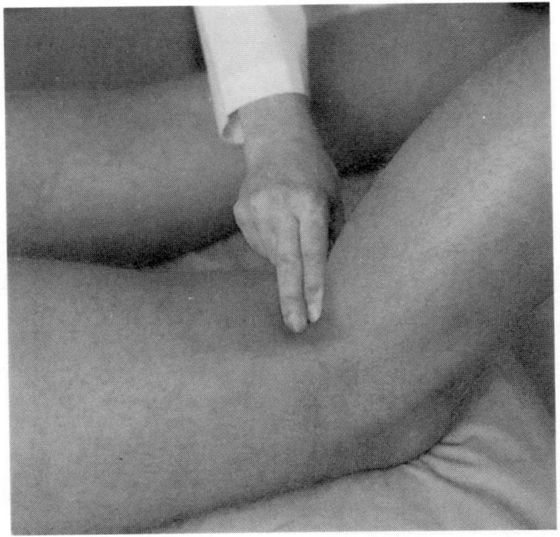

Fig. 13-12
Popliteal pulse site.

Assessment	Normal Findings	Deviations From Normal

Dorsalis pedis pulse: located along the top of the foot in line with the groove between the extensor tendons of the great toe and first toe (Fig. 13-13). Be sure client's foot is relaxed.

Posterior tibial pulse: located on the inner side of each ankle (Fig. 13-14). Place fingers behind and below the medial malleolus (ankle). Have foot relaxed and slightly extended.

The radial pulse may be used to assess heart rate and rhythm (see Chapter 5). To check local circulatory status of tissues, palpate each peripheral artery long enough to note that a pulse is present and assess its character.

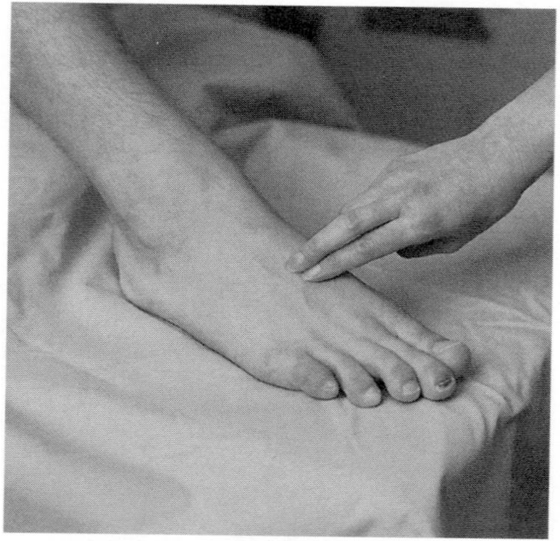

Fig. 13-13
Dorsalis pedis pulse.

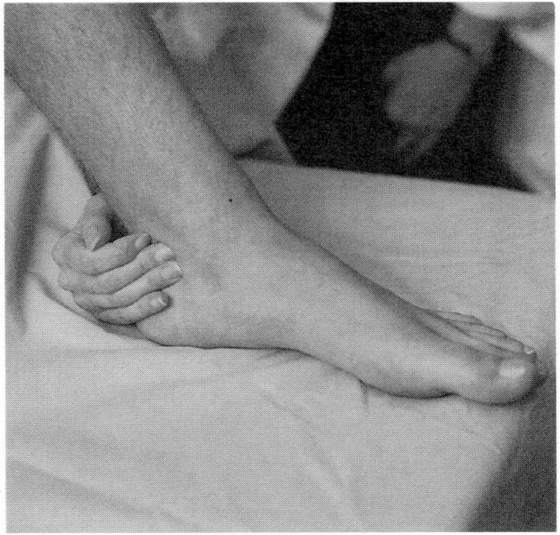

Fig. 13-14
Posterior tibial pulse.

Assessment	Normal Findings	Deviations From Normal
Assess each peripheral pulse for strength and equality (Box 13-1).	Normal pulse is 2+, equal bilaterally.	Absent or diminished pulse may be from a pathologic process interfering with blood flow or obstruction caused by application of external device (e.g., cast, tight bandage).

BOX 13-1 Scale for Measuring Pulse Strength

0	Absent
1+	Pulse is diminished, barely palpable, easy to obliterate
2+	Easily palpable, normal pulse
3+	Full pulse, increased
4+	Strong, bounding pulse, cannot be obliterated

Assess each artery for elasticity of vessel wall.

Wall of artery is easily palpable. After depressing artery, it will spring back to shape when pressure is released.

Sclerotic artery is hard, inelastic, or calcified.

If arterial insufficiency is expected in the hand, perform Allen's test. Have client make a fist as you compress the ulnar and radial arteries simultaneously. Then have the client open the hand while you release the ulnar artery.

Hand should quickly turn pink if ulnar artery is patent.

Failure of color to return indicates arterial occlusion.

! ***Nurse Alert*** *Allen's test should always be performed before drawing an arterial blood sample from the radial artery.*

If it is difficult to palpate a pulse or the pulse is not palpable, use an ultrasound stethoscope over the pulse site:

Connect stethoscope headset to ultrasound probe.

Apply ample amount of conductance gel to client's skin over the pulse site.

Turn stethoscope's volume control to *on*.

Assessment	Normal Findings	Deviations From Normal
Gently apply probe at a 45- to 90-degree angle, pointed in the opposite direction of blood flow, on the skin at the pulse site.		
Adjust volume as needed.	Pulse creates a regular "swooshing" sound.	Pulse is not auscultated.
Assess the skin, nail beds, and lower extremities for color, temperature, and condition. This is a good time to ask the client about history of pain in the legs.	Skin is warm to slightly cool, intact, without obvious varicosities. Client denies pain.	The three P's that characterize an arterial occlusion are **p**ain, **p**allor, and **p**ulselessness. An acute occlusion may also cause **p**aresthesias (Seidel et al., 1995). Venous congestion is characterized by normal or cyanotic color, normal temperature, normal pulse, marked edema, and brown pigmentation around ankles. Pain from arterial insufficiency occurs during exercise and is quickly relieved by rest. Pain from venous insufficiency and musculoskeletal problems occurs during or often hours after exercise. It is re-

lieved by rest, but often pain can be constant.

If arterial occlusion is suspected, have the client lie supine and elevate a leg. Observe for blanching. Then have client sit on edge of bed to lower the extremity.

Slight pallor occurs with elevation. Full color returns when leg again becomes dependent.

Delay in return of full color indicates arterial occlusion.

Examine lower extremities for hair distribution, scars, or lesions.

Hair growth is evenly distributed. (Male clients may have hair loss around calfs from tight-fitting pants or socks.)

Absence of hair growth over legs may indicate circulatory insufficiency. Chronic recurring ulcers of the feet or lower legs are a sign of circulatory insufficiency.

Assess status of peripheral veins by asking client to assume sitting and standing positions. Inspect and palpate for varicosities.

Extremities are clear, without edema or inflammation.

Varicosities are superficial veins that become dilated, especially when legs are in dependent position. Varicosities in the anterior or medial part of the thigh and the posterolateral part of the calf are abnormal.

Assessment	Normal Findings	Deviations From Normal
Palpate lower extremities around feet and ankles for dependent edema. Use your thumb to press firmly 1 to 2 seconds and then release over the medial malleolus or the shins.	Edema is absent.	Depression left in the skin indicates edema and can be a sign of venous insufficiency and right-sided heart failure.
Assess for phlebitis in leg veins. Inspect calves for localized redness, tenderness, and swelling over vein sites. Also check for Homans' sign by supporting the leg, keeping the knee slightly flexed while flexing the foot upward (dorsiflexion).	Absence of pain during calf flexion. Achilles' tendon pain, common in athletes and women who repeatedly wear high-heel shoes, should not be confused with thrombosis. Calf will feel tender in these clients.	Complaint of calf pain during flexion indicates thrombosis. **!** ***Nurse Alert*** *Do not continuously massage a tender or painful calf; this may increase the risk of an embolus.*
Assess the lymphatic drainage of the lower extremities. Palpate the area of the superficial inguinal nodes beginning in the groin area and moving down toward the inner thigh.	A few soft, nontender nodes may be palpable.	Enlarged, hardened, or tender nodes can indicate infection or metastatic disease.

Nursing Diagnoses

Assessment data may reveal defining characteristics for the following nursing diagnoses:

- Decreased cardiac output
- Anxiety
- Activity intolerance
- Fatigue
- Pain
- Knowledge deficit regarding risks for heart or vascular disease and/or medication regimen
- Risk for peripheral neurovascular dysfunction

Pediatric Considerations

- The PMI can be found just lateral to the left midclavicular line and fourth intercostal space in children under 7 years of age and at the left midclavicular line and fifth intercostal space in children over 7 years of age. A child's thin chest wall makes it easy to see and palpate the PMI (Wong, 1995).
- The heart rates of children are more variable than those of adults, reacting with wider swings to stress such as exercise, fever, or tension (Seidel et al., 1995). A heart rate of 200 beats per minute is not uncommon.
- Sinus dysrhythmia (cyclic variation of the heart rate; faster on inspiration and slower on expiration) is common in childhood.
- Fixed splitting, a condition in which the split in S_2 does not change during inspiration, is an important diagnostic sign of atrial septal defect.
- To assess cardiac function in infants, be sure to inspect the color of skin and mucous membranes. A well newborn is pink. An ashy white color indicates shock, and cyanosis of the skin and mucous membranes can indicate congenital heart disease.
- Murmurs are relatively frequent in newborns until about 48 hours of age. Most are benign (Seidel et al., 1995).
- The brachial, radial, and femoral pulses are easy to palpate in newborns. A weak or thin pulse may be caused by reduced cardiac output or peripheral vasoconstriction. A bounding pulse can be caused by patent ductus arteriosus (Seidel et al., 1995).
- Absence of femoral pulse can be a sign of coarctation of the aorta.

Gerontologic Considerations

- With aging the heart rate slows, stroke volume decreases, and cardiac output is reduced by 30% to 40% (Lueckenotte, 1994).
- It may be difficult to locate the PMI, because the chest deepens in its anteroposterior diameter and there may be scoliosis or kyphosis.
- The elderly experience reduced cardiac output and thus the heart reacts less efficiently to stress. Heart failure is a common disorder. Fatigue, restlessness, syncope, and confusion may be early signs of congestive heart failure.
- Heart sounds are not as loud as they are in younger clients.
- Carotid arteries normally become tortuous and dilated because of changes in arterial elasticity.
- Vasomotor tone decreases and baroreceptor sensitivity decreases. Vagal tone increases, which slows heart rate.
- Systolic blood pressure increases in response to loss in elasticity in peripheral vessels and an increase in peripheral vascular resistance.
- Auscultation of the carotid artery is especially important for clients in whom cerebrovascular disease is suspected.
- Dependent edema of the lower extremities is common in older clients.

Cultural Considerations

- Studies suggest that the incidence of heart disease is significantly higher among Jews from Israel. Although the incidence is high, the fatality rates are low (Giger and Davidhizar, 1995).
- African Americans are less susceptible to varicosities than whites.
- African Americans have a higher incidence of hypertension than whites. The onset by age is earlier in African Americans, and the hypertension is more severe.
- The prevalence of hypertension tends to be low among persons of Asian descent, with the exception of Filipinos.

Client Teaching

- Explain risk factors for heart disease, including high dietary intake of saturated fat or cholesterol, lack of regular aerobic exercise, smoking, excess weight, stressful lifestyle, hypertension, and family history of heart disease.

- Refer client (if appropriate) to resources for controlling or reducing risks (e.g., nutritional counseling, exercise class, stress-reduction programs).
- Explain that research shows benefit from reducing dietary intake of cholesterol and saturated fats. The American Heart Association's dietary guidelines to reduce risk factors for coronary artery disease include maintenance of ideal body weight, reduction of dietary fats to 30% to 35% of total kilocalories and no more than 10% as saturated fats, an increase in carbohydrate to 50% to 55% of total kilocalories, use of protein in moderation with less animal protein, limitation of cholesterol to 300 mg or less, and limitation of sodium to 2 to 3 g/day (AHA, 1993).
- Encourage clients to have regular measurement of total blood cholesterol levels and triglycerides. Desirable levels are 150 to 200 mg/100 ml (Bullock and Rosendahl, 1988). More than one cholesterol measurement is needed to assess the blood cholesterol level accurately. Low-density lipoprotein (LDL) cholesterol is the major component of atherosclerotic plaque. An LDL cholesterol level of 160 mg/dl or higher is high risk.
- For clients with heart disease, explain the importance of compliance with the treatment program.
- Teach clients who take heart medication how to measure their own pulse.
- Male clients who have known angina may benefit from taking a daily low dose of aspirin. Consult physician before starting therapy.
- Inform clients of their blood pressure reading. Explain normal readings for the client's age and implications of any abnormalities.
- Instruct clients with risk or evidence of vascular insufficiency in the lower extremities to avoid tight clothing over the lower body or legs, avoid sitting or standing for long periods, avoid crossing legs, walk regularly, and elevate feet when sitting.
- Elderly clients with hypertension may benefit from regular monitoring of blood pressure (daily, weekly, or monthly). Home monitoring kits are available. Teach clients how to use them.
- Advise client with vascular disease to avoid tobacco products, because nicotine causes vasoconstriction.

Breasts

14

Anatomy and Physiology

The breasts are paired mammary glands located on the anterior chest wall. In female adult clients the breasts normally extend in an area from the second or third rib to the sixth or seventh rib and from the sternal margin to the midaxillary line. Each breast consists of glandular and fibrous tissue and subcutaneous and retromammary fat. The glandular tissue is arranged in lobes that radiate about the nipple of each breast. Layers of subcutaneous fibrous tissue provide the breasts with support. An extensive series of lymphatic vessels and channels drain lymph from the breast into the axillary, supraclavicular, and subclavicular nodes. In the axillae the mammary tissue is in direct contact with the axillary lymph nodes. The male breast consists of a small nipple and areola overlying a thin layer of breast tissue that is indistinguishable by palpation from surrounding tissue (Seidel et al., 1995).

Rationale

Breast cancer is the second leading cause of cancer deaths in women (American Cancer Society, 1996a). Early detection is the key to cure. The nurse plays a major role in the assessment of the breasts and the education of women about breast cancer and the need to screen for the presence of masses or irregularities in breast tissue. Because the breasts are associated with reproduction and a woman's sexuality, a high level of anxiety may be expressed by the client during an examination. Diseases of the breast also occur in men, and thus it is important to not overlook this portion of the examination in a male client.

Critical Thinking

Knowledge

Apply the knowledge you have regarding therapeutic communication techniques and human sexuality. The possibility of breast cancer raises considerable anxiety and fear for the female client. Understanding and support is critical for a successful examination.

Refer to knowledge you have regarding developmental changes in the female breast. This will affect your assessment findings.

Experience

It takes practice to be able to recognize changes in breast tissue. Premenopausal female clients frequently have fibrocystic breast disease, a benign condition that involves changes in the breasts such as cyst formation, adenosis, fibrosis, and fibroadenoma formation (Hockenberger, 1993). Use the client as a resource if she has performed breast self-examinations (BSEs) regularly.

Standards

During examination of the breast apply the following principles:

- Teach clients about breast self-examination as you conduct the examination.
- Be methodical as you examine each quadrant and tail of the breast.

Equipment

Small pillow or folded towel
Disposable gloves (only when open lesions are present)
Ruler
Hand mirror
Adequate lighting

Delegation Considerations

The examination of the breast requires problem solving and knowledge application unique to a professional nurse. Delegation of the examination is inappropriate. However, have unlicensed staff report to an RN if a client ever reports presence of a breast mass.

Breast Assessment

Client Preparation

- Initially the client may sit or stand with arms at side. Remove gown down to waist for simultaneous viewing of both breasts. Use a composed and respectful approach during the examination.
- Optionally, use a mirror to assist the woman in learning how to perform a self-examination.
- During palpation have client sit and then lie supine with small pillow placed under upper back.

History

- Determine if woman is over age 40, has a personal or family history of breast cancer, had early-onset menarche (before age 12) or late-age menopause (after age 50), has never had children or gave birth to first child after age 30, or has not breast-fed. All of these findings are risk factors for breast cancer (American Cancer Society, 1996a).
- Ask whether client (either sex) has noticed a lump, thickening, pain, or tenderness of breast; discharge, distortion, retraction, or scaling of nipple; or change in size of breast. Have the client point out any masses.
- If client reports a breast mass, ask about length of time since lump was first noted, whether lump comes and goes or is always present, and whether there have been changes in the lump (e.g., size, relationship to menses, other symptoms).
- Does the client have breast implants?
- Ask the female client whether she performs a monthly BSE. If so, determine time of month she performs it in relation to her menstrual cycle. Have client describe or demonstrate techniques used.
- Does client take oral contraceptives, digitalis, diuretics, steroids, estrogen, or foods high in caffeine? How long have medications been taken?
- Determine date of first day of last menstrual period.
- If client has experienced menopause, review onset, course, and associated problems.
- For pregnant woman determine history of breast sensations, use of supportive brassiere, and preparation procedures for breast-feeding. For a lactating woman determine use of nursing brassiere, nursing routine, use of breast pump, cleansing procedures for breasts, and history of discomfort or other problems involving the nipples.

Assessment	Normal Findings	Deviations From Normal
Make observations in relation to imaginary lines that divide the breast into four quadrants and a tail (Fig. 14-1).		
With client sitting and arms hanging loosely at the sides, inspect the size and symmetry of both breasts.	Breasts extend from the third to the sixth ribs, with the nipple at the level of the fourth intercostal space. One breast is often larger than the other.	Difference in size may be caused by inflammation or a mass.
Inspect the contour and shape of the breasts and note any masses, flattening, retraction, or dimpling.	Breasts vary in shape from convex to pendulous or conical.	Retraction or dimpling results from invasion of underlying ligaments by tumors. Edema may change breast contour.
To bring out retraction or changes in the shape of the breasts, have the client assume three positions:	No retraction present.	If retraction is present, maneuvers will accentuate the retraction.
Raise arms above the head.		
Press hands against the hips.		

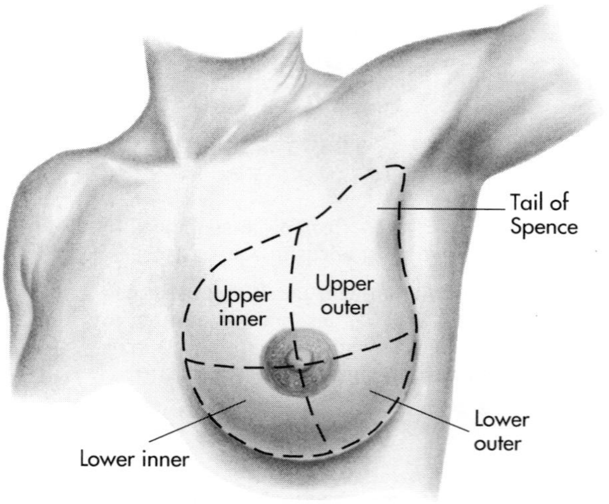

Fig. 14-1
Quadrants of the left breast.

Assessment	Normal Findings	Deviations From Normal
Extend arms straight ahead while sitting and leaning forward.		
Inspect overlying skin for color; texture; venous patterns; and presence of edema, lesions, or inflammation.	Breasts are smooth and the color of neighboring skin. Any venous patterns are the same bilaterally. Venous patterns are easily seen in thin clients or pregnant women.	Unequal contour when comparing both breasts may be caused by an underlying lesion. A peau d'orange appearance (dimpling of the skin that gives it the appearance of the skin of an orange) is caused by lymphedema and is a sign of advanced breast cancer. A unilateral venous pattern may be the result of increased blood flow to an underlying tumor.
In large clients, in particular, lift the breasts to observe the undersurface and lateral aspects for color or texture changes.	Redness and excoriation are caused by rubbing of skin surfaces.	

Assessment	Normal Findings	Deviations From Normal
Inspect nipple and areola for size, color, shape, discharge, and the direction nipples point.	Areolae are round or oval and nearly equal bilaterally. Color ranges from pink to brown. In light-skinned women the areola turns brown during pregnancy and remains dark. In dark-skinned women the areola is brown before pregnancy. Nipples are bilaterally equal or nearly equal in size and point in symmetric directions. They are everted and without drainage. Clear yellow discharge 2 days after childbirth is common.	Rashes or ulcerations are present. Bleeding or discharge from nipple may be the result of an underlying tumor. Peau d'orange may begin in the nipples. Retraction or deviation of the nipple is caused by inward pulling from inflammation or a malignancy.
If nipples are inverted, ask if there is lifetime history of inversion.	Recent inversion or retraction can indicate malignancy.	
Be aware of normal developmental changes in the breasts.	Puberty: Breast buds appear, nipples darken, areola diameter increases, and one breast may grow more rapidly.	

Young adulthood: Breasts reach full normal size, shape is usually symmetric, and one breast may be larger.

Pregnancy: Breasts enlarge to two or three times their normal size, nipples enlarge and may become erect, areolae darken, superficial veins in the breasts become prominent, and a yellowish fluid (colostrum) may be expelled from the nipples.

Menopause: Breasts shrink and tissue becomes softer, and sometimes it becomes flabby.

Palpate lymph nodes with client sitting.

Assessment	Normal Findings	Deviations From Normal
With a female client's arms at her sides, ask her to relax her muscles. Face the client, stand on the side being examined, and support her arm in a flexed position while abducting that same arm from the chest wall.		
Place your hand against the client's chest wall and high in the axillary hollow. With the fingertips, press gently down over the surface of the ribs and muscles. Know the location of axillary lymph nodes (Fig. 14-2). Gently roll soft tissue against the chest wall and muscles.		
Palpate the following areas:		
Edge of the pectoralis major muscle along the anterior axillary line		

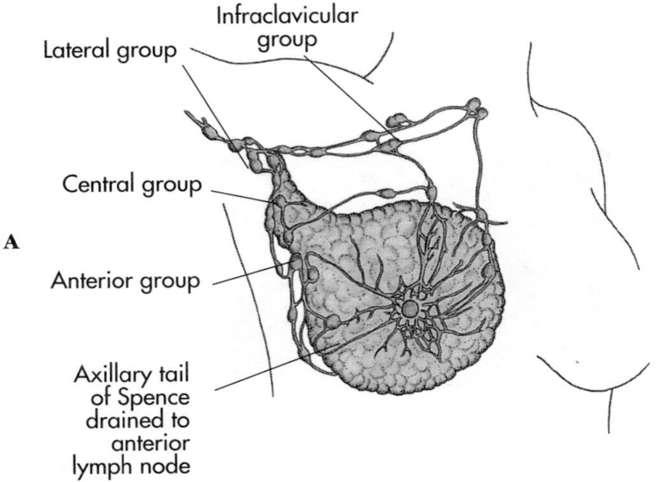

Fig. 14-2
A, Anatomic position of axillary and clavicular lymph nodes in female.

B

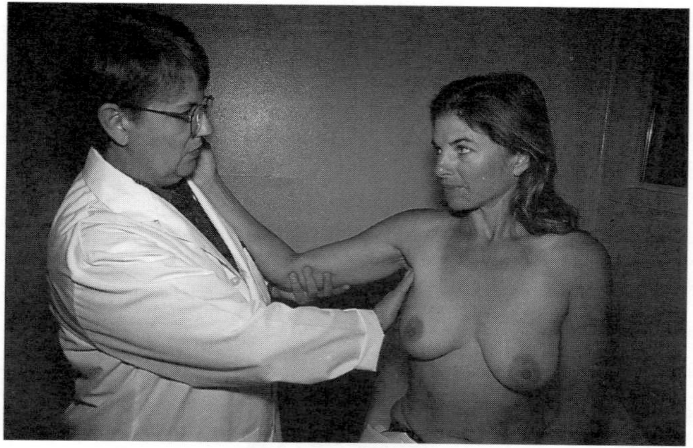

Fig. 14-2, cont'd
B, Position of client during palpation of axilla.

Assessment	Normal Findings	Deviations From Normal
Chest wall in the midaxilla		
Upper part of the humerus		
Anterior edge of the latissimus dorsi muscle along the posterior axillary line		
Upper and lower clavicular ridges (fingers hook over clavicle)	Lymph nodes are not palpable.	
If nodes are palpable, note number, location, consistency, mobility, size, and shape. If node is present, ask client if it is tender.	One or two small, soft, nontender nodes may be normal.	

Assessment	Normal Findings	Deviations From Normal

Palpate breast tissue with client supine and one arm behind the head (alternating with each breast). Have the client raise her hand and place it behind the neck. You may place a small pillow or towel under the shoulder blade to further position breast tissue. During this portion of examination review techniques for BSE carefully.

If client complains of a mass, begin with opposite breast for objective comparison.

Use the pads of the first three fingers to compress breast tissue gently against the chest wall, noting tissue consistency and presence of tenderness (Fig. 14-3). Perform palpation systematically, covering the entire breast and tail in one of two ways:

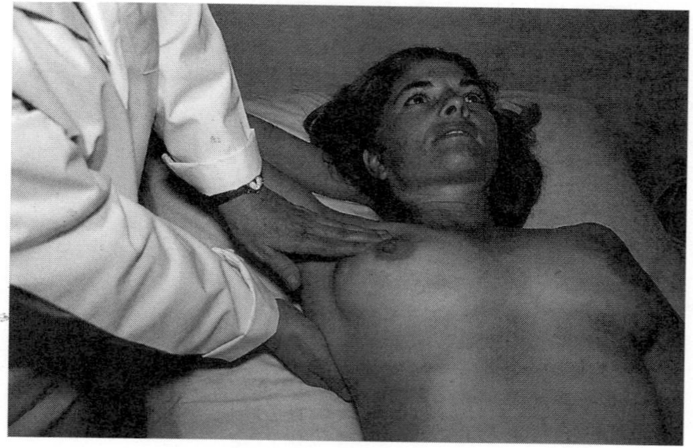

Fig. 14-3
Position of client and examiner for palpation of breast tissue against chest wall.

Clockwise or counterclockwise, forming small circles with the fingers along each quadrant and the tail

Back-and-forth technique with the fingers moving up and down across each quadrant

Breasts of a young client are dense, firm, and elastic. In an older client the tissue may feel stringy and nodular. The inframammary ridge at the lower edge of each breast may feel firm or hard but should not be confused with a tumor. The ridge may enlarge slightly during a menstrual period. During menstruation, there may be an increase in size, nodularity, and tenderness of the breasts.

A palpable, unilateral mass may suggest a malignancy.

Assessment	Normal Findings	Deviations From Normal
While palpating breasts, take the client's fingertips and move them gently over breast tissue to help her learn to feel normal variations of her own breast. Be sure she palpates the inframammary ridge, the lower edge of the breast that may feel firm and hard.		
After light palpation, repeat the examination with deeper palpation.		
Examine any masses further for the following:		
Quadrant location (e.g., upper outer, lower outer, tail)		
Diameter		
Shape (round, discoid, irregular)		
Consistency		
Tenderness		

Mobility

Discreteness (clear or unclear borders)

Fibrocystic masses are usually multiple, bilateral, round, soft (lumpy) to firm in consistency, mobile, and tender. They are well delineated.

A single palpable mass that is hard, nontender, irregular in shape, fixed, and poorly delineated suggests a malignancy.

Support large breasts with one hand and palpate breast tissue with the other against the supporting hand. Note consistency of tissues.

Gently palpate the entire surface of the nipple and areola. Gently compress the nipple and note any discharge. If discharge appears, observe its color and attempt to determine the origin by massaging radially around the areola while watching for discharge through the ducts.

During examination, the nipple may become erect and the areola wrinkled. No masses are present and no discharge should be produced.

Galactorrhea is lactation not associated with childbearing; it can be caused by drugs (e.g., estrogen, phenothiazines, tricyclic antidepressants).

Assessment	Normal Findings	Deviations From Normal
If client has had a mastectomy, palpate unaffected breast in usual manner. Palpate affected area, paying particular attention to the surgical scar. Palpate with two fingers, using small circular motion, for swelling, lumps, thickening, or tenderness.		
Male Breast Assessment		
Inspect breasts for size, symmetry, contour, skin color, texture, and venous patterns.	Enlarged male breast is caused by obesity, glandular enlargement, or chronic use of medication (e.g., digitalis).	
Inspect nipple and areola for color and presence of nodules, edema, and ulceration.		
Palpate breast for same characteristics as with female breasts. The examination can be done more quickly than for a female.	Thin layer of fatty tissue overlying muscle is normal. Obese men have a thicker fatty layer.	For males the same deviations may be present; the smaller amount of breast tissue in males presents lower risk of deviations.

Nursing Diagnoses

Assessment data may reveal defining characteristics for the following nursing diagnoses:

- Anxiety
- Knowledge deficit regarding self-examination of breast
- Impaired skin integrity
- Pain
- Body image disturbance
- Altered sexuality pattern

Pediatric Considerations

- Breasts of infants of both sexes are often enlarged for a brief time after birth.
- The right and left breasts of adolescent females may not develop at the same rate.
- Male adolescents may experience temporary unilateral or bilateral subareolar masses during puberty. These are normal.

Gerontologic Considerations

- Chronic cystic disease diminishes after menopause.
- Adipose tissue increases, glandular tissue atrophies, suspensory ligaments relax, and breasts appear elongated or pendulous.
- Nipples become smaller and flatter.
- Gynecomastia (enlargement of the breast) in men after age 50 is usually unilateral. Causes include testicular or pituitary tumors, cirrhosis, estrogen therapy, and steroidal therapy (Lueckenotte, 1994).

Cultural Considerations

- White women are more likely to develop breast cancer than African-American women (Kosary et al., 1995).
- African-American women are more likely to die of breast cancer than white women. This is likely because of later detection in African Americans and a more aggressive form of tumor (American Cancer Society, 1996a).
- Recently, Japanese Americans have experienced an increased incidence of breast cancer, which may be diet and lifestyle related (Giger and Davidhizar, 1995).

Client Teaching

- All women 20 years of age and older should perform this self-examination monthly (see Appendix J). Always perform examinations around the last day of the menstrual period or the same day each month if the client has reached menopause.

- The American Cancer Society's recommendations (1996a) for breast cancer detection in asymptomatic women include the following:
  - Age 20 to 39: Monthly BSE; clinical breast examination every 3 years
  - Age 40 to 49: Monthly BSE; annual clinical breast examination; mammography every 1 to 2 years; baseline mammogram by age 40
  - Over age 50: Monthly BSE; annual clinical breast examination; annual mammography
- Some controversy exists among physicians regarding the efficacy of routine mammograms.
- Women with a family history of breast cancer should be examined annually by a physician and have an annual mammography.
- Discuss signs and symptoms of breast cancer.

Abdomen

15

Anatomy and Physiology

The abdominal cavity contains vital organs of numerous body systems. The peritoneum, a serous membrane, lines the cavity and protects many of the abdominal structures. The mesentery is a fold of peritoneum that covers most of the small intestine and anchors it to the posterior abdominal wall.

The stomach lies transversely in the upper left abdominal cavity under the costal margin. It is a hollow organ that digests and stores food before passing it through the intestines. The small intestine is 21 feet long and coils through the abdominal cavity, from the pyloric orifice of the stomach to the ileocecal valve at the large intestine. The first 12 inches (30 cm) of the small intestine, the duodenum, forms a C-shaped curve around the head of the pancreas. The pancreatic and common bile duct enter into the duodenum. The next 8 feet of intestine is the jejunum, which joins with the terminal section of the small intestine, the ileum. The small intestine completes digestion through the absorption of water and nutrients and secretion of substances to promote digestion and passage of contents.

The large intestine begins at the cecum, a 2- to 3-inch long pouch, in the lower right abdominal quadrant. The appendix extends from the base of the cecum. The ascending colon rises from the cecum along the right posterior abdominal wall to the undersurface of the liver. Once the colon turns toward the midline, it becomes the transverse colon. The transverse colon crosses the abdominal cavity toward the spleen and turns downward into the descending colon. This final segment of the large intestine travels along the left abdominal wall to the rim of the pelvis, where it turns into the S-shaped sigmoid colon. The rectum extends from the sigmoid to the muscles of the pelvic floor continuing as the anal canal and anus. The large intestine absorbs water, secretes mucus, and eliminates wastes as they course throughout the abdominal cavity.

The kidneys are located deep in the retroperitoneal space in both upper quadrants of the abdomen. Each kidney extends from the T12 to L3 vertebrae. The right kidney is usually lower than the left. These organs selectively filter, reabsorb, and secrete water and electrolytes delivered by means of the circulatory system to maintain fluid and electrolyte balance and eliminate wastes.

The bladder is a hollow, distensible organ that collects and eliminates urine formed by the kidneys. Normally it lies below the symphysis pubis, but once it becomes distended it can become palpable just above the pubic bone.

The liver, one of the most important organs of the body, is located in the right upper quadrant just below the diaphragm. The liver's inferior surface touches the gallbladder, stomach, duodenum, and hepatic curve of the large intestine. The hepatic artery transports blood directly to the liver from the aorta, and the portal vein carries blood from the digestive tract and spleen to the liver. The liver's functions include the formation of serum protein; production of bile; metabolism of fat, carbohydrate, and protein; detoxification of foreign substances; storage of vitamins and iron; production of antibodies; production of blood coagulation factors; and metabolism of bilirubin.

The gallbladder is a saclike organ about 4 inches (10 cm) long that is recessed in the inferior surface of the liver. It concentrates and stores bile from the liver for the eventual emulsification of fats entering the small intestine. Contraction of the gallbladder moves bile through the common bile duct into the duodenum.

The pancreas lies behind and beneath the stomach, with its head along the curve of the duodenum and its tip almost touching the spleen. The organ is both an exocrine gland that secretes digestive enzymes and an endocrine gland that secretes insulin.

The spleen is in the left upper quadrant, lying above the left kidney and just below the diaphragm. The organ consists of lymphoid tissue and functions to filter blood and to manufacture lymphocytes and monocytes. In addition, the spleen contains a capillary and venous network that stores and releases blood.

There are also a number of reproductive organs located within the abdominal cavity. In the female, the vagina and uterus lie in the pelvic cavity between the bladder and rectum. The ovaries and fallopian tubes are located along the lateral pelvic wall at the level of the anterosuperior iliac spine. In the male, the spermatic cords, seminal vesicles, and prostate gland lie along the posterior wall and base of the bladder.

Muscles form and protect the abdominal cavity. In addition, tissues and bones outside the abdominal cavity (e.g., the spine) protect vital organs. These structures may be responsible when clients complain of abdominal pain.

The abdominal aorta passes from the diaphragm through the abdominal cavity, just left of the midline. At the level of the umbilicus it branches into the two common iliac arteries.

Rationale

The abdominal examination primarily includes an assessment of structures of the lower gastrointestinal (GI) tract in addition to the liver, stomach, kidneys, and bladder. Abdominal pain is one of the most common symptoms clients will report when seeking medical care (Table 15-1). An accurate assessment requires a matching of data from the client's history with a careful assessment of the location of physical symptoms. Disturbances in a person's bowel elimination pattern can often be detected during an abdominal assessment. Because many factors influence bowel function (e.g., dietary changes, medications, stress, surgery), the nurse can use assessment findings in caring for a variety of health problems. The nurse's assessment of the abdomen determines the presence or absence of masses, tenderness, organ enlargement, and peristaltic activity.

Assessment of the abdomen involves examination of organs and tissues anteriorly and posteriorly (Fig. 15-1). When assessing the abdomen, the nurse uses a system of landmarks to map out the abdominal region. The abdomen is divided into four equal quadrants, with the xiphoid process (tip of sternum) marking the upper boundary and the symphysis pubis

Table 15-1 Assessing abdominal pain

Abdominal pain can be assessed in a variety of ways to determine its significance:

- Clients may warn you to not touch a specific area; however, they may not have pain if their faces seem relaxed and unconcerned. When you touch they might recoil, but their expression remains unconcerned.
- Clients with an organic cause for abdominal pain are usually not hungry.
- Ask the client to point to the location of the pain. If the finger goes to a fixed point (other than the navel), there is a likelihood that it has physical significance. If the finger goes to the navel and the client seems well, you should consider psychogenic causes.

Common Conditions Producing Abdominal Pain	Pain Characteristics
Appendicitis	Initially periumbilical or epigastric; colicky; later becomes localized to RLQ
Cholecystitis	Severe, unrelenting RUQ or epigastric pain; may be referred to right subscapular area
Pancreatitis	Dramatic, sudden, excruciating LUQ, epigastric or umbilical pain; may be present in one or both flanks; may be referred to left shoulder
Perforated gastric or duodenal ulcer	Abrupt RUQ; may be referred to shoulders
Intestinal obstruction	Abrupt, severe, spasmodic; referred to epigastrium, umbilicus
Leaking abdominal aneurysm	Steady throbbing midline over aneurysm; aneurysm may radiate to back, flank
Ectopic pregnancy	Lower quadrant; referred to shoulder; with rupture is agonizing
Pelvic inflammatory disease	Lower quadrant; increases with activity
Renal stones	Intense; flank, extending to groin and genitals; may be episodic

Modified from Seidel HM et al: *Mosby's guide to physical examination*, ed 3, St Louis, 1995, Mosby.

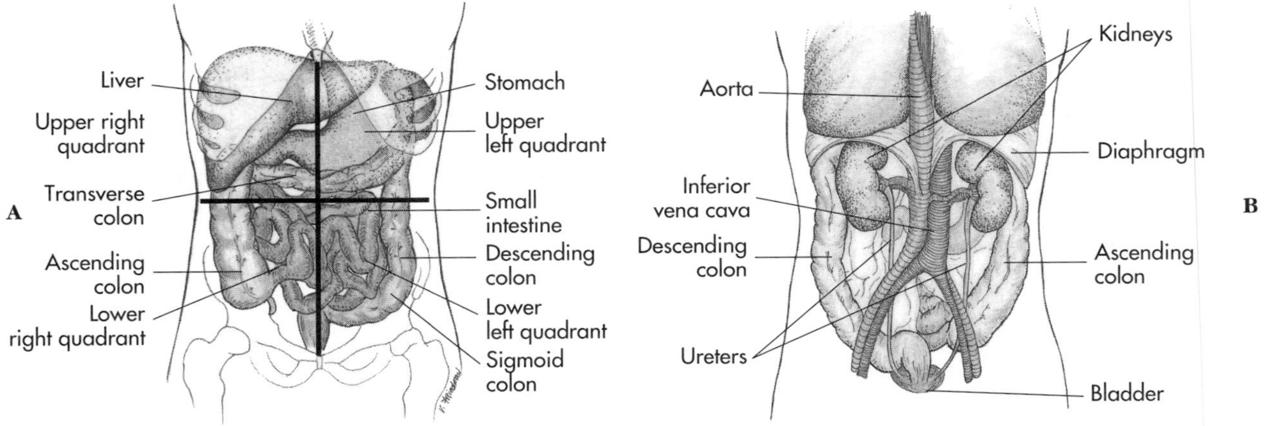

Fig. 15-1
Anterior **(A)** and posterior **(B)** views of the abdomen.

delineating the lowermost boundary. Two imaginary lines cross at the umbilicus to form the quadrants. Assessment findings are recorded in relation to these four quadrants. For example, pain may be noted in the lower left quadrant (LLQ).

Critical Thinking

Knowledge

Apply your knowledge of the physiology of the organs comprising the abdominal cavity. This will improve your ability to anticipate assessment findings and make accurate diagnostic conclusions.

Experience

It will be more difficult to detect abnormalities in those clients who are obese. If you are uncertain about any findings, have a more experienced practitioner confirm your assessment.

Standards

As you examine the abdomen apply the following principles:

- Be sure client is comfortable and has an empty bladder.
- Auscultation should be performed before palpation and percussion. Manipulation of the abdominal organs can change the character of bowel sounds.
- Be methodical in localizing findings according to the abdominal quadrants.

Equipment

Stethoscope
Adequate lighting
Small ruler
Tape measure
Marking pencil
Small pillow

Delegation Considerations

The abdominal examination requires problem solving and knowledge application unique to a professional nurse. Delegation of the skill is inappropriate. However, unlicensed assistive personnel can learn to detect changes in abdominal distention and pain and should know to report these changes to an RN. Changes in bowel habits might also first be noticed by assistive personnel and should be reported.

Abdominal Assessment

Client Preparation

- The room should be warm, and the client's upper chest and legs should be draped.
- Expose the abdomen from just above the xiphoid process down to the symphysis pubis.
- Make sure lighting is good.
- The client lies supine with arms down at the side and knees slightly bent. Small pillows can be placed under the knees for support and relaxation of abdominal muscles (McConnell, 1990).
- A small pillow may also be placed under the head to relax the abdominal muscles.
- Keep your hands and the stethoscope warm to help the client relax.

History

- If the client has abdominal or low back pain, assess the character of pain in detail (type, quality, location, severity, onset, frequency, aggravating factors, precipitating factors, and course).
- Ask about the client's normal bowel habits and stool character. Ask whether the client uses laxatives or cathartics frequently.
- Ask whether the client has had abdominal surgery, trauma, or GI diagnostic tests.
- Ask whether the client has had a recent weight change or intolerance to diet (e.g., nausea, vomiting, cramping), especially in last 24 hours.
- Assess for belching, difficulty in swallowing, flatulence, bloody emesis (hematemesis), black or tarry stools (melena), heartburn, diarrhea, or constipation.
- Inquire about family history of cancer, kidney disease, alcoholism, hypertension, or heart disease.
- Determine if female client is pregnant; note last menstrual period.
- Assess client's usual intake of alcohol.
- Ask whether the client takes antiinflammatory medication (e.g., aspirin, ibuprofen, steroids) or antibiotics that may cause GI upset or bleeding.
- Review client's history for the following risk factors for hepatitis B virus (HBV) exposure: health care occupation, hemodialysis, intravenous drug user, household or sexual contact with HBV carrier, heterosexual person with more than

one sex partner in previous 6 months, sexually active homosexual or bisexual male, international traveler in area of high HBV infection rate (Reece, 1993).

Assessment Techniques

Assessment	Normal Findings	Deviations From Normal
Inspection		
Throughout the examination observe the client's movement and positioning.		Lying still with knees drawn up, moving restlessly to find a comfortable position, splinting the abdomen, and lying on one side or sitting with knees drawn to chest are behaviors indicative of abdominal pain.
Ask client to locate any tender areas, and assess these areas last to minimize discomfort and anxiety.		
Stand at client's right side and inspect from above the abdomen to detect abnormal shadows and movement.	Helps to focus the examination if abnormalities appear.	

Sit down and inspect the abdomen from a lower position to observe the skin over abdomen for color, scars, venous patterns, and stretch marks (striae).

Skin is the same color as the rest of body but may be more pale if not exposed to the sun. Venous patterns are normally faint except in thin clients. Striae (stretch marks) usually result from stretching of tissue by obesity or pregnancy. New stretch marks are pink or blue in color and turn silvery white over time.

Generalized color changes such as jaundice or cyanosis can be seen across the abdomen. Striae can be caused by ascites. Engorged, prominent veins can be caused by cirrhosis or abdominal malignancy. Artificial opening may indicate an ostomy or drainage site resulting from surgery. Scars indicate past trauma or surgery. Bruising may indicate accidental injury, physical abuse, or a type of bleeding disorder.

! ***Nurse Alert*** *If a scar is from surgery, consider extent to which normal anatomy has been altered.*

If a series of bruises is noted, ask if client self-administers injections (e.g., insulin, heparin).

Assessment	Normal Findings	Deviations From Normal
To check prominent abdominal veins, compress a section of vein with two fingers next to each other; remove one finger and observe for filling. Repeat procedure, removing other finger.	Blood fills from above to lower abdomen.	Blood fills from lower to upper abdomen, indicating obstruction of inferior vena cava.
Continue inspection and look for evidence of lesions.	Normal skin changes are present (see Chapter 6).	Transient skin rash is common for hepatitis. Generalized rash (often pruritic) with red, macular, and papular lesions that develop usually abruptly is likely caused by a drug reaction (Lewis et al., 1996). Nodules may indicate intraabdominal lymphoma (Seidel et al., 1995).
Note the position, shape, color, and presence of inflammation, discharge, or protruding masses from the umbilicus.	Normal umbilicus is flat or concave hemisphere, midway between xiphoid process and symphysis pubis. Color is the same as surrounding skin. No discharge is present.	A bluish discoloration around the umbilicus (Cullen's sign) can indicate intraabdominal bleeding. Underlying masses can cause protruding of umbilicus (clarify if client has known umbilical hernia). An everted, pouched-out umbilicus can indicate distention.

Inspect for contour, symmetry, and surface motion of the abdomen, noting any masses or bulging. After viewing from the seated position, move to a standing position behind the client's head to look at contralateral areas of the abdomen.

A flat abdomen forms a horizontal plane from the xiphoid process to the symphysis pubis. A round abdomen is evenly convex, with maximum height at umbilicus. A concave or scaphoid abdomen seems to sink into the muscular wall. The concave abdomen is common in thin adults.

Presence of a mass or asymmetry may indicate an underlying pathology.

Inspect for distention. If the abdomen appears distended, ask the client to roll onto the side and inspect for bulging flank; ask client whether abdomen feels unusually tight.

Generalized symmetric distention, resulting in the entire abdomen protruding, can be caused by a heavy meal, obesity, or gas. Gas does not cause bulging of the flanks. Do not confuse distention with obesity, which is marked by rolls of adipose tissue along the flanks and client denial of tightness.

Distention from ascites causes flanks to bulge; when client rolls onto side, a protuberance forms on the dependent side.

Assessment	Normal Findings	Deviations From Normal
If abdominal distention is expected, measure abdomen's girth by placing a tape measure around abdomen at umbilicus. Use a marking pencil to indicate where the tape measure was applied.	Consecutive measurements show no change or decrease in girth.	Consecutive measurements show increase in girth.
While observing contour, ask client to take a deep breath and hold it.	Contour remains smooth and symmetric.	Enlarged organs in the upper abdominal area (e.g., liver, spleen) may descend below the rib cage to cause a bulge.
Ask client to raise head (not shoulders).	Abdominal musculature remains flat.	Superficial wall masses, hernias, and muscle separations will become apparent during this maneuver.
Inspect abdomen for normal respiratory movement.	Males breathe more abdominally than costally. Females breathe more costally. Smooth, even movement occurs with respiration.	Tightening of abdominal muscles during breathing with reduced ventilatory excursion may indicate guarding from abdominal pain.

Note presence of peristaltic movement or aortic pulsation by looking across the abdomen from the side.

Peristaltic movement may be visible in thin clients; otherwise no movement is present. Aortic pulsations occur with each beat of systole and appear in the midline above the umbilicus.

Pronounced peristaltic wave is abnormal; may indicate an obstruction. Marked pulsation of aorta may indicate increased pressure or aneurysm.

Auscultation

! ***Nurse Alert*** *If the client has a nasogastric tube to intermittent suction, turn the suction off momentarily before auscultation.*

Place the warmed diaphragm of the stethoscope first over the LLQ. Apply very light pressure. Ask the client not to speak. It may take 5 minutes of continuous listening before the examiner determines bowel sounds are absent.

Assessment	Normal Findings	Deviations From Normal
Listen for bowel sounds and note their frequency and character.	Bowel sounds are high-pitched, soft gurgling or clicking sounds that occur irregularly 5 to 35 times per minute (Seidel et al., 1995). It normally takes 5 to 20 seconds to hear a bowel sound. Each lasts about ½ second to several seconds.	Absent sounds indicate a cessation of GI motility that may be a result of bowel obstruction, paralytic ileus, or peritonitis. Hyperactive sounds are loud and growling, indicating increased GI motility from conditions such as inflammation, anxiety, diarrhea, bleeding, and excess ingestion of laxatives or certain foods.
Continue to listen for bowel sounds in all four quadrants.		
Record the client's bowel sounds as normal or audible, absent, hyperactive, or hypoactive.		
Using the stethoscope's bell, auscultate for bruits in the epigastric region and each of the four quadrants over the aortic, renal, iliac, and	Normally there are no vascular sounds over the aortic, renal, iliac, or femoral arteries.	Presence of a bruit indicates an aneurysm or narrowing of vessel. ***Nurse Alert*** *If bruits are heard, do not palpate the abdomen. Injury to an underly*

femoral arteries (Fig. 15-2) and the thoracic aorta.

ing aneurysm may result. Notify a physician immediately.

Use the diaphragm of the stethoscope to auscultate over the liver and spleen for friction rubs.

Normally no rubs are heard.

A rub is a high-pitched rubbing sound that usually occurs on inspiration. Rubs indicate inflammation of serous tissue.

Percussion

Percuss systematically over all four quadrants and note areas of tympany and dullness. Percuss potentially painful areas last.

Hollow organs such as the stomach, intestine, bladder, and aorta are tympanic. A dull, medium- to high-pitched short sound can be heard over the liver, spleen, pancreas, kidneys, and a distended bladder.

A dull note over an area not occupied by an organ can indicate a tumor.

Use percussion to locate borders of underlying organs.

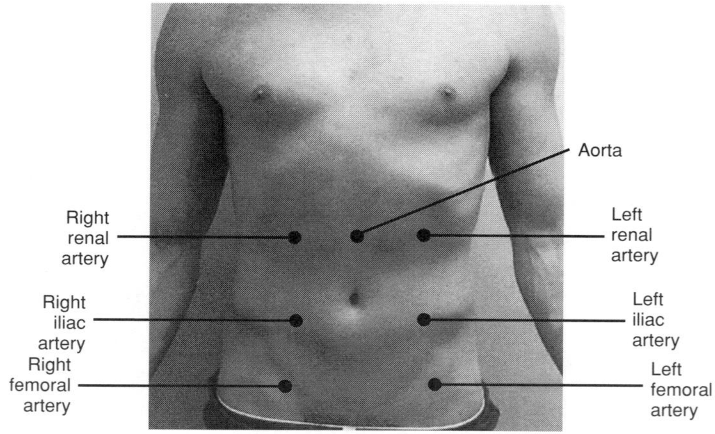

Fig. 15-2
Sites to auscultate for abdominal bruits.
(From Seidel HM et al: *Mosby's guide to physical examination,* ed 3, St Louis, 1995, Mosby.)

Assessment	Normal Findings	Deviations From Normal
Stand on client's right side and begin to percuss at the right iliac crest across from the umbilicus and percuss upward along the right midclavicular line. Note when the percussion note changes from tympanic to dull. Mark liver border with marking pen.	Note changes from tympanic to dull once you percuss the liver's lower border (Fig. 15-3). Usually the border is at the right costal margin or slightly below it.	A lower border can indicate organ enlargement or downward displacement of the organ by the diaphragm.
Percuss the upper border by percussing down from the clavicle along the intercostal spaces at the midclavicular line. Note if sound changes from resonant to dull. Measure distance from upper to lower border.	The liver's upper border is usually at the fifth, sixth, or seventh intercostal space. The distance between the upper and lower liver borders should be 6 to 12 cm (2½ to 5 inches). Liver span is usually greater in males and tall individuals than in females and short persons (Seidel et al., 1991).	Diseases such as cirrhosis, cancer, and hepatitis cause liver enlargement.

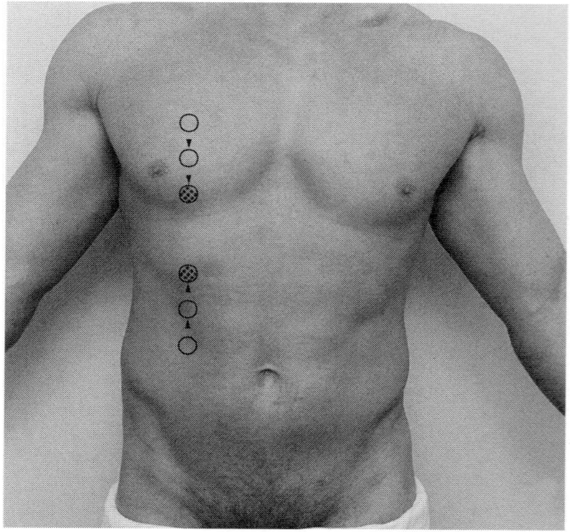

Fig. 15-3
Liver percussion route.
(From Seidel HM et al: *Mosby's guide to physical examination,* ed 3, St Louis, 1995, Mosby.)

Assessment	Normal Findings	Deviations From Normal
With the client sitting or standing, use direct or indirect percussion to assess for kidney inflammation. Use the ulnar surface of the partially closed fist and directly percuss posteriorly over the costovertebral angle at the scapular line.	Nontender.	Inflamed kidney causes tenderness during percussion.
Percuss over the lower left anterior rib cage and left epigastric region.	The stomach's air bubble is tympanic and lower in pitch than tympany of the intestine.	
Palpation		
Palpate the abdomen lightly over each of the four quadrants. Initially avoid areas previously identified as problem spots.		

Assessment	Normal Findings	Deviations From Normal
Lay palm of hand lightly on abdomen, with fingers extended and approximated. Keep the palm and forearm horizontal. Placing the client's hand lightly over the examiner's hand can reduce tickling sensations. With the pads of the fingertips depress lightly ½ inch (1 cm) in a gentle dipping motion.		
Palpate to detect areas of muscular resistance, tenderness, abnormal distention, or superficial masses. During palpation observe client's face for any signs of discomfort.	Abdomen is normally smooth with consistent softness and nontender without masses. A distended bladder may be felt just below the umbilicus and above the symphysis pubis.	Tightening or guarding by the client can occur with peritonitis, cholecystitis, and perforated ulcer. Tumors are palpable, especially in thin clients.
If you feel resistance, determine if it is voluntary or involuntary. Place a pillow under the client's knees and have the client breathe slowly through the mouth. Feel for relaxation of the abdominal muscles.	Muscles relax on expiration.	Tenseness remains, likely because of an involuntary response to rigidity. Rigidity develops from peritoneal irritation.

Avoid quick jabs during palpation. Complete light palpation over those areas reported tender by the client.

! ***Nurse Alert*** *Note that if the hands are cold, if the client is ticklish, or if you palpate too deeply the client may tense or guard the abdomen.*

Use deep palpation to delineate abdominal organs and to detect less obvious masses. Be sure the fingernails are short. Depress the hands 1 to 3 inches (2.5 to 7.5 cm) into the abdomen. Never use deep palpation over tender organs, areas of bruits, or a surgical incision. Move the fingers back and forth over the abdominal contents.

Deep pressure may cause tenderness in the healthy client over the cecum, sigmoid colon, aorta, and midline near the xiphoid process (Seidel et al., 1995). No masses are felt.

Note the characteristics of any deep mass, including size, location, shape, consistency, tenderness, pulsation, and mobility.

A deep mass can be a cyst or cancerous tumor.

Assessment	Normal Findings	Deviations From Normal
If tenderness is found, test for rebound tenderness: press the hand slowly and deeply into the involved area and then release quickly.	No increase in pain.	Pain elicited with release of the hand is a positive rebound test. Can occur in clients with peritoneal inflammation or injury causing bile, blood, or enzymes to enter the peritoneal cavity.
Have the client lift the head from the examining table, causing contraction of abdominal muscles.	Masses in the abdominal wall will continue to be palpable.	
Palpate around the umbilicus and umbilical ring.	Area is free from bulges, nodules, and granulation.	
Palpate the liver's lower edge as follows:		
Stand at the client's right side.		
Place your left hand under the client's right posterior thorax at the eleventh and twelfth ribs. Apply upward pressure (Fig. 15-4).		

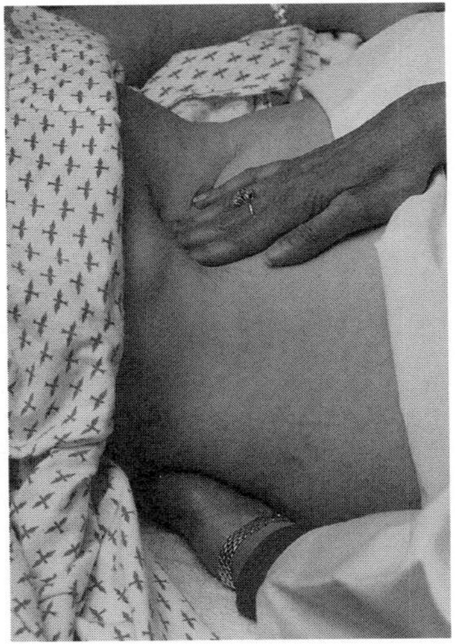

Fig. 15-4
Liver palpation.

Assessment	Normal Findings	Deviations From Normal
With the fingers of the right hand pointing toward the right costal margin, place your hand on the RUQ well below the liver's lower border.		
Press gently in and up with the right hand, while asking the client to inhale deeply. Try to feel the liver's edge as it descends.	The liver is usually difficult to palpate in a normal adult. If palpable, the liver is firm, nontender, and smooth and has a regular contour with a sharp edge.	Liver is palpable; enlargement can be caused by hepatitis, cirrhosis, and cancer. In hepatitis the liver enlarges. In cirrhosis the liver has a firm, nontender border. However, over time the liver becomes less palpable. In carcinoma the liver becomes hard with nodules and an irregular border. It can be tender or nontender.
Palpate below the liver margin at the lateral border of the rectus muscle.	Normal gallbladder is not palpable.	Gallbladder is palpable and tender, indicating cholecystitis.
If gallbladder disease is suspected, ask client to take a deep breath during palpation.		Client will experience pain and quickly stop inspiration (Murphy's sign) as the inflamed gallbladder contacts your examining fingers.

While standing on client's right side, reach across with your left hand and place it beneath client and over the left costovertebral angle. Press upward with left hand.

Place palm of right hand with fingers extended on client's abdomen below the left costal margin. Press fingertips inward toward spleen while asking client to take a deep breath. Palpate edge of the spleen as it moves downward toward your fingers.

A normal spleen is not palpable.

Spleen is enlarged and may be the result of portal hypertension or hemolytic anemia.

! ***Nurse Alert*** *Never vigorously palpate an enlarged spleen, because excessive manipulation can cause it to rupture.*

To palpate for aortic pulsation, use the thumb and forefinger of one hand. Palpate slowly but deeply into the upper abdomen just left of the midline.

A normal aortic pulsation is palpable.

An aortic aneurysm causes pulsation to expand laterally.

Assessment	Normal Findings	Deviations From Normal
To assess for an ascitic fluid wave, ask the client or colleague for assistance. This procedure requires three hands (Seidel et al., 1995): Have client lie supine. Have client or another nurse press the edge of the hand and forearm firmly along the vertical midline of the abdomen. Place your hands on each side of the abdomen and strike one side sharply with your fingertips. Feel for the impulse of a fluid wave with the fingertips of your other hand.		With ascites, a fluid wave is easily palpated.

Nursing Diagnoses

Assessment data may reveal defining characteristics for the following nursing diagnoses:

- Constipation
- Colonic constipation
- Diarrhea
- Pain
- Altered nutrition: less or more than body requirements
- Knowledge deficit regarding risks for colon cancer, use of laxatives, and/or diet management

Pediatric Considerations

- Distraction is important to help children relax when assessing them. Involve the child's parents. It might be helpful to do an abdominal examination first, especially if there is risk of the child becoming agitated.
- A child may confuse the pressure of palpation with pain. Children are also often ticklish.
- The abdomen of an infant or child should be rounded and dome shaped. Abdominal and chest movements are synchronous.
- Pulsations in the epigastric area are common in infants and children.
- Distended veins across the abdomen may indicate abdominal or vascular obstruction or abdominal distention.
- An umbilical hernia, which forms a visible and palpable bulge, is common in infants. A hernia will evert during coughing or sneezing.
- The umbilical stump should be dry and odorless.
- Visible peristaltic waves warrant careful evaluation and can indicate intestinal obstruction.
- Bowel sounds are present within 1 to 2 hours of an infant's birth.
- An infant's abdomen may be more tympanic than an adult's, because the infant swallows air during feeding and crying.
- Organs palpable in children include the bladder, cecum, and sigmoid colon.
- Abdominal pain may be revealed by change in the pitch of crying, facial grimacing, and drawing the knees to the abdomen with palpation.
- Up until the age of 4 or 5 a young child's abdomen takes on a potbellied appearance.
- Consider pregnancy in a young adolescent with a mass in the lower abdomen.

Pregnancy Considerations

- Bowel sounds are diminished as a result of reduced peristalsis.

- Complaints of nausea and vomiting are common during the first trimester.
- Constipation is common.
- Assessment includes measurement of fundal height. Have the client empty her bladder. Then assist the client to lie supine with knees slightly bent and head elevated. With a nonstretchable tape measure, measure from the notch of pubis symphysis over the top of the fundus, without tipping the tape back. Measure in centimeters.

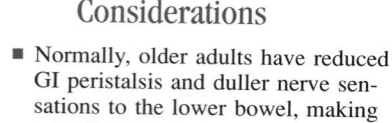

Gerontologic Considerations

- Normally, older adults have reduced GI peristalsis and duller nerve sensations to the lower bowel, making constipation a common problem (Lueckenotte, 1994).
- The abdominal wall is thinner and less firm. Underlying organs are more easily palpated.
- The abdominal contour is often rounded as a result of loss of muscle tone.
- Pain perception is altered; thus older adults may have atypical symptoms such as less severe response to conditions that are typically very painful.

Cultural Considerations

- Native Americans have a high incidence of gallbladder disease (Seidel et al., 1995).
- The number of cancer deaths per 100,000 population caused by colon and rectal cancer is highest in the Czech Republic, Hungary, New Zealand, Singapore, Denmark, and Austria (American Cancer Society, 1996b).
- The highest death rate per 100,000 population for stomach cancer occurs in Costa Rica, with the Russian Federation second.
- Cancer of the stomach, esophagus, and liver occurs more frequently among Japanese Americans than in whites (Giger and Davidhizar, 1995). This may be related to eating dry, salted fish.

Client Teaching

- Explain factors such as diet, regular exercise, limited use of over-the-counter drugs causing constipation, establishment of regular elimination schedule, and a good fluid intake to promote normal bowel elimination.

- Caution the client about the dangers of excessive use of laxatives or enemas.
- If the client has chronic pain, explain measures for pain relief.
- If the client has acute pain, explain activities or positions to avoid.
- If the client is a health care worker or has contact with blood or body fluids of persons infected with hepatitis, encourage the client to receive the series of three vaccine doses.

16 Female and Male Genitalia

Female Genitalia

Assessment of the female genitalia consists of examination of external genitalia and speculum examination of internal genitalia, described separately in the following sections. Speculum examinations are typically performed only by nurse practitioners, midwives, and physicians. However, it is important for a nurse to understand the procedure because a primary care provider will need the nurse's assistance.

Anatomy and Physiology

The female genitalia consist of external and internal sex organs. The external sex organs, referred to collectively as the *vulva,* include the mons veneris, labia majora, labia minora, clitoris, and vaginal opening (Fig. 16-1). The internal sex organs include the vagina, uterus, fallopian tubes, and ovaries.

The mons veneris is a layer of fatty tissue that covers the pubic bone and is covered by pubic hair in the postpubescent female. The two labia majora are fatty folds of skin whose outer surfaces are covered with pubic hair and whose inner surfaces are smooth and hairless. The labia majora extend down from the mons veneris and form the outer boundaries of the vulva. The labia have sensory receptors that are sensitive to touch, pressure, pain, and temperature. The two labia minora, which are just inside the labia majora, are thin folds of pigmented skin that

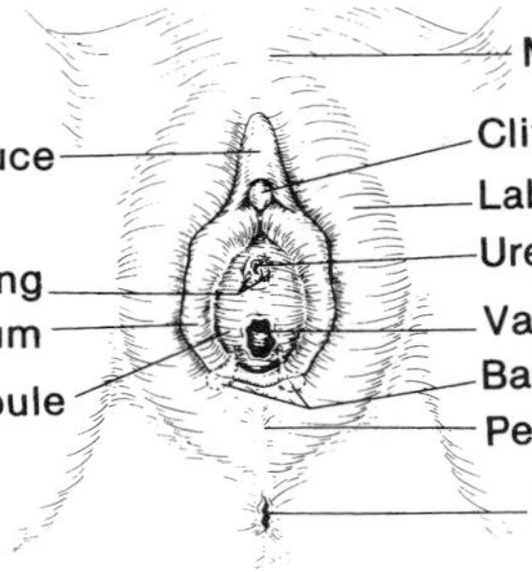

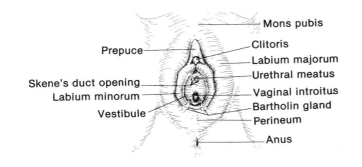

Fig. 16-1
External female genitalia.
(From Bowers AC, Thompson JM: *Clinical manual of health assessment,* ed 4, St Louis, 1992, Mosby.)

extend upward to form the clitoral hood. These inner folds possess many blood vessels and have many sensory nerve endings.

When the clitoral hood is pulled back, the glans of the clitoris is revealed. It looks like a smooth, shiny pea. The clitoris has many nerve endings and is very sensitive to touch, pressure, and temperature.

The vaginal opening, or introitus, is between the urethra and the anus. The hymen is a membranous fold of tissue that partially covers the introitus. It has no known function. It usually remains intact until the first intercourse.

Bartholin's glands are two small ducts that open on the inner surface of the labia minora next to the vaginal opening. The glands secrete a small amount of lubricating fluid.

The vagina is a thin-walled, muscular organ that tilts upward at a 45-degree angle toward the small of the back. The walls of the vagina consist of a thin outer serosa; a middle layer of smooth, involuntary muscle that is continuous with the muscle of the uterus; and an inner layer of moist mucous membrane called *mucosa*. The vagina serves as a passageway for menstrual flow and childbirth.

The uterus is a thick-walled muscular organ located between the urinary bladder and rectum. It is about 3 inches (7.5 cm) long and looks like a small upside-down pear. The fallopian tubes enter the uterus on either side near the top. The wide upper part of the uterus is known as the body. The bottom part, called the cervix, protrudes into the vagina. The inner lining of the cervix contains many glands that secrete varying amounts of mucus that plug the opening to the uterus.

The two fallopian tubes begin at the uterus and end in long fingerlike fimbriae near the ovaries. The chief function of the fallopian tubes is a conduit for the passage of both egg and sperm for fertilization.

The two walnut-size ovaries, one on each side of the uterus, have two functions. They produce eggs that are released into the fallopian tubes, and they secrete female hormones and small amounts of androgen directly into the bloodstream.

Rationale

Examination of the female genitalia should be a part of all preventive health care examinations because of the high incidence of uterine and vaginal cancer. Deaths from uterine (cervix) cancer have declined over the last several decades because of regular checkups and use of the Papanicolaou (Pap) test (American Cancer Society, 1996b). Ovarian cancer still accounts for 4% of all cancers among women and causes more deaths than any other cancer of the female reproductive tract because of its silent nature (American Cancer Society, 1996b). Women should have regular examinations to screen for cancer and sexually transmitted diseases (STDs). The average age of menarche among young girls has declined, and the majority of male and female teenagers are sexually active by age 19 (Wong, 1995).

The speculum examination is performed to assess the internal genitalia for cancerous lesions and other abnormalities and to collect specimens for a Pap smear to test for cervical and vaginal cancer. Women who are, or have been, sexually active or who have reached age 18 years should have annual Pap smears until three or more tests are negative. Thereafter the Pap test may be performed less frequently at the physician's discretion (American Cancer Society, 1996b). Women age 40 and over should have an annual pelvic examination by a health professional. Women at high risk of developing endometrial cancer should have an endometrial tissue sample evaluated at menopause. Pap smear tests are highly effective in detecting uterine cancer early. The test is less effective in detecting endometrial cancer and only rarely uncovers ovarian cancer.

Critical Thinking

Knowledge

Consider the knowledge you have regarding communication techniques, human sexuality, and cultural diversity. The examination of genitalia is intrusive. The client expects you to perform professionally and efficiently. The procedure is embarrassing and can be a source of great anxiety for the client.

Consider the knowledge you have regarding genitourinary function. Signs and symptoms identified during the gynecologic examination may reflect problems involving the urinary system.

Experience

Use your experience in determining a convenient time for conducting examination of the external genitalia. That portion of the examination can be performed during hygiene care, toileting, and during care of an indwelling urinary catheter.

Standards

During the examination of the female genitalia apply the following principles:

- Always use a relaxed approach, keeping the client as comfortable as possible.
- Have a second nurse or care provider present during the speculum examination to assure the client that you will be performing the examination in an ethical manner. Legally, this protects you against any unfounded complaints regarding sexual harassment or abuse.
- Adolescents may prefer to have parents in attendance during the examination. Give them a choice.
- If you suspect sexual abuse, interview and examine the client in private. This will make her more comfortable to report any problems. Presence of a spouse or sexual partner will usually discourage honest reporting.
- A health care provider has a legal obligation to maintain a client's confidentiality (e.g., in the case of an STD) unless required by law to report those who pose a risk to the health or life of innocent parties.

Equipment

Examination table with stirrups
Vaginal speculum of correct size
Adjustable lamp
Sink
Water-soluble lubricant
Clean disposable gloves
Glass microscope slides
Sponge forceps or swabs
Plastic spatulas and/or cytobrush
Specimen bottle with fixative spray

Delegation Considerations

The examination of the genitalia requires problem solving and knowledge application unique to a professional nurse. It is inappropriate to delegate the examination to unlicensed assistive personnel. However, unlicensed personnel will perform perineal hygiene and care for indwelling catheters. Be sure staff know to report problems (e.g., unusual discharge; client complaint of genital tenderness or pain; presence of lesions, masses, or bleeding). Be sure unlicensed staff avoid any attempt to manipulate or inspect the client's genitalia other than that required for hygiene.

Female Genitalia Assessment

Client Preparation

- Have the client empty her bladder before the examination so that a urine specimen may be obtained.
- Because the client may be embarrassed by the lithotomy position, use a calm, reassuring, and attentive approach; position and drape the client carefully, explain each part of the examination in advance, and avoid any delays or interruptions during assessment.
- Maintain eye contact with the client, both before and during the examination as much as possible. Ask if this is the client's first pelvic examination.
- Assist the client to the lithotomy position, in bed or on the examining table for an external genitalia assessment only.
- Assist client into the stirrups if the speculum examination is to be performed. Have the woman stabilize each foot in a stirrup and then have her slide the buttocks down to the edge of the examining table. Place your hand at the edge of the table, and instruct her to move down until touching your hand.
- If the client has pain or deformity of the joints, paralysis, spasticity, or muscle weakness, an alternative position may be necessary to perform the examination. One option is to have only one leg abducted, or the

client can assume a side-lying position on the left side with her right thigh and knee drawn up to her chest. Offer a pillow for the client's head. Drape the client so that one corner of the drape covers the perineal area until the examination begins. Other options include a diamond-shaped position (woman lies on back with knees bent so that both legs are spread flat and the heels meet at the foot of the table; speculum is inserted with handle up), M-shaped position (woman lies on back, knees bent and apart, feet resting on the examination table close to the buttocks; speculum is inserted handle up), or the V-shaped position (woman lies on back with straightened legs spread out to either side of table; speculum is inserted handle up) (Seidel et al., 1995).

History

- If client arrives at the emergency room with emotional or physical manifestations of shock, hysteria, crying, anger, reduced level of consciousness, reported pain in the genital area, and signs of physical trauma, expect rape. This requires immediate medical management. Gather a history of the assault (who, what, where, when, why) and follow agency protocol to ensure a complete medical and legal review (Lewis et al., 1996).
- Has the client had previous illness (e.g., STD) or surgery involving reproductive organs?
- Review menstrual history, including age at menarche, frequency and duration of menstrual cycle, character of flow (e.g., amount, number of pads or tampons used in 24 hours, presence of clots), presence of dysmenorrhea (painful menstruation), pelvic pain, date of last menstrual period (first day of last cycle), and premenstrual symptoms (headaches, weight gain, edema, mood changes, relief measures).
- Ask the client to describe obstetric history, including each pregnancy, history of abortions, and any miscarriages.
- Determine whether client uses safe sex practices. Have the client describe current and past contraceptive practices and problems encountered. Discuss risks of STDs and human immunodeficiency virus (HIV) infection.
- Determine if client has signs and symptoms indicating STD: vaginal discharge, painful or swollen perianal tissues, genital lesions, rectal discharge, dysuria, urinary fre-

quency, lymphadenopathy, malaise, headache, arthralgia.

- Ask if client has had signs of bleeding or pain outside of normal menstrual period or after menopause or has had unusual vaginal discharge (signs of cervical cancer and endometrial cancer).
- Assess if client is between ages of 40 and 50 and has history of condyloma acuminatum infection, herpes simplex, or cervical dysplasia; has multiple sex partners; smokes; has had multiple pregnancies; or was young at first intercourse (risk factors for cervical cancer).
- Assess if client is between ages of 40 and 60 and has history of ovarian dysfunction, cancer of the breast or endometrium, irradiation of pelvic organs, endometriosis, family history of ovarian or breast cancer, or history of infertility or nulliparity (risk factors for ovarian cancer).
- Assess if client is postmenopausal, obese, or infertile; had early menarche (before age 12); had late menopause (after age 50); has history of hypertension, diabetes, or liver disease; or has family history of endometrial, breast, or colon cancer (risk factors for endometrial cancer).
- Does the client have symptoms of genitourinary problems such as dysuria, frequency, urgency, nocturia, hematuria, incontinence, or stress incontinence?
- Assess client's attitudes or feelings about sexual partners and sexual lifestyle.
- For pregnant women, determine expected date of delivery or weeks of gestation, involuntary passage of fluid, presence of bleeding, and associated symptoms.
- Consider factors in general survey that rule out risks for sexual abuse (see Chapter 5).

Assessment	Normal Findings	Deviations From Normal
External Genitalia Adjust light so that the perineal area is well illuminated. *Standard Precautions Alert Glove both hands.* Sit at the end of the examination table or bed. Do not touch the perineal area without warning the client. Touch one thigh first and advance to the perineum.		

Assessment	Normal Findings	Deviations From Normal
Inspect quantity and distribution of hair growth; look for presence of lice or nits.	Preadolescent has no pubic hair except for fine body hair. During adolescence hair grows along the labia, becoming darker, coarser, and curlier as it spreads over the pubic symphysis. In an adult, hair grows in a triangle over the perineum and along the medial surfaces of the thighs. Hair is free of lice or nits.	Unusual growth or distribution of hair can indicate hormonal problems. See Chapter 6 for description of lice.
Inspect the surface characteristics of the labia majora.	The perineal skin is smooth, clean, and slightly darker than other skin. The labia majora may be gaping or closed and appear dry or moist. They are usually symmetric. After menopause, the labia majora become thinner. After childbirth, the labia majora are separated and the labia minora are more prominent.	Unusual change in skin color or pigmentation is one sign of sexual abuse. White, chalky, malodorous discharge within labial folds can indicate poor hygiene habits.

Explain that the next phase of the examination is to inspect deeper perineal structures.

With nondominant hand, gently place thumb and index finger inside labia minora and retract tissues outward. Be sure to maintain a firm hold during retraction.

Inspect characteristics of labia minora and mucous membranes between labia majora and minora. Note any inflammation, edema, lesions, or lacerations.

Mucous membranes appear dark pink and moist. The labia minora are normally thinner than the labia majora, and one side may be larger. Inner surface should be moist and dark pink. In virgins, the labia minora lie together. After childbirth or intercourse, the labia tend to gape or fall to the side.

Scarring in genital area can indicate sexual abuse. Vesicular lesions, moist ulcerations, and crusting of erosions are progressive signs of herpes simplex virus, type 2. The perineal area can also be inflamed. Discrete single or multiple papillary growths that are white to gray appearing on the vulva are manifestations of condylomata acuminata (Lewis et al., 1996).

Use other hand to palpate the labia minora between your thumb and second finger.

Tissue should feel soft without tenderness.

Assessment	Normal Findings	Deviations From Normal
Inspect the clitoris for size, shape, and color. Look for inflammation, irritation, or discharge in tissue folds.	The size of the clitoris is variable, but the clitoris normally does not exceed 2 cm in length and 0.5 cm in diameter.	Enlargement of the clitoris may indicate a masculinizing condition (Seidel et al., 1995). An inflamed clitoris appears bright cherry red. The clitoris is a common site for syphilitic lesions, which appear as small open ulcers that drain serous material.
Observe urethral orifice carefully for color and position; note any discharge, polyps, or fistulas.	Urethral orifice is normally intact without inflammation. The urethral meatus is anterior to the vaginal orifice and is pink. It often appears as an irregular slit or opening in the midline.	Inflammation and reported irritation are signs of repeated urinary tract infections or insertion of foreign objects. Dysuria, hematuria, enuresis, and frequent urinary tract infections are signs and symptoms of sexual abuse.
If inflammation is suspected, check for urethral discharge by placing index finger inside vaginal orifice and gently milking the urethra from inside outward.	Urethral discharge is a sign of STD.	

Standard Precautions Alert *If urethral drainage is present, change to a clean pair of gloves afterwards.*

Note the condition of the hymen.

In virgins the hymen may restrict the opening of the vagina. Only remnants of the hymen remain after sexual intercourse.

Inspect appearance of vaginal introitus; look for inflammation, edema, discoloration, discharge, fistulas, and lesions.

Vaginal introitus is usually a thin vertical slit or a large orifice. Tissue is moist. In women who have had several vaginal childbirths, the opening often extends upward, interfering with the view of the urethra.

Discoloration of tissues with vaginal odor and pain can indicate sexual abuse. Vulvar trauma with erythema and extension of injury to anal area are signs of rape. Foul-smelling discharge can be symptomatic of vaginal infection. *Candida,* a common yeast infection, causes white, curdlike discharge with mild to severe itching and erythema of the labia. *Trichomonas vaginalis* causes a copious, frothy, gray/green discharge and foul odor, with severe itching with or without erythema of the vulva.

Assessment	Normal Findings	Deviations From Normal
With the labia still retracted, examine Skene's and Bartholin's glands. Inform client you are going to insert one finger in her vagina and that she will feel pressure.		
With the palm facing upward, insert index finger of examining hand into vagina as far as second joint. Exert upward pressure, milking Skene's glands by moving the finger outward. Look for discharge and note any tenderness. Repeat on other side. Note the color, odor, and consistency of any discharge present.	Normally, no discharge or tenderness is present.	Discharge appears, indicating infection. **!** ***Nurse Alert*** *Protocol may require collection of urethral discharge for a culture analysis.*
If inflammation and edema are found near the posterior end of the introitus, suspect infection of Bartholin's glands. Palpate the glands one side at a time with thumb and index finger between labia majora and introi-	Bartholin's glands normally cannot be palpated.	Painful swelling, hot to touch, indicates abscess of the gland. A nontender mass suggests a Bartholin cyst (Seidel et al., 1995).

tus. Note swelling, tenderness, masses, or discharge.

Standard Precautions Alert *If drainage is present, change gloves.*

With a gloved index and middle finger in the vaginal orifice, ask the client to strain downward as if voiding. This maneuver checks for muscular support.

Some nulliparous women can squeeze fairly tightly; multiparous women less so. During straining there should be no bulging of tissue through the vaginal orifice.

Vaginal walls bulge, blocking the introitus. A portion of the vaginal wall and bladder may prolapse or fall into the orifice anteriorly; this is a cystocele. Bulging of the posterior wall may be caused by prolapse of the rectum (rectocele).

Nurse Alert *Any expected prolapse should be reported to a physician immediately.*

Then ask the client to bear down while watching for urinary incontinence.

No incontinence noted.

Inspection and palpation of the perineum and anal area (see Chapter 17) may be done at this time.

Surface is smooth. Tissue will feel thick and smooth in nulliparous women and thinner and rigid in multiparous women.

Assessment	Normal Findings	Deviations From Normal
If rectal examination is to be included, proceed with this assessment at this time (see Chapter 17).		
Speculum Examination		
Be sure client is comfortable in stirrups or in lithotomy position.		
Select the proper size speculum (a small speculum will fit women less sexually active, a medium size is best for sexually active women, and a large size works well for women who have delivered children vaginally).		
Warm the speculum by placing it under running water, if you plan to obtain a cytology specimen. Otherwise, water-soluble lubricant can be used. Lubricant can interfere with Pap smear studies.		

Standard Precautions Alert Apply a pair of disposable gloves.

Sit on a stool facing the client's perineum. Adjust light source over your shoulder to the examination site. Explain to the client what you are doing during the examination. Have the client breathe slowly to relax.

Insert speculum:

Hold the speculum in your dominant hand.

If the client has never had a speculum examination, first insert two fingers of nondominant hand gently just inside the vaginal introitus. Look for any abnormalities.

Then with the same two fingers, press down on the perineal body just inside the introitus.

Assessment	Normal Findings	Deviations From Normal

After checking to be sure that the speculum blades are closed, introduce the closed speculum obliquely (rotated 50 degrees counterclockwise from the vertical position) past the fingers (Fig. 16-2, *A*). Client may feel some discomfort as vaginal opening is stretched.

The speculum is inserted downward at a 45-degree angle toward the examination table to avoid trauma to the urethra (this maneuver corresponds with the normal downward slope of the vaginal canal). Do not pull pubic hair or pinch the labia.

A

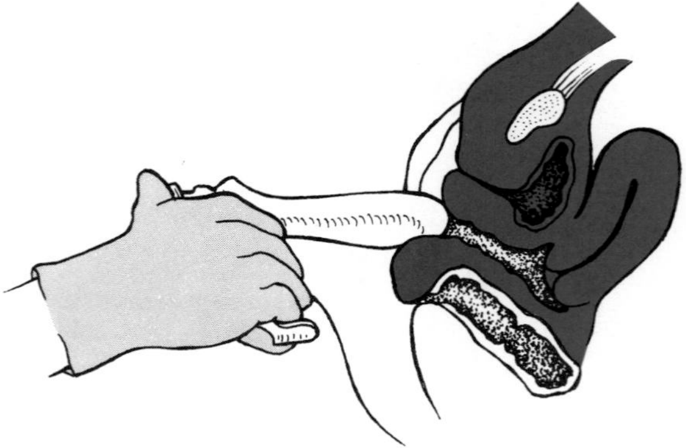

Fig. 16-2
Speculum insertion.

After the wide portions of the blades have passed the introitus, remove your fingers and rotate the speculum so that the blades are horizontal (Fig. 16-2, *B*).

Insert the speculum the length of the vaginal canal.

Open the blades slowly after full insertion and the speculum is moved to visualize the cervix (Fig. 16-2, *C*).

When the cervix is in full view, the blades are locked in the open position by pressing on the thumbpiece or tightening the thumbscrew.

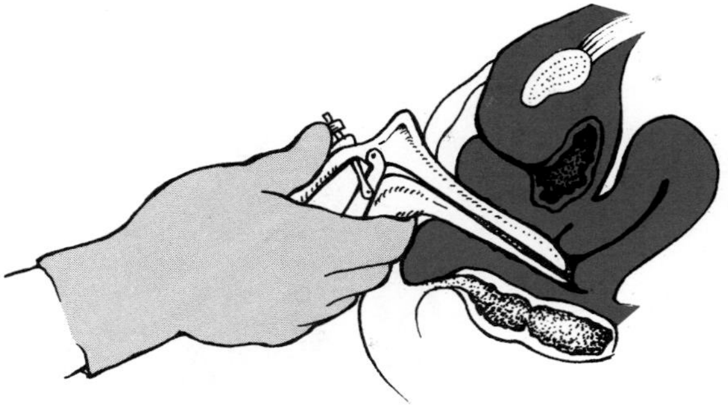

Fig. 16-2, cont'd
For legend see p. 368.

Continued

C

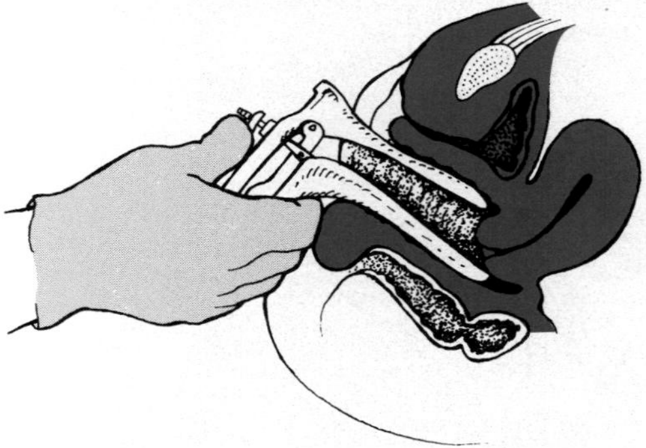

Fig. 16-2, cont'd
For legend see p. 368.

Assessment	Normal Findings	Deviations From Normal
Inspect the cervix for color, appearance of the os or opening, size, surface characteristics, discharge, and symmetry.	Cervix is glistening pink, smooth, and round. Diameter is about 1 inch (2.5 to 3 cm) in a young woman and smaller in an older adult. Cervix is midline without lesions. The cervix becomes bluish during pregnancy.	A pale cervix indicates anemia. An enlarged cervix may indicate an infection. Presence of friable tissue, red patchy areas, granular areas, and white patches can indicate inflammation, infection (e.g., STD), or carcinoma (Seidel et al., 1995).
If discharge is present, note the color, odor, amount, and consistency.		
Describe any irregularities or lesions as being in a 12 o'clock position, 6 o'clock position, and so forth around the cervix.	The os is usually small and closed in women who have not had children or larger and slightly curved after childbirth. In multiparous women the cervical os may have gaps.	

Assessment	Normal Findings	Deviations From Normal
Pay careful attention to the position of the cervix. Is it horizontal?	Cervix in the horizontal position indicates a uterus in mid position.	A cervix pointing anteriorly indicates a retroverted uterus. One pointing posteriorly indicates an anteverted uterus. A pelvic mass, pregnancy, or adhesions can cause deviation to the right or left.
Collect Pap smear specimens from two sites (Table 16-1): ectocervix (outer cervix) and endocervix. Be sure spatula and cytobrush are rotated completely around the cervix.		
With both specimens, apply cells and secretions to glass microscope slides, apply fixative solution, and label with the client's name and the specimen source. Send to laboratory as soon as possible.	Normal results on the Pap smear are negative.	See Appendix L for classification of cytologic findings of Pap tests.

Table 16-1 Methods for obtaining pap smears

Location		Technique
Outer cervix (ectocervix)	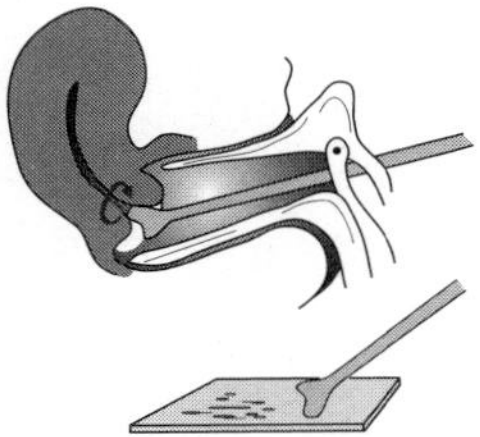	Use plastic spatula. Place tip of longer arm in os. Rotate spatula 360 degrees, scraping outer surface of cervix. Apply cells to glass slide. Apply fixative solution and label slide.
Endocervix	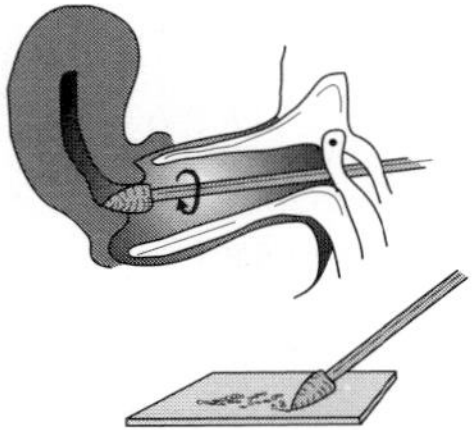	Use cervical brush (cytobrush). WARNING: Do *not* use on pregnant clients. Gently insert brush through os. Rotate brush 180 to 360 degrees. Apply cells by rolling and twisting brush on glass slide. Apply fixative solution and label slide.

Assessment	Normal Findings	Deviations From Normal
Inspect the vaginal walls while withdrawing the speculum with the set screw loose but the blades held open. Rotate it slowly during withdrawal. Inspect the vaginal wall's color, surface characteristics, and secretions.	Vaginal walls are normally pink throughout and free from discharge and lesions. Surface is moist, smooth, or rugated. Secretions are thin, clear or cloudy, and odorless.	White, yellow, gray, or greenish discharge indicates infection. Bleeding may occur in a variety of conditions (e.g., midcycle spotting, delayed menstruation with excessive bleeding, frequent bleeding, intermenstrual or irregular bleeding, postmenopausal bleeding). These conditions may be caused by ovulatory alterations, polyps, intrauterine devices, contraceptive use, and uterine or cervical cancer (Thompson et al., 1993).
As the speculum is withdrawn, the blades tend to close themselves. Avoid pinching the mucosa and maintain downward pressure to avoid trauma to the urethra. Deposit speculum in proper container, and wash hands.		
Proceed to rectal examination (see Chapter 17), or complete this assess-		

ment by cleansing the perineum and anal area to remove any moisture or drainage.

More advanced practitioners will proceed to a bimanual examination and rectovaginal examination.

Nursing Diagnoses

Assessment data may reveal defining characteristics for the following nursing diagnoses:

- Stress or urge incontinence
- Altered urinary elimination
- Sexual dysfunction
- Knowledge deficit regarding birth control methods, effects of menopause, risks for STD, and/or the need for pelvic examinations
- Pain
- Anxiety
- Risk for infection
- Rape-trauma syndrome

Pediatric Considerations

- To examine the genitalia of the newborn, hold infant's legs in a frog position. Labia majora completely cover the clitoris and labia minora at full term.
- Any swelling of the labia majora and minora usually disappears in a few weeks.
- Newborns may have a mucoid whitish vaginal discharge up to 4 weeks after birth. This is caused by passive hormonal transfer from mother to infant (Seidel et al., 1995).
- With children and presexual female adolescents, assessment is of the external genitalia only. To examine the external genitalia of a young child, position child in parent's lap or on examination table in frog position, knees flexed and drawn up.
- A speculum examination is performed only when the child is experiencing bleeding, discharge, trauma, or suspected sexual abuse.
- Sources of perineal irritation in children include bubble baths, soaps, detergents, and urinary tract infec-

tion. A foul odor may be the result of a foreign body.
- Swelling of vulvar tissue should alert the examiner to sexual abuse. Further evidence includes scarring of genital, anal, and perianal areas; unusual changes in skin color; anorectal itching, bleeding, or pain; and genitourinary problems such as rash or sores, vaginal odor, bleeding, and discharge (Seidel et al., 1995).

Pregnancy Considerations

- Examination follows the same procedure as for nonpregnant adult women.
- The cervix gradually becomes soft, and the vulva acquires a bluish color from increased vascularity. Vaginal secretions also increase. The fundus flexes easily on the cervix.
- Estimation of the bony pelvis size is made.

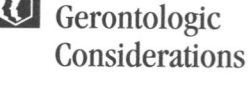

Gerontologic Considerations

- Older women may need more time to assume the lithotomy position and assistance to hold the legs in place.
- Labia become atrophied with advancing age, thus appearing flatter and smaller.
- Pubic hair is gray and sparse.
- Cervix is smaller and paler.
- Vaginal epithelium is thinner, drier, and less vascular, and the cervix and uterus become smaller.
- Dry, scaly, nodular lesions may be malignant changes.

Cultural Considerations

- Female Mexican Americans have a strong social value that women do not expose their bodies to men or even other women. During a pelvic examination a female Mexican-American client may express "feeling hot" because of embarrassment (Giger and Davidhizar, 1995).
- Chinese Americans may view the examination of genitalia as being offensive (Giger and Davidhizar, 1995). The nurse must provide thorough explanations regarding the reason for the procedures used in the examination.
- Until the early 1900s traditional practitioners were not allowed to touch the bodies of Vietnamese female clients except to take their pulse. Figurines were used for the female client to indicate where she

was having problems. Today, many Vietnamese persons still place an emphasis on virginity at the time of marriage and continue to have strong feelings about unmarried young women having pelvic examinations (Giger and Davidhizar, 1995).

- Japanese Americans place a high value on the family system. Family name and honor are important. Be cognizant of the issue of confidentiality and respect. Information should not be shared even with extended family members who appear close to a client (Giger and Davidhizar, 1995).
- Russian Americans generally accept health examination of the genitalia without argument if adequate information and justification are provided and permission has been requested (Giger and Davidhizar, 1995).

Client Teaching

- Instruct the client about purpose and recommended frequency of Pap smears and gynecologic examinations.
- Counsel client with STD about diagnosis and treatment.
- Instruct client on how to perform genital self-examination (GSE):
  - Use a mirror, and position self to see the area covered by the pubic hair.
  - Spread pubic hair apart, looking for bumps, sores, or blisters.
  - Look for any warts, which may appear as small, bumpy spots and then enlarge to fleshy, cauliflower-like lesions.
  - Spread outer vaginal lips apart and look at the clitoris for bumps, blisters, sores, or warts.
  - Look at both sides of the inner vaginal lips.
  - Finally, look at the area around the urinary and vaginal opening for bumps, blisters, sores, or warts.
- Explain warning signs of STD: pain or burning on urination, pain in pelvic area, bleeding between menstruation, an itchy rash around vagina, and vaginal discharge (different from usual).
- Teach ways to prevent STD: preventive measures (e.g., male partner's use of condoms, restricting number of sexual partners, avoiding sex with persons who have several other partners, perineal hygiene measures).
- Explain risk factors for cervical, endometrial, and ovarian cancer (see history section).
- Tell clients with STDs that they

must inform sexual partners of the need for an examination.

- Reinforce the importance of perineal hygiene.
- Explore with clients alternate sources of sexual satisfaction.
- Discuss optional forms of birth control.

Male Genitalia

Examination of the male genitalia includes assessing the integrity of the external genitalia and inguinal ring and canal.

Anatomy and Physiology

The external male genitalia are the penis and scrotum. The male internal sex organs include the testicles, which produce hormones and sperm; the epididymis and vas deferens, a system of ducts that transport sperm; and the prostate gland, seminal vesicles, and Cowper's glands, whose secretions become part of the ejaculated semen (Fig. 16-3).

The penis consists of the shaft, which is composed primarily of erectile tissue, and the glans, which has both erectile and sensory tissue. The penile shaft comprises three parallel tubes: two corpora cavernosa, which lie side by side, and beneath them a single corpus spongiosum, which surrounds the urethra.

The anterior end of the corpus spongiosum fits over the corpora cavernosa and is called the *glans*. The glans resembles an acorn. The area where the glans arises abruptly from the shaft is called the *corona,* meaning crown. If the male is uncircumcised, the skin of the shaft continues forward and forms a loose-fitting hood over the glans. This hood is called the *foreskin* or *prepuce*. On the undersurface the glans is attached to the prepuce by a thin fold of skin called the *frenulum*.

The scrotum is a thin, loose sac of skin that protects the two testicles. It is located at the base of the penis. The scrotum is divided into two compartments, each containing a testis, epididymis, and part of the vas deferens. The testis, epididymis, and parts of the vas deferens that are in the scrotum are considered internal organs even though they are outside the body cavity.

The left testicle usually hangs lower than the right testicle. The testicles have two main functions: to produce sperm and to produce hormones. The sperm drain into the epididymis, a duct that lies just outside the testicle. The vas deferens is a long tube from each testicle that goes up and out of the scrotum. It curves

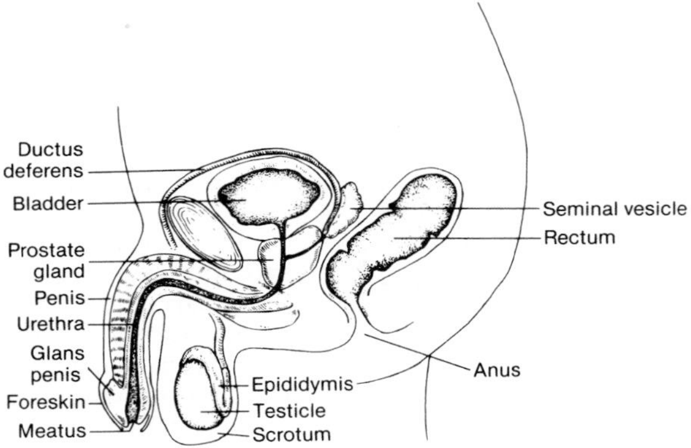

Fig. 16-3
Male sex organs.

around the urinary bladder and then turns downward and opens into an enlargement 4 inches (10 cm) long called the *ampulla*. The ampulla is a reservoir for the sperm before they are discharged into the ejaculatory duct, which carries them through the prostate into the posterior urethra. The urethra goes from the bladder to the penis tip and carries urine or semen.

The prostate is about the size of a chestnut and surrounds the urethra at the bladder neck. It produces the major volume of ejaculatory fluid. The ejaculatory ducts and a portion of the urethra pass through it.

Rationale

Because of the high incidence of STD in adolescents and young adults, the genitalia should be assessed routinely during health promotion examinations. In addition, although testicular tumors make up about 0.7% of all forms of cancer in men, it is important for men to know how to perform testicular self-examinations.

Critical Thinking

Knowledge

Refer to the knowledge you have regarding communication techniques, human sexuality, and cultural diversity. As is the case with the female genitalia examination, the male examination can cause the male client considerable embarrassment. The client will expect you to perform professionally and efficiently.

Refer to the knowledge you have regarding normal genitourinary function.

Experience

Use your experience to find a convenient time during hygienic care or catheter care to perform the male genitalia examination.

Standards

Refer to the female genitalia examination standards for the proper approach to use in making the client feel comfortable, having a second care provider in attendance (preferably a male), and maintaining the confidentiality of examination findings.

Equipment

Disposable gloves
Cotton swab applicator
Tongue blade

Delegation Considerations

The examination of the male genitalia requires problem solving and knowledge application unique to a professional nurse. However, unlicensed assistive personnel will provide routine hygiene and catheter care to clients. It is important for staff to know to observe for unusual discharge, color change, presence of lesions, and the client's report of genital pain. Any changes should be reported to an RN. Instruct staff not to manipulate the genitalia more than is required for routine hygiene.

Male Genitalia Assessment

Client Preparation

- Ask client whether he needs to empty his bladder.
- Make sure the room is warm.
- Have the client lie supine with the chest, abdomen, and lower legs draped. The client may also stand during the examination.
- Because the client may feel anxious during the examination, particularly

with a female nurse, help him relax, and explain each step of the examination. Have a second nurse in attendance to assure the client that you, as the examiner, will perform in an ethical manner. Legally, this protects you against any unfounded complaints regarding sexual harassment or abuse. Examine the genitalia carefully and completely but also briskly. Often adolescents and men are fearful of having an erection during the examination.

History

- Assess normal urinary elimination pattern: frequency of voiding; history of nocturia; character and volume of urine; daily fluid intake; symptoms of burning, urgency, and frequency; difficulty starting stream; and hematuria.
- Assess client's sexual history and use of safe sex habits (e.g., use of condoms, number of sexual partners). Are there concerns about sexual partner or sexual lifestyle?
- Does client have difficulty achieving erection or ejaculation?
- Determine whether the client has had previous surgery or illness involving urinary or reproductive organs, including STD.
- Has client noted penile pain or swelling, lesions of genitalia, or urethral discharge (signs and symptoms of STD)?
- Has client noted heaviness or painless enlargement of testis or irregular lumps (signs and symptoms of testicular cancer)?
- Review medications that might influence sexual performance: diuretics, sedatives, antihypertensive agents, tranquilizers.
- Assess client's knowledge of testicular self-examination. Does the client conduct a self-examination routinely?

Assessment Techniques

Assessment	Normal Findings	Deviations From Normal
Standard Precautions Alert Apply disposable gloves. Assess the sexual maturity of the client; note character and distribution of pubic hair, size of penis, and size and condition of scrotal tissues.	First sign of puberty, an increase in genital and pubic hair development, is variable but usually starts around 9 to 10 years of age. During preadolescence there is no pubic hair except for fine body hair. By puberty, pubic hair extends from the base of the penis over the symphysis pubis and becomes coarse and curly. There is no hair covering the penis. The penis slowly lengthens, reaching to at least the bottom of the scrotum. The scrotal skin becomes wrinkled and darker than surrounding skin.	Slow development of sexual maturity may indicate hormonal imbalance.
Inspect the skin covering the genitalia for lice, rashes, excoriations, or lesions.	Skin is clear, without lesions.	*Pediculus pubis* is a form of lice that may attach eggs to pubic hair. Spread by sexual contact, the infesta-

tion results in the lice biting, which causes intense itching. Scratching may cause secondary infection.

! ***Nurse Alert*** *Lice are highly contagious.*

If lice are present, dispose of gloves and reapply another pair.

Explain that the next portion of examination involves manipulation of the genitalia. Manipulate the genitalia gently to avoid discomfort.

Inspect structures of the penis. Begin by inspecting the dorsal vein.

Normally apparent along shaft.

In uncircumcised males, retract the foreskin to reveal the glans and urethral meatus.

In uncircumcised males, foreskin retracts easily. A bit of white, cheesy smegma may be seen over the glans. If client is circumcised, glans is exposed and no smegma will be present. Glans and meatus are without inflammation.

Phimosis is a tightening of the foreskin, causing difficulty in retracting the tissue. It is the result of infection and congenital abnormality.

Assessment	Normal Findings	Deviations From Normal
Note position of meatus and observe for discharge, lesions, edema, and inflammation.	The meatus is slitlike and normally positioned just millimeters from the the tip of the glans.	In some congenital conditions the meatus is displaced along the penile shaft. In hypospadias the meatus is located on the ventral surface of the glans or penile shaft.
Inspect the glans around its entire circumference for signs of lesions. Look carefully along undersurface.	Glans is smooth and pink without lesions.	Syphilitic chancres usually occur on the glans. They are painless lesions with indurated borders and a clear base. Herpetic lesions appear as superficial vesicles on the glans, foreskin, scrotum, or penile shaft. They are often painful. Herpetic lesions rupture to form shallow, moist ulcerations. Condyloma acuminatum (genital warts) are soft, reddish or gray lesions that develop on the foreskin, glans penis, penile shaft, and scrotum. Penile cancer is rare but may be mistaken for a condyloma acuminatum.

Palpate any lesion gently to note tenderness, size, consistency, and shape.		
Compress the glans gently between the thumb and index finger. Observe the opening of the urethral meatus and note the color and any discharge. (Client can be asked to perform this measure for you.)	Opening is glistening and pink.	Bright erythema or discharge indicates inflammation.
Inspect the shaft of the penis, not overlooking its undersurface, for any lesions, scars, or areas of edema.	No lesions or edema.	A client who has lain in bed for a prolonged time may develop dependent edema in the penile shaft. Lesions resulting from STD can be found on penile shaft.
Gently palpate the shaft between thumb and first two fingers to note any localized areas of hardness or tenderness.	Penis should be soft and free of nodules.	

Assessment	Normal Findings	Deviations From Normal
If abnormal discharge from meatus is present, obtain specimen by gently milking penis from base to urethra. Brush culture swab across meatus. (Client again may assist with this procedure.)	Discharge may indicate a sexually transmitted infection.	
Pull retracted foreskin down to its original position at this point in the examination.		
! ***Nurse Alert*** *This is a good time to begin discussion of genital examination.*		
Be particularly gentle when touching the scrotum. Inspect the scrotum's size, color, shape, and symmetry, and observe for lesions and edema.	Scrotum hangs freely from perineum behind penis. The left testis may normally be lower than the right. The skin of the scrotum is normally loose; surface may be coarse. There are no lesions.	Lumps in scrotal skin are commonly caused by sebaceous cysts (Seidel et al., 1995). Edema of scrotum may be from fluid retention caused by cardiac, hepatic, or renal disease.
Gently lift scrotum to view posterior surface.	The skin color is often more deeply pigmented than body skin. The	

scrotum normally contracts in cold temperatures and relaxes in warm temperatures.

While the client retracts the penis upward, gently palpate the testes between thumb and first two fingers and note size, shape, and consistency; ask client whether palpation reveals any unusual tenderness. Continue palpation of epididymis, a cordlike structure along posterolateral surface of testicle.

Testes should be sensitive to gentle compression but not tender. The testes are normally oval and approximately ½ to 1 inch (1 to 2.5 cm) in diameter. The testes feel smooth, rubbery, and free from nodules; the epididymides feel smooth, nontender, and resilient.

An infection, tumor, or cyst may cause changes in texture or size of testes. Infection will cause tenderness. Palpable, painless, pea-size lumps involving testis may indicate testicular tumor. In diabetic neuropathy the testes are insensitive to painful stimuli (Seidel et al., 1995).

Have client palpate testes at this time to become familiar with consistency of normal tissue.

Continue the examination by palpating the vas deferens separately as it forms the spermatic cord toward the inguinal ring.

Vas deferens feels smooth and discrete, without nodules or swelling.

Lumpiness may be caused by changes from diabetes.

Assessment	Normal Findings	Deviations From Normal
Assess cremasteric reflex by stroking the inner thigh with the end of a tongue blade or your finger.	Testicle and scrotum rise on the stroked side.	
Ask client to stand for assessment of the inguinal ring and canal:		
During inspection, ask the client to bear down as if having a bowel movement.		
Inspect both inguinal areas for signs of obvious bulging.	Abdominal muscles tighten and scrotum lowers as client bears down. No bulging or protrusion is observed in scrotal sac or inguinal area.	Indirect inguinal hernia (most common) appears as soft swelling in area of internal ring with pain on straining. Direct inguinal hernia forms bulge that is usually painless.
Palpate the inguinal ring and canal to be sure a hernia is not present:		
Have client relax and take a deep breath. Begin by gently inserting the examining finger into the		

lower scrotal sac and carry it upward along the vas deferens into the inguinal canal (Fig. 16-4).

Follow the spermatic cord up to the inguinal ring.

Do not force finger into inguinal canal.

When the finger reaches the farthest point along the canal, ask client to cough and strain down.

Repeat on left side.

As client strains, no bulging pressure will be felt against fingertips; a tightening around the finger is normal.

Indirect inguinal hernia comes down inguinal canal and touches fingertip on examination. Direct inguinal hernia pushes against side of finger on examination.

Palpate the prostate gland during rectal examination (see Chapter 17).

A

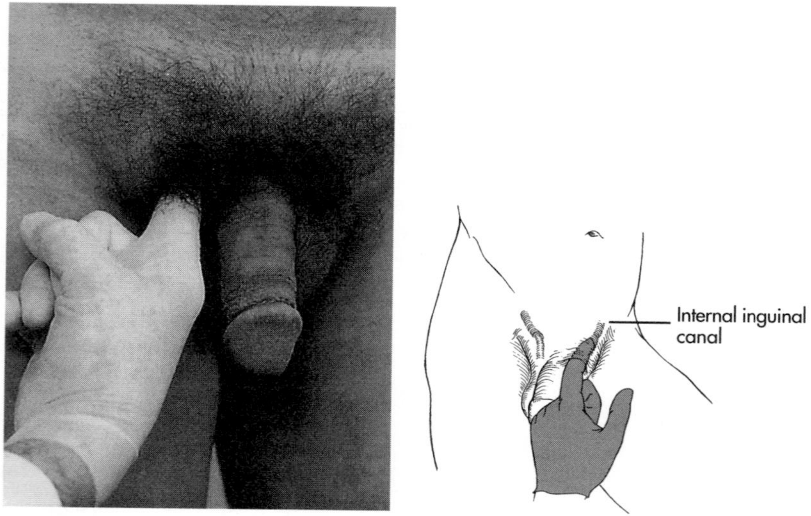

B

Fig. 16-4
A, Right inguinal hernia check. **B,** Left inguinal hernia check.

Nursing Diagnoses

Assessment data may reveal defining characteristics for the following nursing diagnoses:

- Pain
- Sexual dysfunction
- Knowledge deficit regarding testicular self-examination and risks of STD
- Altered urinary elimination
- Impaired tissue integrity

Pediatric Considerations

- Examine newborns for congenital anomalies; note size of penis, placement of urethral opening, and other anomalies.
- The foreskin in an uncircumcised infant is usually tight. It should retract enough to permit a good urinary stream. Uncircumcised infants (2 to 3 months of age) should not have foreskin retracted too far to inspect the urethra because of risk of tearing membrane. The foreskin becomes fully retractable by 3 or 4 years of age (Seidel et al., 1995).
- Undescended testes are common in premature infants.
- The scrotum in infants often appears large in relation to the rest of the genitalia.
- If either testis is not palpable, check to see if in inguinal canal. Alert physician.
- In children the testes should be about 1 cm (½ inch) in size.
- With adolescents, genital examination may be left until last because adolescents are more likely to be embarrassed. The examiner should proceed calmly as with all other segments of the examination. Note degree of maturation.

Gerontologic Considerations

- The size and firmness of the testes generally decrease with age.
- Scrotum becomes more pendulous because of loss of muscular tone.

Cultural Considerations

- Testicular cancer occurs most frequently among whites and is rare in African Americans.

Client Teaching

- If the client expresses interest or concern about STDs, contraceptive techniques, physiologic functioning, and other matters of human sexuality, the nurse may choose to provide information after the examination. Measures to prevent STDs include the following:

- Use of condoms
- Avoiding sex with partner who becomes infected
- Restricting number of sexual partners
- Avoiding sex with persons who have multiple partners

■ Instruct client on genital and testicular self-examination (see Appendix K).

Rectum and Anus

17

For both male and female clients, assessment of the rectum and anus can generally best be performed immediately after assessment of the genitalia. For males, rectal assessment includes assessment of the prostate gland.

Anatomy and Physiology

The rectum is the terminal portion of the lower gastrointestinal tract. Basically, it is a hollow tube, 4 to 6 inches (10 to 15 cm) in length containing folds of mucus-lined tissue. The rectum extends from the sigmoid colon to the muscles of the pelvic floor, where it continues as the anal canal. The anal canal is 1 to 1½ inches (2.5 to 4 cm) in length and is normally kept closed by the internal and external sphincters. The urge to defecate occurs when the rectum fills with feces, causing reflex stimulation that relaxes the internal sphincter. Defecation occurs as the external sphincter, under voluntary control, relaxes. Defecation ensures the elimination of solid wastes.

In males the prostate gland is located at the base of the bladder. The gland surrounds the urethra and is palpable, because its posterior surface comes in contact with the anterior rectal wall.

Rationale

The primary purpose of the rectal examination is for determining the presence of masses or irregularities of the rectal walls. The integrity of the external anal sphincter can also be assessed. The examination includes screening for rectal cancer. Incidence rates for colon and rectal cancer have fallen in recent years (American Cancer Society, 1996b). In males the rectal examination also provides access to assess the condition of the prostate gland. The incidence of prostate cancer in the United States is on the rise because of improved detection. It is currently the second leading cause of death in men (American Cancer Society, 1996b).

Critical Thinking

Knowledge

During this examination consider the emotional impact cancer has on clients. Use communication techniques to allay the client's anxiety. Also be mindful that if there is a likelihood the client has cancer, ethical principles must be applied to be sure the client is a participant in deciding a course of treatment.

Experience

It takes practice to be able to palpate the prostate and to accurately assess changes in its size and condition. Whenever you detect abnormalities have an experienced practitioner confirm your findings until you acquire more experience.

Standards

Apply the following principles during the rectal and anal examination:

- Maintain the client's comfort and privacy, because the examination can be embarrassing.

Equipment

Disposable gloves
Lubricant
Examination light

Delegation Considerations

Examination of the rectum and anus requires problem solving and knowledge application unique to a professional nurse. Delegation of the examination to unlicensed assistive personnel is inappropriate. However, because staff assist clients with toileting be sure they are instructed to report problems such as blood in the stool, difficulty starting urinary stream (in males), and change in clients' bowel habits.

Rectal and Anal Assessment

Client Preparation

- Use a calm, gentle approach. Explain what will happen, step by step.
- Drape client so that only anal area is exposed.
- The female client is assessed in the lithotomy position if rectal assessment follows vaginal examination. Otherwise the female should assume a side-lying or Sims' position.
- The male client is asked to stand and bend forward with hips flexed and upper body resting across the examination table.
- Nonambulatory male clients may be assessed in the Sims' position.

History

- Has the client experienced bleeding from the rectum, black or tarry stools (melena), rectal pain, or change in bowel habits (constipation or diarrhea)?
- Determine whether the client has personal history of colorectal cancer, polyps, or inflammatory bowel disease. Note if client is over age 40.
- Assess dietary habits for high fat intake or deficient fiber content that may be linked to bowel cancer.
- Has the client ever undergone screening for colorectal cancer (digital exam, stool blood slide test, proctosigmoidoscopy)?
- Assess medication history for use of laxatives or cathartics, codeine, or iron preparations, which can alter elimination patterns.
- Ask if male client has experienced weak or interrupted urine flow, inability to urinate, difficulty in starting or stopping urine stream, polyuria, nocturia, hematuria, or dysuria.
- Assess client's family history: colon cancer, familial polyposis, Gardner's syndrome, Peutz-Jeghers syndrome (risks for colorectal cancer).

Assessment Techniques

Assessment	Normal Findings	Deviations From Normal
Standard Precautions Alert *Apply disposable gloves.*		
Inspect the perianal tissues and sacrococcygeal areas. Look for lumps, rashes, inflammation, excoriation, and scars.	Skin is smooth and uninterrupted.	Fungal infection can cause perianal irritation.
Palpate surrounding tissue.	Area is nontender.	
With nondominant hand retract buttocks to inspect the anal area for skin characteristics, lesions, external hemorrhoids, fissures and fistulas, inflammation, rashes, or excoriations.	Anal tissues are moist and hairless compared with perianal skin. Tissue is coarser and more darkly pigmented. The anus is held closed.	External hemorrhoids appear as dilated veins that look like reddened protrusions. Pilonidal cysts are located in the midline, superficial to the coccyx and lower sacrum, and look like dimples with a sinus tract opening. Perianal abscesses appear as areas of swelling with erythema of the anus, internally and externally. Abscesses are painful and tender.

Ask client to bear down as if having a bowel movement (note presence of internal hemorrhoids or fissures). Use clock referents (e.g., 12 o'clock and 6 o'clock) to describe location of findings.

No protrusion of tissue.

Hemorrhoids may protrude. Rectal mucosa may prolapse through the anal ring as the client strains. A prolapse is pink and looks like a doughnut or rosette (Seidel et al., 1995).

Apply lubricant to gloved index finger of nondominant hand.

! ***Nurse Alert*** *Some institutions do not permit nurses to perform digital examinations.*

Press finger pad against the anal opening (Fig. 17-1). Ask client to bear down as though having a bowel movement. As the anal sphincter relaxes, insert fingertip gently into the anal canal directed toward the umbilicus. While your finger is inserted, explain that client may have sensation of need to have a bowel movement.

! ***Nurse Alert*** *To avoid mucosal tissue injury, never force digital insertion.*

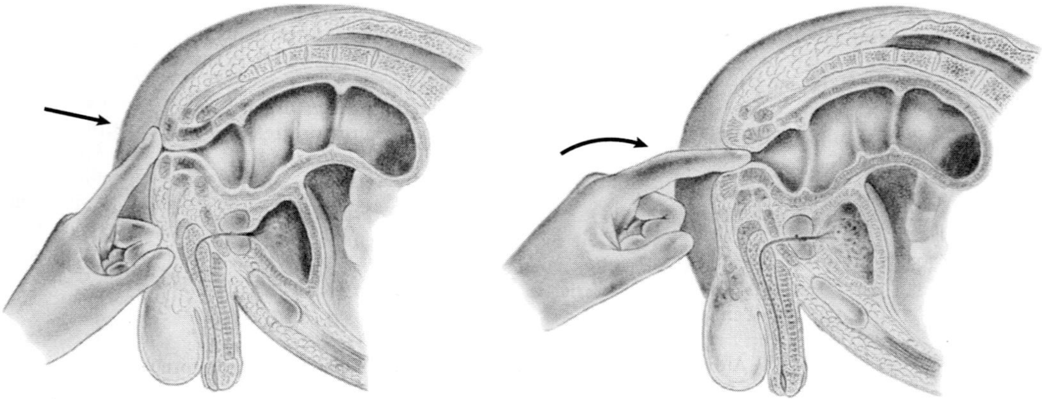

Fig. 17-1
Palpation of rectum.
(From Seidel HM et al: *Mosby's guide to physical examination,* ed 3, St Louis, 1995, Mosby.)

Assessment	Normal Findings	Deviations From Normal
Have client tighten the external sphincter around the finger and note the tone of the anal sphincter.	Muscles close snugly and evenly around finger, without discomfort to client.	Weakened sphincter indicates a neurologic problem. Acute rectal pain may be caused by fissures, inflamed hemorrhoids, or hard constipated stool.
Continue examination, being aware of the course of the anal canal. The canal extends in a line toward the umbilicus before turning into the mucus-lined rectum. The anus contains a rich supply of sensory nerve fibers. At the junction of the anal canal and rectum, the rectum balloons out and turns posteriorly into the hollow of the coccyx and sacrum. Rotate examination finger to palpate the muscular anal ring. Feel for any tissue irregularities.	Anal ring should feel smooth.	

Assessment	Normal Findings	Deviations From Normal
Beyond the anal canal, palpate each side of the rectal wall for tenderness, irregularities, polyps, masses, or nodules.	Wall feels even and smooth. Stool is commonly found in rectum.	Masses can be benign or malignant. A cancerous tumor is usually felt as a polypoid mass with nodular raised edges. The consistency is stony and contour is irregular (Seidel et al., 1995). **!** ***Nurse Alert*** *Report any masses to the physician.*
Once the finger is advanced fully, have the client bear down again. This will cause any high lesions to descend against your fingertip.		This could indicate a metastatic lesion.
In male clients turn the hand so that the finger palpates the anterior rectal wall. Warn the client that he may feel the urge to urinate, but will not. Male prostate is palpable anteriorly as a rounded, heart-shaped structure, 1 to 1½ inches (2.5 to 4 cm) in diameter, divided into two lobes by a	Gland is firm, without bogginess, tenderness, or nodules.	Hardness or nodules may indicate presence of a cancerous lesion. Prostate enlargement is classified by amount of projection into the rectum: grade I is 1 to 2 cm protrusion; grade II, 2 to 3 cm; grade III, 3 to 4 cm; grade IV, more than 4 cm (Seidel et al., 1995).

small groove, firm, and nontender. It often is described as feeling like a pencil eraser. There is normally less than 1 cm protrusion into the rectum. Palpate prostate gland to determine size, shape, firmness, tenderness, or lesions (Fig. 17-2).

In females the cervix may be palpable through the anterior rectal wall. Do not mistake the cervix or an inserted tampon for a rectal tumor.

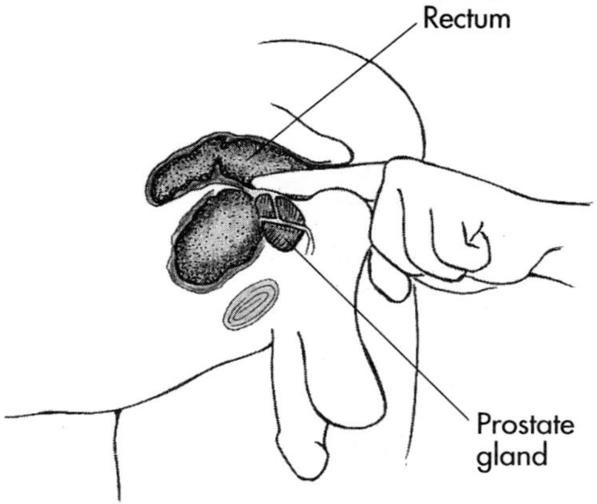

Fig. 17-2
Palpation of prostate.

Assessment	Normal Findings	Deviations From Normal
Gently withdraw finger and examine for fecal material.	Stool should be soft and brown.	Blood or pus is abnormal. Blood can appear in feces for a variety of reasons, including ingestion of iron, steroids, and aspirin-containing medications; anal fissures; coagulation disorders; peptic ulcers; swallowed blood; foreign body trauma; and hemorrhoids. Test stool on gloved finger for occult blood. Stool characteristics can indicate disease: intermittent pencil-shaped stools are caused by spasmodic rectal contractions; persistent pencil-shaped stools indicate permanent stenosis; pipestem and ribbon stools indicate lower rectal stricture (Seidel et al., 1995).
Complete the examination by cleansing the anal and perineal area.		

Nursing Diagnoses

Assessment data may reveal defining characteristics for the following nursing diagnoses:

- Knowledge deficit regarding risks for colorectal cancer or prostatic cancer
- Pain
- Constipation
- Diarrhea
- Anxiety

Pediatric Considerations

- In the neonate, passage of meconium stool within the first 48 hours of life indicates anal patency.
- Rectal examinations are deferred in infants and children unless an abnormality is suspected.
- Routinely inspect the anal region and perineum, examining buttocks for redness, masses, and evidence of change in firmness.
- Perirectal redness and irritation are often caused by pinworms, *Candida,* or other diaper irritants.
- Asymmetric creases in the buttocks may indicate congenital hip dislocation.
- Parents should be assured that toilet training is individualized for children and cannot begin until the child has mature neurologic and muscular development.

Gerontologic Considerations

- Older clients may only be able to assume left lateral side-lying position.
- Sphincter tone is often reduced.
- Most older men have some degree of prostatic enlargement. The gland will feel smooth, rubbery, and symmetric. An annual examination is recommended to monitor recurrent urinary tract infections and to ensure that carcinoma does not exist.

Cultural Considerations

- Performance of the rectal examination is an invasive procedure. Review the cultural considerations regarding touch, summarized in Chapter 16.

Client Teaching

- Discuss the American Cancer Society's guidelines for early detection of colorectal cancer, including digital rectal examinations performed yearly after 40 years of age; stool blood slide tests (guaiac test) performed yearly after 50 years of age; and proctosigmoidoscopy, involving visual inspection of the rectum and lower colon with a flexible, hollow, lighted tube. Proctosigmoidoscopy is performed by a physician every 3 to 5 years after 50 years of age (American Cancer Society, 1996b).

- Discuss diet plan to reduce fat and increase fiber content.
- Warn client about problems caused by overuse of laxatives, cathartics, codeine, and enemas.
- Discuss with male client the American Cancer Society's guidelines for early detection of prostatic cancer: digital rectal examination performed annually after age 40 and prostate-specific antigen blood test performed annually after age 50; if either test result is suspicious, a prostate ultrasound should be performed.

Musculoskeletal System 18

Musculoskeletal assessment can be conducted as a separate examination or integrated appropriately with other parts of the total physical examination. The nurse can also integrate this assessment with other nursing care as the client moves about or performs any type of physical activity.

Anatomy and Physiology

Physical performance requires bones, muscles, and joints that function smoothly and effortlessly. The musculoskeletal system is the body's main line of defense against external forces. The system is a bony structure with its joints held together by ligaments, attached to muscles by tendons, and cushioned by cartilage. The musculoskeletal system provides support, protection, body movement, hematopoiesis, heat production, and mineral storage.

There are four types of bones: long bones (e.g., humerus, femur), short bones (e.g., phalanx), flat bones (e.g., scapula), and irregular bones (e.g., vertebra) (Thibodeau and Patton, 1993). Bones serve differing needs such as bearing weight and offering protection to underlying structures.

Bones differ not only in size and shape but also in the types of bone tissue that comprise them. Compact bone is dense and solid in appearance, whereas cancellous bone is spongy. Bone is anatomically organized so that its great strength and minimal weight result from the interrelationships of its structural components (Thibodeau and Patton, 1993).

An articulation or joint is a point of contact between bones. Although most joints (e.g., diarthrodial) allow considerable movement, others are completely immovable or allow limited motion. It is the existence of movable joints that permits us to perform complex, highly coordinated, and purposeful movements. Most joints are diarthrodial—freely moving articulations that are enclosed by a capsule of fibrous articular cartilage, ligaments, and cartilage covering opposing bones. Each articular cavity is lined with a synovial membrane that secretes synovial fluid. Bursae develop in the spaces of connective tissue between tendons, ligaments, and bones to promote motion and reduce friction. Table 18-1 describes the classification of joints.

Bones and joints cannot move themselves. Skeletal muscle tissue attaches to the skeleton and is responsible for voluntary body movement. Skeletal muscle cells have several characteristics that permit them to function: excitability (capable of responding to nerve signals), contractility (capable of contracting to produce movement), and extensibility (capable to extend or stretch to allow muscles to return to resting length). Muscles perform a function that is often overlooked. Muscle cells, like all cells, produce body heat through catabolism. Because of the highly active nature of muscle cells, skeletal muscle contractions produce a major share of total body heat.

Rationale

The integrity of the musculoskeletal system is vital for persons to move about freely and care for themselves. Disorders of the musculoskeletal system can range from alterations causing minor discomfort, such as sprained ligaments, to life-threatening conditions, such as muscular dystrophy. The musculoskeletal system is complex in that it is influenced by endocrine and neurologic function. The nurse's examination includes assessment of the bones; supportive tissues, such as cartilage, tendons, and fasciae; muscles; and joints. The nurse gives particular attention to areas of limited or absent movement to determine the

Table 18-1 Classification of joints

Type of Joint	Example	Description
Synarthrosis		No movement is permitted
Suture	Cranial sutures	United by thin layer of fibrous tissue
Synchondrosis	Joint between the epiphysis and diaphysis of long bones	A temporary joint in which the cartilage is replaced by bone later in life
Amphiarthrosis		Slightly movable joint
Symphysis	Symphysis pubis	Bones are connected by a fibrocartilage disk
Syndesmosis	Radius-ulna articulation	Bones are connected by ligaments
Diarthrosis (synovial)		Freely movable; enclosed by joint capsule, lined with synovial membrane
Ball and socket	Hip	Widest range of motion, movement in all planes
Hinge	Elbow	Motion limited to flexion and extension in a single plane
Pivot	Atlantoaxis	Motion limited to rotation
Condyloid	Wrist between radius and carpals	Motion in two planes at right angles to each other, but no radial rotation
Saddle	Thumb at carpal-metacarpal joint	Motion in two planes at right angles to each other, but no axial rotation
Gliding	Intervertebral	Motion limited to gliding

From Seidel HM et al: *Mosby's guide to physical examination,* ed 3, St Louis, 1995, Mosby.

level and extent of a client's disability. The client may exhibit problems resulting from disease of bones or joints, trauma, endocrine imbalance affecting muscle function, or disorders of the nerves that innervate the musculoskeletal system.

Critical Thinking

Knowledge

Refer to the knowledge you have regarding anatomy and physiology of the skeletal and muscular system. A detailed understanding will help you recognize alterations and anticipate how changes in other body systems affect muscular and skeletal function.

Refer to the knowledge you have regarding changes in musculoskeletal function as a result of aging. Although this applies to all body systems, age-related changes can significantly affect an older client's mobility and make an examination challenging. The older adult will require special consideration in your examination.

Experience

It will be very helpful to learn how to combine elements of the musculoskeletal examination with other body system examinations. For example, when examining the head and neck it would be easy to assess range of motion (ROM) and muscle strength for major joints and muscle groups.

Most people have experienced some type of injury to their musculoskeletal system, such as a sprained ankle, bruised hand, or injured finger. Remember that pain is associated with such an injury and requires you to carefully support and examine the affected area.

Standards

During examination of the musculoskeletal system apply the following principles:

- Know the normal ROM for each joint.
- Never move or force a joint beyond the client's current ROM.
- Use caution when examining a sports injury.
- Support the full length of the body part being examined.
- Consider the client's level of fatigue or the existence of symptoms such as shortness of breath in determining how extensive an examination can be performed.

Equipment

Goniometer (usually available from physical therapy department)
Tape measure

Delegation Considerations

Physical examination of the musculoskeletal function requires problem solving and knowledge application unique to a professional nurse. For this skill, delegation is inappropriate. However, unlicensed assistive personnel often assist clients with ambulation, transfer, and positioning. The staff member should be trained in recognizing problems with gait and ROM. The nurse should inform unlicensed personnel about the following:

Clients at risk for gait problems
The importance of never moving or forcing a joint beyond the client's current ROM
Clients with muscular weakness, who require special assistance with transfer and ambulation
The need to report any problems noted in ROM, appearance of joint, or muscle strength to an RN

Musculoskeletal Assessment

Client Preparation

- Depending on the muscle groups assessed, the client sits, lies supine, or stands.
- Be sure the client's muscles and joints are fully exposed and free to move. Keep client warm and comfortable.

History

- Ask if client is involved in competitive sports (particularly one involving collision and contact), fails to warm up adequately, is in poor physical condition, or has had a rapid growth spurt (adolescents). Does the client wear protective equipment?
- Review client history (particularly females) for heavy alcohol use, cigarette smoking, constant dieting, calcium intake less than 500 mg daily, thin and light body frame, nulliparous state, occurrence of menopause before age 45, postmenopausal state, bilateral oophorectomy, and family history of osteoporosis (risk factors for osteoporosis).
- Ask the client to describe history of problems in bone, muscle, or joint function, including history of recent falls, trauma, lifting heavy objects, and bone or joint disease with sudden or gradual onset. In addition,

have clients point out the locations of alterations.

- Assess the nature and extent of any stiffness or pain, including location; duration; severity; type of pain; and predisposing, aggravating, and relieving factors.
- Ask whether the client has noticed a change in ability to perform self-care tasks such as bathing, feeding, dressing, toileting, and ambulating or social functions such as household chores, work, recreation, and sexual activities.
- Assess height decrease of women over age 50 by subtracting current height from recall of maximum adult height. This is done to predict osteoporosis (Reed and Birge, 1988).

Assessment Techniques

Assessment	Normal Findings	Deviations From Normal
Inspection and Palpation		
Inspect gait as client walks into examination room and stands. Observe for foot dragging, shuffling or limping, balance, presence of obvious deformity in lower extremities, and position of the trunk in relation to the legs.	Gait is normal, with arms swinging freely at sides. Head and face lead body, and balance is good. Toes should point straight ahead.	Dragging of the foot, shuffling, or unsteady gait may indicate neurologic problem (see Chapter 19). Dragging of the foot might also be caused by localized injury or deformity.
Stand behind client and observe postural alignment (position of hips relative to shoulders). Look at client's	Posture is erect. Head is held erect, with hips and shoulders aligned in parallel. There is an even contour of	Posture is stooped, angled to the side, which may indicate posturing to minimize pain. Lordosis is an abnor-

ability to stand erect and note symmetry of body parts. Look sideways at cervical, thoracic, and lumbar curves (Fig. 18-1).

shoulder, level scapulae and iliac crests, with alignment of head over gluteal folds. Normal cervical, thoracic, and lumbar curves are present.

mal posturing with a swayback or increased curvature of the lumbar spine. Kyphosis, or hunchback, is an exaggeration of the posterior curvature of the thoracic spine. Scoliosis is lateral spinal curvature.

Note client's base of support and weight-bearing stability.

Weight is evenly distributed; the client stands on right and left heels and toes. Pregnant woman's base of support is shifted forward with a compensatory lordosis and forward cervical flexion.

If you detect a problem or wish to inspect gait more closely, refer to neurologic exam (see Chapter 19).

Make a general observation of the extremities. Look at overall size, gross deformity, bony enlargement, alignment, and symmetry.

Bilateral symmetry in length, circumference, alignment, and the position and number of skin folds.

Asymmetry may indicate trauma, previous surgery, or skeletal deformity.

A

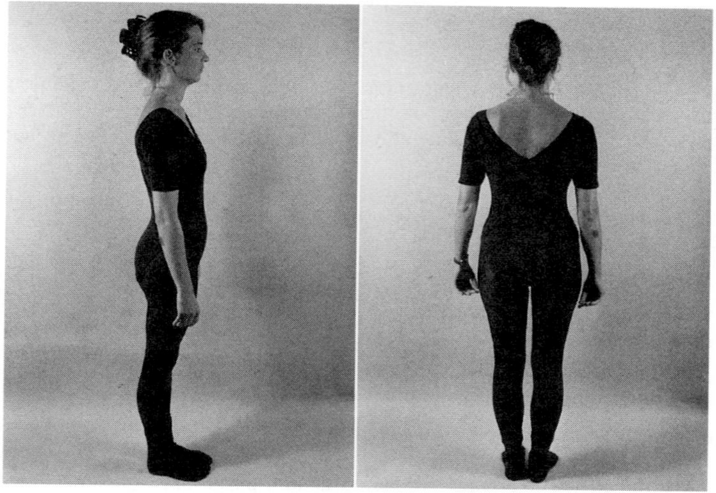

B

Fig. 18-1
Postural positions. **A,** Side view. **B,** Posterior view.

Assessment	Normal Findings	Deviations From Normal
Conduct similiar gross examination of muscles. Note size and presence of fasciculations or spasms.	Muscle size is approximately symmetric bilaterally. Dominant forearm may be larger in laborers or athletes. There is no atrophy or hypertrophy.	Serious muscle sprain is indicated by marked swelling, hemorrhage, pain, and loss of function. Atrophy of muscles can be the result of disuse from paralysis. A fracture of the bone can cause muscle contractions and spasms leading to shortening of tissue around the bone.
Inspect the skin and subcutaneous tissues overlying muscles, bones, and joints for discoloration, swelling, or masses.	Tissue tends to conform to shape of body part, without swelling or masses.	Bluish or black discoloration of tissues indicates hematoma or bruising. Bursitis is an inflamed bursa, characterized by swelling, pain on movement, and erythema. Rheumatoid arthritis causes swelling and enlargement of soft tissue involving diarthrodial joints (e.g., fingers, feet) (Fig. 18-2).

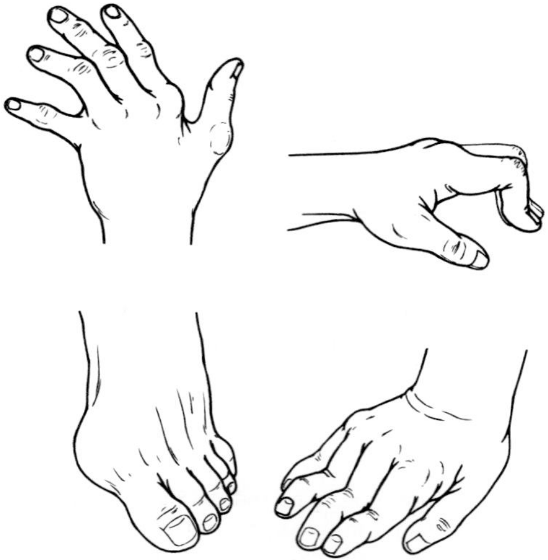

Fig. 18-2

Typical deformities of rheumatoid arthritis.

(From Lewis SM et al: *Medical-surgical nursing*, ed 4, St Louis, 1996, Mosby.)

Assessment	Normal Findings	Deviations From Normal
Gently palpate all bones, joints, and surrounding muscles in a complete examination (e.g., client with arthritis or other systemic problem). In a focused assessment, palpate only an involved area. Note any heat, tenderness, edema, crepitus, or resistance to pressure.	Muscle tone is firm. No discomfort occurs when pressure is applied. No deformities or crepitus.	Rheumatoid arthritis causes joints to sometimes feel warm to the touch. A fracture is indicated by edema, pain, loss of function, color changes, and paresthesia. **!** *Nurse Alert Palpate any inflamed joints last.*

Assessment	Normal Findings	Deviations From Normal
Range of Joint Motion and Muscle Tone and Strength		
! *Nurse Alert When client has obvious traumatic injury to the bone or joint, do not assess ROM. A physician or qualified practitioner will assess more fully the extent of injury.*		
Assist client in putting each major joint through its full ROM (Table 18-2). Observe equality of motion in same body parts:		
Give client adequate space to move each muscle group.		
Active motion: Instruct client in moving each joint through its normal range.	Full active ROM is present in all joints with good muscle tone. ROM is equal between contralateral joints.	
Passive motion: Have client relax and move the same joints passively until the end of the range is felt. Support extremity at joint.		

Table 18-2 Terminology for normal range of motion positions

Term	Range of Motion	Examples of Joints
Flexion	Movement decreasing angle between two adjoining bones; bending of limb	Elbow, fingers, knee
Extension	Movement increasing angle between two adjoining bones	Elbow, knee, fingers
Hyperextension	Movement of body part beyond its normal resting extended position	Head
Pronation	Movement of body part so that front or ventral surface faces downward	Hand, forearm
Supination	Movement of body part so that the front or ventral surface faces upward	Hand, forearm
Abduction	Movement of extremity away from midline of body	Leg, arm, fingers
Adduction	Movement of extremity toward midline of body	Leg, arm, fingers
Internal rotation	Rotation of joint inward	Knee, hip
External rotation	Rotation of joint outward	Knee, hip
Eversion	Turning of body part away from midline	Foot
Inversion	Turning of body part toward midline	Foot
Dorsiflexion	Flexion of toes and foot upward	Foot
Plantar flexion	Bending of toes and foot downward	Foot

Assessment	Normal Findings	Deviations From Normal
Do not force any joint through its ROM.		
If a joint appears to have increased or limited ROM, measure precise degree of motion with goniometer:		
Position center of protractor at center of joint being measured.		
Extend each arm of goniometer along body parts extending from joint.		
Measure joint angle before moving joint.		
Take joint through its full ROM, and measure angle again (Fig. 18-3).	ROM angle is full for measured joint.	Decreased ROM can be the result of chronic contracture or deformity (painless) or from painful conditions such as muscle strain, sprain, or fracture.
Compare reading with normal degree of joint movement.		

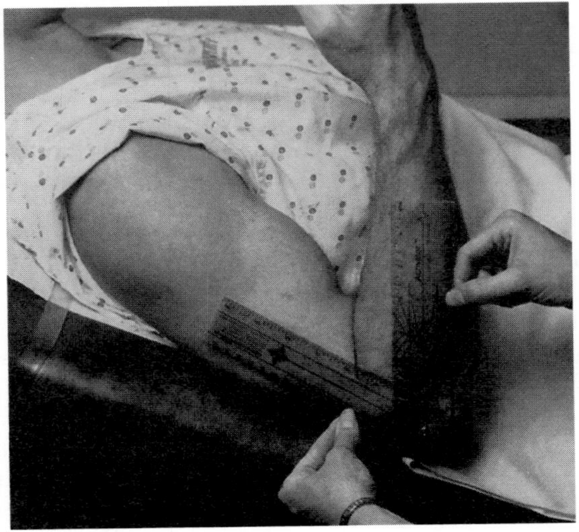

Fig. 18-3
Measuring ROM with goniometer.

Assessment	Normal Findings	Deviations From Normal
While measuring ROM, note any instability of joint:		
Palpate for unusual movement of joint during its movement. Note any deformity.		
Palpate joint for swelling, stiffness, tenderness, and heat; note any redness.	No discomfort should occur when applying pressure to bones and joints. There are no nodules or evidence of swelling.	Swelling can indicate cyst, bony overgrowth, arthritic changes, hematoma, or fracture.
While assessing ROM, ask client to allow extremity to relax or hang limp. Support extremity and move limb through ROM to detect muscular resistance. It may help to palpate muscle mass being tested.	Normal tone causes mild, even resistance to movement through entire ROM.	Increased tone (hypertonicity) occurs with sudden movement of joint causing considerable resistance. Hypotonic muscle moves without resistance; muscle feels flabby.
Assess muscle strength. Be sure client is in a stable position, one that will allow active contraction of muscle groups. Assess muscle strength by ap-		

plying gradual increase in pressure to muscle group. Have client resist pressure applied by trying to move against resistance (e.g., flex elbow). Have client maintain resistance until told to stop. Compare symmetric groups. For example:

Place hand on client's upper jaw (Fig. 18-4) as client turns head laterally against resistance (neck muscles).

Place hands over client's deltoid muscle with client's arm abducted to 90 degrees; have client hold position against resistance (deltoid muscle).

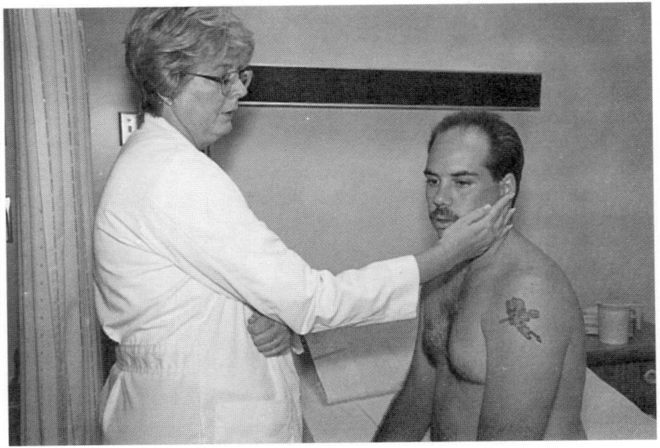

Fig. 18-4
Testing muscle strength.

Assessment	Normal Findings	Deviations From Normal
Place hand on dorsal surface of client's neutrally positioned foot as client tries to bend foot up (ankle and foot). **!** *Nurse Alert Client's position should not be one that would easily cause a loss of balance or a fall.*	Muscle strength is bilaterally symmetric with resistance to opposition. Dominant arm may be slightly stronger than nondominant arm.	
Rate muscle strength on a scale of 0 to 5: 0 No voluntary contraction 1 Slight contractility, no movement 2 Full ROM, passive 3 Full ROM, active 4 Full ROM against gravity, some resistance 5 Full ROM against gravity, full resistance		

If muscle weakness is noted, measure muscle size by placing a tape measure around muscle body's circumference and compare with opposite side.	Circumference is symmetric bilaterally. Dominant side of upper or lower extremity may be larger in athletes or laborers.	Reduced circumference indicates muscle atrophy. A muscle that is atrophied or reduced in size may feel soft and boggy on palpation.

Nursing Diagnoses

Assessment data may reveal defining characteristics for the following nursing diagnoses:

- Pain
- Impaired physical mobility
- Self-care deficit (bathing/hygiene, dressing/grooming, feeding, toileting)
- Risk for injury

Pediatric Considerations

- Fully undress an infant and observe the posture and spontaneous generalized movements.
- In the neonate the spine is gently rounded rather than the characteristic S shape. Hyperflexibility of the joints is characteristic of Down syndrome.
- Arms and legs should flex symmetrically in infants. The axillary, gluteal, femoral, and popliteal creases should also be symmetric, and the limbs should move freely (Seidel et al., 1995).
- Newborns have some resistance to full extension of the elbows, hips, and knees.
- A newborn's hands should open periodically with the fingers fully extended. When the hand is fisted, the thumb is positioned inside the fingers.
- Infants should be checked for hip dislocation throughout the first 12 months of life (this requires a special examination technique).
- An infant has a bowlegged pattern until 18 to 24 months of age.
- Young children have a lumbar curvature of the spine and a protuberant abdomen.
- Toddlers usually have a wide-based gait until 2 years of age.
- Watch children during play to assess musculoskeletal function.

Gerontologic Considerations

- The older adult fatigues easily; has a slower reaction time as a result of a decrease in nerve conduction and muscle tone; and may not display smooth, coordinated movement. Allow clients in this age-group adequate time for rest during the physical examination.
- Older adults walk with smaller steps and a wider base of support.
- Older clients lose height because intervertebral space narrows.
- ROM is limited.
- The client's posture may display increased dorsal kyphosis, with flexion of the hips and knees. Extremities may appear long if the trunk has diminished in length.
- It is especially important to assess an older adult's functional abilities (Table 18-3).

Cultural Considerations

- Motor development of African-American infants is often advanced over that of whites; thus African-American children under 3 years of age may reach developmental milestones earlier. White children start to catch up by 3 years of age (Seidel et al., 1995).
- There is a high prevalence of arthritis, including rheumatoid arthritis, among selected American Indians (Giger and Davidhizar, 1995).
- Osteoporosis is less prevalent in African-American women than in white women. This may be because of differences in adult bone mass (Pollitzer and Anderson, 1990).

Client Teaching

- Instruct the client about correct posture. Consult with a physical therapist about exercises to improve the client's posture.
- To reduce bone demineralization, instruct the client on a proper exercise program (e.g., walking) to be followed three or more times a week. Also encourage intake of calcium to meet the recommended daily allowance. Increased vitamin D will aid calcium absorption. Recommendations for calcium supplements are 1000 mg before and 1500 mg after menopause.
- Explain to clients with low back pain that they can benefit from modification of worker risk factors (e.g., lifting heavy weights, use of protective equipment), regular aerobic exercise, exercises that

Table 18-3 Functional assessment: musculoskeletal assessment

Activity to Observe	Indicators of Weakened Muscle Groups
Rising from lying to sitting position	Rolling to one side and pushing with arms to raise to elbows; grabbing a siderail or table to pull to sitting
Rising from chair to standing	Pushing with arms to supplement weak leg muscles; upper torso thrusts forward before body rises
Walking	Lifting leg farther off floor with each step; shortened swing phase; foot may fall or slide forward; arms held out for balance or move in rowing motion
Climbing steps	Holding handrail for balance; pulling body up and forward with arms; uses stronger leg
Descending steps	Lowering weakened leg first; often descends sideways holding rail with both hands; may watch feet
Picking up item from floor	Leaning on furniture for support; bending over at waist to avoid bending knees; uses one hand on thigh to assist with lowering and raising torso
Tying shoes	Using footstool to decrease spinal flexion
Putting on and pulling up trousers or stockings	Difficulty may indicate decreased shoulder and upper arm strength; these activities often performed in sitting position until clothing is pulled up
Putting on sweater	Putting sleeve on weaker arm or shoulder first; uses internal or external shoulder rotation to get remaining arm in sleeve
Zipping dress in back	Difficulty with this indicates weakened shoulder rotation

From Seidel HM et al: *Mosby's guide to physical examination,* ed 3, St Louis, 1995, Mosby.

Continued

Table 18-3 Functional assessment: musculoskeletal assessment—cont'd

Activity to Observe	Indicators of Weakened Muscle Groups
Combing hair	Difficulty indicates problems with grasp, wrist flexion, pronation and supination of forearm, and elbow rotation
Pushing chair away from table while seated	Standing and easing chair back with torso; difficulty indicates problems with upper arm, shoulder, lower arm strength, and wrist motion
Buttoning button or writing name	Difficulty indicates problem with manual dexterity and finger-thumb opposition

From Seidel HM et al: *Mosby's guide to physical examination,* ed 3, St Louis, 1995, Mosby.

strengthen the back and increase trunk flexibility, and learning how to lift properly. Use of nonsteroidal antiinflammatory drugs and muscle relaxants is questionable (Malter et al., 1994).

- For clients with osteoporosis, instruct on proper body mechanics and ROM (e.g., swimming) and moderate weight-bearing exercises (e.g., walking, light weight lifting) to minimize trauma and subsequent bone fractures.
- Instruct older adults on the use of assistive devices such as zippers on clothing instead of buttons, elevated chairs to minimize bending of hips and knees, and use of crutches and walkers.
- Instruct older adults to pace activities to compensate for loss in muscle strength.
- Discuss pain-relief measures such as relaxation, massage, distraction, and heat applications.
- For clients with an unstable gait, discuss safety precautions in the home such as removal of throw rugs and installation of grab bars alongside stairs.

Neurologic System

19

Assessment of the neurologic system includes assessing the following areas: mental and emotional status, behavior and appearance, language function, intellectual function, cranial nerve function, sensory function, motor function, and reflexes. Full assessment of neurologic functions can be complex in part because of the various factors that influence neurologic function such as oxygenation, metabolic balance, and circulatory status. The examination can be time consuming, but neurologic measurements can be integrated with other parts of the physical examination; for example, mental and emotional status can be observed while taking the nursing history, and reflexes can be measured while the musculoskeletal system is assessed. The nurse's judgment is necessary in determining the extent of a neurologic examination.

Anatomy and Physiology

The central nervous system, composed of the brain and spinal cord, coordinates and controls body functions through the reception, storage, processing, and transmission of information. The peripheral nervous system, composed of motor (efferent) and sensory (afferent) nerves, carries information to and from the central nervous system. The motor division has two subdivisions: the somatic, or voluntary, nervous system and the autonomic, or involuntary, nervous system. Sympathetic and parasympathetic branches of the autonomic nervous system regulate nervous activity. The neurologic system is responsible for initiation and coordination of movement, reception and perception of sensory stimuli, organization of thought processes, control of cognitive and voluntary behaviors such as speech, and storage of memory. The neurologic system is closely integrated with all other body systems.

The brain is composed of the cerebrum, cerebellum, and brainstem and continues with the spinal cord, which extends from the foramen magnum to the lower border of the first lumbar vertebra. The two cerebral hemispheres comprise the greatest mass of the cerebrum. The outer layer, or cortex, integrates sensory and motor function and enables one to conduct higher-level functions dealing with behavior, learning, and language. Each lobe of the brain has distinct functions:

- Frontal lobe: Voluntary skeletal movement and speech formation, emotions, affect, drive, and self-awareness.
- Parietal lobe: Processes and interprets tactile (temperature, pressure, pain, size, shape, texture, and two-point discrimination), visual, gustatory, olfactory, and auditory sensations. Comprehension of written words and awareness of body position (proprioception) are also a function.
- Temporal lobe: Perception and interpretation of sounds and determination of their source. Also responsible for comprehension of the spoken word and written language. The lobe also integrates taste, smell, and balance, as well as behavior, emotion, and personality.
- Occipital lobe: Contains primary vision center.
- Limbic system: Mediates behavior that determines survival, such as aggression, affection, fear, and mating.

The cerebellum functions with the cerebrum in the integration of voluntary movement. By processing nerve impulses from the eyes, ears, touch receptors, and musculoskeleton, the cerebellum integrates with the vestibular system, sensory data for muscle tone, equilibrium, and posture.

The brainstem consists of the midbrain, pons, and medulla. It lies as a pathway between the brain and spinal cord. Nuclei from the 12 cranial nerves arise from the brainstem. The brainstem controls important vital functions such as respiratory, circulatory, and vasomotor activities; controls reflexes such as swallowing, coughing, pupillary response, and vomiting; and acts as a relay center for ascending and descending spinal tracts.

The spinal cord contains fibers, grouped into tracts, that run through the spinal cord carrying sensory, motor, and autonomic impulses between higher centers in the brain and the body. Myelinated fibers of the spinal cord contain the ascending (sensory) and descending (motor) tracts. The gray matter contains the nerve cell bodies, comprising the anterior and posterior horns of the spinal cord. The ascending tracts mediate various sensations by transmitting precise information about the type of stimulus and its location. The posterior (dorsal) column spinal tract carries the nerve fibers for discriminatory sensations (e.g., touch, joint position, two-point discrimination, deep pressure, vibration). The spinothalamic tracts carry nerve fibers for sensations of light and crude touch, pressure, temperature, and pain. The descending tracts originate in the brain and carry impulses to various muscle groups with inhibitory or facilitatory actions. The tracts also send impulses for the control of muscle tone and posture.

Thirty-one pairs of spinal nerves arise from the spinal cord and exit at each intervertebral foramen (Fig. 19-1). The sensory and motor fibers of each spinal nerve supply and receive information in a specific part of the body called a *dermatome*. Within the spinal cord, each spinal nerve separates into a ventral and dorsal root. Motor fibers of the ventral root carry impulses from the spinal cord to the muscles and glands. The sensory fibers of the dorsal root carry impulses from sensory receptors of the body to the spinal cord.

Rationale

The integrity of the nervous system is necessary for an individual's survival and the function of almost all bodily functions. The nurse's assessment primarily focuses on a client's sensory, motor, affective, and intellectual capacities. Disturbances in any of these functions can cause serious physical and psychological compromise and may make clients incapable of caring for themselves. Neurologic disorders often place them at significant risk for injury. Neurologic deficits can have an impact on a client's self-concept and create a significant threat to the life-

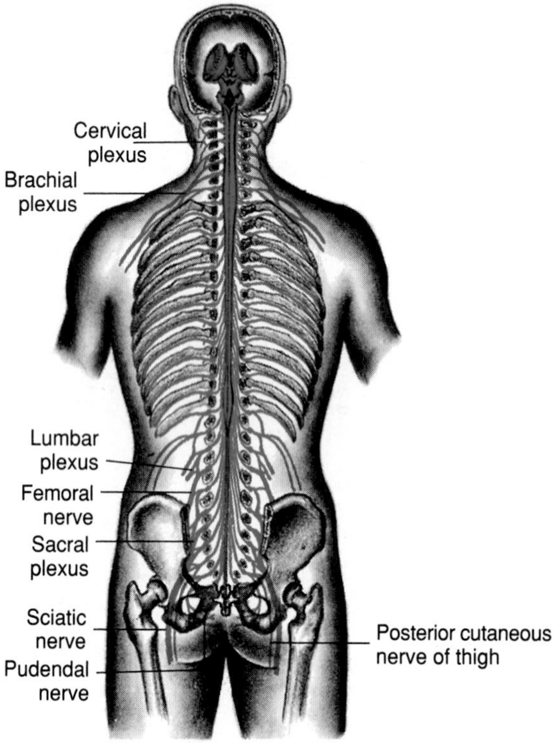

Fig. 19-1
Posterior view of exiting spinal nerves in relation to vertebrae.

style of clients and their family members.

Critical Thinking

Knowledge

It is important to refer to the knowledge you have regarding neurologic anatomy and physiology. Clinical signs and symptoms can help localize any type of neurologic pathology.

Refer to the knowledge you have regarding communication techniques. Clients with neurologic alterations may have visual, auditory, cognitive, and speech impairments, all of which can affect their ability to communicate.

Refer to the knowledge you have regarding psychology and normal behavior. Neurologic problems can create subtle and sometimes obvious behavioral changes.

Experience

Because the neurologic system is so complicated, it is useful to learn to combine different aspects of the examination during a review of other body systems. This takes practice. For example, examination of the cranial nerves can occur while examining the eyes, ears, pharynx, and head and neck; certain motor functions can be assessed while examining the musculoskeletal system.

Standards

Because neuropathways cross within either the brain or spinal cord, remember that physical signs on one side of the body generally indicate a problem on the opposite side.

When testing neurologic function, be sure the client is aroused to the highest level of consciousness possible.

When clients have a reduced level of consciousness it is unnecessary to raise your voice. Speak in a clear and normal tone of voice.

When testing motor function, be sure to demonstrate the maneuver you wish the client to attempt. Poor performance can result from lack of understanding the maneuver rather than neurologic impairment.

To ensure an objective assessment, consider the client's cultural and educational background, values, beliefs, previous experiences, and current level of coping. Such factors influence a client's response to questions.

Equipment

Reading material
Vials containing aromatic substances (e.g., vanilla, coffee)
Familiar objects (coin or paper clip)

Tongue blades (2)
Snellen chart
Penlight
Vials containing sugar or salt
Two test tubes, one filled with hot water and one filled with cold water
Cotton balls or cotton-tipped applicators
Tuning fork
Reflex hammer

Delegation Considerations

The neurologic examination requires problem solving and knowledge application unique to a professional nurse. Delegation of the skill is inappropriate. However, unlicensed assistive personnel should know to inform the nurse of any changes in a client's behavior or level of consciousness. When caring for clients with motor or sensory limitations, inform unlicensed care providers of the safety precautions needed to prevent injury to the client.

Neurologic Assessment

Client Preparation

- During the mental and emotional assessment, a client may assume a comfortable sitting or lying position.
- A client sits during cranial nerve assessment.
- Assessment of sensory, motor, and reflex function can require the client to assume various positions.

History

- Determine if the client is taking prescribed analgesics, sedatives, hypnotics, antipsychotics, antidepressants, or nervous system stimulants as medications. Also determine if the client uses illicit street drugs.
- Assess specifically the client's use of alcohol or sedative-hypnotics, which can cause tremors, ataxia, and changes in peripheral nerve function.
- Determine if client has recent history of seizures or convulsions. Clarify sequence of events that occur during a seizure (aura, fall to ground, motor activity, loss of consciousness); character of any symptoms; and relationship of seizure to time of day, fatigue, or emotional stress.
- Screen the client for headaches (including migraines), tremors, dizziness, vertigo, numbness or tingling of a body part, visual changes, weakness, pain, or changes in speech (combinations of these symptoms can indicate neurologic pathology). Determine onset, duration, precipitating factors, and other concomitant symptoms.

- Discuss with the client's spouse, family members, or friends any recent changes in the client's behavior (e.g., increased irritability, mood swings, memory loss).
- Assess client for history of changes in vision, hearing, smell, taste, and touch.
- If an older adult client displays sudden acute confusion (delirium), review history for drug toxicity (anticholinergics, diuretics, digoxin, cimetidine, sedatives, antihypertensives, antidysrhythmics), serious infections, metabolic disturbances, heart failure, and severe anemia.
- Has the client had a history of head or spinal cord trauma, meningitis, congenital anomalies, neurologic disease, or psychiatric counseling?
- If client exhibits behavioral changes, screen for evidence of depression (e.g., troubling thoughts or feelings, change in outlook on life, feeling hopeless, reduced energy level, change in eating habits, spends more time sleeping, talks about hurting self).

Assessment Techniques

Assessment	Normal Findings	Deviations From Normal
❗ ***Nurse Alert*** *Screen neurologic function when client has no major symptom complex or has no recent history of head or spinal cord injury or disease. (Assess mental status, including level of consciousness and orientation, pupillary reflexes, movement of extremities, sensation, and deep tendon reflexes.)*		

Assessment	Normal Findings	Deviations From Normal
Mental and Emotional Status		
Much of this assessment can be accomplished through general interaction with the client throughout other parts of the assessment by posing questions and remaining observant of the client at all times to determine appropriateness of emotions and thoughts expressed.		
For clients who are alert and responsive to conversation, conduct a mental status examination. Folstein's Mini–Mental State (MMS) is a good tool (see Chapter 5).	Client demonstrates immediate recall of past events; is able to perform cognitive exercises. Maximum score on MMS is 30.	Depressed clients without dementia usually score between 24 and 30. A score of 21 or less is found in clients with dementia, delirium, schizophrenia, or an affective disorder (Lueckenotte, 1996; Seidel et al., 1995).
If client's alertness is questioned, assess level of consciousness and orientation by directing questions and giving instructions that require a response. Be sure client is fully awake		

before testing. Note appropriateness of emotions, responses, and ideas expressed:

Use the Glasgow Coma Scale (GCS) to measure consciousness objectively (Table 19-1).

GCS score is 13 or higher.

Client shows confusion or reduced responsiveness. Disorientation or confusion may result from pain, fever, substance abuse, electrolyte imbalance, side effects or toxic effects of medications, circulatory shock, severe anemia, hypoxia, diabetic coma, or liver failure. Any sudden change in responsiveness or orientation requires immediate notification of the physician.

! ***Nurse Alert*** *The GCS can be misleading in clients with sensory losses. Clients are responsive but unable to sense painful stimuli over certain areas of the body.*

Rephrase or ask similar question if it is uncertain whether client understands.

Table 19-1 Glasgow coma scale

Action	Response	Score
Eyes open	Spontaneously	④
	To speech	3
	To pain	2
	None	1
Best verbal response	Oriented	⑤
	Confused	4
	Inappropriate words	3
	Incomprehensible sounds	2
	None	1
Best motor response	Obeys commands	⑥
	Localized pain	5
	Flexion withdrawal	4
	Abnormal flexion	3
	Abnormal extension	2
	Flaccid	1
	Total Score	⑮

Assessment	Normal Findings	Deviations From Normal
If client's responses are inappropriate, ask short, to-the-point questions regarding information the client knows (e.g., "Tell me your name," "Tell me where you live," "What is the name of this place?").	Client is able to respond to questions correctly with little hesitancy.	Client is slow to respond and difficult to arouse, fails to answer all questions correctly, or is unable to respond.
If client is unable to respond to questions of orientation, offer simple commands (e.g., "Squeeze my fingers," "Move your toes.").	Client responds appropriately to command.	Client fails to respond to command. Inability to move extremity (especially on one side) indicates motor deficit rather than change in level of consciousness.
When client fails to respond to command, test response to painful stimuli by applying firm pressure with thumb over root of client's fingernail. ❗ ***Nurse Alert*** *Do not pinch skin, because this can cause bruising.*	Client withdraws hand from painful stimulus.	There is no response to pain, indicating severe lowering of consciousness. Alterations in level of consciousness may be manifested as the following (in order of increasing alteration): Irritability, short attention span, or dulled perception of environment Disorientation

Assessment	Normal Findings	Deviations From Normal
		Inability to recall name or time of day Inability to follow even simple commands such as "Move your toes." Responsive only to painful stimuli Completely unresponsive to verbal and painful stimuli (comatose)
Behavior and Appearance During initial general survey (see Chapter 5) and throughout previous assessment, observe the client's mannerisms and actions, noting verbal and nonverbal behavior. Does client respond appropriately to directions, and what type of mood is displayed? Does client cooperate with examination?	The client should behave in a manner expressing concern and interest in the examination. Client should make eye contact with you. Client normally is anxious or concerned about findings.	Euphoria or lack of concern is exhibited.

Observe client's appearance: personal hygiene, cleanliness, choice of clothing and appropriateness to setting and type of weather, and use and appropriateness of makeup.	Client is well groomed and shows appropriate dress for weather.	Appearance is unkempt, choice of clothing is inappropriate for weather, makeup is excessive. May be result of emotional problem, psychiatric disturbance, or organic brain syndrome. **! *Nurse Alert*** *Variations in appearance may result from cultural preference, inability to attend to or perform self-care, inability to keep clothing clean, or poor self-image.*
Language		
Observe manner of client's speech. Note voice inflection, tone, and volume.	The client's voice should have inflections, be clear and strong, and increase in volume appropriately. Speech should be fluent and articulate.	Speech is slow and slurred.
When it is clear that communication with a client is unclear (e.g., misuse of words, hesitations, creation of new words), assess the following:		
Ask the client to name familiar objects to which you point.	Client names objects correctly.	

Assessment	Normal Findings	Deviations From Normal
Ask the client to respond to simple verbal and written commands such as "Stand up" or "Sit down."	Client can follow commands.	
Ask the client to read simple sentences out loud.	Client reads sentences correctly.	Inability of client to understand spoken or written words may indicate a form of aphasia (expressive, receptive, or global).
Intellectual Function		
Use an approach that does not threaten the client or make the client feel uncomfortable. Using a casual manner, ask questions about concepts or ideas with which the client is familiar.		
Ask client to repeat a short series of numbers forward and then backward (e.g., 7, 3, 1 and 1, 3, 7). Gradually increase the number of digits until client fails to repeat digits correctly.	Immediate recall is evidenced by client repeating series of five to eight digits forward and four to six backward.	Immediate recall is impaired; associated possibly with depression or diffuse brain disease.

Refer to MMS examination for test of short-term memory, registration, and recall (see Chapter 5).	Client is able to name three objects and recall them later during the examination.	Client is unable to recall objects. Impairment can be related to various neurologic or psychiatric disorders.
Have client recall verifiable events occurring during the same day, such as what was eaten for breakfast or form of transport used to arrive at clinic or hospital. Confirm the client's answers with family or friends if necessary.	Client recalls events.	Loss of immediate and recent memory with retention of remote memory suggests organic brain syndrome (Seidel et al., 1995).
Ask client to recall previous medical history or family history of illness. You may also ask when client's birthday or a special day in history is. Ask open-ended questions rather than simple *Yes* or *No* questions.	Client should have immediate recall of such information.	
Have client follow a series of commands (e.g., tap your head, smile, raise one finger) or repeat a short story you relate.	Client's attention span is normal.	Easy distraction, confusion, or impaired memory may be caused by fatigue, anxiety, or medication effects.

Assessment	Normal Findings	Deviations From Normal
Ask client to identify analogies or associations between terms or simple concepts (go from simple to complex):		
What is similar about these objects: a plane and a bird, a tree and a rose, a river and a lake?		
Complete the following comparison: A dog is to a beagle as a cat is to a ________.		
What is the difference between these two objects: a computer and a typewriter, a doctor and a nurse?	Client makes correct analogy or association.	Inability to describe similarities or differences can be caused by pathology of the cerebral cortex or by lower intelligence.
Ask the client (without paper and pencil) to perform simple arithmetic calculations: Subtract 6 from 40 and 6 from that answer, etc. Add 9 to 60 and 9 to that, etc.	Calculations should be completed within a minute, with few errors.	Impairment of arithmetic skills can be associated with depression and diffuse brain disease.

Ask client a series of questions designed to measure judgment and reasoning: Ask what client knows about reason for hospitalization, plans for the future, or how the client would react if he or she suddenly became ill at home.

Client exhibits clear reasoning; evaluates situation and offers appropriate response.

Explanations are incongruent; judgment is impaired.

Have client explain meaning of simple proverb (e.g., "A stitch in time saves nine," "Don't count your chickens before they're hatched."). Note if the client's explanation is relevant and concrete.

Abstract reasoning is intact, as evidenced by adequate interpretation of phrase.

Abstract reasoning can be impaired by organic brain syndrome, brain damage, or lack of intelligence.

! ***Nurse Alert*** *The client's ability to perform intellectual functions has implications for the remainder of the neurologic examination. You may have to skip or delay parts of the examination that require feedback if the client is confused or irritable.*

Cranial Nerve Function

Assess the function of each of the 12 cranial nerves (Table 19-2). Many of the tests can be integrated during earlier portions of the physical examination.

Deviations from normal include the following:

Inability to identify aroma or agnosia (CN I)

Table 19-2 Cranial nerve function and assessment

Number	Name	Type	Function	Method
I	Olfactory	Sensory	Sense of smell	Ask client to identify different nonirritating aromas such as coffee and vanilla.
II	Optic	Sensory	Visual acuity	Use Snellen chart or ask client to read printed material while wearing glasses.
III	Oculomotor	Motor	Extraocular eye movement	Assess directions of gaze.
			Pupil constriction and dilation	Measure pupil reaction to light reflex and accommodation.
IV	Trochlear	Motor	Upward and downward movement of eyeball	Assess directions of gaze.
V	Trigeminal	Sensory and motor	Sensory nerve to skin of face	Lightly touch cornea with wisp of cotton. Assess corneal reflex. Measure sensation of light pain and touch across skin of face.
			Motor nerve to muscles of jaw	Palpate temples as client clenches teeth.
VI	Abducens	Motor	Lateral movement of eyeballs	Assess directions of gaze.

VII	Facial	Sensory and motor	Facial expression	As client smiles, frowns, puffs out cheeks, and raises and lowers eyebrows, look for asymmetry.
			Taste	Have client identify salty or sweet taste on front of tongue.
VIII	Auditory	Sensory	Hearing	Assess ability to hear spoken word.
IX	Glossopharyngeal	Sensory and motor	Taste	Ask client to identify sour or sweet taste on back of tongue.
X	Vagus	Sensory and motor	Sensation of pharynx	Ask client to say "Ah." Observe palate and pharynx movement.
			Movement of vocal cords	Assess speech for hoarseness.
XI	Spinal accessory	Motor	Movement of head and shoulders	Ask client to shrug shoulders and turn head against passive resistance.
XII	Hypoglossal	Motor	Position of tongue	Ask client to stick out tongue to midline and move it from side to side.

Assessment	Normal Findings	Deviations From Normal
		Reduced visual acuity (CN II) Abnormal direction of gaze, pupil reacts slowly to light or is nonreactive (CN III) Abnormal direction of gaze in upward and downward diagonals (CN IV) Absent corneal reflex, absent sensation of light touch across skin of face, client unable to clench teeth (CN V) Abnormal direction of gaze laterally (CN VI) Inability to smile symmetrically, absent or one-sided blinking and raising of eyebrows, irregular or unequal facial movement, inability

Sensory Function

Perform all sensory testing with client's eyes closed and be sure not to give client cues as to correct response (e.g., pattern in which body part is stimulated).

to identify taste on front of tongue (CN VII)

Inability to hear spoken word (CN VIII)

Inability to identify taste on back of tongue, absent gag reflex (CN IX)

Unequal or absent rise of uvula and soft palate as client says "Ah," absent gag reflex (CN X)

Inability to shrug shoulders against resistance (CN XI)

Tongue deviates to side (CN XII)

Assessment	Normal Findings	Deviations From Normal
Ask client to say when a particular stimulus is perceived. Be sure to test sensation bilaterally. Perform the following tests on the client's hands, lower arms, feet, and lower legs. If impairment is found, describe by the distribution of major peripheral nerves or dermatomes (Fig. 19-2): Light touch: Apply light wisp of cotton to sensitive points along the skin's surface (face, neck, top of hands). Ask client to voice when sensation is felt.		

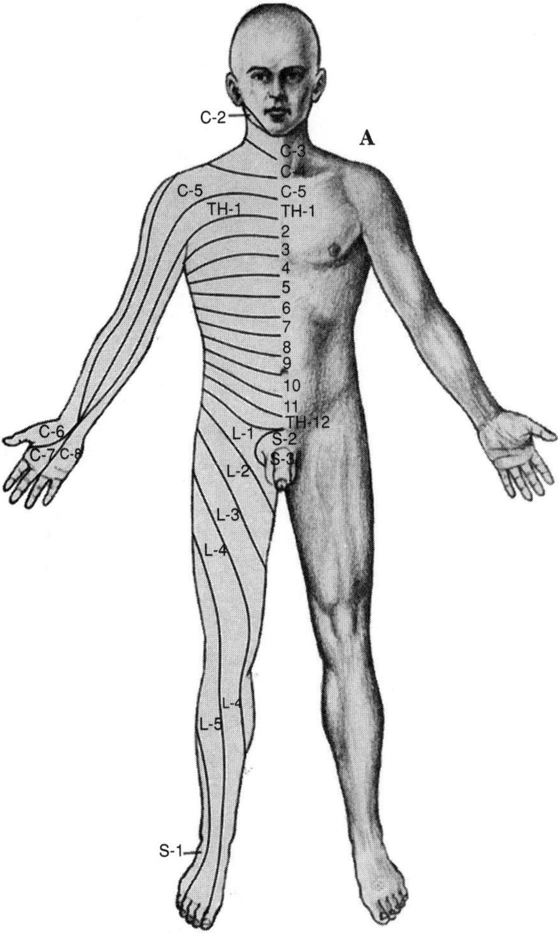

Fig. 19-2
A, Anterior view of sensory dermatomes.
(From Thompson JM et al: *Mosby's clinical nursing*, ed 3, St Louis, 1993, Mosby.)

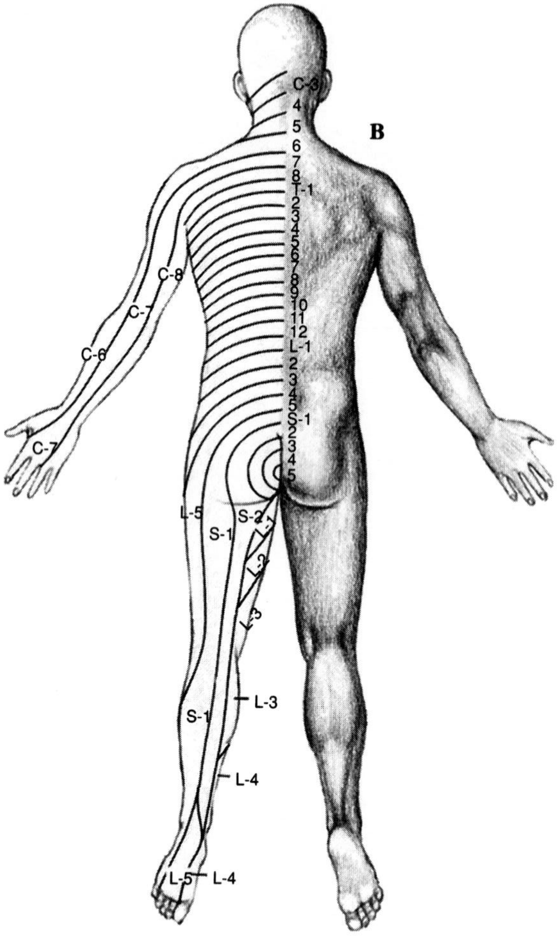

Fig. 19-2, cont'd
B, Posterior view.

Pain: Break one end of a tongue blade. Alternately apply the sharp and blunt ends of the tongue blade to the skin's surface. Note areas of numbness or increased sensitivity by asking if client feels a "sharp" or "dull" sensation.

Vibration: Apply stem of vibrating tuning fork to the distal interphalangeal joint of fingers and interphalangeal joint of great toe, elbow, and wrist. Have client say when vibration is first felt and when vibration stops. Be sure client feels vibration and not just pressure.

Assessment	Normal Findings	Deviations From Normal
Position: Grasp finger or toe, holding it by its sides with thumb and index finger. Alternate moving finger or toe up and down. Ask client to state when finger (or toe) is up or down. Perform on both sides and with fingers and toes.		
Temperature: Touch skin with test tube filled with hot or cold water. Ask client if sensation of hot or cold is felt. (Omit if pain sensation is normal.)		
Two-point discrimination: Take two broken tongue blades. Lightly apply one or both tongue blade tips simultaneously to skin's surface. Ask client if one or two pricks are felt. Find distance at which client can no longer distinguish two points.	Sensation for touch, pain, vibration, and position is intact. Client can discriminate two points as close as 2 to 8 mm (fingertips), 8 to 12 mm (palms), 40 mm (forearms), and 75 mm (upper arms and thighs) (Barkauskas et al., 1994).	Impaired sensory reception can be the result of local peripheral nerve injury, spinal cord injury, or disturbance in sensory cortex.

Test the client's cognitive ability to interpret sensations:

Place a coin or paper clip in client's hand and ask client to identify object.	Client is cognitively able to interpret sensation and identify object (stereognosis).	Client incorrectly identifies object.
Draw a letter or number with the end of a tongue blade on the client's palm. Have the client identify the figure.	Client is able to readily recognize figure or letter drawn on palm (graphesthesia).	Letter or number cannot be identified. Inability to perform these tests may indicate lesion of the sensory cortex or posterior columns of spinal cord (Seidel et al., 1995).

Motor Function

Assess gait, stance, gross muscle movement, involuntary muscle movement, and muscle strength and tone following procedures described in musculoskeletal assessment (see Chapter 18).

Assessment	Normal Findings	Deviations From Normal
To further assess gait, ask client to walk a straight line with eyes open, then turn and walk back with eyes closed. Note gait sequence, arm movements, and degree of steadiness. **!** *Nurse Alert Stand near client with your arms extended out, but not touching client.*	Client walks with first heel striking the floor and then moving to full contact with the floor. Second heel pushes off, leaving the ground. Body weight transfers from first heel to the ball of its foot. Leg swing accelerates as weight is removed from second foot. Second foot is lifted and travels ahead of the weight-bearing first foot, swinging through. Second foot slows in preparation for heel strike. Balance is steady.	Client shuffles, staggers, reels, has leg lag, or has foot flop. Gait abnormalities may be caused by alterations such as pinched sciatic nerve (foot flop), hemiparesis (dragging or circling stiffly), cerebellar ataxia (wide based and staggering), or sensory ataxia (wide based, feet thrown forward and out, client watches ground).
Test client's coordination and fine motor skills. In each of the following tests, demonstrate the maneuver first, then have the client repeat the maneuver, noting smoothness, rhythm, and speed: Ask client to sit. Demonstrate for client method for rapidly strik-		

ing thigh with palm of hand, evenly, without hesitation. Then have client repeat.

Next demonstrate and have client alternately strike thigh with hand supinated and then pronated.

Stand in front of client, holding your index finger stationary 2 feet away from client's face. Ask client to touch your finger with index finger and then to touch own nose alternately.

Client performs all maneuvers smoothly, rhythmically, and with increasing speed.

Stiff, slow, or nonrhythmic movement can indicate proprioception or cerebellar dysfunction. Tremors of hand may appear.

Test lower extremities for coordination by asking the client to lie supine. Place your hand at ball of client's foot. Ask client to tap hand with foot as quickly as possible. Note speed and smoothness of movement.

Taps foot evenly and quickly without hesitation.

Assessment	Normal Findings	Deviations From Normal
Have client stand with feet close together, arms at the sides, eyes closed. Note presence of swaying. (Stand close to client with arms outstretched to catch client in case of fall.)	Slight swaying is expected but not to cause risk of falling.	Loss of balance (positive Romberg's test) indicates cerebellar ataxia or vestibular (CN VIII) dysfunction.
Ask client to close eyes and stand on one foot and then the other. (Continue to stand close by client.)	Balance maintained for 5 seconds with slight swaying.	Loss of balance occurs almost immediately.

Reflexes

Assess deep tendon reflexes (Table 19-3). Reflexes should be symmetrical on both sides of body. Reflexes are graded on the following scale:

0	No response
1+	Low normal with slight muscle contraction
2+	Normal, visible muscle twitch and movement of arm/leg
3+	Brisker than normal but may not indicate disease
4+	Hyperactive, very brisk; spinal cord disorder suspected

Have client relax extremity to be tested and avoid voluntary movement.

Position limb to slightly stretch the muscle being tested.

Absent reflexes may indicate neuropathy or lower motor neuron disease. Hyperactive reflexes suggest an upper motor neuron disorder.

Table 19-3 Common reflexes

Type	Procedure	Normal Reflex
Deep Tendon Reflexes		
Biceps	Flex the client's arm up to 45 degrees at the elbow with palms down; place your thumb in the antecubital fossa at the base of the biceps tendon and your fingers over the biceps muscle; strike the thumb with the reflex hammer	Flexion of arm at elbow
Triceps	Flex the client's arm at the elbow up to 90 degrees, holding the arm across the chest, or hold the upper arm horizontally and allow the lower arm to go limp; strike the triceps tendon, just above the elbow	Extension at elbow
Patellar	Have the client sit with legs hanging freely over the side of the table or chair or have the client lie supine and support knee in a flexed 90-degree position; briskly tap the patellar tendon just below the patella	Extension of lower leg
Achilles'	Have the client assume the same position as for patellar reflex; slightly dorsiflex the client's ankle by grasping the toes in the palm of your hand; strike Achilles' tendon just above the heel at the ankle malleoli	Plantar flexion of foot
Plantar (Babinski)	Have the client lie supine with legs straight and feet relaxed; take the handle end of the reflex hammer and stroke the lateral aspect of the sole from the heel to the ball of the foot, curving across the ball to the medial side	Bending of the toes downward

Cutaneous Reflexes		
Gluteal	Have the client assume a side-lying position; spread apart the client's buttocks and lightly stimulate the perineal area with a cotton-tipped applicator	Contraction of anal sphincter
Abdominal	Have the client stand or lie supine; stroke the abdominal skin with the base of a cotton-tipped applicator over the lateral borders of the rectus abdominal muscles toward the midline; repeat the test in each abdominal quadrant	Rectus abdominal muscles contract with pulling of umbilicus toward the stimulated side
Cremasteric	Stroke the inner upper thigh of the male client, using a cotton-tipped applicator	Scrotum elevates on stimulated side

Assessment	Normal Findings	Deviations From Normal
Palpate each tendon to locate correct point for stimulation. Hold reflex hammer loosely so it can swing freely between thumb and fingers. Tap tendon briskly (Fig. 19-3).		

A

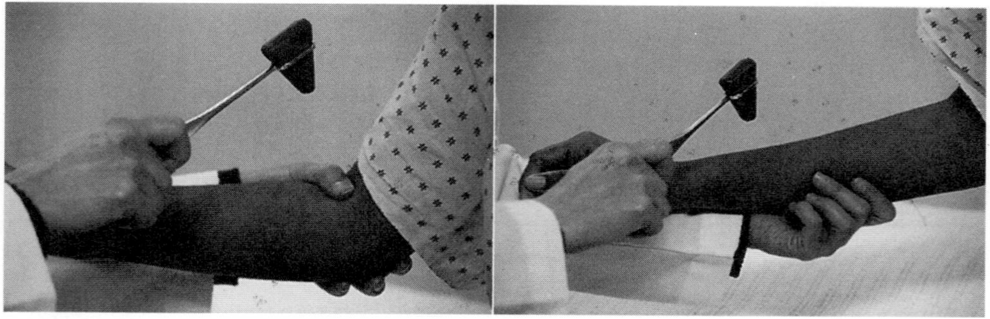

B

Fig. 19-3
Checking reflexes. A, Biceps. B, Brachioradial.
(From Seidel HM et al: *Mosby's guide to physical examination,* ed 3, St Louis, 1995, Mosby.)

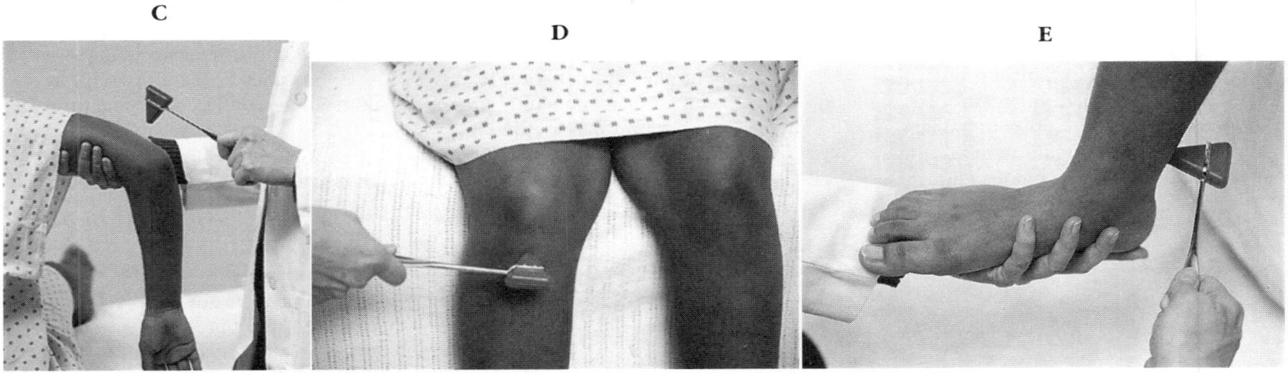

Fig. 19-3, cont'd
C, Triceps. **D,** Patellar. **E,** Achilles'.
(From Seidel HM et al: *Mosby's guide to physical examination,* ed 3, St Louis, 1995, Mosby.)

Assessment	Normal Findings	Deviations From Normal
Compare symmetry of reflex from one side of body to the other. If necessary, distract client during testing to increase reflex response by asking the client to clench teeth while testing upper extremities or asking the client to interlock hands and pull outward during testing lower extremities.		

Nursing Diagnoses

Assessment data may reveal defining characteristics for the following nursing diagnoses:

- Impaired verbal communication
- Altered thought processes
- Altered cerebral tissue perfusion
- Risk for injury
- Sensory/perceptual alterations (auditory, gustatory, tactile, olfactory)
- Risk for aspiration related to absent gag reflex
- Impaired swallowing
- Impaired physical mobility

Pediatric Considerations

- Parents should act as resources for information regarding any recent change in child's behavior, attention span, or school performance.
- Memory testing may begin at about 4 years of age. The number of words or numbers a child can repeat in order varies by age.

- Use of the Denver Developmental Screening Test (DDST) can determine whether the child is developing language and personal-social skills as expected.
- Use a Snellen, "E," or picture chart to test child's visual acuity.
- To assess cranial nerves, often games must be played to elicit response, such as imitating the examiner puffing out the checks or making facial expressions.
- Observe child eating a cookie or cracker to assess jaw strength.
- In sensory testing children can point to areas touched. Superficial pain is usually not tested because of child's fear of sharp objects.
- Observe children at play, noting gait and fine motor coordination. The child can hop or do the heel-to-toe test in an improvised game.
- Young children have a wide-based gait. The school-age child walks with feet closer together.
- There are a number of reflexes to assess an infant's developmental status, including the following:
  - Rooting reflex: Infant turns head toward side of face stroked (disappears at 3 to 12 months of age).
  - Grasp reflex: Infant flexes the hand or toes when light touch is applied to the palm of the hand or the sole of the foot (disappears at 3 months of age).
  - Moro's reflex: Sudden jarring of infant while lying down causes infant to suddenly extend and abduct extremities. Crying also is elicited (disappears at 3 to 4 months of age).
  - Dance reflex: Infant is held upright so that the feet touch a flat surface to stimulate walking movement (disappears at 3 to 4 weeks of age).

Gerontologic Considerations

- The older adult may need additional time to respond to questions requiring the use of memory, judgment, or other cognitive functions.
- Commonly, older clients show symptoms of forgetfulness resulting from normal neurologic changes. Sudden confusion, however, is usually unrelated to age. The older client is at greater risk of confusion from acute conditions such as dehydration, infection, drug toxicity, hyponatremia, and hypoglycemia.
- Delirium is an acute disturbance of consciousness that is accompanied

by a change in cognition. It cannot be accounted for by a preexisting or evolving dementia. Delirium develops over a short period of time, usually hours to days, and tends to fluctuate during the course of the day. Usually it is a direct physiologic consequence of a general medical condition. Client has reduced clarity of awareness of environment, ability to focus or shift attention is impaired, person is easily distracted, there is an accompanying change in cognition (recent memory impaired, disorientation to time and place, language disturbance), and the client has perceptual alterations (e.g., illusions, hallucinations) (American Psychiatric Association, 1994).

- Deterioration of intellectual function should not be found unless the client has a disease of the central nervous system.
- Some problem-solving skills deteriorate with aging, but this may be related to disuse. Recent memory deteriorates before remote memory.
- See Chapters 8 and 9 regarding the older adult's limitations resulting from visual and hearing impairment.
- Atrophy of the taste buds is normal in older clients.
- Conduction velocity in peripheral nerves declines with age.
- The tactile and vibratory senses are blunted, and therefore more strong stimuli are required to test this sense.
- Proprioception in the older adult becomes increasingly less functional with age.
- Older clients have reduced pain sensation bilaterally.
- A normally slow reaction time may cause coordination testing to be less rhythmic in older adults.
- Slight swaying when the client stands with feet together and eyes closed is normal for an older client.
- Reflexes are normally less brisk or even absent in older clients.
- Reflex response diminishes in the lower extremities before the upper extremities are affected (Seidel et al., 1991).

Cultural Considerations

- Many Mexican Americans believe that health represents a state of equilibrium in the universe wherein the forces of "hot," "cold," "wet," and "dry" must be balanced. Headaches may have a causative agent thought to have a hot or cold quality. If a headache is seen to be caused by a "hot" factor, cold herbs may be placed on the temples to absorb the heat. Paralysis is thought to be caused when cold air enters the body (Giger and Davidhizar, 1995).

- Cerebrovascular disease mortality is the highest for Japanese living in Japan, intermediate for Japanese living in Hawaii, and lowest for Japanese living on the U.S. mainland (Yano et al., 1985).

Client Teaching

- Explain to the client's family and friends the implications of any behavioral or mental impairment shown by the client.
- For clients with sensory or motor impairments, explain measures to ensure the client's safety (e.g., use of ambulation aids, using caution when applying ice packs or heating pads).
- Teach older clients to observe skin surfaces for areas of trauma.
- See Chapters 8 and 9 regarding instructions for clients with hearing and vision loss.
- If client has reduced corneal reflex, advise on use of ophthalmic drops to keep cornea moistened.
- If a client has difficulty swallowing, instruct family on ways to properly prepare food or assist client with feeding.
- Teach older adult to plan enough time to complete tasks, because reaction time is slowed.
- Gait is characterized by short, uncertain steps. Shuffling may also occur.

20 Nutrition

A nutritional assessment includes four components: physical measurements and anthropometry, laboratory tests, dietary history and health history, and clinical observations. This chapter summarizes some techniques previously described in earlier chapters of this text.

Rationale

Nurses are in an excellent position to recognize signs of poor nutrition and to take steps to initiate change. Close daily contact with clients and families enables nurses to make observations about clients' physical status, food intake, weight gain or loss, and responses to therapy. A nutritional assessment is designed to identify clients' nutritional deficiencies that adversely affect health, to assist in planning and delivering nutritional care, and to evaluate the efficacy of nutritional care.

Critical Thinking

Knowledge

Refer to the knowledge you have regarding principles of nutrition and the function of the gastrointestinal system. Clients will exhibit alterations that involve either a change in dietary intake or a change in the physiologic systems that influence food digestion, absorption, and elimination.

Be aware of developmental variables influencing normal nutritional needs, as well as the influence of culture on dietary preferences.

Experience

Consider the factors that influence your own appetite and selection of foods. This personal experience will help you in identifying a client's food preferences, dietary habits, and problems that result when nutrition is inadequate.

Assessment can be very effective if performed while a client is eating or while preparing food in the home.

Standards

When performing a nutritional assessment apply the following principles:

- Collaborate closely with a clinical dietitian if one is available.
- When assessing a client's typical diet history, assess not only the foods he or she eats but also how they are prepared.

Equipment

Tongue blade
Penlight
Scale (weight bearing or stretcher)
Tape measure
Skin fold caliper

Delegation Considerations

The nutritional assessment involves problem solving and knowledge application unique to a professional nurse. Delegation of the assessment is inappropriate. However, trained unlicensed assistive personnel can measure and report height and weight values and assist in measuring intake and output (I&O) and estimating solid food intake. Staff should also be informed of clients at risk for eating problems and to report to the RN when a client's appetite and dietary intake change.

Nutritional Assessment

Client Preparation

- Ideally, client will stand during measurement of height and weight (see Chapter 5).
- Client may sit or lie in bed during remainder of nutritional assessment.
- Client should wear a loose-fitting gown for access to upper extremities.
- Involve a friend or family member who helps in preparing food for the client (when applicable).

History

- Refer to Chapter 5 for data included within a general diet history.

- Obtain a diet history, including usual intake of food and liquids, food preferences, snacks, and normal meal times. It may be helpful to give the client or family member a dietary log to complete for a week to establish food patterns over time. (See Appendix M for the U.S. food guide pyramid.)
- Determine how foods are normally prepared (e.g., fried, baked).
- Determine if client is on a prescribed diet or independently follows a weight-loss or special diet. How long has the client followed the diet?
- Ask if client has noticed a recent weight loss or gain and over what time period.
- Does client have any physical limitations affecting the ability to feed self (e.g., weak grasp, reduced hand-eye coordination)?
- Does client's current physical status increase metabolic demands, such as burns, sepsis, major skeletal trauma, or fever?
- Does client have a physical intolerance to foods or fluids, such as nausea, vomiting, anorexia, abdominal cramping, or diarrhea?
- Is client taking any medications that might influence appetite (e.g., captopril, chemotherapy, steroids, antibiotics, insulin, lithium)?
- Is client taking any medications that may interact with nutrients to decrease medication function (e.g., vitamin K–rich foods such as dark green vegetables, coumarin anticoagulants)?
- Does the client follow any cultural, ethnic, or religious traditions that influence the type and intake of food?
- Ask if client has any difficulties in being able to purchase food, travel to grocery store, or maintain utilities to prepare food.
- Determine if client ingests alcohol; determine frequency and amount.

Assessment	Normal Findings	Deviations From Normal
Review findings from physical examination and note clinical signs of client's nutritional status (e.g., condition of muscles; gastrointestinal function; condition of skin, nails, and mucous membranes; ability to chew and swallow) (Table 20-1).	Review of systems reveals good condition of integument and musculoskeletal systems. Gastrointestinal function is normal with no palpable masses. Client has own teeth or properly fitting dentures. Client is energetic, sleeps well, and has good attention span.	See abnormalities listed in Table 20-1.
Obtain client's height and weight (see Chapter 5). **! *Nurse Alert*** *If client is unable to stand, the armspan or distance from fingertip to fingertip with arms fully outstretched at shoulder level approximates height for the mature adult.*		
Convert weight to kilograms (2.2 lb = 1 kg).		

Table 20-1 Clinical signs of nutritional status

Body Area	Signs of Good Nutrition	Signs of Poor Nutrition
General appearance	Alert, responsive	Listless, apathetic, cachectic
Weight	Normal for height, age, body build	Overweight or underweight (special concern for underweight)
Posture	Erect, arms and legs straight	Sagging shoulders, sunken chest, humped back
Muscles	Well-developed, firm, good tone, some fat under skin	Flaccid, poor tone, underdeveloped, tender, edematous, wasted appearance, cannot walk properly
Nervous control	Good attention span, not irritable or restless, normal reflexes, psychologic stability	Inattentive, irritable, confused, burning and tingling of hands and feet (paresthesia), loss of position and vibratory sense, weakness and tenderness of muscles (may result in inability to walk), decrease or loss of ankle and knee reflexes, absent vibratory sense
Gastrointestinal function	Good appetite and digestion, normal regular elimination, no palpable organs or masses	Anorexia, indigestion, constipation or diarrhea, liver or spleen enlargement
Gums	Good pink color, healthy, red, no swelling or bleeding	Spongy, bleed easily, marginal redness, inflamed, gums receding

Tongue	Good pink color or deep reddish in appearance, not swollen or smooth, surface papillae present, no lesions	Swelling, scarlet and raw, magenta color, beefy (glossitis), hyperemic and hypertrophic papillae, atrophic papillae
Teeth	No cavities, no pain, bright, straight, no crowding, well-shaped jaw, clean, no discoloration	Unfilled caries, absent teeth, worn surfaces, mottled (fluorosis), malpositioned
Eyes	Bright, clear, shiny, no sores at corner of eye-lids, membranes moist and healthy pink color, no prominent blood vessels or mound of tissue or sclera, no fatigue circles beneath	Eye membranes pale (pale conjunctivae), redness of membrane (conjunctival infection), dryness, signs of infection, Bitot's spots, redness and fissuring of eyelid corners (angular palpebritis), dryness of eye membrane (conjunctival xerosis), dull appearance of cornea (corneal xerosis), soft cornea (keratomalacia)
Neck (glands)	No enlargement	Thyroid enlargement
Nails	Firm, pink	Spoon shape (koilonychia), brittle, ridged
Legs, feet	No tenderness, weakness, or swelling; good color	Edema, tender calf, tingling, weakness
Skeleton	No malformations	Bowlegs, knock-knees, chest deformity at diaphragm, beaded ribs, prominent scapulae

From Williams SR: Nutritional assessment and guidance in prenatal care. In Worthington-Roberts BS, Williams SR, eds: *Nutrition in pregnancy and lactation,* ed 5, St Louis, 1993, Mosby.

Assessment	Normal Findings	Deviations From Normal
Calculate ideal body weight (IBW): Males: 47.7 kg (106 lb) for the first 5 feet, then add 2.25 kg/2.5 cm or 6 lb per additional inch in height Females: 45 kg (100 lb) for the first 5 feet, then add 2.25 kg/2.5 cm or 5 lb per additional inch in height	Client ranges 10% above or 10% below IBW.	Client ranges exceed 10% above or 10% below IBW.
Another approach for assessing height/weight balance is calculation of the body mass index (BMI) (Fig. 20-1), derived by dividing a person's weight (in kilograms) by the height (in meters squared).	Normal BMI for women is 19 to 23. Normal BMI for men is 20 to 25.	Women with a BMI value of 23 to 29 are classified as being overweight; a value over 30 indicates obesity. Men with a BMI value of 25 to 30 are classified as overweight; a value over 30 indicates obesity.

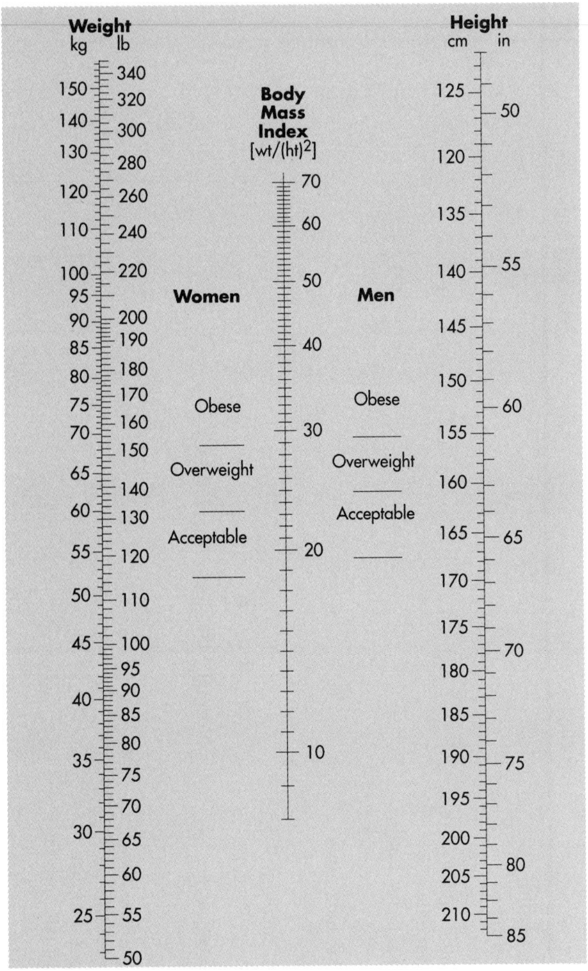

Fig. 20-1
Nomogram for determining BMI. Use by placing a ruler or other straight edge between the column for height and the column for weight, connecting an individual's numbers for these two variables.
(From Bray G: Obesity: definition, diagnosis and disadvantages, *Med J Aust* 142, 1985.)

Assessment	Normal Findings	Deviations From Normal
Using tape measure, determine smallest portion of wrist distal to styloid process by measuring circumference in centimeters. Divide the wrist circumference into the client's height to calculate the *r* value for body frame size: Women: small > 11; medium 10.1 to 11.0; large < 10.1 Men: small > 10.4; medium 9.6 to 10.4; large < 9.6		
With client's nondominant arm relaxed, measure circumference at midpoint of arm in centimeters (between tip of acromial process of scapula and olecranon process of ulna). Record as mid–upper arm circumference (MAC) to estimate muscle wasting.	Normal MAC (see Appendix C).	

With thumb and forefinger, pinch a double fold of fat lengthwise about 1 cm above midpoint of the MAC. With other hand, place teeth of calipers on either side of fat fold. Place calipers below fingers so pressure is exerted from calipers and not fingers. Record three separate readings in millimeters and then average to obtain a skin-fold measure (estimate of subcutaneous fat).	Triceps skin fold (TSF): men 12.5 mm; women 16.5 mm.	TSF greater than 15 mm in men and 25 mm in women.
Calculate midarm muscle circumference (MAMC) to estimate skeletal muscle mass.	Normal MAMC (see Appendix C).	$MAMC = MAC - (TSF \times 3.14)$
Review common laboratory tests to evaluate client's nutritional status. Pay special attention to albumin (indicator for chronic malnutrition), transferrin (indicator of protein and calorie malnutrition), prealbumin, retinol-binding protein, total iron-binding capacity, and hemoglobin.	No single laboratory or biochemical test is diagnostic for malnutrition. Most plasma proteins have a >7-day half-life and will not reflect changes in less than a week. Consider all of the client's clinical symptoms when reviewing laboratory results.	

Assessment	Normal Findings	Deviations From Normal
Determine client's caloric needs using the Harris-Benedict equation for basal energy expenditure (BEE): Male: BEE = 66 + 13.7W (weight in kilograms) + 5H (height in centimeters) − 6.8A (age of client) Female: BEE = 65.5 + 9.6W + 1.7H − 4.7A	Client's daily food intake ranges from 1600 to 1800 kcal/day (Health and Welfare Canada, 1992; USDA, 1990). Dietary fat intake averages 30% or less of total calories, with saturated fat less than 10%.	Client's food intake is less than 1500 kcal or exceeds 2500 kcal/day. Dietary fat intake is 36% or more of total calories, with saturated fat 13% or more.

Nursing Diagnoses

Assessment data may reveal defining characteristics for the following nursing diagnoses:

- Altered nutrition: less than body requirements
- Altered nutrition: more than body requirements
- Altered nutrition: risk for more than body requirements
- Risk for infection
- Altered oral mucous membranes
- Risk for impaired skin integrity
- Impaired swallowing
- Diarrhea
- Self-care deficit: feeding

Pediatric Considerations

- Growth is most rapid during an infant's first year of life.
- Some aspects of the assessment could produce anxiety in children. Potential concerns, such as how calipers are to be used, should be explained.

- Refer to adjusted height and weight tables based on a child's developmental age and sex (see Appendix D).
- TSF thickness is not routinely measured unless child is at a weight greater than the 90th percentile. It is often difficult to differentiate fat folds from lean muscle tissue in children (Seidel et al., 1991).
- Toddlers need fewer calories but an increased amount of protein in relation to body weight. Calcium and phosphorus are needed for bone growth. Recommend a minimum of two servings from the milk group, four servings daily from the fruit and vegetable group, four servings from the bread and cereal group, 1 to 3 oz from the meat group, and 1 to 2 tsp of margarine or butter.
- For school-agers, recommend two servings daily from the milk group, 2 to 3 oz from the meat group, four or more servings from the fruit and vegetable group, three to four servings from the bread group, and 1 to 2 tsp of margarine or butter.
- For adolescents, recommend three or more servings from the milk group, two or more servings from the meat group, four or more servings from the vegetable and fruit group, four to six or more servings from the bread group, and 1 to 2 tbsp of margarine or butter.

Gerontologic Considerations

- Older adults have a decreased need for calories as the metabolic rate slows.
- Older adults are particularly prone to fluid imbalance and inadequate intake of fiber nutrients (Ebersole and Hess, 1994).
- A reduction in the number of taste buds can reduce an older adult's sense of taste and thus reduce appetite.
- Basic tips for older adults in following dietary guidelines include eating a variety of foods; maintaining ideal weight; avoiding excess fat, saturated fat, and cholesterol; eating foods with adequate starch and fiber; avoiding excess sugar, sodium, and salt; and drinking alcohol in moderation.
- Review the following factors with an older adult to determine the risk for poor nutritional health: has an illness or condition that makes client change the kind and/or amount of food eaten, or has fewer than two meals per day; eats few fruits/vegetables/milk products; has three

or more drinks of beer/liquor/wine almost daily; has tooth or mouth problems; does not have enough money to buy food needed; eats alone most of the time; takes three or more different prescribed over-the-counter drugs; has lost or gained 10 pounds in the last 6 months; is not physically able to shop/cook/feed self (score of 3 to 5 indicates moderate risk; 6 or more indicates high risk) (*Nutrition Interventions Manual,* 1992).

Cultural Considerations

- Prevalence of overweight increases with age, for both men and women, but to a greater degree in women. African Americans and Hispanics have a greater prevalence of being overweight than do whites (Kumanyika, 1993).
- Japanese Americans frequently prepare their food using soy sauce as a seasoning; it is high in sodium.
- There is a growing incidence of childhood obesity among Mexican Americans, which may be related to mothers believing that a fat baby is a healthy baby (Giger and Davidhizar, 1995).
- Lactose intolerance is found in over 66% of Mexican Americans and is very common in African Americans, some American Indian tribes, and Orientals (Giger and Davidhizar, 1995).
- G6PD is an enzyme constituent of the red blood cells and is involved in the hexose monophosphate pathway, which accounts for 10% of glucose metabolism of the red blood cells. Deficiency of the enzyme causes red blood cells to hemolyze. G6PD deficiency occurs in different forms. The A variety is found in 35% of African Americans. The B variety is found in 65% of African Americans who have the deficiency and in nearly all non–African Americans who have the deficiency. There is also a Chinese disorder and a Mediterranean variety of the deficiency (Giger and Davidhizar, 1995).
- Elderly Russian women often have a problem with obesity because of the lack of fresh fruits and vegetables in their country. Many culturally prepared foods are high in fat and salts (Giger and Davidhizar, 1995).

Client Teaching

- Instruct adolescents on how vigorous exercise increases needs for kilocalories, fluid, and iron. Stress the need for fluid during exercise.

Discuss common myths about nutrition in sports (steak and eggs before competition, sport drinks, carbohydrate loading, high-fat meals).

- Have client develop a 1-week menu to learn how to integrate recommended food groups into daily diet.
- Instruct older clients on effect certain medications might have on appetite.
- Explain to clients how to read daily reference values (DRVs), found on nutritional labeling. DRVs are based on the percentages of 2000 kcal or the highest amount that is recommended (Potter and Perry, 1997).

21 Completing the Examination

Recording and Reporting the Physical Assessment Findings

- When recording information gathered in a physical assessment, the examiner must condense and organize information into a meaningful written summary.
- Standardized forms are usually available in institutions and allow all health professionals to review the client's status.
- The summary of the assessment is a legal document, and thus information must be presented by incorporating the following characteristics: accuracy, conciseness, thoroughness, currentness, organization, and confidentiality.
- During the examination it is wise to take brief notes about findings and the client's concerns. Measurements such as vital signs, extent of edema, and the size of the liver should be written down as they are obtained.
- Do not try to record all data during the examination, because it may detract attention away from the client.
- Conduct the examination in an efficient sequence (this may mean combining assessments of body

systems), but record your results by the categories on the assessment form used by your institution.

- Review entries made during the examination for accuracy and thoroughness.
- Communicate significant findings to appropriate medical and nursing personnel. This depends on the seriousness and urgency of need for intervention. Record the findings communicated to other health care providers.

Organization of Assessment Information

- Refer to Chapter 2 for a summary of how a history and physical assessment are organized.

Guidelines for Description of Findings

- The report of a client's physical assessment should leave no questions in the mind of readers as to the client's current physical and psychologic condition. Data should be concise and accurate enough so that subsequent examiners can compare their data with the baseline database. Helpful guidelines for recording details of the client's examination include the following:

  A client's presenting problem or illness helps an examiner anticipate what an assessment will reveal. Record both expected and unexpected findings with integration of subjective and objective data. One way to record expected findings is to indicate the absence of symptoms (e.g., no cough, shortness of breath, dyspnea).

  Record unexpected findings (such as pain) by their quality or character.

  Relate physical findings to the processes of inspection, palpation, percussion, and auscultation. This makes the process of data gathering clear to the reader.

  Refer to topographic or anatomic landmarks when describing findings. The location of the apical pulse, a breast mass, the site of abdominal pain, or the liver span measurement must be measured to provide a comparison for future assessments. For example, "The apical impulse is 4 cm from the midsternal line at the fifth intercostal space."

Assessment findings are sometimes reported as variations by degree. Extent of edema, pulse amplitude, and heart murmur intensity are examples of findings reported on incremental scales.

Organs, masses, and lesions are consistently recorded on the basis of seven characteristics: texture, size, shape, mobility, tenderness, color, and location. In addition, characteristics such as heat or induration and scarring or discharge may be noted.

Discharge from any site is always described by color, consistency, odor, and amount.

Drawings or illustrations may prove helpful in describing the location of findings. A picture of the abdomen divided into quadrants may be useful in drawing the location of a lesion or mass. Similarly, a stick figure can be used to compare findings in extremities, such as pulse amplitude or reflexes.

Recording Conclusions

- After organizing and recording all information from the examination, review findings and consider the client's signs and symptoms, both overt and subtle. It may be necessary to repeat an assessment or have a colleague confirm a finding.

Do not be afraid to rely on previous experience in examining clients. A nurse becomes more expert at formulating nursing diagnoses after examining hundreds of clients. The nurse's intuition, coupled with scientific knowledge of a client's presenting condition, helps to ensure that all possible questions have been asked and assessments gathered.

- Review all available assessment data and consider the patterns that emerge from the physical findings. Selection of accurate nursing diagnoses is critical to ensure that an appropriate plan of care is developed for the client.

References

AHCPR Panel for the Prediction and Prevention of Pressure Ulcers in Adults: *Pressure ulcers in adults: prediction and prevention,* Clinical Practice Guideline No 3, AHCPR Pub No 92-0047, Rockville, Md, 1992, AHCPR, PHS, USDHHS.

American Cancer Society: *Breast cancer facts and figures,* Atlanta, 1996a, The Society.

American Cancer Society: *1996 cancer facts and figures,* Atlanta, 1996b, The Society.

American Heart Association: *Dietary treatment for hypercholesterolemia: handbook for counselors,* vol 70-2001, Dallas, 1993, The Association.

American Nurses Association: *Nursing and social policy statement,* Kansas City, Mo, 1980, The Association.

American Psychiatric Association: *Diagnostic and statistical manual of mental disorders,* ed 4, Washington, 1994, American Psychiatric Association.

American Thoracic Society: Control of tuberculosis in the United States, *Am Rev Resp Dis* 146(6):1623, 1992.

Barkauskas VH et al: *Health and physical assessment,* St Louis, 1994, Mosby.

Bates B: *A guide to physical examination,* ed 5, Philadelphia, 1990, JB Lippincott.

Bowers AC, Thompson JM: *Clinical manual of health assessment,* ed 4, St Louis, 1992, Mosby.

Bray G: Obesity: definition, diagnosis and disadvantages, *Med J Aust* 142, 1985.

Bullock BI, Rosendahl PP: *Pathophysiology: adaptations and alterations in function,* ed 2, Boston, 1988, Little, Brown.

Burnside IM: *Nursing and the aged: a self-care approach,* ed 3, New York, 1988, McGraw-Hill.

Carnevali DL, Thomas MD: *Diagnostic reasoning and treatment decision making in nursing,* Philadelphia, 1993, JB Lippincott.

Carpenito LJ: *Nursing diagnosis: application to clinical practice,* Philadelphia, 1995, JB Lippincott.

Caulker-Burnett I: Primary care screening for substance abuse, *Nurs Pract* 19(6):42, 1994.

Centers for Disease Control and Prevention: A strategic plan for the elimination of tuberculosis in the United States, *MMWR* 38(suppl 13):1, 1989.

Clore ER: Dispelling the common myths about pediculosis, *J Pediatr Health Care* 3:28, 1989.

Crowell DH et al: Race, ethnicity, and birth weight, Hawaii 1983 to 1986, *Hawaii Med J* 51(9):242, 1992.

Ebersole P, Hess P: *Toward healthy aging,* ed 3, St Louis, 1994, Mosby.

Erickson RS et al: Accuracy of chemical dot thermometers in critically ill adults and young children, *Nurs Res* 28(1):23, 1996.

Facione NC, Facione P: Externalizing the critical thinking in knowledge development and clinical judgment, *Nurs Outlook* 44:129, 1996.

Flory C: Skin assessment, *RN* 55:22, 1992.

Folstein MF, Folstein S, McHugh PR: Mini–Mental State; a practical method for grading the cognitive state of patients for the clinician, *J Psychiatr Res* 12:189, 1975.

Forgacs P: The functional basis of pulmonary sounds, *Chest* 73:399, 1978.

Giger JN, Davidhizar RE: *Transcultural nursing: assessment and intervention,* ed 2, St Louis, 1995, Mosby.

Gordon M: *Manual of nursing diagnoses: 1991-1992,* St Louis, 1991, Mosby.

Gordon M: Nursing diagnosis and the diagnostic process, *Am J Nurs* 76:1298, 1976.

Gordon M: *Nursing diagnosis, process and application,* ed 2, New York, 1987, McGraw-Hill.

Hardy MA: A pilot study of the diagnosis and treatment of impaired skin integrity: dry skin in older persons, *Nurs Diagn* 1(2):57, 1990.

Haviland S, O'Brien J: *Orthop Nurs* 8(4):11, 1989.

Hazinski MF: Children are different. In Hazinski MF, ed: *Nursing care of the critically ill child,* St Louis, 1984, Mosby.

Health and Welfare Canada, Minister of Supply and Services Canada, Cat No H39-252/1992E, Ottawa, 1992.

Hockenberger SJ: Fibrocystic breast disease: every woman is at risk, *Plast Surg Nurs* 13(1):37, 1993.

Holtzclaw B: The febrile response in critical care: state of the science, *Heart Lung* 21(5):482, 1992.

Hulsey TC et al: Birth weights of infants of black and white mothers without pregnancy complications, part 1, *Am J Obstet Gynecol* 164(5):1299, 1991.

Ivey AE: *Intentional interviewing and counseling: facilitating client development,* ed 2, Pacific Grove, Calif, 1988, Brooks/Cole.

Janken JK, Lewis-Cullinan CL: Auditory sensory/perceptual alterations: suggested revision of defining characteristics, *Nurs Diagn* 1(4):147, 1990.

Joint National Committee on Detection, Evaluation, and Treatment of High Blood Pressure; National High Blood Pressure Education Program; National Heart, Lung and Blood Institute; National Institutes of Health: *Fifth report of the Joint National Committee on Detection, Evaluation, and Treatment of High Blood Pressure,* NIH Pub No 93-1088, Bethesda, Md, January 1993, NIH.

Kataoka-Yahiro M, Saylor C: A critical thinking model for nursing judgment, *J Nurs Educ* 33(8):351, 1994.

Kinney MR et al: *AACN's clinical reference for critical care nursing,* ed 3, St Louis, 1993, Mosby.

Kneisl CR, Wilson HS: *Handbook of psychosocial nursing care,* Menlo Park, Calif, 1984, Addison Wesley.

Kolonel LN: Cancer incidence among Filipinos in Hawaii and the Philippines, *Nat Cancer Inst Monogr* 69:93, 1985.

Kosary CL et al: *SEER cancer statistics review, 1973-1992: tables and graphs,* NIH Pub No 95-2789, Bethesda, Md, 1995, National Cancer Institute.

Kumanyika SK: Special issues regarding obesity in minority populations, *Ann Intern Med* 119:722, 1993.

Lewis SM et al: *Medical-surgical nursing: assessment and management of clinical problems,* ed 4, St Louis, 1996, Mosby.

Lueckenotte A: *Gerontologic nursing,* St Louis, 1996, Mosby.

Lueckenotte A: *Pocket guide to gerontologic assessment,* St Louis, 1990, Mosby.

Lueckenotte A: *Pocket guide to gerontologic assessment,* ed 2, St Louis, 1994, Mosby.

Maklebust J: Impact of AHCPR pressure ulcer guidelines on nursing practice, *Decubitus* 4(2):46, 1991.

Malasanos L et al: *Health assessment,* ed 4, St Louis, 1990, Mosby.

Malter LA et al: The effectiveness of four interventions for the prevention of low back pain, *JAMA* 272(16):1286, 1994.

Master S, Terpstra JK: Recognition and diagnosis. In Schnoll SH, Horvatich PK, Terpstra JK: *Prescribing drugs with abuse liability,* Richmond, Va, 1992, DSAM, MCV-VCU.

McConnell E: Auscultating bowel sounds, *Nurs 90* 20:106, 1990.

McKenry LM, Salerno E: *Mosby's pharmacology in nursing,* ed 19, St Louis, 1995, Mosby.

Merz ML et al: Tooth diameters and arch perimeters in a black and white population, *Am J Orthod Dentofacial Orthop* 100(1):53, 1991.

Monrroy LSA: Nursing care of Raza/Latina patients. In Orque MS, Block B, Monrroy LSA, eds: *Ethnic nursing care: a multicultural approach,* St Louis, 1983, Mosby.

Moss VA, Taylor WK: *ADRN J* 53(5):1158, 1991.

NANDA: *Taxonomy I revised 1990 with official nursing diagnoses,* St Louis, 1997, North American Nursing Diagnosis Association.

National High Blood Pressure Education Program; National Heart, Lung, and Blood Institute, National Institutes of Health: *The fifth report of the Joint National Committee on Detection, Evaluation, and Treatment of High Blood Pressure,* NIH Pub No 93-1088, Bethesda, Md, January 1993, NIH.

Nutrition interventions manual for professionals caring for older Americans, Greer, Margolis, Mitchell, Grunwald, & Associates, Inc, Nutrition Screening Initiative, 1010 Wisconsin Ave NW, Suite 800, Washington, DC, 20007, 1992.

Paul R: The art of redesigning instruction. In Willsen J, Binker AJA, eds: *Critical thinking: how to prepare students for a rapidly changing world*, Santa Rosa, Calif, 1993, Foundation for Critical Thinking.

Pires M, Muller A: Detection and management of early tissue pressure indicators: a pictorial essay, *Progressions* 3(3):3, 1991.

Pollitzer W, Anderson J: Ethnic and genetic differences in bone mass: a review with a hereditary versus environmental perspective, *Am J Clin Nutr* 52:181, 1990.

Pontious S et al: Accuracy and reliability of temperature measurement by instrument and site, *J Pediatr Nurs* 9(2):114, 1994.

Potter PA, Perry AG: *Fundamentals of nursing: concepts, process, and practice,* ed 4, St Louis, 1997, Mosby.

Reece SM: Immunization strategies for the elimination of hepatitis B, *Nurs Pract* 18:2, 1993.

Reed AT, Birge SJ: Screening for osteoporosis, *J Gerontol Nurs* 14(7):18, 1988.

Rocereto L: Selected health beliefs of Vietnamese refugees, *J Sch Health* 51(1):63, 1981.

Rossi L, Leary E: Evaluating the patient with coronary artery disease, *Nurs Clin North Am* 27(1):171, 1992.

Seidel HM et al: *Mosby's guide to physical examination,* ed 2, St Louis, 1991, Mosby.

Seidel HM et al: *Mosby's guide to physical examination,* ed 3, St Louis, 1995, Mosby.

Smoller J, Smoller BR: Skin malignancies in the elderly: diagnosable, treatable, and potentially curable, *J Gerontol Nurs* 18(5):19, 1992.

Stanley SR: *Orthop Nurs* 8(1):33, 1989.

Thibodeau GA, Patton K: *Anatomy and physiology,* ed 2, St Louis, 1993, Mosby.

Thompson JM et al: *Mosby's clinical nursing,* ed 3, St Louis, 1993, Mosby.

Thompson SM et al: *Mosby's manual of clinical nursing,* ed 2, St Louis, 1989, Mosby.

Trelease CC: *Ostomy/Wound Manage* 20:46, 1988.

US Department of Agriculture and US Department of Health and Human Services: *Nutrition and your health: dietary guidelines for Americans,* USDA/DHHS Home and Garden Bull No 232, Washington, DC, 1990, US Government Printing Office.

Wilkins RL, Hodgkin JE, Lopez B: *Lung sounds: a practical guide,* St Louis, 1988, Mosby.

Williams SR: Nutritional assessment and guidance in prenatal care. In Worthington-Roberts BS, Williams SR, eds: *Nutrition in pregnancy and lactation,* ed 5, St Louis, 1993, Mosby.

Wong DL: *Whaley and Wong's nursing care of infants and children,* ed 5, St Louis, 1995, Mosby.

Yano K et al: Coronary heart disease, hypertension, and stroke among Japanese American men in Hawaii: the Honolulu heart program, *Hawaii Med J* 44(8):297, 1985.

Yip R et al: Race and birth weight: the Chinese example, *Pediatrics* 87(5):688, 1991.

APPENDIXES

Red Flags for Suspicion of Substance Abuse

APPENDIX A

- Clients who frequently miss appointments
- Clients who frequently request written excuses for work
- Clients who have chief complaints of insomnia, "bad nerves," or pain that does not fit a particular pattern
- Clients who often report lost prescriptions (e.g., tranquilizers or pain medications) or ask for frequent refills
- Clients who make frequent emergency room visits
- Clients who have a history of changing doctors or who bring in medication bottles prescribed by several different providers
- Clients with histories of gastrointestinal bleeds, peptic ulcers, pancreatitis, cellulitis, or frequent pulmonary infections
- Clients with frequent sexually transmitted diseases, complicated pregnancies, multiple abortions, or sexual dysfunction
- Clients who complain of chest pains or palpitations or who have histories of admissions to rule out myocardial infarctions
- Clients who give histories of activities that place them at risk for human immunodeficiency virus (HIV) infections (multiple sexual partners, multiple rapes)
- Clients with family history of addiction; history of childhood sexual, physical, or emotional abuse; social and financial or marital problems

Modified from Master S, Terpstra JK: Recognition and diagnosis. In Schnoll SH, Horvatich PK, Terpstra JK: *Prescribing drugs with abuse liability,* Richmond, Va, 1992, DSAM, MCV-VCU.

APPENDIX B

Adult Height and Weight Tables*

Men					Women				
Height					Height				
Feet	Inches	Small Frame (lbs)	Medium Frame (lbs)	Large Frame (lbs)	Feet	Inches	Small Frame (lbs)	Medium Frame (lbs)	Large Frame (lbs)
5	2	128-134	131-141	138-150	4	10	102-111	109-121	118-131
5	3	130-136	133-143	140-153	4	11	103-113	111-123	120-134
5	4	132-138	135-145	142-156	5	0	104-115	113-126	122-137
5	5	134-140	137-148	144-160	5	1	106-118	115-129	125-140
5	6	136-142	139-151	146-164	5	2	108-121	118-132	128-143

5	7	138-145	142-154	149-168	5	3	111-124	121-135	131-147
5	8	140-148	145-157	152-172	5	4	114-127	124-138	134-151
5	9	142-151	148-160	155-176	5	5	117-130	127-141	137-155
5	10	144-154	151-163	158-180	5	6	120-133	130-144	140-159
5	11	146-157	154-166	161-184	5	7	123-136	133-147	143-163
6	0	149-160	157-170	164-188	5	8	126-139	136-150	146-167
6	1	152-164	160-174	168-192	5	9	129-142	139-153	149-170
6	2	155-168	164-178	172-197	5	10	132-145	142-156	152-173
6	3	158-172	167-182	176-202	5	11	135-148	145-159	155-176
6	4	162-176	171-187	181-207	6	0	138-151	148-162	158-179

Source of basic data: 1979 Build Study, Society of Actuaries and Association of Life Insurance Medical Directors of America, 1980.
*Desirable weights for persons 25-29 years old (in indoor clothing).
Weight in pounds according to frame (in indoor clothing weighing 5 lb for men and 3 lb for women; shoes with 1-inch heels).

APPENDIX C

Mid–Upper-Arm Muscle Circumference and Triceps Skin Fold Percentiles

Mid–upper-arm muscle circumference percentiles (cm)

	Female Percentiles					Male Percentiles				
Age (yr)	5th	25th	50th	75th	95th	5th	25th	50th	75th	95th
1	10.5	11.7	12.4	13.9	14.3	11.0	11.9	12.7	13.5	14.7
2	11.1	11.9	12.6	13.3	14.7	11.1	12.2	13.0	14.0	15.0
3	11.3	12.4	13.2	14.0	15.2	11.7	13.1	13.7	14.3	15.3
4	11.5	12.8	13.8	14.4	15.7	12.3	13.3	14.1	14.8	15.9
5	12.5	13.4	14.2	15.1	16.5	12.8	14.0	14.7	15.4	16.9

6	13.0	13.8	14.5	15.4	17.1	13.1	14.2	15.1	16.1	17.7
7	12.9	14.2	15.1	16.0	17.6	13.7	15.1	16.0	16.8	19.0
8	13.8	15.1	16.0	17.1	19.4	14.0	15.4	16.2	17.0	18.7
9	14.7	15.8	16.7	18.0	19.8	15.1	16.1	17.0	18.3	20.2
10	14.8	15.9	17.0	18.0	19.7	15.6	16.6	18.0	19.1	22.1
11	15.0	17.1	18.1	19.6	22.3	15.9	17.3	18.3	19.5	23.0
12	16.2	18.0	19.1	20.1	22.0	16.7	18.2	19.5	21.0	24.1
13	16.9	18.3	19.8	21.1	24.0	17.2	19.6	21.1	22.6	24.5
14	17.4	19.0	20.1	21.6	24.7	18.9	21.2	22.3	24.0	26.4
15	17.5	18.9	20.2	21.5	24.4	19.9	21.8	23.7	25.4	27.2
16	17.0	19.0	20.2	21.6	24.9	21.3	23.4	24.9	26.9	29.6
17	17.5	19.4	20.5	22.1	25.7	22.4	24.5	25.8	27.3	31.2
18	17.4	19.1	20.2	21.5	24.5	22.6	25.2	26.4	28.3	32.4
19-25	17.9	19.5	20.7	22.1	24.9	23.8	25.7	27.3	28.9	32.1
25-35	18.3	19.9	21.2	22.8	26.4	24.3	26.4	27.9	29.8	32.6
35-45	18.6	20.5	21.8	23.6	27.2	24.7	26.9	28.6	30.2	32.7
45-55	18.7	20.6	22.0	23.8	27.4	23.9	26.5	28.1	30.0	32.6
55-65	18.7	20.9	22.5	24.4	28.0	23.6	26.0	27.8	29.5	32.0
65-75	18.5	20.8	22.5	24.4	27.9	22.3	25.1	26.8	28.4	30.6

Values derived by formula calculation. Data derived from the Health and Nutrition Examination Survey data of 1971-1974, using same population samples as those of the National Center for Health Statistics (NCHS) growth percentiles for children. Adapted from Frisancho AR: New norms of upper limb fat and muscle areas for assessment of nutritional status, *Am J Clin Nutr* 34:2540, 1981.

Triceps skin fold percentiles (mm)

	Female Percentiles					Male Percentiles				
Age (yr)	5th	25th	50th	75th	95th	5th	25th	50th	75th	95th
1	6	8	10	12	16	6	8	10	12	16
2	6	9	10	12	16	6	8	10	12	15
3	7	9	11	12	15	6	8	10	11	15
4	7	8	10	12	16	6	8	9	11	14
5	6	8	10	12	18	6	8	9	11	15
6	6	8	10	12	16	5	7	8	10	16
7	6	9	11	13	18	5	7	9	12	17
8	6	9	12	15	24	5	7	8	10	16
9	8	10	13	16	22	6	7	10	13	18
10	7	10	12	17	27	6	8	10	14	21
11	7	10	13	18	28	6	8	11	16	24
12	8	11	14	18	27	6	8	11	14	28
13	8	12	15	21	30	5	7	10	14	26
14	9	13	16	21	28	4	7	9	14	24
15	8	12	17	21	32	4	6	8	11	24
16	10	15	18	22	31	4	6	8	12	22
17	10	13	19	24	37	5	6	8	12	19

18	10	15	18	22	30	4	6	9	13	24
19-25	10	14	18	24	34	4	7	10	15	22
25-35	10	16	21	27	37	5	8	12	16	24
35-45	12	18	23	29	38	5	8	12	16	23
45-55	12	20	25	30	40	6	8	12	15	25
55-65	12	20	25	31	38	5	8	11	14	22
65-75	12	18	24	29	36	4	8	11	15	22

Data derived from the Health and Nutrition Examination Survey data of 1971-1974, using same population samples as those of the National Center for Health Statistics (NCHS) growth percentiles for children. Adapted from Frisancho AR: New norms of upper limb fat and muscle areas for assessment of nutritional status, *Am J Clin Nutr* 34:2540, 1981.

APPENDIX D

Physical Growth Curves for Children

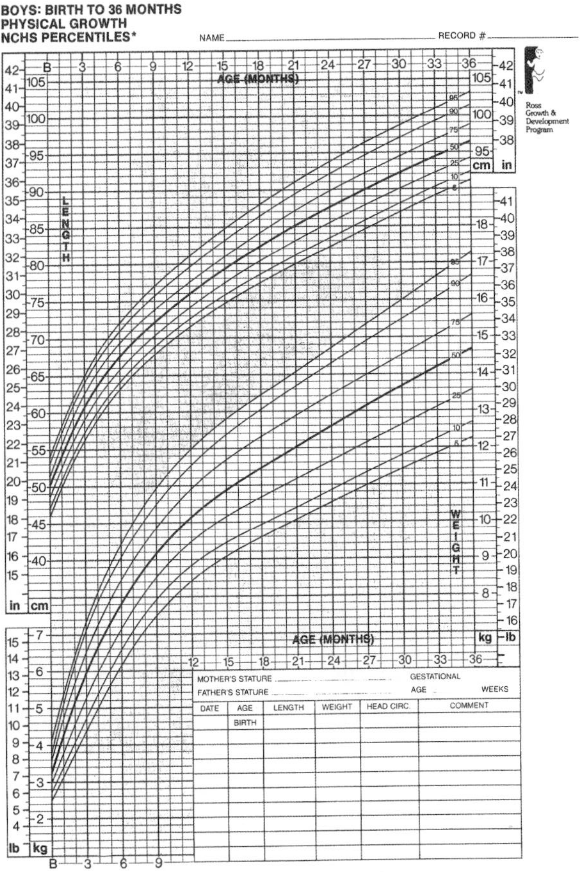

Courtesy Ross Laboratories, Columbus, Ohio.

BOYS: BIRTH TO 36 MONTHS
PHYSICAL GROWTH
NCHS PERCENTILES*

NAME ____________________ RECORD # ____________

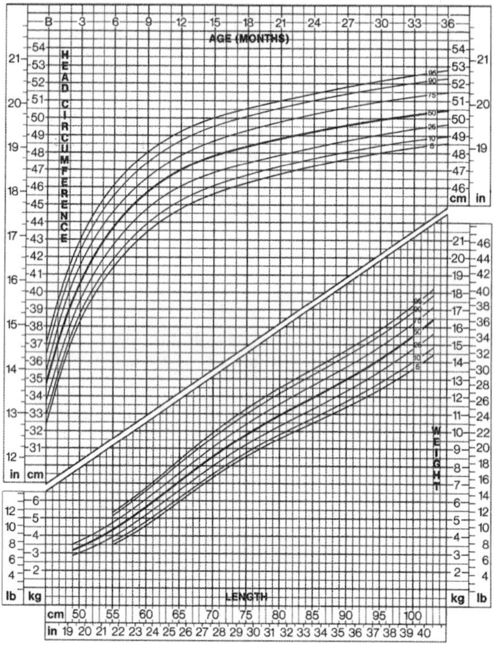

DATE	AGE	LENGTH	WEIGHT	HEAD CIRC	COMMENT

*Adapted from: Hamill PVV, Drizd TA, Johnson CL, Reed RB, Roche AF, Moore WM: Physical growth: National Center for Health Statistics percentiles. AM J CLIN NUTR 32:607-629, 1979. Data from the Fels Research Institute, Wright State University School of Medicine, Yellow Springs, Ohio.

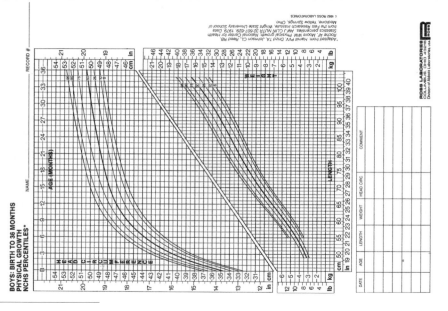

ROSS LABORATORIES
COLUMBUS, OHIO 43216
Division of Abbott Laboratories, USA

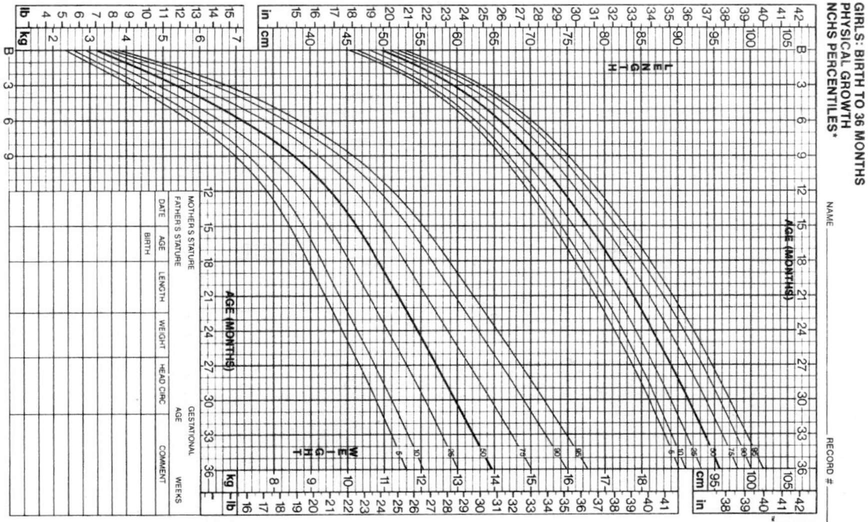

*Adapted from: Hamill PVV, Drizd TA, Johnson CL, Reed RB, Roche AF, Moore WM. Physical growth: National Center for Health Statistics percentiles. AM J CLIN NUTR 32:607-629, 1979. Data from the Fels Research Institute, Wright State University School of Medicine, Yellow Springs, Ohio

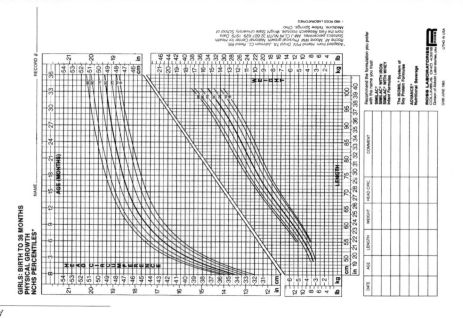

GIRLS: BIRTH TO 36 MONTHS
PHYSICAL GROWTH
NCHS PERCENTILES*

NAME ______________________ RECORD # ______________

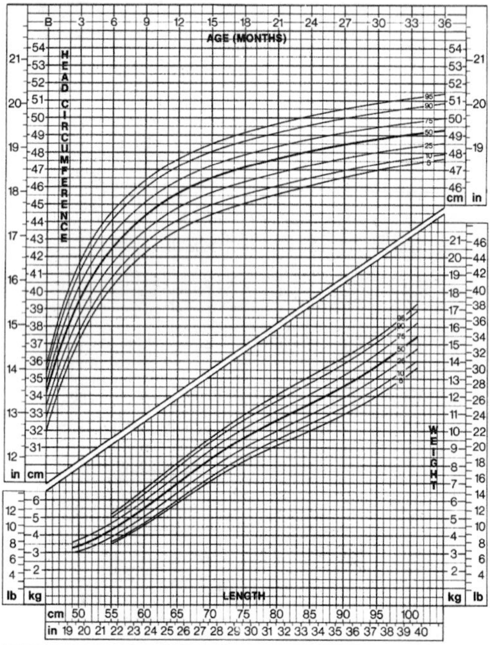

DATE	AGE	LENGTH	WEIGHT	HEAD CIRC.	COMMENT

Recommend the formulation you prefer with the name you trust

SIMILAC®
SIMILAC® WITH IRON
SIMILAC® WITH WHEY
Infant Formulas

The ISOMIL® System of Soy Protein Formulas

ADVANCE®
Nutritional Beverage

ROSS LABORATORIES
COLUMBUS, OHIO 43216
Division of Abbott Laboratories, USA

G106 JUNE 1983 LITHO IN USA

*Adapted from: Hamill PVV, Drizd TA, Johnson CL, Reed RB, Roche AF, Moore WM: Physical growth: National Center for Health Statistics percentiles. AM J CLIN NUTR 32:607-629, 1979. Data from the Fels Research Institute, Wright State University School of Medicine, Yellow Springs, Ohio.

Giger and Davidhizar's Transcultural Assessment Model

Culturally Unique Individual	Communication
1. Place of birth	1. Voice quality
2. Cultural definition What is . . .	a. Strong, resonant b. Soft
3. Race What is . . .	c. Average d. Shrill
4. Length of time in country (if appropriate)	2. Pronunciation and enunciation a. Clear

Schematic design by Geneva Turner, PhD, CFLE; Joyce Newman Giger, EdD, RN, CS, FAAN; and Susan Wieczorek, MSN, RN. From Bobak IM, Jensen MD: *Maternity and gynecologic care,* ed 5, St Louis, 1993, Mosby.

Continued

Communication—cont'd

   b. Slurred
   c. Dialect (geographical)
3. Use of silence
   a. Infrequent
   b. Often
   c. Length
      (1) Brief
      (2) Moderate
      (3) Long
      (4) Not observed
4. Use of nonverbal
   a. Hand movement
   b. Eye movement
   c. Entire body movement
   d. Kinesics (gestures, expression, or stances)
5. Touch
   a. Startles or withdraws when touched
   b. Accepts touch without difficulty
   c. Touches others without difficulty
6. Ask these and similar questions:
   a. How do you get your point across to others?
   b. Do you like communicating with friends, family, and acquaintances?
   c. When asked a question, do you usually respond (in words or body movement, or both)?
   d. If you have something important to discuss with your family, how would you approach them?

Space

1. Degree of comfort
   a. Moves when space invaded
   b. Does not move when space invaded
2. Distance in conversations
   a. 0 to 18 inches
   b. 18 inches to 3 feet
   c. 3 feet or more
3. Definition of space
   a. Describe degree of comfort with closeness when talking with or standing near others.

b. How do objects (e.g., furniture) in the environment affect your sense of space?
4. Ask these and similar questions:
   a. When you talk with family members, how close do you stand?
   b. When you communicate with co-workers and other acquaintances, how close do you stand?
   c. If a stranger touches you, how do you react or feel?
   d. If a loved one touches you, how do you react or feel?
   e. Are you comfortable with the distance between us now?

Social Organization

1. Normal state of health
   a. Poor
   b. Fair
   c. Good
   d. Excellent
2. Marital status
3. Number of children
4. Parents living or deceased?
5. Ask these and similar questions:
   a. How do you define social activities?
   b. What are some activities that you enjoy?
   c. What are your hobbies, or what do you do when you have free time?
   d. Do you believe in a Supreme Being?
   e. How do you worship that Supreme Being?
   f. What is your function (what do you do) in your family unit/system?
   g. What is your role in your family unit/system (father, mother, child, advisor)?
   h. When you were a child, what or who influenced you most?
   i. What is/was your relationship with your siblings and parents?

Schematic design by Geneva Turner, PhD, CFLE; Joyce Newman Giger, EdD, RN, CS, FAAN; and Susan Wieczorek, MSN, RN. From Bobak IM, Jensen MD: *Maternity and gynecologic care*, ed 5, St Louis, 1993, Mosby.

Continued

Social Organization—cont'd

j. What does work mean to you?
k. Describe your past, present, and future jobs.
l. What are your political views?
m. How have your political views influenced your attitude toward health and illness?

Time

1. Orientation to time
   a. Past-oriented
   b. Present-oriented
   c. Future-oriented
2. View of time
   a. Social time
   b. Clock-oriented
3. Physiochemical reaction to time
   a. Sleeps at least 8 hours a night
   b. Goes to sleep and wakes on a consistent schedule
   c. Understands the importance of taking medication and other treatments on schedule
4. Ask these and similar questions:
   a. What kind of timepiece do you wear daily?
   b. If you have an appointment at 2 PM, what time is acceptable to arrive?
   c. If a nurse tells you that you will receive a medication in "about a half hour," realistically, how much time will you allow before calling the nurses' station?

Environmental Control

1. Locus-of-control
   a. Internal locus-of-control (believes that the power to affect change lies within)
   b. External locus-of-control (believes that fate, luck, and chance have a great deal to do with how things turn out)
2. Value orientation
   a. Believes in supernatural forces
   b. Relies on magic, witchcraft, and prayer to affect change

c. Does not believe in supernatural forces
d. Does not rely on magic, witchcraft, or prayer to affect change
3. Ask these and similar questions:
a. How often do you have visitors at your home?
b. Is it acceptable to you for visitors to drop in unexpectedly?
c. Name some ways your parents or other persons treated your illnesses when you were a child.
d. Have you or someone else in your immediate surroundings ever used a home remedy that made you sick?
e. What home remedies have you used that worked? Will you use them in the future?
f. What is your definition of "good health"?
g. What is your definition of illness or "poor health"?

Biologic Variations

1. Conduct a complete physical assessment noting:
   a. Body structure (small, medium, or large frame)
   b. Skin color
   c. Unusual skin discolorations
   d. Hair color and distribution
   e. Other visible physical characteristics (e.g., keloids, chloasma)
   f. Weight
   g. Height
   h. Check lab work for variances in hemoglobin, hematocrit, and sickle phenomena if Black or Mediterranean
2. Ask these and similar questions:
   a. What diseases or illnesses are common in your family?

Schematic design by Geneva Turner, PhD, CFLE; Joyce Newman Giger, EdD, RN, CS, FAAN; and Susan Wieczorek, MSN, RN. From Bobak IM, Jensen MD: *Maternity and gynecologic care,* ed 5, St Louis, 1993, Mosby.

Continued

Biologic Variations—cont'd

b. Describe your family's typical behavior when a family member is ill.
c. How do you respond when you are angry?
d. Who (or what) usually helps you to cope during a difficult time?
e. What foods do you and your family like to eat?
f. Have you ever had any unusual cravings for:
   (1) White or red clay dirt?
   (2) Laundry starch?
g. When you were a child what types of foods did you eat?
h. What foods are family favorites or are considered traditional?

Nursing Assessment

1. Note whether the client has become culturally assimilated or observes own cultural practices.
2. Incorporate data into plan of nursing care:
   a. Encourage the client to discuss cultural differences; people from diverse cultures who hold different world views can enlighten nurses.
   b. Make efforts to accept and understand methods of communication.
   c. Respect the individual's personal need for space.
   d. Respect the rights of clients to honor and worship the Supreme Being of their choice.
   e. Identify a clerical or spiritual person to contact.
   f. Determine whether spiritual practices have implications for health, life, and well-being (e.g., Jehovah's Witnesses may refuse blood and blood derivatives; an Orthodox Jew may eat only kosher food high in sodium and may not drink milk when meat is served).
   g. Identify hobbies, especially when devising interventions for a short or extended convalescence or for rehabilitation.
   h. Honor time and value orientations and differences in these areas. Allay anxiety and apprehension if adherence to time is necessary.

i. Provide privacy according to personal need and health status of the client (NOTE: The perception and reaction to pain may be culturally related).
j. Note cultural health practices
   (1) Identify and encourage efficacious practices.
   (2) Identify and discourage dysfunctional practices.
   (3) Identify and determine whether neutral practices will have a long-term ill effect.
k. Note food preferences
   (1) Make as many adjustments in diet as health status and long-term benefits will allow and that dietary department can provide.
   (2) Note dietary practices that may have serious implications for the client.

Schematic design by Geneva Turner, PhD, CFLE; Joyce Newman Giger, EdD, RN, CS, FAAN; and Susan Wieczorek, MSN, RN. From Bobak IM, Jensen MD: *Maternity and gynecologic care,* ed 5, St Louis, 1993, Mosby.

APPENDIX F

Temperature Conversion Chart

Convert Fahrenheit to Centigrade

Subtract 32 from the Fahrenheit reading and multiply the result by $5/9$.

$C = (F - 32°) \times 5/9$ Example: $40° C = (104° F - 32° F) \times 5/9$

Convert Centigrade to Fahrenheit

Multiply the centigrade reading by $9/5$ and add 32 to the product.

$F = (9/5 \times C) + 32°$ Example: $104° F = (9/5 \times 40° C) + 32°$

Skin Lesions, Skin Malignancies, and Pressure Ulcers

APPENDIX G

Types of Primary Skin Lesions

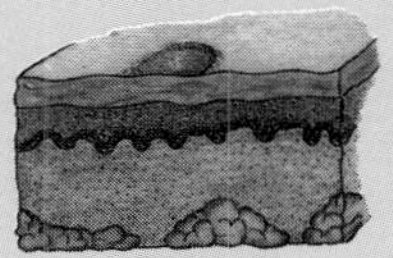

Macule: flat, nonpalpable change in skin color, smaller than 1 cm (e.g., freckle, petechia)

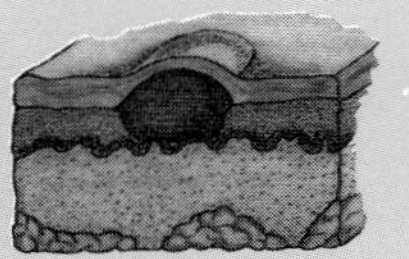

Papule: palpable, circumscribed, solid elevation in skin, smaller than 0.5 cm (e.g., elevated nevus)

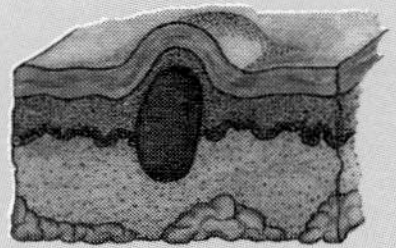

Nodule: elevated solid mass, deeper and firmer than papule, 0.5 to 0.2 cm (e.g., wart)

Continued

Types of Primary Skin Lesions—cont'd

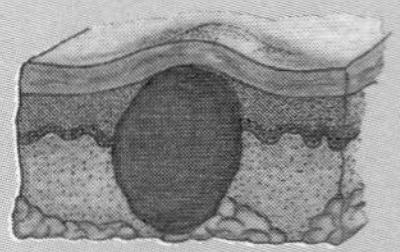

Tumor: solid mass that may extend deep through subcutaneous tissue, larger than 1 to 2 cm (e.g., epithelioma)

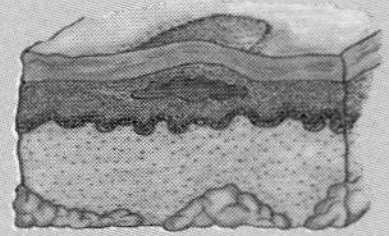

Wheal: irregularly shaped, elevated area or superficial localized edema, varies in size (e.g., hive, mosquito bite)

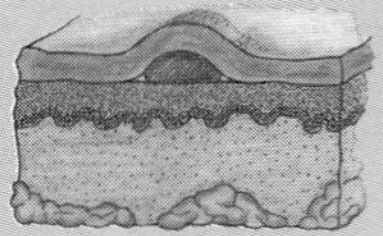

Vesicle: circumscribed elevation of skin filled with serous fluid, smaller than 0.5 cm (e.g., herpes simplex, chickenpox)

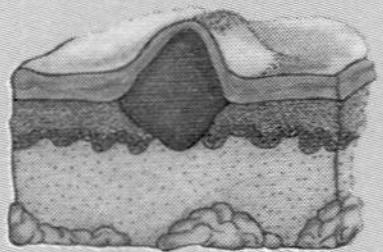

Pustule: circumscribed elevation of skin similar to vesicle but filled with pus, varies in size (e.g., acne, staphylococcal infection)

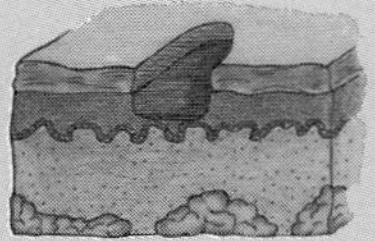

Ulcer: deep loss of skin surface that may extend to dermis and frequently bleeds and scars, varies in size (e.g., venous stasis ulcer)

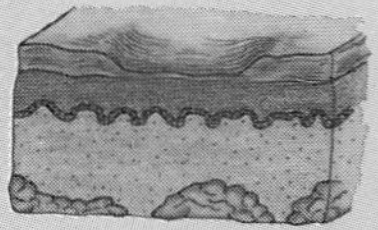

Atrophy: thinning of skin with loss of normal skin furrow with skin appearing shiny and translucent, varies in size (e.g., arterial insufficiency)

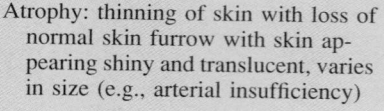

Skin Malignancies in the Older Adult

Basal Cell Carcinoma

0.5-cm to 1.0-cm crusted lesion that may be flat or raised and may have a rolled, somewhat scaly border.
Frequently there are underlying, widely dilated blood vessels that can be seen clinically within the lesions.

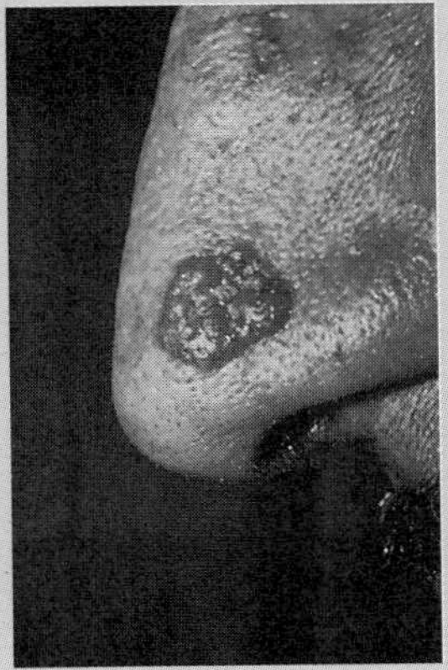

Modified from Smoller J, Smoller BR: Skin malignancies in the elderly: diagnosable, treatable, and potentially curable, *J Gerontol Nurs* 18(5):19, 1992. Illustrations from Belcher AE: *Cancer nursing,* St Louis, 1992, Mosby; Habif TP: *Clinical dermatology,* ed 3, St Louis, 1996, Mosby; and Zitelli B, Davis H: *Atlas of pediatric physical diagnosis,* ed 2, St Louis, 1991, Mosby.

Continued

Skin Malignancies in the Older Adult—cont'd

Squamous Cell Carcinoma

Occurs more often on mucosal surfaces and nonexposed areas of skin, compared to basal cell.

0.5-cm to 1.5-cm scaly lesions, may be ulcerated or crusted. Frequently appear and grow more rapidly than basal cell.

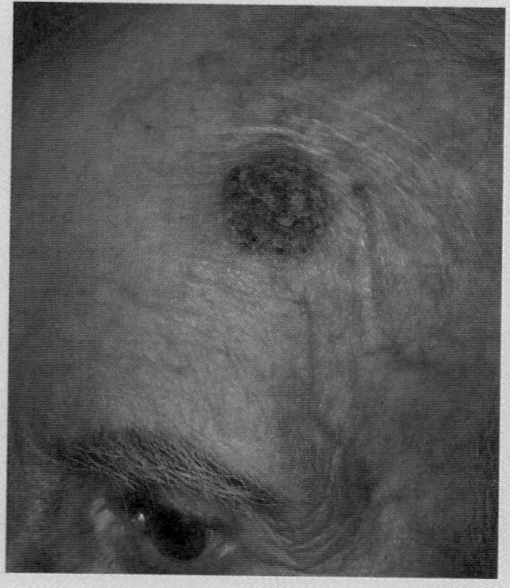

Melanoma

0.5-cm to 1.0-cm brown, flat lesions that may arise on sun-exposed or nonexposed skin. Variegated pigmentation, irregular borders, and indistinct margins.

Ulceration, recent growth, or recent change in longstanding mole are ominous signs.

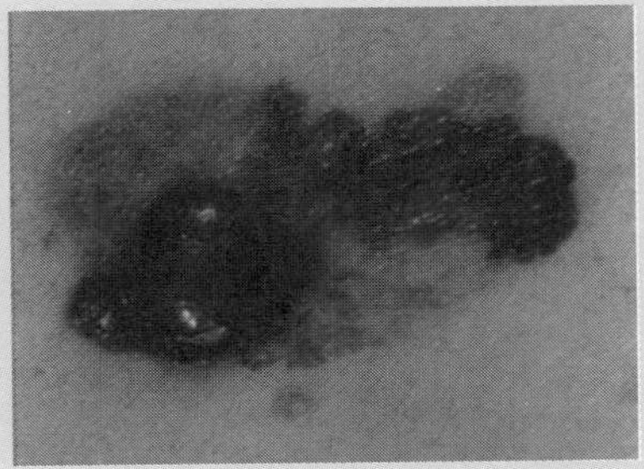

Modified from Smoller J, Smoller BR: Skin malignancies in the elderly: diagnosable, treatable, and potentially curable, *J Gerontol Nurs* 18(5):19, 1992. Illustrations from Belcher AE: *Cancer nursing,* St Louis, 1992, Mosby; Habif TP: *Clinical dermatology,* ed 3, St Louis, 1996, Mosby; and Zitelli B, Davis H: *Atlas of pediatric physical diagnosis,* ed 2, St Louis, 1991, Mosby.

Pressure Ulcers in Stages

A

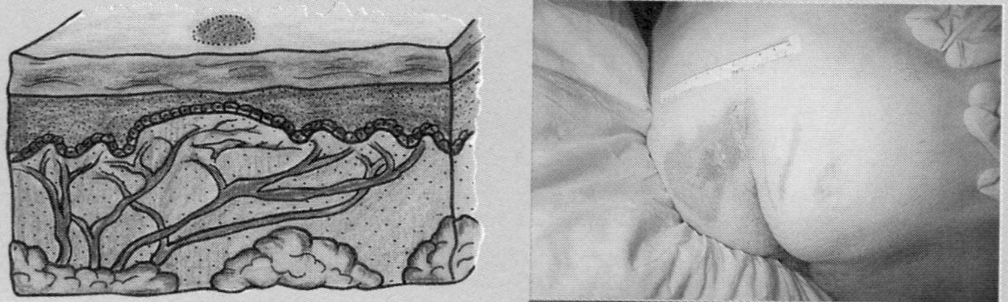

B

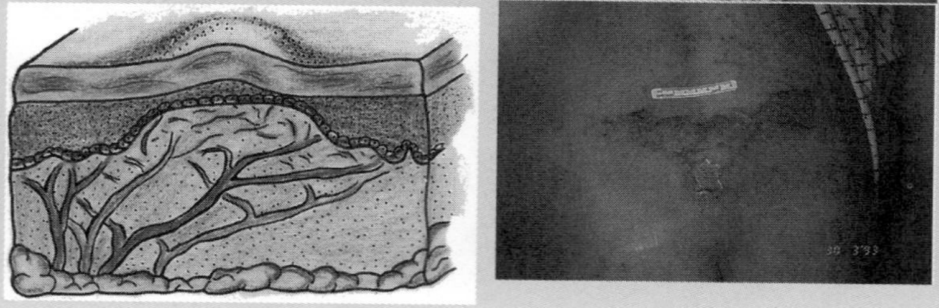

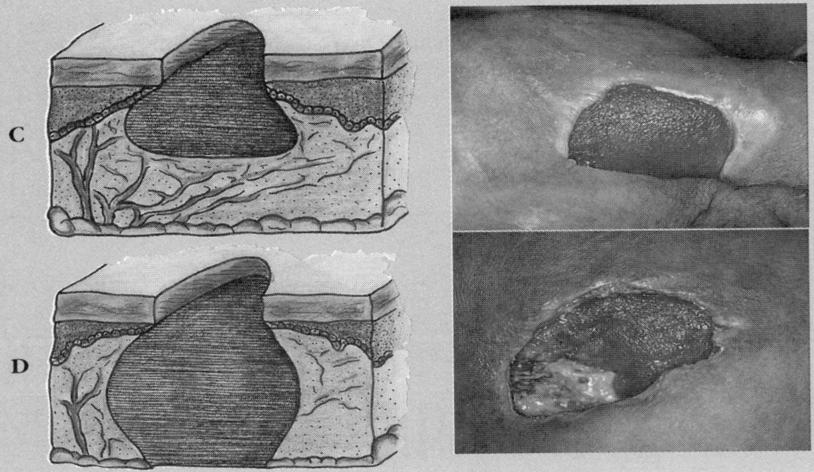

Diagram of Stages. **A,** Stage I pressure ulcer. **B,** Stage II pressure ulcer. **C,** Stage III pressure ulcer. **D,** Stage IV pressure ulcer. (Courtesy Laurel Wiersma, RN, MSN, Clinical Nurse Specialist, Barnes Hospital, St Louis, Mo.)

APPENDIX H

Recommended Schedule for Immunization of Healthy Infants and Children[a] in the United States

Recommended Age[b]	Immunization(s)[c]	Comments
Birth	HBV[d]	
1-2 months	HBV[d]	
2 months	DTP, Hib, OPV	DTP and OPV can be initiated as early as 4 weeks after birth in areas of high endemicity or during outbreaks
4 months	DTP, Hib, OPV	2-month interval (minimum of 6 weeks) recommended for OPV
6 months	DTP, (Hib[e])	
6-18 months	HBV,[d] OPV	

12-15 months	Hib, MMR	MMR should be given at 12 months of age in high-risk areas; if indicated, tuberculin testing may be done at the same visit
15-18 months	DTaP or DTP	The fourth dose of diphtheria-tetanus-pertussis vaccine should be given 6 to 12 months after the third dose of DTP and may be given as early as 12 months of age, provided that the interval between doses 3 and 4 is at least 6 months and DTP is given; DTaP is not currently licensed for use in children younger than 15 months
4-6 years	DTaP or DTP, OPV	DTaP or DTP and OPV should be given at or before school entry; DTP or DTaP should not be given at or after the seventh birthday
11-12 years	MMR	MMR should be given at entry to middle school or junior high school unless 2 doses were given after the first birthday
14-16 years	Td	Repeat every 10 years throughout life

From American Academy of Pediatrics, Committee on Infectious Diseases: *1994 Red Book: report of the Committee on Infectious Diseases,* ed 23, Elk Grove Village, Ill, 1994, The Academy.

[a]Table is not completely consistent with all package inserts. For products used, also consult manufacturer's package insert for instructions on storage, handling, dosage, and administration. Biologics prepared by different manufacturers may vary, and package inserts of the same manufacturer may change from time to time. Therefore the practitioner should be aware of the contents of the current package insert.

[b]These recommended ages should not be construed as absolute. For example, 2 months can be 6 to 10 weeks. However, MMR usually should not be given to children younger than 12 months. If measles vaccination is indicated, monovalent measles vaccine is recommended, and MMR should be given subsequently at 12 to 15 months.

[c]Vaccine abbreviations: *HBV,* hepatitis B virus vaccine; *DTP,* diphtheria and tetanus toxoids and pertussis vaccine; *DTaP,* diphtheria and tetanus toxoids and acellular pertussis vaccine; *Hib, Haemophilus influenzae* type b conjugate vaccine; *OPV,* oral poliovirus vaccine (containing attenuated poliovirus types 1, 2, and 3); *MMR,* live measles, mumps, and rubella viruses vaccine; *Td,* adult tetanus toxoid (full dose) and diphtheria toxoid (reduced dose), for children $\geq$7 years and adults.

[d]An acceptable alternative to minimize the number of visits for immunizing infants of HBsAg-negative mothers is to administer dose 1 at 0 to 2 months, dose 2 at 4 months, and dose 3 at 6 to 18 months.

[e]Hib: dose 3 of Hib is not indicated if the product for doses 1 and 2 was PedvaxHIB (PRP-OMP).

APPENDIX I

Routine Primary Immunization Schedule for Infants and Children in Canada

Age	Immunization Against				
2 months	Diphtheria	Pertussis	Tetanus	Poliomyelitis	*Haemophilus influenzae* b[1]
4 months	Diphtheria	Pertussis	Tetanus	Poliomyelitis	*Haemophilus influenzae* b
6 months	Diphtheria	Pertussis	Tetanus	Poliomyelitis[2]	*Haemophilus influenzae* b
12 months	Measles	Mumps	Rubella		
18 months	Diphtheria	Pertussis	Tetanus	Poliomyelitis	*Haemophilus influenzae* b
4-6 years	Diphtheria	Pertussis	Tetanus	Poliomyelitis	
14-16 years	Diphtheria[3]		Tetanus[3]	Poliomyelitis[2]	

From National Advisory Committee on Immunization: *Canadian immunization guide,* ed 4, Canada, 1993, Authority of the Minister of National Health and Welfare, Health Protection Branch, Laboratory Centre for Disease Control.

[1]Hib schedule shown is for HbOC or PRP-T vaccine. If PRP-OMP is used, give at 2, 4, and 12 months of age.

[2]Omit this dose if OPV is used exclusively.

[3]Td (tetanus and diphtheria toxoid), a combined absorbed "adult-type" preparation for use in persons ≥ 7 years of age, contains less diphtheria toxoid than preparations given to younger children and is less likely to cause reactions in older persons. Repeat every 10 years throughout life.

Breast Self-Examination

Instruct client on breast self-examination. All women 20 years and older should perform this self-examination monthly using the following steps:

- Stand before a mirror. Look at both breasts for anything unusual, such as discharge from the nipples, puckering, dimpling, or scaling of the skin.
- To note changes in the shape of the breasts, perform the following measures (see the illustration):
  - Watch in the mirror while raising the arms above the head.
  - Press hands firmly on the hips and bow slightly toward the mirror when pulling the shoulders and elbows forward.

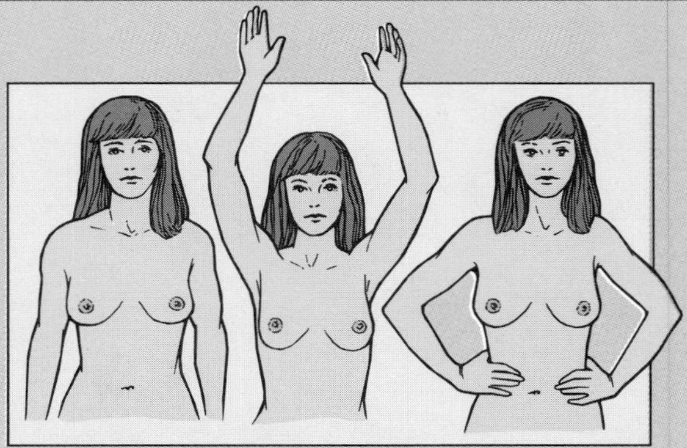

Illustrations from Payne WA, Hahn DB: *Understanding your health,* ed 2, St Louis, 1989, Mosby.

- In the shower or in front of the mirror, palpate each breast. Raise the right arm and use three or four fingers of the left hand to explore the breast carefully (see the illustration). Then start at the outer edge, pressing the flat part of the fingers in small circles, moving the circles slowly around the breast, gradually working toward the nipple (see the illustration). Pay close attention to the area between the breast and armpit and feel for unusual lumps or masses. Repeat the process for the left breast.
- Gently palpate each nipple, looking for discharge (see the illustration). Caution against pinching.
- Repeat the third and fourth steps lying down. Lie flat on the back with the right arm over the head and a small pillow under the right shoulder. Palpate the right breast (see the illustration). Repeat the process on the left breast.
- Call your physician if you find a lump.

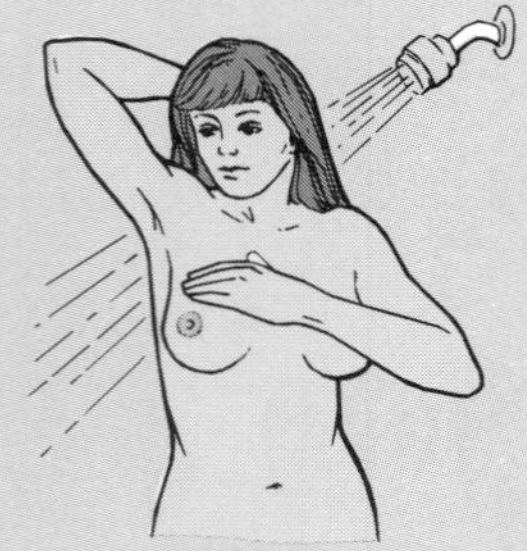

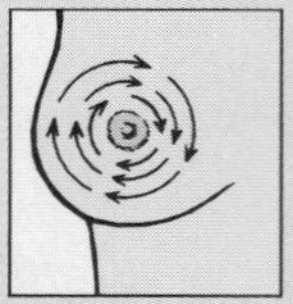

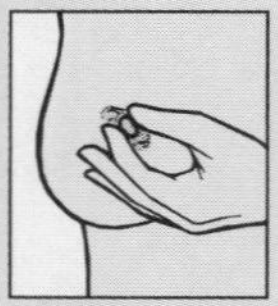

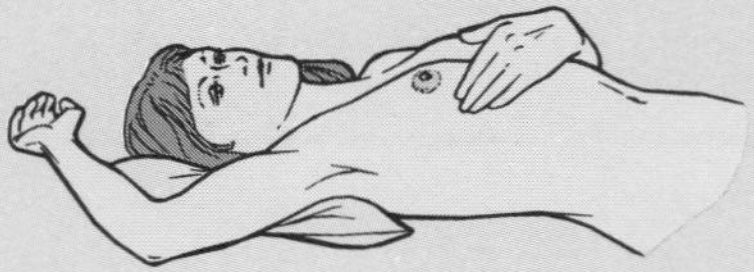

Illustrations from Payne WA, Hahn DB: *Understanding your health,* ed 2, St Louis, 1989, Mosby.

Male Genital Self-Examination

All men 15 years and older should perform this examination monthly using the following steps:

Genital Examination

Perform the examination after a warm bath or shower when the scrotal sac is relaxed.

Stand naked in front of a mirror and hold the penis in your hand and examine the head. Pull back the foreskin if uncircumcised.

Testicular Self-Examination

Look for swelling or lumps in the skin of the scrotum while looking in the mirror.

Illustrations from Seidel HM et al: *Mosby's guide to physical examination*, ed 3, St Louis, 1995, Mosby.

Genital Examination—cont'd

Inspect and palpate the entire head of the penis in a clockwise motion, looking carefully for any bumps, sores, or blisters. Look also for any bumpy warts (see the illustration).

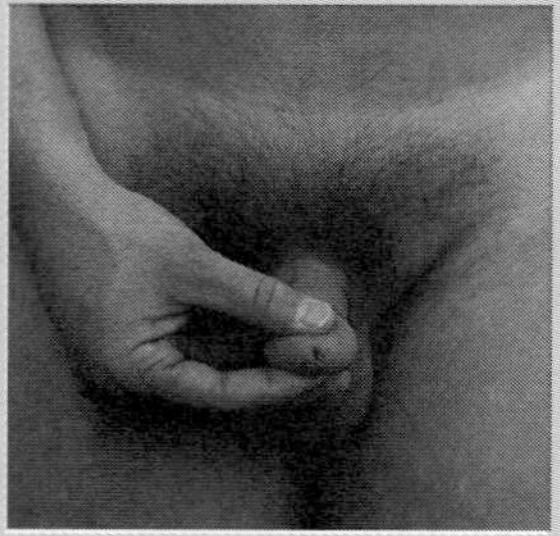

Testicular Self-Examination—cont'd

Use both hands, placing the index and middle fingers under the testicles and the thumb on top (see the illustration).

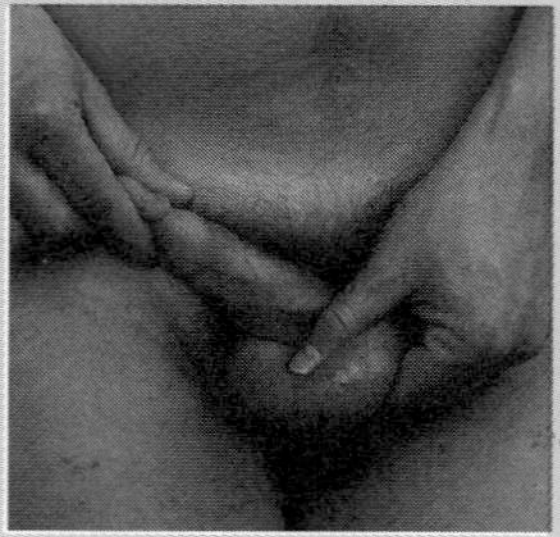

All men 15 years and older should perform this examination monthly using the following steps:

Genital Examination—cont'd

Look at the opening at the end of the penis for discharge.

Look along the entire shaft of the penis for the same signs.

Be sure to separate pubic hair at the base of the penis and carefully examine the skin underneath.

Testicular Self-Examination—cont'd

Gently roll the testicle, feeling for lumps, thickening, or a change in consistency (hardening).

Find the epididymis (a cordlike structure on the top and back of the testicle; it is not a lump).

Feel for small, pea-sized lumps on the front and side of the testicle. The lumps are usually painless and are abnormal.

Call your physician if you find a lump.

Illustrations from Seidel HM et al: *Mosby's guide to physical examination*, ed 3, St Louis, 1995, Mosby.

APPENDIX L

Classification of Cytologic Findings of Pap Tests

Papanicolaou Class	Dysplasia	CIN	Bethesda System
Class I			
Normal smear	Negative	Negative	Within normal limits
Class II			
Atypical cells, no dysplasia	Reactive atypia Koilocytosis or HPV Mild dysplasia	Koilocytosis or HPV CIN 1	Regeneration, repair Inflammation Low-grade squamous intraepithelial lesion

Class III			
Abnormal cells consistent with dysplasia	Moderate dysplasia	CIN 2	
Class IV			
Abnormal cells consistent with CIS	Severe dysplasia, CIS	CIN 2 CIN 3	High-grade squamous intraepithelial lesion
Class V			
Abnormal cells consistent with invasive or squamous cell origin	Squamous cell carcinoma	Squamous cell carcinoma	Squamous cell carcinoma

From Stenchever MA: *Office gynecology,* St Louis, 1992, Mosby.
CIN, Cervical intraepithelial neoplasia; *CIS,* carcinoma in situ; *HPV,* human papilloma virus.

APPENDIX M

U.S. Food Guide Pyramid

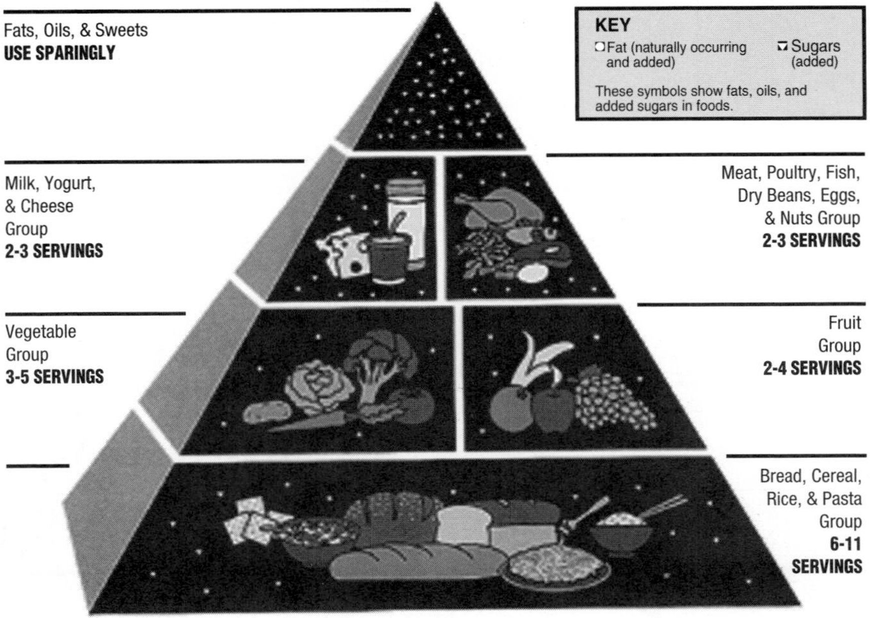

Fats, Oils, & Sweets
USE SPARINGLY
KEY
Fat (naturally occurring and added)
Sugars (added)
These symbols show fats, oils, and added sugars in foods.
Milk, Yogurt, & Cheese Group
2-3 SERVINGS
Meat, Poultry, Fish, Dry Beans, Eggs, & Nuts Group
2-3 SERVINGS
Vegetable Group
3-5 SERVINGS
Fruit Group
2-4 SERVINGS
Bread, Cereal, Rice, & Pasta Group
6-11 SERVINGS

APPENDIX N

Canada's Food Guide to Healthy Eating

Healthy Canada

Health and Welfare Canada | Santé et Bien-être social Canada

Canada's Food Guide to Healthy Eating

Enjoy a variety of foods from each group every day.

Choose lower-fat foods more often.

Grain Products
Choose whole grain and enriched products more often.

Vegetables & Fruit
Choose dark green and orange vegetables and orange fruit more often.

Milk Products
Choose lower-fat milk products more often.

Meat & Alternatives
Choose leaner meats, poultry and fish, as well as dried peas, beans and lentils more often.

Canada

Canada's Food Guide to Healthy Eating

FOR PEOPLE FOUR YEARS AND OVER

Different People Need Different Amounts of Food

The amount of food you need every day from the 4 food groups and other foods depends on your age, body size, activity level, whether you are male or female and if you are pregnant or breast-feeding. That's why the Food Guide gives a lower and higher number of servings for each food group. For example, young children can choose the lower number of servings, while male teenagers can go to the higher number. Most other people can choose servings somewhere in between.

Grain Products
5–12
SERVINGS PER DAY

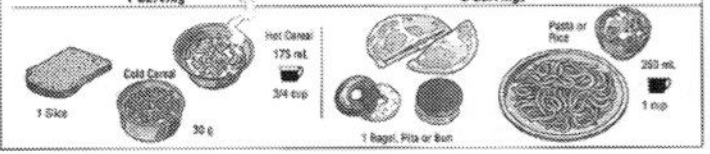

Vegetables & Fruit
5–10
SERVINGS PER DAY

Milk Products
SERVINGS PER DAY
Children 4–9 years: 2–3
Youth 10–16 years: 3–4
Adults: 2–4
Pregnant & Breast-feeding Women: 3–4

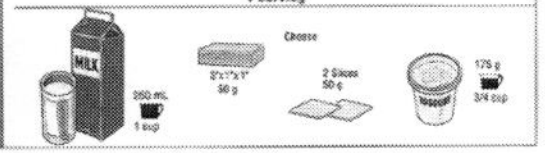

Meat & Alternatives
2–3
SERVINGS PER DAY

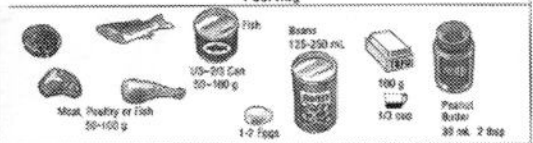

Other Foods

Taste and enjoyment can also come from other foods and beverages that are not part of the 4 food groups. Some of these foods are higher in fat or Calories, so use these foods in moderation.

*Enjoy eating well, being active and feeling good about yourself. That's VITALIT*É

ISBN 0-662-19648-1

APPENDIX O

Normal Reference Laboratory Values

Blood, plasma, or serum values

Test	Reference Range: Conventional Values	Reference Range: SI Units*
Acetoacetate plus acetone	0.30-2.0 mg/dl	3-20 mg/l
Acetone	Negative	Negative
Acid phosphatase	Adults: 0.10-0.63 U/ml (Bessey-Lowry) 0.5-2.0 U/ml (Bodansky) 1.0-4.0 U/ml (King-Armstrong) Children: 6.4-15.2 U/L	28-175 nmol/s/L

Activated partial thromboplastin time (APTT)	30-40 sec	30-40 sec
Adrenocorticotropic hormone (ACTH)	6 AM 15-100 pg/ml	10-80 ng/L
	6 PM <50 pg/ml	<50 ng/L
Alanine aminotransferase (ALT)	5-35 IU/L	5-35 U/L
Albumin	3.2-4.5 g/dl	35-55 g/L
Alcohol	Negative	Negative
Aldolase	Adults: 3.0-8.2 Sibley-Lehninger units/dl	22-59 mU/L at 37° C
	Children: approximately 2 × adult values	
	Newborns: approximately 4 × adult values	
Aldosterone	Peripheral blood:	
	Supine: 7.4 ± 4.2 ng/dl	0.08-0.3 nmol/L
	Upright: 1-21 ng/dl	0.14-0.8 nmol/L
	Adrenal vein: 200-800 ng/dl	
Alkaline phosphatase	Adults: 30-85 ImU/ml	
	Children and adolescents:	
	<2 years: 85-235 ImU/ml	
	2-8 years: 65-210 ImU/ml	
	9-15 years: 60-300 ImU/ml (active bone growth)	
	16-21 years: 30-200 ImU/ml	

*The use of the System of International Units (SI) was recommended at the 30th World Health Assembly in 1977 to implement an international language of measurement. Because this system is being adopted by numerous laboratories, many of the common values are expressed in both conventional and SI units. SI units are calculated by multiplying the conventional unit by a number factor. The SI measurement system uses *moles* as the basic unit for the amount of a substance, *kilograms* for its mass, and *meter* for its length.

Continued

Blood, plasma, or serum values—cont'd

Test	Reference Range	
	Conventional Values	SI Units*
Alpha-aminonitrogen	3-6 mg/dl	2.1-3.9 mmol/L
Alpha-1-antitrypsin	>250 mg/dl	
Alpha fetoprotein (AFP)	<25 ng/ml	
Ammonia	Adults: 15-110 µg/dl	47-65 µmol/L
	Children: 40-80 µg/dl	
	Newborns: 90-150 µg/dl	
Amylase	56-190 IU/L	25-125 U/L
	80-150 Somogyi units/ml	
Angiotensin-converting enzyme (ACE)	23-57 U/ml	
Antinuclear antibodies (ANA)	Negative	
Antistreptolysin O (ASO)	Adults: ≤160 Todd units/ml	
	Children:	
	Newborns: similar to mother's value	
	6 months-2 years: ≤50 Todd units/ml	
	2-4 years: ≤160 Todd units/ml	
	5-12 years: ≤200 Todd units/ml	
Antithyroid microsomal antibody	Titer < 1:100	

Antithyroglobulin antibody	Titer < 1:100	
Ascorbic acid (vitamin C)	0.6-1.6 mg/dl	23-57 μmol/L
Aspartate aminotransferase (AST, SGOT)	12-36 U/ml	0.10-0.30 μmol/s/L
	5-40 IU/L	5-40 U/L
Australian antigen (hepatitis-associated antigen, HAA)	Negative	Negative
Barbiturates	Negative	Negative
Base excess	Men: −3.3 to +1.2	0 ± 2 mmol/L
	Women: −2.4 to +2.3	0 ± 2 mmol/L
Bicarbonate (HCO_3^-)	22-26 mEq/L	22-26 mmol/L
Bilirubin		
Direct (conjugated)	0.1-0.3 mg/dl	1.7-5.1 μmol/L
Indirect (unconjugated)	0.2-0.8 mg/dl	3.4-12.0 μmol/L
Total	Adults and children: 0.1-1.0 mg/dl	5.1-17.0 μmol/L
	Newborns: 1-12 mg/dl	
Bleeding time (Ivy method)	1-9 min	
Blood count (see Complete blood count)		

Continued

Blood, plasma, or serum values—cont'd

Test	Reference Range	
	Conventional Values	SI Units*
Blood gases (arterial)		
pH	7.35-7.45	
PCO_2	35-45 mm Hg	4.7-6.0 kPa
HCO_3^-	22-26 mEq/L	21-28 nmol/L
PO_2	80-100 mm Hg	11-13 kPa
O_2 saturation	95%-100%	
Blood urea nitrogen (BUN)	5-20 mg/dl	3.6-7.1 mmol/L
Bromide	Up to 5 mg/dl	0-63 mmol/L
Bromosulfophthalein (BSP)	<5% retention after 45 min	
CA 15-3	<22 U/ml	
CA-125	0-35 U/ml	
CA 19-9	<37 U/ml	
C-reactive protein (CRP)	<6 μg/ml	
Calcitonin	<50 pg/ml	<50 pmol/L
Calcium (Ca)	9.0-10.5 mg/dl (total)	2.25-2.75 mmol/L
	3.9-4.6 mg/dl (ionized)	1.05-1.30 mmol/L
Carbon dioxide (CO_2) content	23-30 mEq/L	21-30 mmol/L

Carboxyhemoglobin (COHb)	3% of total hemoglobin	
Carcinoembryonic antigen (CEA)	<2 ng/ml	0.2-5 μg/L
Carotene	50-200 μg/dl	0.74-3.72 μmol/L
Chloride (Cl)	90-110 mEq/L	98-106 mmol/L
Cholesterol	150-250 mg/dl	3.90-6.50 mmol/L
Clot retraction	50%-100% clot retraction in 1-2 hours, complete retraction within 24 hours	
Complement	C_3: 70-176 mg/dl	0.55-1.20 g/L
	C_4: 16-45 mg/dl	0.20-0.50 g/L
Complete blood count (CBC)		
Red blood cell (RBC) count	Men: 4.7-6.1 million/mm^3	
	Women: 4.2-5.4 million/mm^3	
	Infants and children: 3.8-5.5 million/mm^3	
	Newborns: 4.8-7.1 million/mm^3	
Hemoglobin (Hgb)	Men: 14-18 g/dl	8.7-11.2 mmol/L
	Women: 12-16 g/dl (pregnancy: >11 g/dl)	7.4-9.9 mmol/L
	Children: 11-16 g/dl	1.74-2.56 mmol/L
	Infants: 10-15 g/dl	
	Newborns: 14-24 g/dl	2.56-3.02 mmol/L

Continued

Blood, plasma, or serum values—cont'd

Test	Reference Range: Conventional Values	Reference Range: SI Units*
Hematocrit (Hct)	Men: 42%-52%	
	Women: 37%-47% (pregnancy: >33%)	
	Children: 31%-43%	
	Infants: 30%-40%	
	Newborns: 44%-64%	
Mean corpuscular volume (MCV)	Adults and children: 80-95 μ^3	80-95 fl
	Newborns: 96-108 μ^3	
Mean corpuscular hemoglobin (MCH)	Adults and children: 27-31 pg	0.42-0.48 fmol
	Newborns: 32-34 pg	
Mean corpuscular hemoglobin concentration (MCHC)	Adults and children: 32-36 g/dl	0.32-0.36
	Newborns: 32-33 g/dl	
White blood cell (WBC) count	Adults and children >2 years: 5,000-10,000/mm^3	
	Children ≤2 years: 6,200-17,000/mm^3	
	Newborns: 9000-30,000/mm^3	
Differential count		
Neutrophils	55%-70%	
Lymphocytes	20%-40%	

Monocytes	2%-8%	
Eosinophils	1%-4%	
Basophils	0.5%-1%	
Platelet count	150,000-400,000/mm^3	
Coombs' test		
Direct	Negative	Negative
Indirect	Negative	Negative
Copper (Cu)	70-140 μg/dl	11.0-24.3 μmol/L
Cortisol	6-28 μg/dl (AM)	170-635 nmol/L
	2-12 μg/dl (PM)	82-413 nmol/L
CPK isoenzyme (MB)	<5% total	
Creatinine	0.7-1.5 mg/dl	<133 μmol/L
Creatinine clearance	Men: 95-104 ml/min	<133 μmol/L
	Women: 95-125 ml/min	
Creatinine phosphokinase (CPK)	5-75 mU/ml	12-80 units/L
Cryoglobulin	Negative	Negative
Differential (WBC) count (see Complete blood count)		
Digoxin	Therapeutic level: 0.5-2.0 ng/ml	40-79 μmol/L
	Toxic level: >2.4 ng/ml	

Continued

Blood, plasma, or serum values—cont'd

Test	Reference Range: Conventional Values	Reference Range: SI Units*
Erythrocyte count (see Complete blood count)		>119 µmol/L
Erythrocyte sedimentation rate (ESR)	Men: up to 15 mm/hour	
	Women: up to 20 mm/hour	
	Children: up to 10 mm/hour	
Ethanol	80-200 mg/dl (mild to moderate intoxication)	17-43 mmol/L
	250-400 mg/dl (marked intoxication)	54-87 mmol/L
	>400 mg/dl (severe intoxication)	>87 mmol/L
Euglobulin lysis test	90 min-6 hours	
Fats	Up to 200 mg/dl	
Ferritin	15-200 ng/ml	15-200 µg/L
Fibrin degradation products (FDP)	<10 µg/ml	
Fibrinogen (factor I)	200-400 mg/dl	5.9-11.7 µmol/L
Fibrinolysis/euglobulin lysis test	90 min-6 hours	
Fluorescent treponemal antibody (FTA)	Negative	Negative
Fluoride	<0.05 mg/dl	<0.027 mmol/L
Folic acid (Folate)	5-20 µg/ml	14-34 mmol/L

Follicle-stimulating hormone (FSH)	Men: 0.1-15.0 ImU/ml	
	Women: 6-30 ImU/ml	
	Children: 0.1-12.0 ImU/ml	
	Castrate and postmenopausal: 30-200 ImU/ml	
Free thyroxine index (FTI)	0.9-2.3 ng/dl	
Galactose-1-phosphate uridyl transferase	18.5-28.5 U/g hemoglobin	
Gammaglobulin	0.5-1.6 g/dl	
Gamma-glutamyl transpeptidase (GGTP)	Men: 8-38 U/L	5-40 U/L at 37° C
	Women: <45 years: 5-27 U/L	
Gastrin	40-150 pg/ml	40-150 ng/L
Glucagon	50-200 pg/ml	14-56 pmol/L
Glucose, fasting (FBS)	Adults: 70-115 mg/dl	3.89-6.38 mmol/L
	Children: 60-100 mg/dl	
	Newborns: 30-80 mg/dl	
Glucose, 2-hour postprandial (2-hour PPG)	<140 mg/dl	
Glucose-6-phosphate dehydrogenase (G-6-PD)	8.6-18.6 IU/g of hemoglobin	
Glucose tolerance test (GTT)	Fasting: 70-115 mg/dl	
	30 min: <200 mg/dl	
	1 hour: <200 mg/dl	
	2 hours: <140 mg/dl	
	3 hours: 70-115 mg/dl	
	4 hours: 70-115 mg/dl	

Continued

Blood, plasma, or serum values—cont'd

Test	Reference Range: Conventional Values	Reference Range: SI Units*
Glycosylated hemoglobin	Adults: 2.2%-4.8%	
	Children: 1.8%-4.0%	
	Good diabetic control: 2.5%-6%	
	Fair diabetic control: 6.1%-8%	
	Poor diabetic control: >8%	
Growth hormone	<10 ng/ml	<10 μg/L
Haptoglobin	100-150 mg/dl	16-31 μmol/L
Hematocrit (Hct)	Men: 42%-52%	
	Women: 37%-47% (pregnancy: >33%)	
	Children: 31%-43%	
	Infants: 30%-40%	
	Newborns: 44%-64%	
Hemoglobin (HgB)	Men: 14-18 g/dl	8.7-11.2 mmol/L
	Women: 12-16 g/dl (pregnancy: >11 g/dl)	7.4-9.9 mmol/L
	Children: 11-16 g/dl	
	Infants: 10-15 g/dl	
	Newborns: 14-24 g/dl	

Hemoglobin electrophoresis	Hgb A_1: 95%-98%	
	Hgb A_2: 2%-3%	
	Hgb F: 0.8%-2%	
	Hgb S: 0	
	Hgb C: 0	
Hepatitis B surface antigen (HB_sAG)	Nonreactive	Nonreactive
Heterophil antibody	Negative	Negative
HLA-B27	None	None
Human chorionic gonadotropin (HCG)	Negative	Negative
Human placental lactogen (HPL)	Rise during pregnancy	
5-Hydroxyindoleacetic acid (5-HIAA)	2.8-8.0 mg/24 hours	
Immunoglobulin quantification	IgG: 550-1900 mg/dl	5.5-19.0 g/L
	IgA: 60-333 mg/dl	0.6-3.3 g/L
	IgM: 45-145 mg/dl	0.45-1.5 g/L
Insulin	4-20 μU/ml	36-179 pmol/L
Iron (Fe)	60-190 μg/dl	13-31 μmol/L
Iron-binding capacity, total (TIBC)	250-420 μg/dl	45-73 μmol/L
Iron (transferrin) saturation	30%-40%	
Ketone bodies	Negative	Negative
Lactic acid	0.6-1.8 mEq/L	

Continued

Blood, plasma, or serum values—cont'd

Test	Reference Range: Conventional Values	Reference Range: SI Units*
Lactic dehydrogenase (LDH) isoenzymes	90-200 ImU/ml	0.4-1.7 μmol/s/L
	LDH-1: 17%-27%	
	LDH-2: 28%-38%	
	LDH-3: 19%-27%	
	LDH-4: 5%-16%	
	LDH-5: 6%-16%	
Lead	120 μg/dl or less	<1.0 μmol/L
Leucine aminopeptidase (LAP)	Men: 80-200 U/ml	
	Women: 75-185 U/ml	
Leukocyte count (see Complete blood count)		
Lipase	Up to 1.5 units/ml	0-417 U/L
Lipids		
Total	400-1000 mg/dl	4-8 g/L
Cholesterol	150-250 mg/dl	3.9-6.5 mmol/L
Triglycerides	40-150 mg/dl	0.4-1.5 g/L
Phospholipids	150-380 mg/dl	1.9-3.9 mmol/L

Lithium		
Long-acting thyroid-stimulating hormone (LATS)	Negative	Negative
Magnesium (Mg)	1.6-3.0 mEq/L	0.8-1.3 mm/L
Methanol	Negative	Negative
Mononucleosis spot test	Negative	Negative
Nitrogen, nonprotein	15-35 mg/dl	10.7-25.0 mmol/L
Nuclear antibody (ANA)	Negative	Negative
5′-Nucleotidase	Up to 1.6 units	27-233 nmol/s/L
Osmolality	275-300 mOsm/kg	
Oxygen saturation (arterial)	95%-100%	0.95-1.00 of capacity
Parathormone (PTH)	<2000 pg/ml	
Partial thromboplastin time, activated (APTT)	30-40 sec	
PCO_2	35-45 mm Hg	
pH	7.35-7.45	7.35-7.45
Phenylalanine	Up to 2 mg/dl	<0.18 mmol/L
Phenylketonuria (PKU)	Negative	Negative
Phenytoin (Dilantin)	Therapeutic level: 10-20 μg/ml	
Phosphatase (acid)	0.10-0.63 U/ml (Bessey-Lowry)	0.11-0.60 U/L
	0.5-2.0 U/ml (Bodansky)	
	1.0-4.0 U/ml (King-Armstrong)	

Continued

Blood, plasma, or serum values—cont'd

Test	Reference Range	
	Conventional Values	SI Units*
Phosphatase (alkaline)	Adults: 30-85 ImU/ml	20-90 units/L
	Children and adolescents:	
	<2 years: 85-235 ImU/ml	
	2-8 years: 65-210 ImU/ml	
	9-15 years: 60-300 ImU/ml (active bone growth)	
	16-21 years: 30-200 ImU/ml	
Phospholipids (see Lipids)		
Phosphorus (P, PO_4)	Adults: 2.5-4.5 mg/dl	0.78-1.52 mmol/L
	Children: 3.5-5.8 mg/dl	1.29-2.26 mmol/L
Platelet count	150,000-400,000/mm^3	
PO_2	80-100 mm Hg	
Potassium (K)	3.5-5.0 mEq/L	3.5-5.0 mmol/L
Progesterone	Men, prepubertal girls, and postmenopausal women: <2 ng/ml	6 nmol/L
	Women, luteal: peak >5 ng/ml	>16 nmol/L
Prolactin	2-15 ng/ml	2-15 μg/L

Prostate-specific antigen (PSA)	<4 ng/ml	
Protein (total)	6-8 g/dl	55-80 g/L
Albumin	3.2-4.5 g/dl	35-55 g/L
Globulin	2.3-3.4 g/dl	20-35 g/L
Prothrombin time (PT)	11.0-12.5 sec	11.0-12.5 sec
Pyruvate	0.3-0.9 mg/dl	34-103 μmol/L
Red blood cell count (see Complete blood count)		
Red blood cell indexes (see Complete blood count)		
Renin		
Reticulocyte count	Adults and children: 0.5%-2% of total erythrocytes Infants: 0.5%-3.1% of total erythrocytes Newborns: 2.5%-6.5% of total erythrocytes	
Rheumatoid factor	Negative	Negative
Rubella antibody test		
Salicylates	Negative Therapeutic: 20-25 mg/dl (to age 10: 25-30 mg/dl) Toxic: >30 mg/dl (after age 60: >20 mg/dl)	 1.4-1.8 mmol/L >2.2 mmol/L
Schilling test (vitamin B_{12} absorption)	8%-40% excretion/24 hours	

Continued

Blood, plasma, or serum values—cont'd

Test	Reference Range: Conventional Values	Reference Range: SI Units*
Serologic test for syphilis (STS)	Negative (nonreactive)	
Serum glutamic oxaloacetic transaminase (SGOT, AST)	12-36 U/ml 5-40 IU/L	0.10-0.30 μmol/s/L
Serum glutamic-pyruvic transaminase (SGPT, ALT)	5-35 IU/L	0.05-0.43 μmol/s/L
Sickle cell	Negative	
Sodium (Na^+)	136-145 mEq/L	136-145 mmol/L
Sugar (see Glucose)		
Syphilis (see Serologic tests for syphilis, Fluorescent treponemal antibody, Veneral Disease Research Laboratory)		
Testosterone	Men: 300-1200 ng/dl Women: 30-95 ng/dl Prepubertal boys and girls: 5-20 ng/dl	10-42 nmol/L 1.1-3.3 nmol/L 0.165-0.70 nmol/L
Thymol flocculation	Up to 5 units	
Thyroglobulin antibody (see Antithyroglobulin antibody)		

Thyroid-stimulating hormone (TSH)	1-4 μU/ml Neonates: <25 μIU/ml by 3 days	5 mU/L
Thyroxine (T_4)	Murphy-Pattee: Neonates: 10.1-20.1 μg/dl 1-6 years: 5.6-12.6 μg/dl 6-10 years: 4.9-11.7 μg/dl >10 years: 4-11 μg/dl Radioimmunoassay: 5-10 μg/dl	50-154 nmol/L
Thyroxine-binding globulin (TBG)	12-28 μg/ml	129-335 nmol/L
Toxoplasmosis antibody titer		
Transaminase (see Serum glutamic-oxaloacetic transaminase, Serum glutamic pyruvic transaminase)		
Triglycerides	40-150 mg/dl	0.4-1.5 g/L
Triiodothyronine (T_3)	110-230 ng/dl	1.2-1.5 nmol/L
Triiodothyronine (T_3) resin uptake	25%-35%	
Tubular phosphate reabsorption (TPR)	80%-90%	
Urea nitrogen (see Blood urea nitrogen)		
Uric acid	Men: 2.1-8.5 mg/dl Women: 2.0-6.6 mg/dl Children: 2.5-5.5 mg/dl	0.15-0.48 mmol/L 0.09-0.36 mmol/L

Continued

Blood, plasma, or serum values—cont'd

Test	Reference Range	
	Conventional Values	SI Units*
Venereal Disease Research Laboratory (VDRL)	Negative	Negative
Vitamin A	20-100 g/dl	0.7-3.5 μmol/L
Vitamin B_{12}	200-600 pg/ml	148-443 pmol/L
Vitamin C	0.6-1.6 mg/dl	23-57 μmol/L
Whole blood clot retraction (see Clot retraction)		
Zinc	50-150 μg/dl	

Test	Reference Range	
	Conventional Values	SI Units*
Acetone plus acetoacetate (ketone bodies)	Negative	Negative
Addis count (12-hour)	Adults: WBCs and epithelial cells: 1.8 million/12 hours RBCs: 500,000/12 hours Hyaline casts: Up to 5000/12 hours Children: WBCs: <1 million/12 hours RBCs: <250,000/12 hours Casts: >5000/12 hours Protein: <20 mg/12 hours	Negative
Albumin	Random: ≤8 mg/dl 24-hour: 10-100 mg/24 hours	Negative 10-100 mg/24 hr

*The use of the System of International Units (SI) was recommended at the 30th World Health Assembly in 1977 to implement an international language of measurement. Because this system is being adopted by numerous laboratories, many of the common values are expressed in both conventional and SI units. SI units are calculated by multiplying the conventional unit by a number factor. The SI measurement system uses *moles* as the basic unit for the amount of a substance, *kilograms* for its mass, and *meter* for its length.

Continued

Urine values—cont'd

Test	Reference Range: Conventional Values	Reference Range: SI Units*
Aldosterone	2-16 μg/24 hours	5.5-72 nmol/24 hours
Alpha-aminonitrogen	0.4-1.0 g/24 hours	28-71 nmol/24 hours
Amino acid	50-200 mg/24 hours	
Ammonia (24-hour)	30-50 mEq/24 hours	30-50 nmol/24 hours
	500-1200 mg/24 hours	
Amylase	≤5000 Somogyi units/24 hours	6.5-48.1 U/hr
	3-35 IU/hour	
Arsenic (24-hour)	<50 μg/L	<0.65 mol/L
Ascorbic acid (vitamin C)	Random: 1-7 ng/dl	0.06-0.40 mmol/L
	24-hour: >50 mg/24 hours	>0.29 mmol/24 hours
Bacteria	None	None
Bence Jones protein	Negative	Negative
Bilirubin	Negative	Negative
Blood or hemoglobin	Negative	Negative
Borate (24-hour)	<2 mg/L	<32 μmol/L
Calcium	Random: 1 + turbidity	1 + turbidity
	24-hour: 1-300 mg (diet dependent)	

Catecholamines (24-hour)	Epinephrine: 5-40 μg/24 hours	<55 nmol/24 hours
	Norepinephrine: 10-80 μg/24 hours	
	Metanephrine: 24-96 μg/24 hours	<590 nmol/24 hours
	Normetanephrine: 75-375 μg/24 hours	0.5-8.1 μmol/24 hours
Chloride (24-hour)	140-250 mEq/24 hours	140-250 mmol/24 hours
Color	Amber-yellow	Amber-yellow
Concentration test (Fishberg test)	Specific gravity: >1.025	>1.025
	Osmolality: 850 mOsm/L	>850 mOsm/L
Copper (CU) (24-hour)	Up to 25 μg/24 hours	0-0.4 μmol/24 hours
Coproporphyrin (24-hour)	100-300 μg/24 hours	150-460 nmol/24 hours
Creatine	Adults: <100 mg/24 hours or <6% creatinine	
	Pregnant women: ≤12%	
	Infants < 1 year: equal to creatinine	
	Older children: ≤30% of creatinine	
Creatinine (24-hour)	15-25 mg/kg body wt/24 hours	0.13-0.22 nmol/kg^{-1} body wt/24 hours
Creatinine clearance (24-hour)	Men: 90-140 ml/min	90-140 ml/min
	Women: 85-125 ml/min	85-125 ml/min
Crystals	Negative	Negative
Cystine or cysteine	Negative	Negative
Delta-aminolevulinic acid (ΔALA)	1-7 mg/24 hours	10-53 μmol/24 hours

Continued

Urine values—cont'd

	Reference Range	
Test	Conventional Values	SI Units*
Epinephrine (24-hour)	5-40 μg/24 hours	
Epithelial cells and casts	Occasional	Occasional
Estriol (24-hour)	>12 mg/24 hours	
Fat	Negative	Negative
Fluoride (24-hour)	<1 mg/24 hours	0.053 mmol/24 hours
Follicle-stimulating hormone (FSH) (24-hour)	Men: 2-12 IU/24 hours Women: During menses: 8-60 IU/24 hours During ovulation: 30-60 IU/24 hours During menopause: >50 IU/24 hours	
Glucose	Negative	Negative
Granular casts	Occasional	Occasional
Hemoglobin and myoglobin	Negative	Negative
Homogentisic acid	Negative	Negative
Human chorionic gonadotropin (HCG)	Negative	Negative
Human placental lactogen (HPL)		
Hyaline casts	Occasional	Occasional

17-Hydroxycorticosteroids (17-OCHS) (24-hour)	Men: 5.5-15.0 mg/24 hours	8.3-25 μmol/24 hours
	Women: 5.0-13.5 mg/24 hours	5.5-22 μmol/24 hours
	Children: lower than adult values	
5-Hydroxyindoleacetic acid (5-HIAA, serotonin) (24-hour)	Men: 2-9 mg/24 hours	10-47 μmol/24 hours
	Women: lower than men	
Ketones (see Acetone plus acetoacetate)		
17-Ketosteroids (17-KS) (24-hour)	Men: 8-15 mg/24 hours	21-62 μmol/24 hours
	Women: 6-12 mg/24 hours	14-45 μmol/24 hours
	Children:	
	12-15 yr: 5-12 mg/24 hours	
	<12 yr: <5 mg/24 hours	
Lactose (24-hour)	14-40 mg/24 hours	41-116 μm
Lead	<0.08 g/ml or <120 g/24 hours	0.39 μmol/L
Leucine aminopeptidase (LAP)	2-18 U/24 hours	
Magnesium (24-hour)	6.8-8.5 mEq/24 hours	3.0-4.3 mmol/24 hours
Melanin	Negative	Negative
Odor	Aromatic	Aromatic
Osmolality	500-800 mOsm/L	38-1400 mmol/kg water
pH	4.6-8.0	4.6-8.0

Continued

Urine values—cont'd

	Reference Range	
Test	Conventional Values	SI Units*
Phenolsulfonphthalein (PSP)	15 min: at least 25%	At least 0.25
	30 min: at least 40%	At least 0.40
	120 min: at least 60%	At least 0.60
Phenylketonuria (PKU)	Negative	Negative
Phenylpyruvic acid	Negative	Negative
Phosphorus (24-hour)	0.9-1.3 g/24 hours	29-42 mmol/24 hours
Porphobilinogen	Random: negative	Negative
	24-hour: up to 2 mg/24 hours	
Porphyrin (24-hour)	50-300 mg/24 hours	
Potassium (K^+) (24-hour)	25-100 mEq/24 hours	25-100 nmol/24 hours
Pregnancy test	Positive in normal pregnancy or with tumors producing HCG	Positive in normal pregnancy or with tumors producing HCG
Pregnanediol	After ovulation: >1 mg/24 hours	
Protein (albumin)	Random: ≤8 mg/dl	
	10-100 mg/24 hours	>0.05 g/24 hours

Sodium (Na^+) (24-hour)	100-260 mEq/24 hours	100-260 nmol/24 hours
Specific gravity	1.010-1.025	1.010-1.025
Steroids (see 17-Hydroxycorticosteroids, 17-Ketosteroids)		
Sugar (see Glucose)		
Titratable acidity (24-hour)	20-50 mEq/24 hours	20-50 mmol/24 hours
Turbidity	Clear	Clear
Urea nitrogen (24-hour)	6-17 g/24 hours	0.21-0.60 mol/24 hours
Uric acid (24-hour)	250-750 mg/24 hours	1.48-4.43 mmol/24 hours
Urobilinogen	0.1-1.0 Ehrlich U/dl	0.1-1.0 Ehrlich U/dl
Uroporphyrin	Negative	Negative
Vanillylmandelic acid (VMA) (24-hour)	1-9 mg/24 hours	<40 μmol/day
Zinc (24-hour)	0.20-0.75 mg/24 hours	

Index

A

In page references, "t" indicates tables; "f" indicates figures; "b" indicates boxes.

B

D

E